Instructor's Resource Manual

DALE R. BUSKE

St. Cloud State University

Excursions IN MODERN MATHEMATICS

Sixth Edition

PETER TANNENBAUM

PEARSON

Prentice Hall

Upper Saddle River, NJ 07458

Editor-in-Chief: Sally Yagan
Acquisitions Editor: Chuck Synovec
Supplement Editor: Joanne Wendelken
Executive Managing Editor: Kathleen Schiaparelli
Senior Managing Editor: Nicole M. Jackson
Assistant Managing Editor: Karen Bosch Petrov
Production Editor: Robert Merenoff
Supplement Cover Manager: Paul Gourhan
Supplement Cover Designer: Christopher Kossa
Manufacturing Buyer: Ilene Kahn
Manufacturing Manager: Alexis Heydt-Long

© 2007 Pearson Education, Inc.
Pearson Prentice Hall
Pearson Education, Inc.
Upper Saddle River, NJ 07458

The author and publisher of this book have used their best efforts in preparing this book. These efforts include the development, research, and testing of the theories and programs to determine their effectiveness. The author and publisher make no warranty of any kind, expressed or implied, with regard to these programs or the documentation contained in this book. The author and publisher shall not be liable in any event for incidental or consequential damages in connection with, or arising out of, the furnishing, performance, or use of these programs.

Printed in the United States of America

10 9 8 7 6 5 4 3 2

ISBN 0-13-187381-4

Pearson Education Ltd., *London*
Pearson Education Australia Pty. Ltd., *Sydney*
Pearson Education Singapore, Pte. Ltd.
Pearson Education North Asia Ltd., *Hong Kong*
Pearson Education Canada, Inc., *Toronto*
Pearson Educación de Mexico, S.A. de C.V.
Pearson Education—Japan, *Tokyo*
Pearson Education Malaysia, Pte. Ltd.

Table of Contents

Answers to Exercises

An Instructor Guide

Excursions in Modern Mathematics can serve as the text for a variety of mathematics courses. This Instructor's Resource Manual is intended to give (to the newly initiated and perhaps even the experienced teacher) an overview of the text (goals and desired outcomes), ideas for use in the classroom, and worksheets.

Choice of Content

A variety of content from the text may be used depending on instructor needs and wants. Covering all 16 chapters in a semester course is not realistic for the vast majority of instructors. Typically, about half of the chapters can be covered in a standard 15-week semester. Of course, this number can vary depending on the depth of coverage desired in each chapter.

The text is geared to allow for various depths of coverage. For example, in about one week (three 50-minute class periods), an instructor could give an overview of a chapter and assign only "Walking" exercises. A more typical approach would be to spend four to five class periods per chapter, assign "Walking" and "Jogging" problems and, perhaps, a project or paper. More in-depth coverage could be achieved, for example, with the use of "Running" problems and/or Excel projects found at the text website http://www.prenhall.com/tannenbaum/. Each chapter allows for an instructor to take many "excursions" into other areas if they wish. However, an instructor teaching the course for the first time would be well advised to resist this temptation. The 6th edition of the Student Resource Manual contains four "mini-excursions" for a more in-depth look at selected topics.

While all chapters in the text are independent, some chapters work very well together. For example, chapters 13 and 14 are tightly connected. Other good pairs are chapters 1 and 2, chapters 3 and 4, and chapters 5 and 6. The book is organized into four parts consisting of four chapters each. Choosing to cover chapters from all four parts and make a coherent course may be difficult. A new instructor to the text may wish to focus on two or three of the four parts.

While nearly uniform in their level of difficulty, not all chapters are of the same difficulty. Chapters 9, 12 and 15 stand out as slightly more challenging for students than others.

Approach

In reading the text for the first time, an instructor may be struck by the well-conceived approach taken by the author - whether it be the historical motivation (e.g. chapter 4), the classical, yet modern examples discussed (e.g. chapter 13), the avoidance of the term "function," or the applications. Further, it will soon become clear that the author has a substantial gift for writing.

There are other ideas, however, that may not be obvious at first. Consider, for example, the use of the algorithm to replace the formula. The reader will note few "shaded boxes" containing formulas in the text. For example, the discussion around the concept of standard deviation in chapter 14 revolves around the meaning of the standard deviation and the steps used in computing it.

There are other consistent threads found in the text: methods of enumeration, factorials, recursive and explicit descriptions of sequences, subscript notation, and modeling to name a few. These ideas can help to tie together 16 seemingly unrelated chapters.

It should also be noted that the author does not insult the intelligence of the (student) reader. An understanding of ideas from high school mathematics is assumed. For example, in chapter 9 the author uses the quadratic equation with little introduction. Throughout the exercises, the ability to solve linear equations, work with percentages, understand scientific notation, etc... is assumed.

Exercises

Great caution should be used in assigning exercises from the text. "Running" problems are just that. Instructors should think hard about any running problems they assign and should work out solutions to these in advance. The same can be said for a few "Jogging" problems. In any case, it may be wise to compare solutions with those given in this manual. For many problems, there is more than one valid approach possible.

It should also be noted that exercises are included in odd/even pairs. However, be aware that the differences in these pairs are not always as straightforward as one might guess.

Having made these observations, it should be pointed out that the exercises found in this text are some of the best found anywhere. Instructors looking for a text in which students (and instructors!) need to *think* to solve problems will be very happy with the exercises in *Excursions*. A blind following of examples from the reading will not solve many exercises in this book!

Projects & Papers

Several projects and papers are included in this edition of the text. Many of these projects require access to reference materials. An instructor assigning such a project should be certain that students have reasonable access to these references and, if need be, that such references are put on reserve for all students to access. In order to not pursue an "excursion" too much, narrowing the scope may be necessary for several projects. It would also be wise for an instructor to state specific expectations of what is to be turned in for each project. One source of additional project ideas ("excursions" if you will) are internet links found at the text's website.

Student Calculator Needs

A scientific calculator is sufficient to be successful in using this text. Many exercises can be done without the aid of a calculator. No exercises require a graphing calculator.

Technology

Various technologies can easily be incorporated into the course as desired. Microsoft *Excel* is a natural tool of choice in chapters such as 4, 9, and 14. More information (along with many exercises) on incorporating *Excel* into every chapter of the text can be found at the text website.

Applets suited to the course can be of great instructional help in computationally intensive chapters such as 1, 2, 4, and 12. For example, computing the Banzhaf power index and the Shapley-Shubik power index for four or more players can be quite tedious. However, many useful examples include four or more players. Moreover, useful concepts are easier to describe when the computational details are not the focus. More on the use of the applets tied to the text can be found at the text website http://www.prenhall.com/tannenbaum/.

Testing Materials

While multiple-choice testing materials (in both print and electronic form) are available, it is unlikely (and also not recommended) that instructors choose to solely assess in this manner. These materials can, however, should spawn ideas for other types of questions one can ask on quizzes and exams. Of course, learning from this text should be assessed using a multitude of methods.

Exams, when they are given, should not cover too many chapters. Because the material is so independent, exams covering more than two chapters may not allow for proper student focus. Further, because so many students that take such a course have an aversion to mathematics, one or two exams in a semester-long course may raise the stakes too high and cause widespread panic. Again, multiple assessments are encouraged. Writing quality exams for this course can be more difficult than in a standard algebra or calculus course. It should be noted that substantially more time is required to write such an exam.

Supplemental Materials

A set of *Powerpoint* presentations for each chapter can be found at the text website http://www.prenhall.com/tannenbaum/. These presentations can (and should!) be modified as the instructor wishes.

A Student Resource Manual is available for students and contains hints to odd exercises and fully worked out solutions to odd numbered exercises. Also included are learning outcomes and suggested skills that students should master for each chapter.

A large collection of classroom materials for the textbook developed at Virginia Commonwealth University can be found online at http://www.prenhall.com/tannenbaum_inotes/. The materials are in Microsoft *Word* format allowing for easy editing to fit the needs of your particular course. These materials can help make a course more interactive and less lecture-based. Some of these worksheets appear (in some form or another) in this manual.

Request for Additional Materials

If you have developed classroom materials for this course that are successful in engaging students and lead to student learning and if you are willing to share those materials, drop me an e-mail at drbuske@stcloudstate.edu and we will attempt to include them in future editions of the supplementary materials.

Enjoy using the text. I do.

Dale R. Buske
St. Cloud State University
drbuske@stcloudstate.edu

Chapter 1 – The Mathematics of Voting

Learning Outcomes

Students will

➡ construct and interpret a preference schedule for an election involving preference ballots.

➡ implement the plurality, Borda count, plurality-with-elimination, and pairwise comparisons vote counting methods.

➡ rank candidates using recursive and extended methods.

➡ identify fairness criteria as they pertain to voting methods.

➡ understand the significance of Arrows' impossibility theorem.

Skill Objectives

➡ Construct and interpret preference schedules for elections involving preference ballots.

➡ Determine the winner of an election using preference ballots using the
 - plurality method.
 - Borda count method.
 - plurality-with-elimination method.
 - method of pairwise comparisons.

➡ Rank candidates using
 - extended methods.
 - recursive methods.

➡ Identify fairness criteria violations.

➡ Count the number of pairwise comparisons in a given election.

➡ Count the number of votes needed to win an election.

➡ State Arrow's impossibility theorem.

Ideas for the Classroom

Poll the class on a topic of common interest having three seemingly equally favorable candidates/options. Create and hand out preference ballots for the election. In class, create a preference schedule directly by having students raise hands for each of the six possible rankings.

Construct an example having four candidates in which each wins using a different voting method discussed in the chapter (similar to the MAS election). To develop your example, use the applet found at the text's website http://www.prenhall.com/tannenbaum/. One possible example is given in the preference schedule below (*A* wins under the plurality-with-elimination, *B* wins using Borda count, *C* wins using pairwise comparisons, *D* wins using plurality).

Number of Voters	7	7	8	5
1st choice	*A*	*C*	*D*	*B*
2nd choice	*B*	*B*	*C*	*A*
3rd choice	*C*	*A*	*B*	*C*
4th choice	*D*	*D*	*A*	*D*

Ask students how many total Borda points are given out in the election described in the preference schedule above. Do not allow them to use calculators. Show them two methods of finding this number ($65 + 78 + 76 + 51 = 270$; $(4 + 3 + 2 + 1)(7 + 7 + 8 + 5) = (10)(27) = 270$).

Count the number of pairwise comparisons needed for an election with four candidates (see preference schedule above). Ask how many would be needed for an election with five (and six) candidates. Have students spot a pattern and develop a formula based on that pattern.

Have students propose a ranking system using the Borda count and pairwise comparisons. Rank the candidates in the election described in the preference schedule above using extended Borda count and extended pairwise comparisons.

Worksheets

Counting the Counting of Votes

More Counting of the Counting of Votes

The Commish

The Commish II

Counting the Counting of Votes

Votes for the president of the Math Club (as discussed in the text) are listed in the following preference schedule.

Number of Voters	14	10	8	4	1
1st choice	A	C	D	B	C
2nd choice	B	B	C	D	D
3rd choice	C	D	B	C	B
4th choice	D	A	A	A	A

1. If the members had voted differently, explain why there are 24 different columns that *could* have appeared in the preference schedule for the Math Club election?

2. If the method of pairwise comparisons were used to decide the outcome of the Math Club election, how many head-to-head match-ups would need to be evaluated?

3. In an election with four candidates (such as the Math Club election), what is the maximum number of elimination rounds that might be needed to determine a winner using plurality with elimination?

4. If the Borda count were used to decide the outcome of the Math Club election, Dave (candidate D) would receive $14 \times 1 + 10 \times 2 + 8 \times 4 + 4 \times 2 + 1 \times 2 = 81$ points. This number is found by several multiplications and additions.

   a) How many multiplications were used to find Dave's Borda point total?

   b) How many additions were used to find Dave's Borda point total?

   c) How many multiplications are used to determine the final Borda count (for all candidates) of the Math Club election?

   d) How many additions are used to determine the final Borda count of the Math Club election?

5. What is the maximum number of additions that would be used to determine the final Borda count for an election having four candidates? *Hint*: There could be a maximum of 24 columns in the preference schedule.

Fill in the following table.

Number of Candidates	4	5	6	7
Maximum number of columns possible in the preference schedule	24			
Number of head-to-head comparisons needed in applying the method of pairwise comparisons				
Maximum possible number of elimination rounds to determine a winner using plurality with elimination				
Maximum possible number of additions used to determine one player's Borda count				
Maximum possible number of additions used to determine the final Borda count				

More Counting of the Counting of Votes

Recursive ranking of candidates in an election can take a lot of time and effort. In this activity, we quantify just how much effort is needed.

1. In an election with four candidates, what is the maximum number of elimination rounds needed to rank the candidates using recursive plurality with elimination?

2. In an election with four candidates, what is the maximum number of head-to-head match-ups needed to rank the candidates using recursive pairwise comparisons?

3. The votes for the president of the Math Club are listed in the following preference schedule.

Number of Voters	14	10	8	4	1
1st choice	A	C	D	B	C
2nd choice	B	B	C	D	D
3rd choice	C	D	B	C	B
4th choice	D	A	A	A	A

a) How many additions are used to rank the candidates using recursive Borda count?

b) How many multiplications are used to rank the candidates using recursive Borda count?

c) What is the maximum number of additions needed in applying the recursive Borda count ranking method to an election having four candidates?

The Commish

The National Football League is in the process of selecting a new commissioner. They have narrowed the field to four candidates – Aikman, Bradshaw, Csonka, and Ditka. Each of the league's 32 owners has voted using a preferential ballot. Even so, no commissioner has been chosen.

Ballot	Ballot	Ballot	Ballot	Ballot	Ballot	Ballot	Ballot	Ballot	Ballot	Ballot	Ballot
1st A	1st D	1st B	1st A	1st C	1st D	1st A	1st C	1st D	1st D	1st C	1st A
2nd B	2nd C	2nd A	2nd B	2nd B	2nd C	2nd B	2nd B	2nd C	2nd C	2nd B	2nd B
3rd C	3rd B	3rd C	3rd C	3rd D	3rd B	3rd C	3rd D	3rd B	3rd B	3rd D	3rd C
4th D	4th A	4th D	4th D	4th A	4th A	4th D	4th A	4th A	4th A	4th A	4th D

Ballot	Ballot	Ballot	Ballot	Ballot	Ballot	Ballot	Ballot	Ballot	Ballot	Ballot	Ballot
1st A	1st C	1st A	1st D	1st C	1st C	1st D	1st A	1st D	1st D	1st A	1st B
2nd B	2nd B	2nd B	2nd C	2nd B	2nd B	2nd C	2nd B	2nd C	2nd C	2nd B	2nd A
3rd C	3rd D	3rd C	3rd B	3rd D	3rd D	3rd B	3rd C	3rd B	3rd B	3rd C	3rd C
4th D	4th A	4th D	4th A	4th A	4th A	4th A	4th D	4th A	4th A	4th D	4th D

Ballot	Ballot	Ballot	Ballot	Ballot	Ballot	Ballot	Ballot
1st B	1st A	1st B	1st A	1st D	1st C	1st A	1st D
2nd A	2nd B	2nd A	2nd B	2nd C	2nd B	2nd B	2nd C
3rd C	3rd C	3rd C	3rd C	3rd B	3rd D	3rd C	3rd B
4th D	4th D	4th D	4th D	4th A	4th A	4th D	4th A

Summarize the results of the election using a **preference schedule**:

Number of Voters	11			
1st choice	A	D		
2nd choice	B	C		
3rd choice	C	B		
4th choice	D	A		

1. Ms. Preponderance was the first to cast a ballot. She argues that the winner of the election should be the candidate receiving a **plurality** of the first-place votes. Which candidate received the most first-place votes?

2. Owner **Borda** argues that the winner of the election should be decided using a point system. He suggests that the candidates receive 4 points for each first-place vote, 3 points for each second-place vote, 2 points for each third-place vote, and 1 point for each fourth-place vote. How many Borda points did each candidate receive? Mark the winning candidate with an X.

Candidate	Borda Points	Winning Candidate
Aikman		
Bradshaw		
Csonka		
Ditka		

3. The owner of the **Eliminators** suggests that the commissioner should be decided by eliminating the most unfit candidate (that person having the fewest first-place votes) in three rounds of instant runoff elections.

    Using this elimination method of determining a winner, which candidate would be eliminated in Round 1?

    Describe the preferences of the voters in the second round. You should assume that, except for any eliminated candidate, the preferential order remains the same on each ballot.

Number of Voters	11			
1st choice	A			
2nd choice	C			
3rd choice	D			

    Which candidate would be eliminated in Round 2?

    Describe the preferences of the voters in the third round.

Number of Voters	11			
1st choice				
2nd choice				

    Which candidate is selected as commissioner using this elimination process?

4. The owner heading the competition committee sets up a round-robin tournament for the four finalists. Each candidate will be pitted against each other candidate in a series of one-on-one matches. The preference ballots determine the winner of each **pairwise comparison**. For example, Csonka would beat Bradshaw 17-15 in a head-to-head election since C is above B on 17 of the ballots.

Head-to-Head Match	Winner, Score
A vs. B	
A vs. C	
A vs. D	
B vs. C	C, 15-17
B vs. D	
C vs. D	

    If a candidate receives 1 point for a victory, half a point for a tie, and no points for a loss in this tournament, which candidate would be selected as commissioner using this process?

5. In your opinion, which candidate (Aikman, Bradshaw, Csonka, or Ditka) should be elected commissioner? Defend your choice.

The Commish II

Chaos has broken out in the National Football League as owners decide which of four candidates (Aikman, Bradshaw, Csonka, or Ditka) will be the next commissioner. In fact, depending on the technique used to count the ballots, several lawsuits could be filed. As the judge hearing these cases, you need to render a defensible decision.

The votes of the 32 owners have been summarized for you in the following **preference schedule**:

Number of Voters	11	10	7	4
1st choice	A	D	C	B
2nd choice	B	C	B	A
3rd choice	C	B	D	C
4th choice	D	A	A	D

The following four rules of fairness (the election laws) must be used in judging the cases.

Majority Criterion – If a choice receives a majority of the first-place votes in an election, then that choice should be the winner of the election.

The Condorcet Criterion – If there is a choice that in head-to-head comparisons is preferred by the voters over each of the other choices, then that choice should be the winner of the election.

The Monotonicity Criterion – If choice X is a winner of an election and, in a reelection, the only changes in the ballots are changes that only favor X, then X should remain a winner of the election.

Independence-of-Irrelevant-Alternatives Criterion – If choice X is a winner of an election and one (or more) of the other choices is disqualified and the ballots recounted, then X should still be a winner of the election.

Case 1 – Csonka vs. NFL

Background: Having the most first-place votes, Aikman has been selected as NFL commissioner. Csonka argues that he is a better candidate than Aikman and would win an election between the two.

1. Defend a ruling in favor of Csonka.

Case 2 – Ms. Preponderance vs. NFL

Background: Using owner Borda's point system to select a winning candidate in the election has resulted in Bradshaw being selected as NFL commissioner. Ms. Preponderance argues that this is unjust and that Aikman should be the winner of the election.

2. Defend a ruling in favor of Ms. Preponderance.

Case 3 – Ditka vs. NFL

Background: Adopting a method of plurality with elimination, it appeared that the NFL would elect Ditka as the next commissioner. This vote counting technique works by eliminating the most unfit candidate (that candidate having the fewest first-place votes) in three rounds of instant runoff elections. Before the results of the election could be verified by the NFL's accounting firm, Aikman found himself wrapped up in a steroid scandal and all references to his candidacy were scratched from the ballots. By the time the accounting firm finally tallied the results Ditka was no longer the winner.

3. Which candidate had the most to gain from the NFL winning this case?

4. Defend a ruling in favor of Ditka.

Chapter 2

Learning Outcomes

Students will

➡ represent a weighted voting system using a mathematical model.

➡ use the Banzhaf and Shapley-Shubik power indices to calculate the distribution of power in a weighted voting system.

Skill Objectives

➡ Effectively use weighted voting terminology.

➡ Construct mathematical models of weighted voting systems.

➡ Identify the presence of dictators, veto power, and dummies in a weighted voting system.

➡ Compute Banzhaf and Shapley-Shubik power indices.

➡ Compute factorials (by hand and with a calculator).

➡ Determine possible values of the quota q for a weighted voting system.

➡ Count the number of coalitions having a particular property.

Ideas for the Classroom

Prompt: Imagine a U.S. Supreme Court consisting of 4 conservatives, 3 moderates, and 2 liberals. Model this weighted voting system.

Prompt: In 2005, NARAL (National Abortion and Reproductive Rights League) described the U.S. Senate as consisting of 29 fully pro-choice senators, 21 mixed-choice senators, and 50 anti-choice senators. Describe the U.S. Senate as a weighted voting system (assume all members vote as a block on abortion issues) using appropriate notation.

Discuss $[q, 6, 3, 1, 1]$.
- What values of the quota q lead to legitimate weighted voting systems?
- When $q = 6$, point out how one player is a dictator (and the rest are dummies).
- When $q = 7$ or 8, point out how one player has veto power.
- When $q = 9$, point out how two players have veto power but two players are dummies.
- When $q = 10$, point out how two players have veto power but no players are dummies.
- When $q = 11$, point out how players share power equally.

To develop the formula for the number of possible coalitions containing N voters ($2^N - 1$), experiment with groups of 3, 4, and 5 students. Select three students to represent the players in the weighted voting system (assign each a number of votes based on the last digit of their student ID number). Ask each if they would like to form a coalition (prompting yes or no responses). Describe the coalition formed and give its weight. Then, ask how many choices each student had when they answered and apply the multiplication rule. Note that if all of them had said "no" then a coalition would not have been formed so we discount that possibility. Repeat with 4 and perhaps 5 students to spot a pattern.

Repeat the above activity to develop the formula for the number of possible sequential coalitions having N voters. In this case, ask the students for the number of options as to who votes first, second, third, etc..

Consider a weighted voting system having four players $P_1, P_2, P_3,$ and P_4. Suppose that the winning coalitions are as follows: $\{P_1, P_2\}$, $\{P_1, P_2, P_3\}$, $\{P_1, P_2, P_4\}$, $\{P_1, P_2, P_3, P_4\}$. Determine the Banzhaf power distribution.

Prompt: In any weighted voting system having N players what is the maximum number of players that can have veto power? Can you give such an example?

Prompt: In any weighted voting system having N players, what is the minimum number of winning coalitions possible? Can you give such an example?

Don't forget that applets exist at the textbook website http://www.prenhall.com/tannenbaum/ that will allow you to calculate Banzhaf and Shapley-Shubik power distributions with ease.

Worksheets

Is a Dummy Always a Dummy?

Comparing Measures of Power

Is a Dummy Always a Dummy?

The weighted voting system [37:14, 13, 12, 12, 6] represents a partnership among five people (P_1, P_2, P_3, P_4, and P_5). You are player P_5 (the one with 6 votes). With so few votes, you feel like a dummy. Are you? Does your answer depend on which measure of power (Banzhaf or Shapley-Shubik) is used?

1. Are there any coalitions of size 1 that are winning coalitions?

2. Are there any coalitions of size 2 that are winning coalitions?

3. Are there any coalitions of size 3 that are winning coalitions? If so, are you a part of any of them?

4. Are there any coalitions of size 4 that are winning coalitions? If so, are you (with your 6 votes) ever a critical player in these? Explain.

5. Are you a critical player in the grand coalition? Explain.

6. Do you have any Banzhaf power? That is, are you a (Banzhaf) dummy? Why or why not?

7. What is the largest number of votes you could have in order to be a (Banzhaf) dummy?

For the remaining questions, use the applet found at http://www.prenhall.com/tannenbaum/ to compute Banzhaf and Shapley-Shubik power distributions.

8. Use the applet to calculate the Banzhaf power index of each player in this weighted voting system.

9. Use the applet to calculate the Shapley-Shubik power index of each player. Are you still a (Shapley-Shubik) dummy?

10. Vary the quota and weights in the given weighted voting system. Can you find any examples in which you are a dummy according to one power index, but not according to the other?

Comparing Measures of Power

A weighted voting system with three players has the winning coalitions listed below.

Winning Coalitions: $\{P_1, P_2\}$, $\{P_1, P_3\}$, $\{P_2, P_3\}$, $\{P_1, P_2, P_3\}$

1. Underline the critical players in each coalition. *Hint*: Remember that a critical player is one whose desertion turns a winning coalition into a losing coalition.

2. Determine the Banzhaf power distribution for this system.

   $P_1:$ _____ $P_2:$ _____ $P_3:$ _____

3. Underline the pivotal players in each sequential coalition.
$$\langle P_1, P_2, P_3 \rangle \quad \langle P_2, P_1, P_3 \rangle \quad \langle P_3, P_1, P_2 \rangle$$
$$\langle P_1, P_3, P_2 \rangle \quad \langle P_2, P_3, P_1 \rangle \quad \langle P_3, P_2, P_1 \rangle$$

4. Determine the Shapley-Shubik power distribution for this system.

   $P_1:$ _____ $P_2:$ _____ $P_3:$ _____

5. How do these power distributions compare?

Another weighted voting system with three players has the winning coalitions listed below.

Winning Coalitions: $\{P_1, P_2\}$, $\{P_1, P_3\}$, $\{P_1, P_2, P_3\}$

6. Underline the critical players in each coalition.

7. Determine the Banzhaf power distribution for this system.

   $P_1:$ _____ $P_2:$ _____ $P_3:$ _____

8. Underline the pivotal players in each sequential coalition.
$$\langle P_1, P_2, P_3 \rangle \quad \langle P_2, P_1, P_3 \rangle \quad \langle P_3, P_1, P_2 \rangle$$
$$\langle P_1, P_3, P_2 \rangle \quad \langle P_2, P_3, P_1 \rangle \quad \langle P_3, P_2, P_1 \rangle$$

9. Determine the Shapley-Shubik power distribution for this system.

   $P_1:$ _____ $P_2:$ _____ $P_3:$ _____

10. How do these power distributions compare?

Chapter 3

Learning Outcomes

Students will

➡ state the fair-division problem and identify assumptions used in developing solution methods.

➡ recognize the differences between continuous and discrete fair-division problems.

➡ apply the divider-chooser, lone-divider, lone-chooser, and last-diminisher methods to continuous fair-division problems.

➡ apply the method of sealed bids and the method of markers to a discrete fair-division problem.

Skill Objectives

➡ Quantify players' value systems.

➡ Identify fair shares to a given player.

➡ Apply the following methods to solve continuous fair-division problems:
  - divider-chooser
  - lone-divider
  - lone-chooser
  - last-diminisher

➡ Apply the following methods to solve discrete fair-division problems:
  - sealed bids
  - method of markers

Ideas for the Classroom

Prompt: Doug's little sister Martha has eaten ½ of the vanilla part of a chocolate-vanilla cake. Alan, Brianna, Claire, and Doug all value chocolate twice as much as they value vanilla. What fraction of the original cake would be considered a fair share to each?

Bring a large piece of playdoium (playdoh) to class to divide using the divider-chooser (2 students in front of class), lone-divider (3 & 4 students), lone-chooser (3 & 4 students), and last-diminisher (5 students) methods. At first, use a homogeneous piece of playdoium (all yellow). Then, use a piece that is half yellow and half green (the green is twice as valuable to one student, equally valuable to another, etc.).

Bring that leftover Halloween candy to class to be divided among a random selection of four students that have perfect attendance. Be sure that the candy is not all of the same type. Use the method of markers.

Applets illustrating the method of markers and the method of sealed bids can be found at the textbook website http://www.prenhall.com/tannenbaum/. Illustrating the method of sealed bids using a spreadsheet can also be valuable for students to understand the structure of the process.

The "Hogg 'n the Booty" worksheet is designed to be used in the classroom with students playing their favorite roles. The calculations may best be done on a spreadsheet. Have students round their bids to the nearest $1000.

Worksheets

Cake Cutting 101

More Cake Cutting

Hogg 'n the Booty

Cake Cutting 101

Six players want to divide a cake fairly using the lone-divider method. The divider cuts the cake into six slices: $s_1, s_2, s_3, s_4, s_5, s_6$. The player's value decisions are listed in the table below:

	s_1	s_2	s_3	s_4	s_5	s_6
Player 1	16%	16%	16%	16%	16%	20%
Player 2	12%	25%	20%	15%	13%	15%
Player 3	15%	$16\frac{1}{6}\%$	20%	$19\frac{5}{6}\%$	14.5%	14.5%
Player 4	$16\frac{1}{6}\%$	$16\frac{1}{6}\%$	$16\frac{1}{6}\%$	$16\frac{1}{6}\%$	$16\frac{1}{6}\%$	$16\frac{1}{6}\%$
Player 5	20%	15%	25%	12%	17%	11%
Player 6	25%	15%	20%	14%	12%	14%

1. Which player was the divider?

2. List the bids of each player.

	Player 1	**Player 2**	**Player 3**	**Player 4**	**Player 5**	**Player 6**
Bid		$\{s_2, s_3\}$				

3. Based on the list of bids, distribute the slices to each player.

	Player 1	**Player 2**	**Player 3**	**Player 4**	**Player 5**	**Player 6**
Final Distribution						

4. Explain why each player should feel he/she has a fair share.

5. Would any players want to swap slices in the end? Explain.

6. Using the lone-divider method, how many different fair distributions of this cake are possible?

Suppose instead that the six players place the values listed in the table below on the various slices:

	s_1	s_2	s_3	s_4	s_5	s_6
Player 1	25%	15%	15%	15%	15%	15%
Player 2	$16\frac{1}{6}\%$	$16\frac{1}{6}\%$	$16\frac{1}{6}\%$	$16\frac{1}{6}\%$	$16\frac{1}{6}\%$	$16\frac{1}{6}\%$
Player 3	15%	20%	28%	12%	10%	15%
Player 4	12%	10%	14%	24%	25%	15%
Player 5	14%	12%	15%	28%	11%	20%
Player 6	30%	15%	13%	14%	14%	14%

7. Which player was the divider?

8. List the bids of each player.

	Player 1	**Player 2**	**Player 3**	**Player 4**	**Player 5**	**Player 6**
Bid						

9. Based on the list of bids, distribute the slices to each player.

	Player 1	**Player 2**	**Player 3**	**Player 4**	**Player 5**	**Player 6**
Final Distribution						

10. Explain why each player should feel that he/she has a fair share.

More Cake Cutting

Al, Betty and Carl want to divide a cake that is half chocolate and half strawberry using the lone-chooser method. Al likes both flavors equally well. So does Betty. Carl is allergic to strawberries, though, so he can only eat the chocolate cake. Straws are drawn to determine the chooser.

Act I: Carl is the lone chooser. Al will make the first cut.

1. a) Draw a possible result of the divider-chooser round, where Al is the divider.

Al's share of the cake	Betty's share of the cake

b) Draw slices that Al and Betty might form with their portion of the cake. Then, circle slices that Carl would select.

Al's division of his share	Betty's division of her share

c) Explain why Carl chose as he did.

d) Explain why each player should feel that he/she has a fair share of the cake.

2. a) Draw a second possible result of the divider-chooser round, where Al is the divider.

Al's share of the cake	Betty's share of the cake

   b) Draw slices that Al and Betty might form with their portion of the cake. Then, circle slices that Carl would select.

Al's division of his share	Betty's division of her share

3. In Carl's eyes, what is the least favorable initial division of the cake that Al could possibly make in the divider-chooser round? Explain.

4. Who would Carl prefer to make the initial division of the cake? Explain.

Act II: Al is the lone chooser. Carl will make the first cut.

5. a) Draw a possible result of the divider-chooser round, where Carl is the divider.

Betty's share of the cake	Carl's share of the cake

   b) Draw the slices that Betty and Carl make in their portion of the cake. Then, circle the slices that Al might select.

Betty's division of her share	Carl's division of his share

   c) Explain why Al chose as he did.

   d) Might Carl have received a more favorable share if he had been the lone chooser? Explain.

Act III: Al is the lone chooser. Betty will make the first cut.

6. a) Draw one possible result of the divider-chooser round, where Betty is the divider.

Betty's share of the cake	Carl's share of the cake

b) Draw the slices that Betty and Carl make in their portion of the cake. Then, circle the slices that Al might select.

Betty's division of her share	Carl's division of his share

c) In Carl's eyes, what is the most favorable initial division of the cake that Betty could possibly make in the divider-chooser round? Explain.

.

6. Rank the following roles in Carl's eyes.
   (A) Carl makes the first cut
   (B) Carl is the lone-chooser
   (C) Carl neither makes the first cut nor is the lone-chooser

Hogg 'n the Booty

Uncle Jesse has passed away and left his estate to five cousins – Bo, Luke, Daisy, Coy, and Vance.

The Booty:
Car - 1975 Ford F100 pickup in mint condition
House - 2 BR, 1 BA home set on 2 acres in rural Hazzard county
Business - Moonshine site #2

The Activity:
In this role-playing activity, your instructor will play the role of Mr. Hogg, the executor of the estate. He is charged with evenly dividing Uncle Jesse's three remaining possessions using the method of sealed bids. Five members of the class, playing the roles of his heirs, will privately submit bids to Mr. Hogg for each of Uncle Jesse's items. For simplicity of calculation, all bids placed by the heirs should be rounded to the nearest $1,000.

The Bids:

	Bo	Luke	Daisy	Coy	Vance
Car					
House					
Business					

1. Based on the bids above, determine what each heir considers to be a fair share of Uncle Jesse's estate.

	Bo	Luke	Daisy	Coy	Vance
Total Value of Bids					
Fair Share of Estate					

2. Based on the bids, allocate the booty to each heir by placing an "X" in the appropriate boxes below.

	Bo	Luke	Daisy	Coy	Vance
Car					
House					
Business					

3. Based on the allocation of the booty, how much does cash each heir *receive* from the estate in order to achieve a fair share? Enter negative values if the heir must *give* cash to the estate.

	Bo	**Luke**	**Daisy**	**Coy**	**Vance**
Payment from Estate					

4. What is the surplus cash from this division? How much of it will each heir receive?

5. What is the final allocation of the booty? Include items and any cash payments.

	Bo	**Luke**	**Daisy**	**Coy**	**Vance**
Final Allocation					

Chapter 4

Learning Outcomes

Students will

➡ state the basic apportionment problem.

➡ implement the methods of Hamilton, Jefferson, Adams, and Webster to solve apportionment problems.

➡ state the quota rule and determine when it is satisfied.

➡ identify paradoxes when they occur.

➡ understand the significance of Balinski and Young's impossibility theorem.

Skill Objectives

➡ Compute standard divisors and quotas for a given apportionment problem.

➡ Implement Hamilton's method.

➡ Implement Jefferson's and Adams's methods.

➡ Implement Webster's method.

➡ Identify a paradox when it presents itself.

➡ Identify when the quota rule is satisfied.

➡ State Balinski and Young's impossibility theorem.

Ideas for the Classroom

Illustrate the process of applying Hamilton's, Jefferson's, Adams's, and Webster's methods to apportion the U.S. House of Representatives using a spreadsheet and the 2000 Census data. Go through the process step by step (enter formulas and copy in class rather than simply showing a completed worksheet). For divisor methods, determine the approximate range of modified divisors that can be used. Be sure to comment on the constitutional requirement that each state receive at least one representative.

An illustration of the Population Paradox: 50 seats; Suppose North grows by 9%, South by 2%, and West by 8%.

State	Population
North	167,000
South	166,250
West	666,750

An illustration of the Alabama Paradox: 24 seats expands to 25 seats.

State	Population
North	53
South	99
West	223

An illustration of the New States Paradox: Add a new state East with a population of 392 and add 20 seats.

State	Population
North	168
South	465
West	367

Prompt (See Exercise #60): Define an apportionment method as follows: Give to each state its *upper quota* of seats. Then, take away any extra seats from those states with the smallest fractional parts to their quotas until there no extra seats have been allocated.
(a) Does this method satisfy the quota rule? Explain.
(b) Which apportionment method is this?

Students struggle with knowing when they should make the modified divisor larger or smaller. Use a spreadsheet to argue that when the sum of the rounded quotas is too low, then the standard quotas should be increased which means that the modified divisors should *decrease*. Likewise, when the sum of the rounded quotas is too high, the standard quotas should be decreased which means that the modified divisors should *increase*. Seeing this happen dynamically on a spreadsheet drives the point home.

Students will undoubtedly ask *how much* the modified divisor needs to be modified in Jefferson's, Adams's, and Webster's methods. The approach taken in the text is to use trial and error. Since a large range of modified divisors will work for typical problems, this is a reasonable approach. To investigate this question further, try the worksheet "Stepping towards a modified divisor."

Worksheets

Stepping Towards a Modified Divisor

Answers: 1. (a) greater (b) standard divisor for state *C* is closest; 100.01053% (c) 1001.053 (d) *A*: 4; *B*: 18; *C*: 28
2. (a) less (b) standard divisor for state *A* is closest; 99.937% (c) 49.9685 (d) *A*: 64; *B*: 30; *C*: 106.

Anacrostic – Part 1

Stepping Towards a Modified Divisor

1. A small country consists of three states (*A*, *B*, and *C*). The 50 seats in the legislature are to be apportioned under Webster's method.

State	Population	Standard Quota
A	3,950	3.95
B	17,520	17.52
C	28,530	28.53
Total	50,000	

(a) Will the first choice of modified divisor in this problem need to be greater than or less than the standard divisor? Explain.

(b) The "cut-offs" in this problem are 3.5, 17.5, and 28.5. On a percentage basis, which of the standard quotas are closest to these cut-offs? What percent of the cut-off is this standard quota?

(c) Modify the standard divisor by the percentage found in part (b). What is this modified divisor?

(d) Find the apportionment under Webster's method.

----

2. A small country consists of three states (*A*, *B*, and *C*). The 200 seats in the legislature are to be apportioned under Webster's method.

State	Population	Standard Quota
A	3,173	63.46
B	1,524	30.48
C	5,303	106.06
Total	10,000	

(a) Will the first choice of modified divisor in this problem need to be greater than or less than the standard divisor? Explain.

(b) The "cut-offs" in this problem are 63.5, 30.5, and 106.5. *On a percentage basis*, which of the standard quotas are closest to these cut-offs? What percent of the cut-off is this standard quota?

(c) Modify the standard divisor by the percentage found in part (b). What is this modified divisor?

(d) Find the apportionment under Webster's method.

Anacrostic

-Bill Clinton, 5/29/93

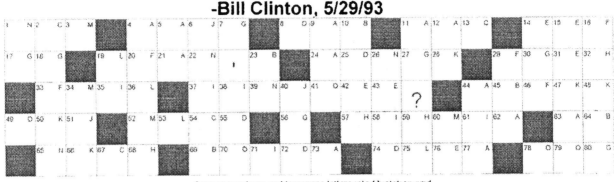

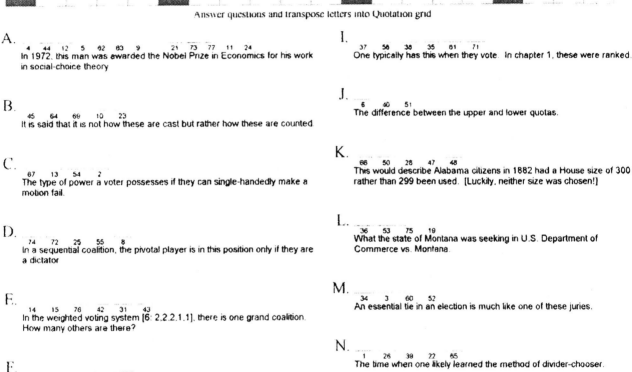

Answer questions and transpose letters into Quotation grid

A.
4 44 12 5 62 63 9   21 73 77 11 24
In 1972, this man was awarded the Nobel Prize in Economics for his work in social-choice theory

B.
45 64 69 10 23
It is said that it is not how these are cast but rather how these are counted.

C.
67 13 54 2
The type of power a voter possesses if they can single-handedly make a motion fail.

D.
74 72 25 55 8
In a sequential coalition, the pivotal player is in this position only if they are a dictator

E.
14 15 76 42 31 43
In the weighted voting system [6: 2,2,2,1,1], there is one grand coalition. How many others are there?

F.
29 20 16 33 46
Apportionment is as American as apple pie and red, _____, and blue.

G.
80 56 7 27 30 17 18
Master the ideas of apportionment and you will find yourself doing this when applying Webster's method.

H.
68 59 57 32
To _____ state should go a fair share of representatives. This is the apportionment problem.

I.
37 58 38 35 61 71
One typically has this when they vote. In chapter 1, these were ranked.

J.
6 40 51
The difference between the upper and lower quotas.

K.
66 50 28 47 48
This would describe Alabama citizens in 1882 had a House size of 300 rather than 299 been used. [Luckily, neither size was chosen!]

L.
36 53 75 19
What the state of Montana was seeking in U.S. Department of Commerce vs. Montana.

M.
34 3 60 52
An essential tie in an election is much like one of these juries.

N.
1 26 39 22 65
The time when one likely learned the method of divider-chooser.

O.
79 70 49 78 41
When the International Olympic Committee votes, they are searching for this.

Chapter 5

Learning Outcomes

Students will

➡ identify and model Euler circuit and Euler path problems.

➡ understand the meaning of basic graph terminology.

➡ classify which graphs have Euler circuits or paths using Euler's circuit theorems.

➡ implement Fleury's algorithm to find an Euler circuit or path when it exists.

➡ eulerize and semi-eulerize graphs when necessary.

➡ recognize an optimal eulerization (semi-eulerization) of a graph.

Skill Objectives

➡ Demonstrate an understanding of basic graph terminology.

➡ Draw a graph modeling a particular situation.

➡ Determine if a given graph has an Euler circuit or an Euler path.

➡ Find an Euler circuit or path for a graph having one.

➡ Find an (optimal) eulerization for a graph that has no Euler circuit.

➡ Find an (optimal) semi-eulerization for a graph that has no Euler path.

Ideas for the Classroom

Count the number of paths from *A* to *H*, *I*, and *J* respectively in the following graphs. Have students develop a conclusion about graphs with similar structure.

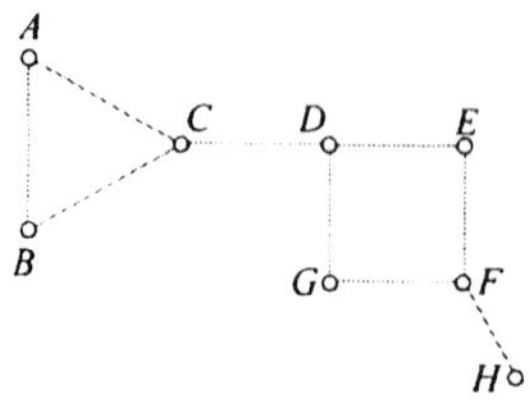

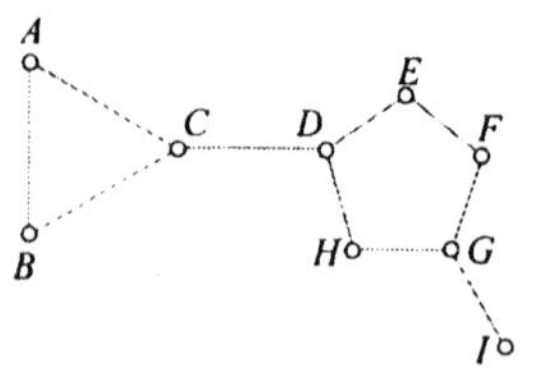

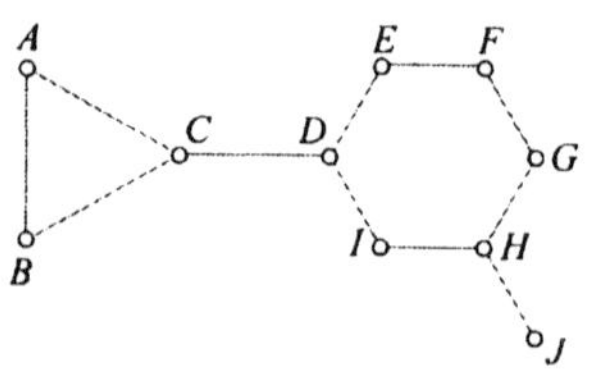

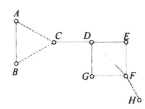

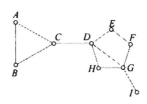

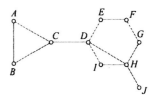

Model your own "bridges" problem. That is, have students develop a graph model (see below right) based on the diagram below. Ask if the associated graph has an Euler circuit. Then, discuss eulerization and semi-eulerization of this graph.

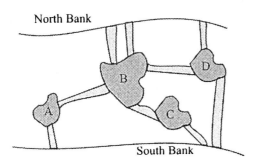

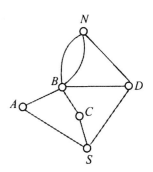

Discuss finding optimal eulerizations of rectangular graphs using the "edge walker" technique. That is, starting at one corner of a rectangular graph, walk around the outside edge of the rectangle adding additional edges as necessary. Exhibit the strategy by applying it to 4-by-5, 4-by-6, and 5-by-5 rectangular graphs.

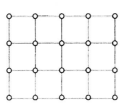

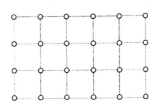

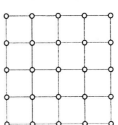

The worksheet on *Tucker's Algorithm* gives an alternative to Fleury's algorithm for finding Euler circuits.

Worksheets

Eulerization and Semi-Eulerization

Tucker's Algorithm

Eulerization and Semi-Eulerization

Circle the graphs below that have an Euler circuit. For each graph that does not have an
Euler circuit, find an optimal eulerization. Then, use Fleury's algorithm to label the edges of
an Euler circuit in the order that you might travel them.

a)

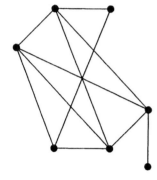

b)

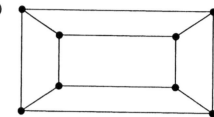

c)

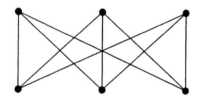

d)

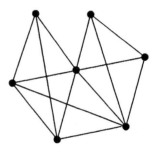

e)

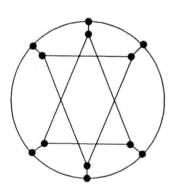

f)

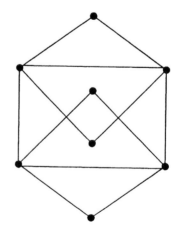

Circle the graphs below that have an Euler path. For each graph that does not have an Euler path, find an optimal semi-eulerization. Then, label the edges of an Euler path in the order that you might travel them.

a)

b)

c)

d)

e)

f)

g)

h)

i)

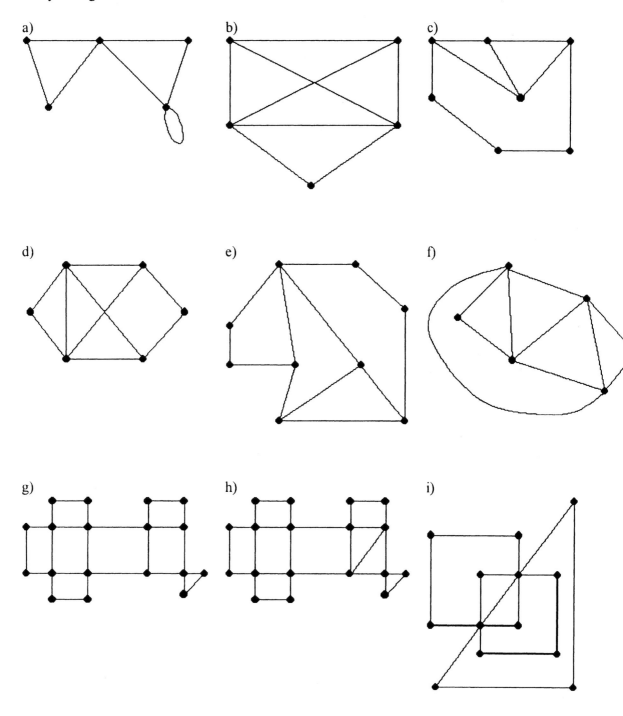

Tucker's Algorithm

Though Fleury's algorithm works perfectly well for finding Euler circuits, other algorithms also exist (see, e.g., Exercise 71 in the text). We investigate an algorithm introduced by Alan Tucker (*The American Mathematical Monthly*, Vol. 83, No. 8. (Oct., 1976), pp. 638-640) used to schedule street sweepers.

The idea behind Tucker's method of finding Euler circuits is to introduce extra vertices in the graph in such a way that every vertex has degree two. For example five "new" vertices (*C'*, *C''*, *E'*, *E''*, and *F'*) have been introduced in the graph below.

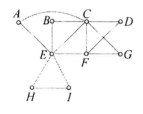 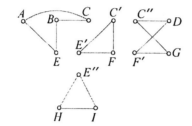

Once every vertex has degree two, the graph consists of many components (each of which are mini-circuits). These components are then put back together again to form an Euler circuit. For example, *E-A-C-B-E* and *E'-C'-F-E'* and *E''-H-I-E''* form the circuit *E-A-C-B-E-C-F-E-H-I-E* and this is joined with *C''-D-F'-G-C''* to form *E-A-C-D-F-G-C-B-E-C-F-E-H-I-E*.

1. Consider the graph shown at the right.
   (a) How many extra vertices must be introduced to apply Tucker's method to the graph?

   (b) Describe three circuits (components) that are constructed in Tucker's method.

   (c) Find an Euler circuit using Tucker's method.

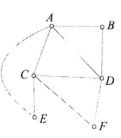

2. Now consider the graph (used in Alan Tucker's original paper) shown at the right.
   (a) How many extra vertices must be introduced to apply Tucker's method to this graph?

   (b) Describe the components that are constructed in applying Tucker's method.

   (c) Find an Euler circuit using Tucker's method.

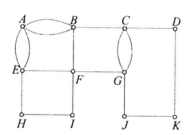

Chapter 6

Learning Outcomes

Students will

➡ identify and model Hamilton circuit and Hamilton path problems.

➡ recognize complete graphs and state the number of Hamilton circuits that they have.

➡ identify traveling-salesman problems and the difficulties faced in solving them.

➡ implement brute-force, nearest-neighbor, repeated nearest-neighbor, and cheapest-link algorithms to find approximate solutions to traveling-salesman problems.

➡ recognize the difference between efficient and inefficient algorithms.

➡ recognize the difference between optimal and approximate algorithms.

Skill Objectives

➡ Find one or more Hamilton circuits or Hamilton paths for a given graph.

➡ Calculate factorials by hand and with a calculator.

➡ Calculate how many edges and Hamilton paths there are in a given complete graph.

➡ Use the brute-force algorithm to find optimal solutions to traveling-salesman problems stated in various contexts.

➡ Use the nearest-neighbor algorithm and repetitive nearest-neighbor algorithm to find approximate solutions to traveling-salesman problems stated in various contexts.

➡ Use the cheapest-link algorithm to find approximate solutions to traveling-salesman problems stated in various contexts.

➡ Draw a graph model for a traveling-salesman problem.

Ideas for the Classroom

Consider the problem of finding the minimum cost Hamilton circuit for the weighted graph that follows.

➤ Apply the nearest-neighbor algorithm starting at vertex *C*.

➤ Apply the repetitive nearest-neighbor algorithm.

➤ Apply the cheapest-link algorithm.

➤ Apply the brute-force algorithm to find the optimal Hamilton circuit. [Find the cost of 12 circuits and illustrate how 12 others are mirror images. This would also be a good time to discuss the number of Hamilton circuits in a complete graph on *N* vertices.]

Point out which algorithms are optimal and which are not and which are efficient and which are inefficient.

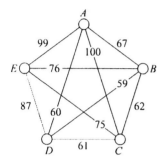

Circuit	Cost
ABCDEA	376
ABCEDA	351
ABDCEA	361
ABDECA	388
ABECDA	339
ABEDCA	391
ACBDEA	407
ACBEDA	385
ACDBEA	395
ACEBDA	370
ADBCEA	355
ADCBEA	358

Illustrate the process of listing all possible Hamilton circuits for a graph (such as that in Exercise 4 shown below) using tree diagrams.

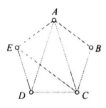

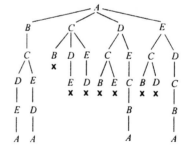

Then, argue in the following manner: First note that edges *AB* and *BC* must be a part of every Hamilton circuit and that *AC* cannot be a part of any Hamilton circuit.

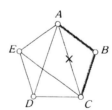

There are 2 possibilities at vertex A: edge AE or edge AD. Each of these alternatives can be completed in only one way.

Make the point that although enumeration using trees will always work, it is not always the best (most efficient) approach.

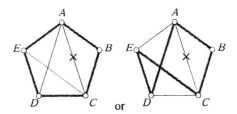

Using a triangular shaped mileage chart for your own state (such as that shown below for Nevada from the Nevada State Library website http://dmla.clan.lib.nv.us/docs/nsla/services/nvmiles.htm), have students apply the nearest-neighbor algorithm. For example, in the Nevada mileage chart, starting at Las Vegas, the nearest-neighbor is clearly North Las Vegas. To discover this, one needs to look across the row for Las Vegas *and* down to the bottom at the end of this row. Then, one would cross out the row and column to proceed.

Nevada Mileage Chart

	AUSTIN	BATTLE MT	BEATTY	BOULDER CITY	CALIENTE	CARLIN	CARSON CITY	ELKO	ELY	EUREKA	FALLON	FERNLEY	GOLDFIELD	HAWTHORNE	HENDERSON	JACKPOT	LAS VEGAS	LAUGHLIN	LOVELOCK	McDERMITT	MESQUITE	MINDEN	NORTH LAS VEGAS	PIOCHE	RENO	SPARKS	TONOPAH	VIRGINIA CITY	WELLS	WEST WENDOVER	WINNEMUCCA
BATTLE MOUNTAIN	89																														
BEATTY	209	289																													
BOULDER CITY	349	437	139																												
CALIENTE	281	352	262	174																											
CARLIN	138	49	347	499	325																										
CARSON CITY	171	233	324	459	418	295																									
ELKO	161	72	370	493	319	23	305																								
ELY	147	218	259	308	134	210	318	187																							
EUREKA	70	141	279	385	211	92	241	115	77																						
FALLON	110	181	311	407	366	248	61	253	257	180																					
FERNLEY	137	184	338	434	393	231	49	256	284	207	27																				
GOLDFIELD	142	231	87	206	215	280	253	297	192	188	201	228																			
HAWTHORNE	149	237	196	335	294	359	124	310	271	220	72	99	129																		
HENDERSON	337	426	126	11	163	465	448	482	297	374	396	423	195	324																	
JACKPOT	279	190	488	512	338	141	450	118	205	233	389	372	421	476	501																
LAS VEGAS	324	413	115	24	150	452	435	469	284	361	383	410	182	311	13	488															
LAUGHLIN	417	506	208	80	243	545	528	552	377	454	476	503	275	404	103	581	93														
LOVELOCK	166	125	395	483	422	174	108	197	313	236	56	59	257	126	452	315	439	532													
McDERMITT	215	126	540	583	478	175	253	198	344	267	201	204	357	273	552	316	539	632	145												
MESQUITE	404	493	195	104	230	532	567	560	363	440	514	541	262	391	93	568	80	173	590	619											
MINDEN	186	248	309	445	406	310	15	320	333	256	76	64	240	111	435	503	422	515	123	268	504										
NORTH LAS VEGAS	326	415	117	26	148	450	437	467	282	359	385	412	184	313	15	486	2	95	441	541	78	424									
PIOCHE	258	327	290	199	25	277	427	294	109	186	366	393	240	319	188	313	175	268	422	453	265	431	173								
RENO	170	217	372	467	426	265	30	289	317	240	60	33	261	132	456	406	443	536	92	237	575	45	445	426							
SPARKS	187	217	369	464	423	262	33	286	314	237	57	30	258	129	453	403	440	533	89	234	572	48	442	432	3						
TONOPAH	117	206	92	231	190	255	228	272	167	163	178	203	25	104	220	396	207	300	323	332	287	215	209	215	236	235					
VIRGINIA CITY	171	233	320	459	418	295	16	305	318	241	61	49	253	124	448	450	435	528	108	253	567	31	437	427	24	27	228				
WELLS	211	122	396	445	269	73	355	50	137	185	303	308	329	360	432	68	419	512	247	248	500	370	417	244	339	338	304	355			
WEST WENDOVER	265	181	377	425	250	132	414	109	118	195	362	365	310	389	413	127	400	493	308	307	481	429	398	225	398	359	285	414	59		
WINNEMUCCA	142	53	351	490	405	102	180	125	271	194	128	131	284	200	479	243	466	559	72	71	548	195	468	380	164	161	259	180	175	234	
YERINGTON	166	230	253	392	351	306	67	302	315	238	58	46	186	57	261	447	368	461	105	250	448	54	370	378	79	76	161	67	352	411	177

Worksheets

Hamilton Circuits

Hamilton Circuits

1. Apply the nearest-neighbor algorithm starting at A to find a Hamilton circuit of reasonably minimal weight in each of the following graphs. For each, name the circuit and find its total weight.

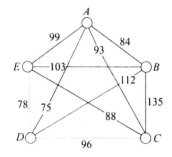

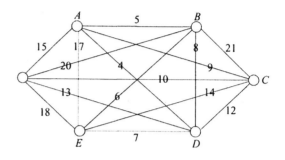

2. Are the same Hamilton circuits produced if the nearest-neighbor algorithms are applied using B as the starting vertex?

3. Apply the repetitive nearest-neighbor algorithm to find a Hamilton circuit of reasonable minimal weight in the graph at the right. Write the circuit assuming that the starting and ending point is A.

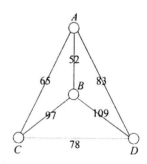

4. Use the cheapest-link algorithm to find a Hamilton circuit of reasonably minimal weight in all three of the above graphs. List the edges in the order you choose them. Write the circuit assuming that the starting and ending point is A.

5. If you were to use the brute-force algorithm to determine the minimal cost Hamilton circuit in each of the three graphs above, how many circuits would need to be checked? [Assume that you plan to take advantage of mirror-image circuits.]

Chapter 7

Learning Outcomes

Students will

➡ identify and use a graph to model minimum network problems.

➡ classify which graphs are trees.

➡ implement Kruskal's algorithm to find a minimal spanning tree.

➡ understand Torricelli's construction for finding a Steiner point.

➡ recognize when the shortest network connecting three points uses a Steiner point.

➡ understand basic properties of the shortest network connecting a set of (more than three) points.

Skill Objectives

➡ Determine whether a graph is a tree or not.

➡ Find one or more or even all of the spanning trees of a given network.

➡ Find a minimal spanning tree for a weighted network.

➡ Determine the shortest network connecting three points.

➡ Compute information about graphs containing 30-60-90° triangles.

➡ Reproduce Torricelli's construction.

Ideas for the Classroom

Allow students to "discover" properties 1-3 of a tree as follows: First, define a tree as a connected graph with no circuits. Then, present a selection of trees (like those below) and the prompts that follow.

Tree 1

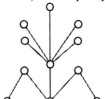
Tree 2

Tree 3

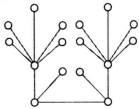
Tree 4

- How many paths are there between any two vertices in a tree?
- How many edges in a tree are bridges?
- How many edges does a tree with *N* edges have?

Count the number of different spanning trees in each of the following networks. You may also want to compute the redundancy *R* of each network.

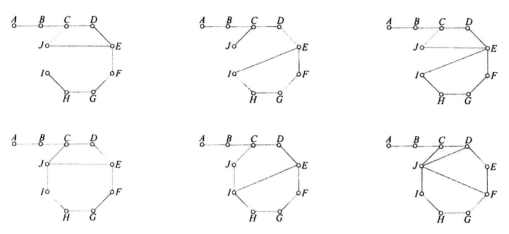

Ans. $4, 5, 4 \times 5 = 20$, $3 + 5 + 3 \times 5 = 23$, $4 + 4 + 4 \times 4 = 24$, $2 + 2 + 4 + 4 \times 4 + 2 \times 6 + 2 \times 2 \times 4 = 52$; The redundancy of the networks are 1, 1, 2, 2, 2, and 3 respectively.

Apply Kruskal's algorithm to a mileage chart consisting of 6-10 cities selected from the state in which you live. Present the mileage data in triangular form as shown below. [Note: The following example has a tie to discuss.]

	St. Cloud	Minneapolis	Duluth	Mankato	Bemidji	Rochester
St. Cloud	*	65	141	115	150	148
Minneapolis		*	149	77	218	83
Duluth			*	227	150	224
Mankato				*	266	83
Bemidji					*	302
Rochester						*

Using a compass and a straightedge, illustrate Torricelli's construction on any triangle *ABC*. Hand out a similar copy of the triangle to allow the students to perform the construction on the same triangle. You will need to remember some high school geometry such as finding the circumcenter of a triangle to do the construction (see figures below).

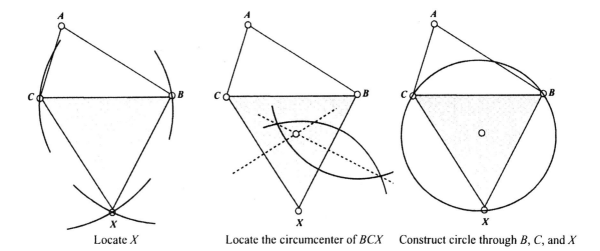

Locate X Locate the circumcenter of BCX Construct circle through B, C, and X

Use hexagonal grid paper (as shown at the right) to illustrate shortest paths.

Place vertices of a triangle ABC on edges e_1, e_2, and e_3 and determine the shortest network.

Then, place two vertices of a triangle ABC on edge e_2 and one on edge e_3 and determine the shortest network.

Ask students to defend their answers.

For more advanced work, experiment with quadrilaterals on hexagonal grid paper.

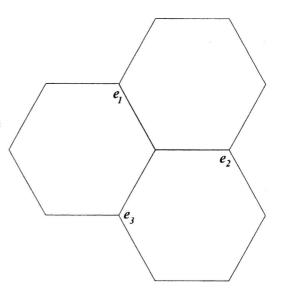

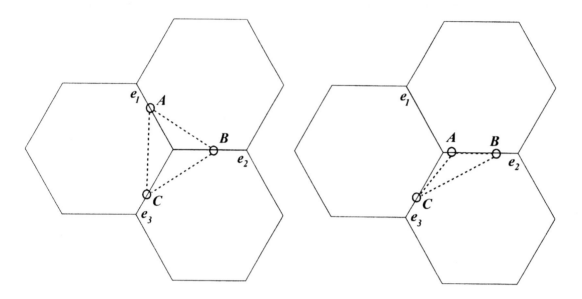

Worksheets

Kruskal's Algorithm

Building a Telephone System

Kruskal's Algorithm

Apply Kruskal's algorithm to find the minimal spanning tree of each of the following networks.

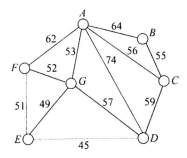

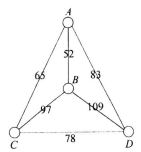

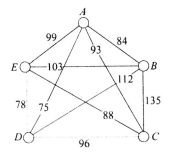

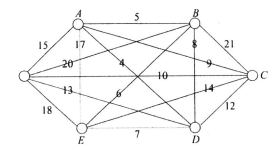

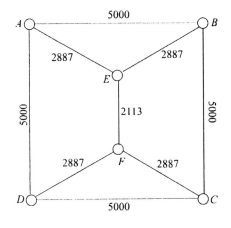

	A	B	C	D
A	-	7	5	2
B	7	-	3	4
C	5	3	-	8
D	2	4	8	-

*This table shows the distance between vertices in the network.

Building a Telephone System

You are the owner of Metro Fiber Optics, and your company is hired to build a phone system in a remote flat, semi-desert area of Australia. In building telephone systems, it is only necessary to lay the cable in such a way that there is one path between any two points.

Given three cities arranged as A, B, and C determine how much cable (in miles) each of these four plans requires. (A "plan" consists of the solid edges shown.)

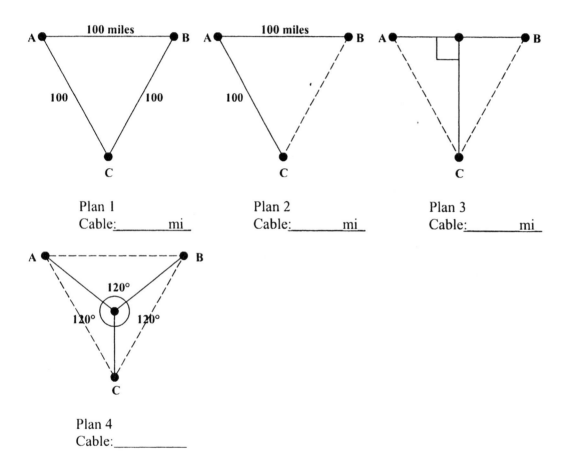

Plan 1
Cable:_____ mi_

Plan 2
Cable:_____ mi_

Plan 3
Cable:_____ mi_

Plan 4
Cable:_____

Given four cities arranged as *A*, *B*, *C*, and *D*, how much cable would it take to build the system using each plan?

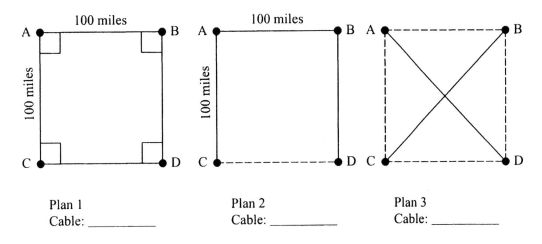

Plan 1
Cable: _____

Plan 2
Cable: _____

Plan 3
Cable: _____

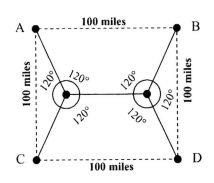

Plan 4
Cable: _____

Chapter 8

Learning Outcomes

Students will

➡ understand and use digraph terminology.

➡ schedule a project on *N* processors using the priority-list model.

➡ apply the backflow algorithm to find the critical path of a project.

➡ implement the decreasing-time and critical-path algorithms.

➡ recognize optimal schedules and the difficulties faced in finding them.

Skill Objectives

➡ Find indegrees, outdegrees, vertex-sets, arc-sets, cycles, etc. for a given digraph.

➡ Use digraphs to model real-life situations.

➡ Use a given priority list to schedule a project on *N* processors.

➡ Use the decreasing-time algorithm to schedule a project on *N* processors.

➡ Apply the backflow and critical-path algorithms.

➡ Schedule independent tasks and determine how close the result is to optimal.

Ideas for the Classroom

Complete the table for the digraph shown at the right.

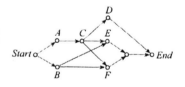

Vertex	Degree	Indegree	Outdegree	Vertex is incident to	Vertex is incident from
A					
B					
C					
D					
E					
F					

Prompt: Four candidates are interviewing for a toy store job with Mr. Frump. To narrow the field to two, Mr. Frump has a contest to determine which pair of candidates can assemble a new toy the quickest. The assembling of the toy involves 7 tasks (*A*, *B*, *C*, *D*, *E*, *F*, and *G*). Team 1 (Allison and Brent) and Team 2 (Charmaine and Dan). The rules of the contest specify that each task must be done by a single member of the team and that no team member can remain idle if there is a task to be done. The precedence relations for the tasks are shown in the following project digraph.

Team 1 has practiced a lot, and both Allison and Brent are able to complete each task in the following time (in minutes): *A*(1), *B*(3), *C*(1), *D*(9), *E*(4), *F*(4), and *G*(9).

Team 2 did not practice as much so Charmaine and Dan are able to complete each task in the following time: *A*(2), *B*(4), *C*(2), *D*(10), *E*(5), *F*(5), and *G*(10).

- Find an optimal schedule for Team 1.
- Find an optimal schedule for Team 2.
- Which team will win the contest?
- What would happen if Team 1 slowed their work a little on task C, each taking 2 minutes rather than 1 minute?

Prompts: True or False?
- A schedule in which none of the processors is idle must be an optimal schedule.
- In an optimal schedule, none of the processors is idle.
- In an optimal schedule of independent tasks, none of the processors is idle.

More-is-less paradox. Use the critical-path algorithm to schedule a project with 8 tasks using 2 processors according to the following project digraph. Then, using 3 processors, use the critical-path-algorithm to schedule the same project.

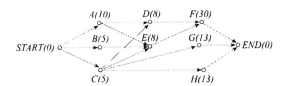

Worksheets

Really Bad Scheduling

Condo Flipping

Really Bad Scheduling

It is sometimes possible to use a really bad priority list. With a really bad priority list, one can schedule independent tasks in such a way as to almost double the optimal completion time. Illustrated below are one optimal and one really bad schedule (having completion time nearly twice as long) using 4 processors.

Priority list 1:

$A(2), B(2), G(4), I(8), C(3),$
$D(3), H(4), E(3), F(3)$

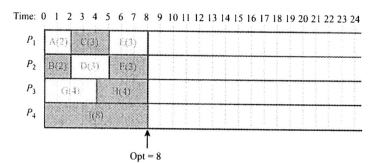

Priority list 2:

$A(2), B(2), C(3), E(3), G(4),$
$H(4), D(3), F(3), I(8)$

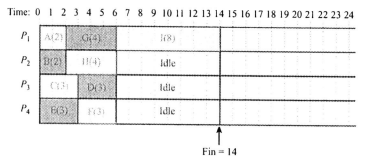

In the following questions, you are to model your solutions after the above example.

1. Using 5 processors, schedule the same project of independent tasks with
   (a) optimal completion time of 10 hours (twice the number of processors)

Priority list 1:

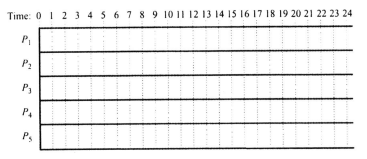

(b) completion time 18 hours (2 hours less than *twice* the optimal completion time).

Priority list 2:

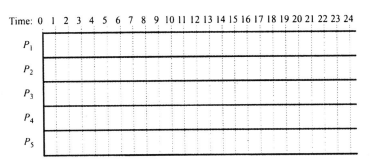

2. Using 6 processors, schedule the same project of independent tasks with
   (a) optimal completion time of 12 hours (twice the number of processors)

Priority list 1:

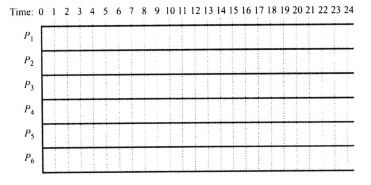

(b) completion time 22 hours (2 hours less than *twice* the optimal completion time).

Priority list 2:

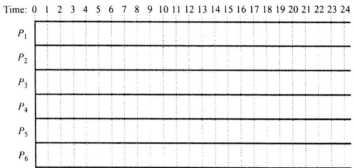

3. Using 7 processors, schedule the same project of independent tasks with
   (a) optimal completion time of 14 hours (twice the number of processors)

Priority list 1:

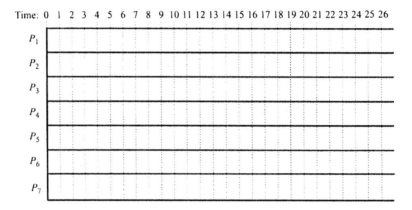

(b) completion time 26 hours (2 hours less than *twice* the optimal completion time).

Priority list 2:

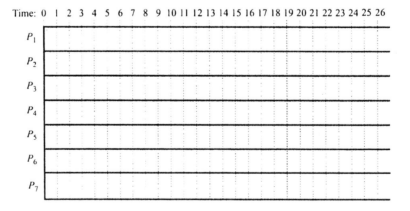

Condo Flipping

Condo flipping refers to a practice where investors buy, lightly renovate, and quickly sell condos to reap a profit. The table below shows the typical tasks performed by one condo flipper, the average time required for each task (measured in days), and the precedence relations between tasks.

JOB	SYMBOL/TIME	PRECEDENCE RELATIONS
Bathroom (clean)	B(8)	P → B
Carpets (shampoo)	C(4)	W → C, S → C
Filters (replace)	F(1)	
General cleaning	G(8)	B → G, K → G, F → G
Kitchen (clean)	K(12)	P → K
Lights (replace bulbs)	L(1)	
Paint	P(32)	L → P
Smoke detectors (battery)	S(1)	G → S
Windows (wash)	W(4)	G → W

1. Draw a project digraph for this situation.

2. Using the priority list *B, C, F, G, K, L, P, S, W*, make a schedule for refurbishing an apartment using two workers. How many days will it take to get the condo ready for resale?

Time: 0 2 4 6 8 10 12 14 16 18 20 22 24 26 28 30 32 34 36 38 40 42 44 46 48 50 52

P_1

P_2

3. Using the priority list *B, C, F, G, K, L, P, S, W*, make a schedule for refurbishing an apartment using two workers. Is this schedule better than that found above?

Time: 0 2 4 6 8 10 12 14 16 18 20 22 24 26 28 30 32 34 36 38 40 42 44 46 48 50 52

P_1

P_2

Chapter 9

Learning Outcomes

Students will

➡ generate the Fibonacci sequence and identify some of its properties.

➡ identify relationships between the Fibonacci sequence and the golden ratio.

➡ define a gnomon and understand the concept of similarity.

➡ recognize gnomonic growth in nature.

Skill Objectives

➡ Use and understand subscript notation.

➡ State and apply the defining characteristics of the Fibonacci numbers.

➡ State and apply basic properties of the golden ratio $\left(e.g.\ \phi^2 = \phi + 1 \right)$.

➡ Evaluate expressions in which order of operations is essential.

➡ Work with scientific notation.

➡ Solve quadratic equations.

➡ Determine when two figures are similar.

➡ Determine parameters of gnomons to given plane figures.

➡ State the *exact* value of the golden ratio $\left(\phi = \dfrac{1+\sqrt{5}}{2} \right)$ and an approximate value (1.618).

Ideas for the Classroom

Motivate the Fibonacci numbers by solving seemingly unrelated problems in which they appear in a solution. A good reference for such problems is
http://www.mcs.surrey.ac.uk/Personal/R.Knott/Fibonacci/fibpuzzles.html. The examples below are taken directly from Ron Knott's website.

- If we want to build a brick wall out of the usual size of brick which has a length twice as long as its height, and if our wall is to be two units tall, how many different patterns can be made using *N*=1,2,3,4,5,... bricks?
- A bee starts at the end of some cells in its hive. It can either start at cell 1 or 2 and moves only to the right (that is, only to a cell with a higher number in it – see diagram below). How many paths are there from the start

to cell number $N = 1, 2, 3, 4, 5, \ldots$?

- Britain has coins of value 1 penny (1p) and 2 pence (2p). In how many ways can we make up $N = 1, 2, 3, 4, 5 \ldots$ pence with just these two coins?

- What is the total resistance of $N = 1, 2, 3, 4, 5 \ldots$ 1 ohm resistors hooked up in a ladder configuration (as shown below)?

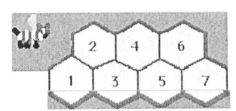 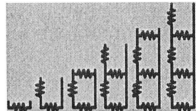

Construct the first 30 Fibonacci numbers using Microsoft Excel (type the value 1 in cells A1 and A2, enter the formula =A1+A2 in cell A3, and then copy this formula down column A):

1, 1, 2, 3, 5, 8, 13, 21, 34, 55, 89, 144, 233, 377, 610, 987, 1597, 2584, 4181, ..., 832040

Prompt: Which Fibonacci numbers are even (divisible by 2)? Which are divisible by 3? By 4? By 5? Do you spot a pattern?

In Excel, you might also make a scatter plot of the first 30 Fibonacci numbers in order to illustrate their explosive (exponential) growth. Further, placing the formula =A2/A1 in cell B2 and copying this formula down column B will allow you to illustrate the fact that $\lim\limits_{N \to \infty} \dfrac{F_{N+1}}{F_N} = \phi$. Placing the formula =A1/A2 in cell C2

and copying this formula down column C will illustrate the related value $\lim\limits_{N \to \infty} \dfrac{F_N}{F_{N+1}}$. In columns D and E,

illustrate how Binet's formula really does generate the Fibonacci numbers. Place the value 1 in cell D1, the formula =D1+1 in cell D2, and then copy this formula down column D. Then, place the formula =(((1+SQRT(5))/2)^D1-((1-SQRT(5))/2)^D1)/SQRT(5) in cell E1 and copy that formula down column E.

In many computer applications such as Microsoft Word, holding the CRTL-SHIFT keys while enlarging a drawing will preserve proportions. Illustrate this in discussing the concept of similarity.

Prompt: Rectangle A is 1 by 2. Rectangle B is 3 by 6. How many times larger is the perimeter of rectangle B? How many times larger is the area of the similar rectangle B?

Rectangle A is a by b. Rectangle B is ra by rb. How many times larger is the perimeter of rectangle B? How many times larger is the area of the similar rectangle B?

Right triangle A has legs of length a by b. Right triangle B has legs of length ra by rb. How many times larger is the perimeter of the similar triangle B? How many times larger is the area of triangle B?

Triangle A has sides of length a, b, and c. Triangle B has sides of length ra, rb, and rc. How many times larger is the perimeter of triangle B? How many times larger is the area of triangle B?

Prompts: Can squares have square gnomons? If so, give an example. If not, explain why not.
Can squares have rectangular gnomons? If so, give an example. If not, explain why not.
Can rectangles have rectangular gnomons? If so, describe such a rectangle. If not, explain why not.
Can rectangles have square gnomons? If so, describe such a rectangle. If not, explain why not.

After discussing the concept of similarity, derive the value of the golden ratio by calculating the length of any diagonal in a regular pentagon (having sides of length 1). Motivate the reason to do this calculation by asking for numbers that they believe are in the "Number Hall of Fame." Some members mentioned might include 0, 1, e, i, -1, and π. Explain that $\sqrt{2}$ has a place in the hall since it is the length of a diagonal of a unit square (a founding irrational member).

A nice applet illustrating properties of the golden rectangle can be found at
http://nlvm.usu.edu/en/nav/frames_asid_133_g_3_t_3.html

Compute the value of $\left(\dfrac{1+\sqrt{5}}{2}\right)^{N} + \left(\dfrac{1-\sqrt{5}}{2}\right)^{N}$ for values $N = 1, 2, 3, \ldots$ and spot a pattern. Steer students toward a conjecture involving the Fibonacci numbers by using the fact that $L_{N} = F_{N-1} + F_{N+1}$ (where L_{N} represents the Nth Lucas number).

Some students are impressed by the fact that there is a Fibonacci Association: http://www.mscs.dal.ca/Fibonacci/ and a quarterly journal devoted to all things Fibonacci (The Fibonacci Quarterly).

The puzzle of the missing area. Consider a square 8 units on a side and cut into four pieces as shown in the accompanying figure.

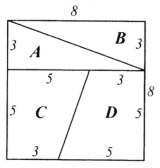

If we rearrange the pieces into a rectangle, as shown in the next figure, we see that although the square has area

$8 \times 8 = 64$, the rectangle has area $13 \times 5 = 65$.

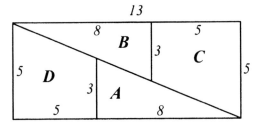

Explain the discrepancies in the areas.

What are the conditions on a and b (see figures below) so that this puzzle is not a puzzle – that is, the areas are the same? [Hint: Look for the golden ratio.]

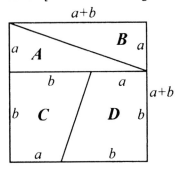

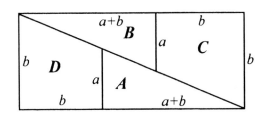

Worksheets

The Geometry of Bark

Digging for Gold

The Geometry of Bark

A **gnomon** to a figure F is a connected figure G which, when attached (without overlap) to F, produces a new figure similar to F.

A good analogy: An O-ring G is a gnomon to a disk F as bark is a gnomon to the (round) cross-section of a tree.

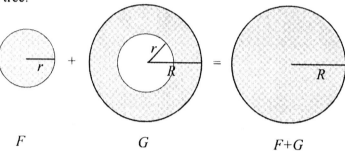

$$F \qquad\qquad G \qquad\qquad F+G$$

The figure above describes **gnomonic growth**. A young tree starts with a small cross-section (figure F). As it ages, it grows bark (figure G) on the outside yielding a tree with a larger, but *similar*, cross-section (figure $F+G$).

1. Imagine a particular variety of tree that has a *square* cross section F. If bark were to grow evenly on all four sides of the tree, what properties would this bark have? That is, describe a gnomon G to F shown below by finding the thickness of the "bark" (labeled as x) on each side of these trees after one growing season.

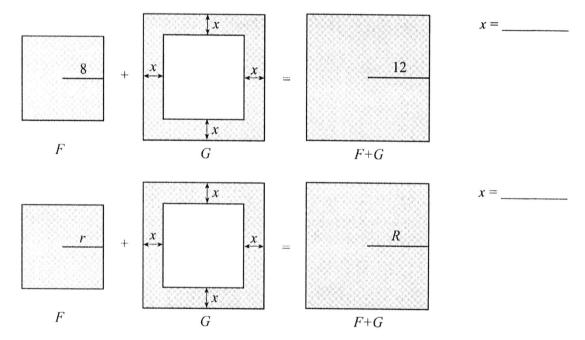

$x =$ _____

$x =$ _____

It is possible that the bark grows faster on two sides of the tree than on the other two sides. Find the value of x so that the "bark" G shown below is a gnomon to a tree having square cross section F.

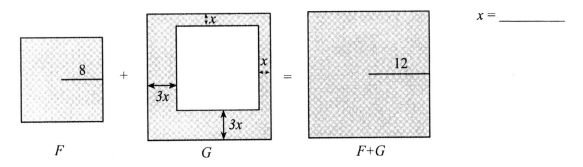

$x =$ _____

Is it possible for the bark to grow at a different rate on all 4 sides of a tree yet retain a similar (square) cross section as it grows? If so, give an example.

In certain climates, bark only grows on three sides of trees. Find the thickness of the bark on each side of the following "square" trees after one growing season.

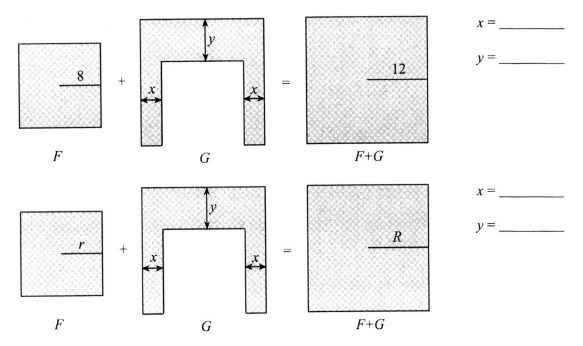

$x =$ _____

$y =$ _____

$x =$ _____

$y =$ _____

Is it possible for bark to grow on 1 or 2 sides of a tree having a square cross section and still yield a similar (square) cross section after one growing season? If so, give an example. If not, explain why not.

2. Now imagine a particular variety of tree that has a *right triangular* cross section *F*.
    Suppose that bark grows on the two shorter sides of the tree. For each of the following,
    find the thickness of the "bark" (the gnomon *G*) on each side that will maintain a similar
    cross section.

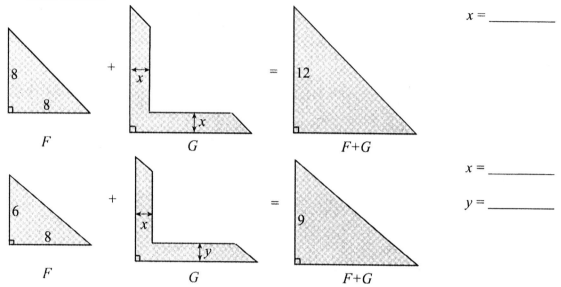

x = _____

x = _____

y = _____

It is possible for bark to grow on one side of a tree having a right triangular cross section
while retaining a similar cross section. Draw one possible way that the bark could grow
on the following cross section *F*. (That is, draw a gnomon *G* that can be added to one
side of this figure *F*).

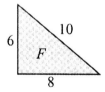

It is also possible for bark to grow on three sides of a tree having a right triangular cross
section while retaining a similar cross section. Illustrate one possible way that the bark
could grow on the following cross section *F*.

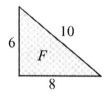

3. Now imagine a tree that has a *rectangular* cross section F (with both an "inner" and an "outer" radius). Suppose that bark grows on two adjacent sides of the tree. Find the thickness of the "bark" (i.e. values of x and y for the gnomon G) on each side that will maintain a similar cross section.

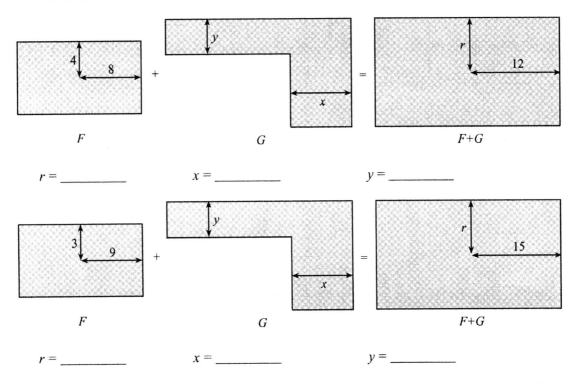

$r =$ _____ $x =$ _____ $y =$ _____

$r =$ _____ $x =$ _____ $y =$ _____

If bark were to grow on all four sides of a rectangular tree, could it grow evenly on all four sides while retaining a similar cross section? If yes, give an example of a rectangular cross section for which this happens. If no, explain why it cannot.

Can bark grow on three sides of a rectangular tree while retaining a similar cross section? If yes, give an example of a rectangular cross section for which this happens. If no, explain why it cannot.

4. Finally, imagine a tree that has an *elliptical* cross section *F*. Like a rectangle, it has both an "inner" and an "outer" radius. Suppose that bark grows on all four sides. Find the thickness of the "bark" (i.e. values of *x* and *y* for the gnomon *G*) on each side that will maintain a similar cross section.

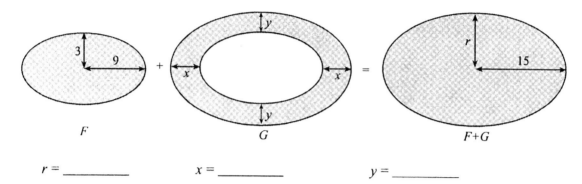

$$r = \underline{\hspace{2cm}} \qquad\qquad x = \underline{\hspace{2cm}} \qquad\qquad y = \underline{\hspace{2cm}}$$

Reflect

Is the following shaded region a gnomon to a disk of radius *r*? That is, could it represent the bark of a round tree? Explain.

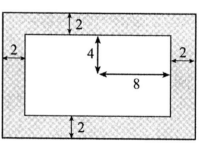

Is the following shaded region a gnomon to a 16-by-8 rectangle? That is, could it represent the bark of a rectangular tree? Explain.

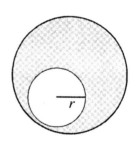

Is the shaded region *G* shown below a gnomon to *F* shown at the right?[1] Explain.

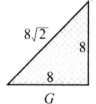

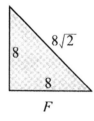

---

[1] This is another way of asking whether a tree having an isosceles right triangle as its cross section can have bark that grows on one side.

Digging for Gold

Find the value(s) of *x* for which a square is gnomon to the rectangle given below.

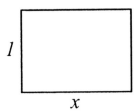

Find the value(s) of *x* for which triangle *G* is gnomon to triangle *F* (see figure below).

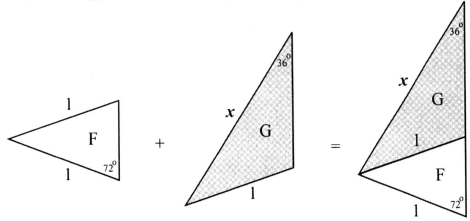

Find the value(s) of *x* for which triangle *G* is gnomon to triangle *F* (see figure below).

Chapter 10

Learning Outcomes

Students will

➡ understand how a transition rule models population growth.

➡ recognize linear, exponential, and logistic growth models.

➡ apply linear, exponential, and logistic growth models to solve population growth problems.

➡ differentiate between recursive and explicit models of population growth.

➡ apply the general compounding formula to answer financial questions.

➡ state and apply the arithmetic and geometric sum formulas in their appropriate contexts.

Skill Objectives

➡ Find a particular term of an arithmetic, geometric, or logistic sequence.

➡ Give a recursive and/or explicit description of a population sequence.

➡ Identify a population model and/or find common differences/ratios.

➡ Compute the sum of a given number of terms in an arithmetic or geometric sequence.

➡ Apply the general compounding formula.

➡ Solve problems involving percentage increases/decreases.

➡ Compute annual yield.

Ideas for the Classroom

The *Sequence Activity* worksheet will illustrate two of the three types of sequences to be studied in this chapter.

The *Growth Models* worksheet nicely motivates the recursive and exponential formulas for linear and exponential growth.

Prompt: A Flor-mart employee earns $40,000 for her first year of employment. She gets a fixed increase in salary each year of $500. Model the employee's salary.

Note: Model the salary recursively and exponentially using an arithmetic sequence S_N.

- Determine first the values of S_0, S_1, S_2, and S_3. Then, spot a pattern.
- Motivate the arithmetic sum formula by asking for the total amount the employee earns in her lifetime.
- Compare this employee's lifetime earnings to the case in which the yearly salary increases by 1.25% (motivates exponential growth and the geometric sum formula).

Prompt: Under current law, there are two types of IRA's (Individual Retirement Accounts). In a **Roth** IRA, you pay tax now and let the deposit accumulate tax-free. In a **traditional** IRA, a deposit grows tax-deferred and tax is paid at the time of withdrawal. Assume the tax is at a rate of 27% both now and at the time of withdrawal.

If a 20-year old student that plans to withdraw the money in 35 years, determine which is the better deal (the Roth or the traditional IRA).

Notes: For calculation purposes, you could assume a 6% annual rate of return and a $1000 deposit. Develop recursive and explicit models for the growth of this population ($r = 1.06$, $P_0 = \$1000$, $N = 35$).
- Discuss the question of what happens when the initial deposit is doubled. [Explain that each $1000 deposit could be put in a different bank.]
- Explain why the answer is that both types of IRAs yield the same amount if the tax rate stays constant. [Think about two piles of money – one being 27% and one being 73% of the principal.]
- Discuss what factors might lead to the Roth IRA being preferred by young people.
- Extend the discussion to include a series of 35 deposits. In so doing, motivate the geometric sum formula.

Compare and contrast growth of money in a piggy bank with that in a fixed-rate bank account or Treasury note.

Illustrate why the arithmetic sum formulas hold by computing the sums $x = 7+11+15+19+\ldots+403$ and $x = 1458 + 486 + 162 + 54 + \ldots + \dfrac{2}{81}$. Note how these sums follow from neat "tricks" of the trade:

Add: $\begin{aligned} x &= 7 \ + \ 11 + \ 15 + \ 19 + \ldots + 403 \\ x &= 403 + 399 + 395 + 391 + \ldots + \ \ 7 \\ \hline 2x &= 410 + 410 + 410 + 410 + \ldots + 410 \end{aligned}$	so that $2x = 100(410)$ and $x = \dfrac{\#terms(\,first\ term + last\ term)}{2}$ $= 20,500$
Subtract: $\begin{aligned} x &= 1458 + 486 + 162 + 54 + \ldots + \dfrac{2}{81} \\ \tfrac{1}{3}x &= \qquad\ \ 486 + 162 + 54 + \ldots + \dfrac{2}{81} + \dfrac{2}{243} \\ \hline \left(1 - \dfrac{1}{3}\right)x &= 1458 \qquad\qquad\qquad\qquad\quad -\dfrac{2}{243} \end{aligned}$	so that $x = \dfrac{first\ term - r \cdot last\ term}{1 - r}$ $= \dfrac{1458 - \dfrac{2}{243}}{1 - \dfrac{1}{3}}$

Prompt: Flor-mart employees earn 60% less than their peers at L-mart. How much of a raise would Flor-mart employees need to receive in order to earn the same as their L-mark peers? 10%? 20%? 60%?

Prompt: A local bank is offering various choices regarding the manner in which it will compound interest. You have $1000 that you wish to deposit at a nominal rate of 100% (that's right, this bank is fictional!). The banks charges a $2 fee for each compounding period k. Based on the options given in the table below, how many compounding periods would be ideal for your deposit?

Compounding Periods	Fee Charged	End Result
1	$2.00	$1,998.00
2	$4.00	$2,246.00
4	$8.00	
8	$16.00	
16		
32		
64		
128		
256		
512		
1024		
2048		
4096		
8192		
16384		
32768		
65536		
131072		
262144		
524288		
1048576		

Answer the above question by constructing a table similar to that above in Excel to help with the calculations. Then, ask the question again supposing that no fee is charged. Reward the student with the best guess as to how much $1000 grows to after 1 year if it is compounded 1,048,576 times. Then, discuss the value of the magical constant e.

Illustrate logistic growth by using Excel to compute and plot 100 terms of a logistic sequence. First, fix the growth parameter $r = 2.5$ and vary the initial population p_0 (e.g. $p_0 = 0.2, 0.3, 0.7, 0.701$). Then, vary the growth parameter using $r = 2.5, 3.1, 3.25, 3.5, 3.56, 3.75, 4$.

Geometrically, illustrate an approximate value of $x = \underbrace{3200 + 1600 + 800 + 400 + ...}_{100 \ terms}$ using an 80 by 80 square.

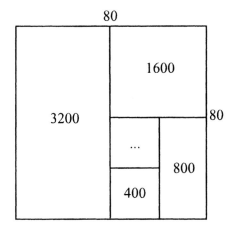

Worksheets

Grouping Sequences

Growth Models

Crime Predictions

Grouping Sequences

Describe the pattern you see and use it to predict what numbers come next.

I)   2, 4, 6, 8, ____, ____, ____, ____, …   pattern:_____

II)   -1, 1, -1, 1, ____, ____, ____, ____, …   pattern:_____

III)   -1, -4, -7, ____, ____, ____, ____, …   pattern:_____

IV)   1, 4, 9, 16, ____, ____, ____, ____, …   pattern:_____

V)   2, 4, 8, 16, ____, ____, ____, ____, …   pattern:_____

VI)   1, ¾, ½, ¼, ____, ____, ____, ____, …   pattern:_____

VII)   1, 0, 1, 0, 1, ____, ____, ____, ____, …   pattern:_____

VIII) 1, $\frac{1}{4}$, $\frac{1}{16}$, ____, ____, ____, ____, …   pattern:_____

IX)   2, -6, 18, ____, ____, ____, ____, …   pattern:_____

X)   5 ½, 6, 6 ½, ____, ____, ____, ____, …   pattern:_____

Sequences I, III, and VI are called **arithmetic** sequences. They describe **linear growth**.

1. What property do sequences I, III, and VI have in common?

2. Identify one other sequence above as arithmetic.

Sequences V, VIII, and IX are called **geometric** sequences. They describe **exponential growth**.

3. What property do sequences V, VIII, and IX have in common?

4. Identify one other sequence above as geometric.

5. Are there any sequences that are both arithmetic and geometric? Is so, what is one?

Growth Models

1. Based on the pattern, determine the next term in each sequence.

$P_1 = 3$ $A_1 = 6$ $C_0 = 8$

$P_2 = 5$ $A_2 = 3$ $C_1 = 7$

$P_3 = 7$ $A_3 = \dfrac{3}{2}$ $C_2 = 6$

$P_4 = 9$ $A_4 = \dfrac{3}{4}$ $C_3 = 5$

$P_5 = 11$ $A_5 = \dfrac{3}{8}$ $C_4 = 4$

$P_6 =$ _____ $A_6 =$ _____ $C_5 =$ _____

$H_0 = \dfrac{2}{9}$ $M_0 = 4$ $D_1 = 3$

$H_1 = \dfrac{2}{3}$ $M_1 = 5$ $D_2 = 3$

$H_2 = 2$ $M_2 = 7$ $D_3 = 6$

$H_3 = 6$ $M_3 = 10$ $D_4 = 18$

$H_4 = 18$ $M_4 = 14$ $D_5 = 72$

$H_5 =$ _____ $M_5 =$ _____ $D_6 =$ _____

2. Which sequences are arithmetic?

3. Which sequences are geometric?

4. Find the indicated term of each sequence.

$P_{20} =$ _____ $A_{14} =$ _____ $C_{30} =$ _____

$H_{15} =$ _____ $M_{15} =$ _____ $D_{10} =$ _____

5. Find a *recursive* description of each sequence. That is, describe each as in terms of the
    preceding term, the $N-1^{st}$, in the sequence.

$P_N = $ _____ $A_N = $ _____ $C_N = $ _____

$H_N = $ _____ $M_N = $ _____ $D_N = $ _____

6. Find an *explicit* description of each sequence. That is, describe each in terms of N.

$P_N = $ _____

$A_N = $ _____

$D_N = $ _____

Crime Predictions

Middletown police cited 70 people for speeding in the year 2000. Due to growth, there are two predictions as to how the number of citations will grow over the next 25 years.

Prediction A: The number of people cited will grow at a rate of 4 people per year.

1. What type of growth is this prediction describing?

2. According to prediction A, how many people will be cited for speeding by the Middletown police in the year 2025?

3. According to prediction A, how many people will be cited for speeding by the Middletown police during the 26-year time period 2000-2025?

Prediction B: The number of people cited will grow at a rate of 4% per year.

4. What type of growth is this prediction describing?

5. According to prediction B, how many people will be cited for speeding by the Middletown police in the year 2025?

6. According to prediction B, how many people will be cited for speeding by the Middletown police during the time period 2000-2025?

Chapter 11

Learning Outcomes

Students will

➡ describe the basic rigid motions of the plane and state their properties.

➡ classify the possible symmetries of any finite two-dimensional shape or object.

➡ classify the possible symmetries of a border pattern.

Skill Objectives

➡ Find the image of a shape under a reflection given the
   - axis of reflection
   - location of the image of one point.
   - location of two fixed points of the reflection.

➡ Find the image of a shape under a rotation given the
   - location of the rotocenter and the angle of rotation.
   - location of the image of two points.
   - image of one point and the angle of rotation.

➡ Find the image of a shape under a translation given the
   - translation vector.
   - image of a point under the translation.

➡ Find the image of a shape under a glide reflection given
   - a description of the translation and reflection.
   - the location of the image of two points.

➡ Give the symmetry type (D_N or Z_N) of finite figures in the plane.

➡ Give the symmetry type (mm, mg, m1, 1m, 1g, 12, 11) of border patterns.

➡ Identify a rigid motion based on its properties.

Ideas for the Classroom

Consider using the following examples to aid in-class discussion.

Suppose that *C* is translated to *C'*. Find the image of *ABC* under this translation. Find the vector (and length) of this translation.

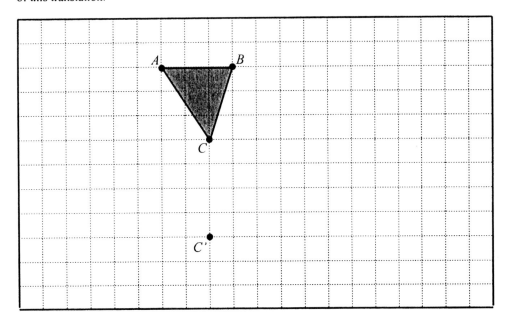

Suppose that *C* is translated to *C'*. Find the image of *ABCD* under this translation. Find the vector (and length) of this translation.

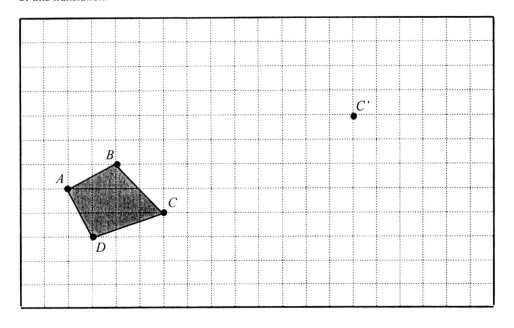

Find the image of *ABC* under the following reflection.

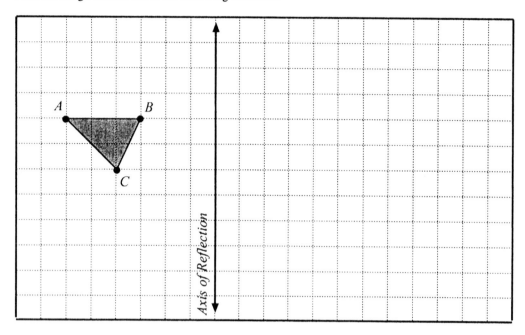

Find the image of *ABCD* under the following reflection.

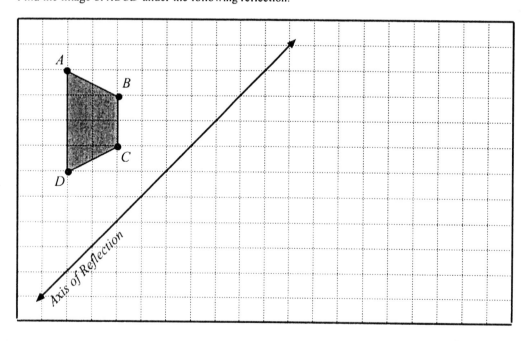

Find the axis of reflection and the image of *ABC* under the following reflection sending *C* to *C'*.

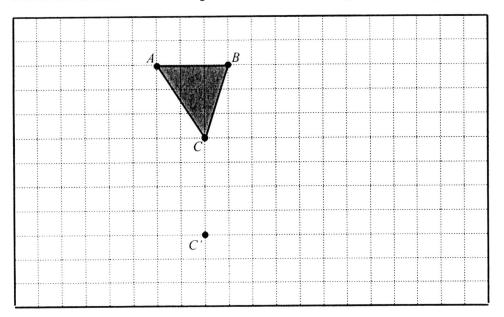

Find the axis of reflection and the image of *ABCDE* under the following reflection sending *E* to *E'*.

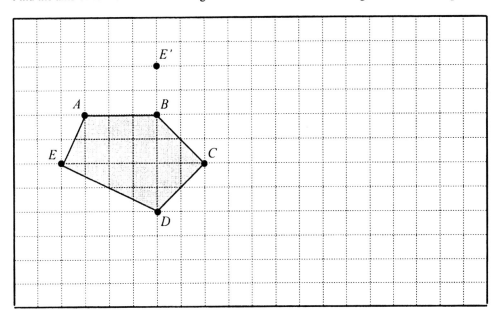

Find the axis of reflection and the image of *ABC* under the following reflection sending *B* to *B'*.

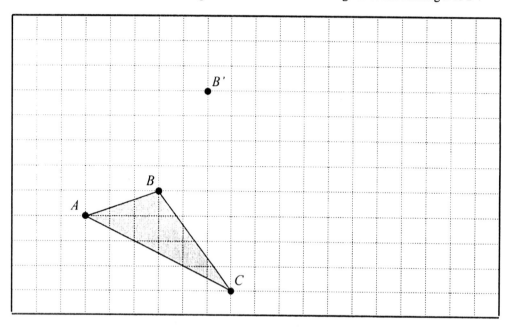

Find the image of *ABCD* under the following glide reflection whose translation is 4 units up and axis of reflection is as shown.

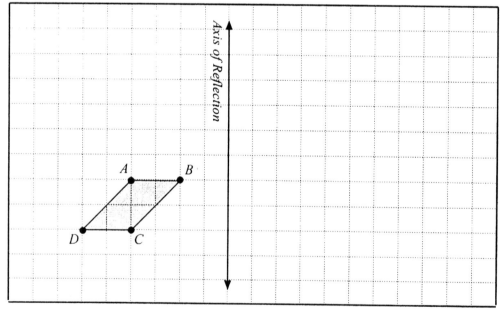

Find the image of *ABC* under a glide reflection that sends *B* to *B'* and *C* to *C'*.

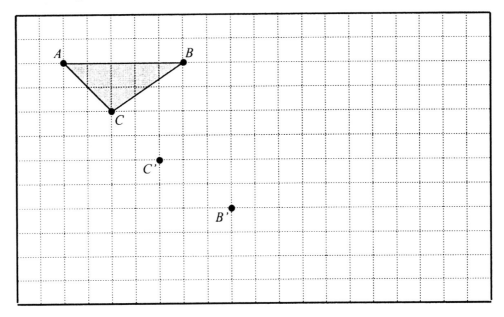

Find the image of *ABCDE* under a glide reflection that sends *B* to *B'* and *C* to *C'*.

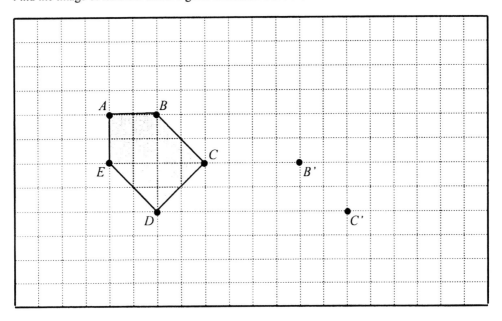

Find the image of *ABCDE* under a glide reflection that sends *C* to *C'* and *D* to *D'*.

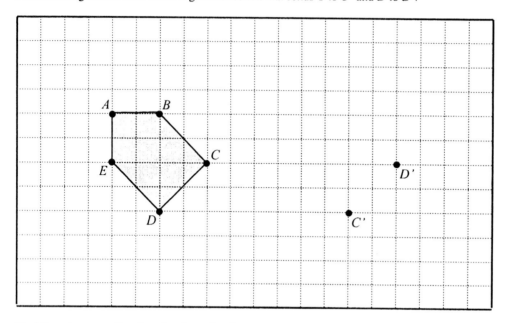

Find the rotocenter *O* and angle of rotation for a rotation that sends *A* to *A'* and *C* to *C'*. Find the image of *ABC*.

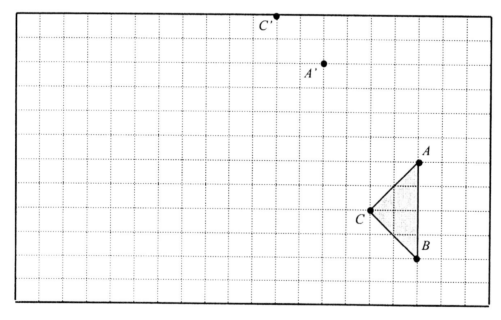

Find the rotocenter O and angle of rotation for a rotation that sends B to B' and C to C'. Find the image of ABC.

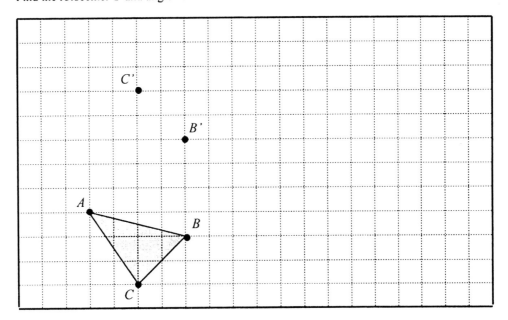

Worksheets

Symmetry Types

Border Patterns

Symmetry Type

Putting objects into categories is an effective way to better understand the world around us. From a biological standpoint, the three objects below could all be placed in the category of living organisms. From a mathematical point of view, these objects appear to be in the same "symmetry family."

We say that two objects or shapes are of the same **symmetry type** if they have exactly the same set of symmetries. The symmetry type of the objects above is D_1. The "D" represents the fact that the objects have the same number of reflection symmetries as rotation symmetries. The "1" represents the fact that each object has exactly 1 reflection (and 1 rotation).

Objects that have rotations but not reflections are put into a different category. Such objects are said to have symmetry type "Z." For example, the objects above each have 3 rotations and no reflections so are said to be of type Z_3.

Classify each of the objects below according to their symmetry type.

Classifying Border Patterns

There are seven types (categories) of border patterns. The classification system assigns to each border pattern a two-symbol code.

Seven Types of Border Patterns			
1m	1g	12	11
mm	mg		m1

The first symbol signifies if there is vertical (**m**idline) symmetry or not:

m = vertical symmetry
1 = no vertical symmetry

The second symbol signifies if the pattern has these additional symmetries:

m = horizontal (**m**idline) symmetry
g = glide reflectional symmetry
2 = half-turn symmetry
1 = no additional symmetry

A flowchart for classifying border patterns:

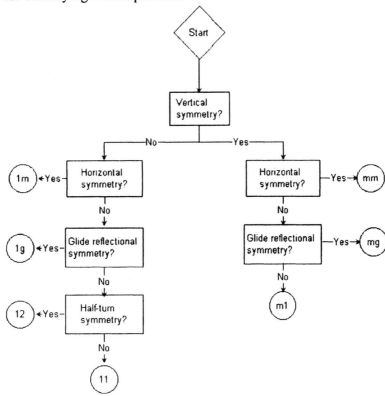

Fill in each box with Yes/No in order to determine the correct border pattern type.

Symmetry Type							
Pattern							
Half Turns							
Glide Reflections							
Horizontal Reflections							
Vertical Reflections							
Translations							

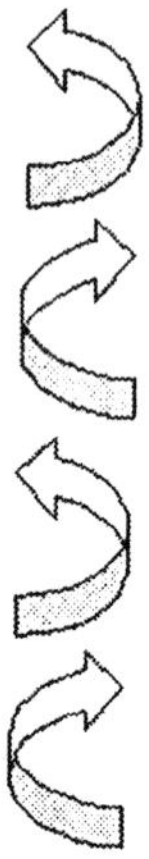

Chapter 12

Learning Outcomes

Students will

- explain the process by which fractals such as the Koch snowflake and the Sierpinski Gasket are constructed.

- recognize self-similarity (or symmetry of scale) and its relevance.

- describe how random processes can create fractals such as the Sierpinski Gasket.

- explain the process by which the Mandelbrot set is constructed.

Skill Objectives

- Calculate the perimeter and area of the figure found at any step in the construction of a given fractal.

- Draw the outcome of a particular step in the construction of a fractal.

- Play the chaos game.

- Add and multiply complex numbers.

- Construct the Mandelbrot sequence for a given seed s and identify it as escaping, periodic, or attracted.

Ideas for the Classroom

Matryoshka dolls can be used to illustrate the idea of symmetry on different scales.

While Mandelbrot sequences can easily be generated using computer algebra packages such as Maple or Mathematica, it is also possible to generate them using Microsoft *Excel* using the *Analysis Toolpak Add-In* (Look under *Options* for the list of *Add-Ins*). The IMSUM and IMPRODUCT functions are the key to constructing Mandelbrot sequences in *Excel*.

Consider playing the Chaos game on a regular hexagon (using a standard die). The resulting figure will be the Sierpinski Hexagon. One choice of possible vertices is $(-2,0)$, $(-1, -\sqrt{3})$, $(1, -\sqrt{3})$, $(2,0)$, $(1, \sqrt{3})$, $(-1, \sqrt{3})$.

The classic website for the Chaos game and for exploring the Mandelbrot set is located at Boston University: http://math.bu.edu/DYSYS/.

Discuss the "box" fractal described in the figures below. Be sure to discuss items such as the number of rectangles, perimeter, and area at stage N of construction.

Construction of Box Fractal:

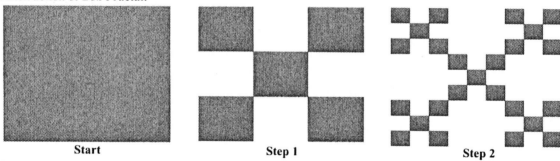

Start   Step 1   Step 2

Box Fractal:

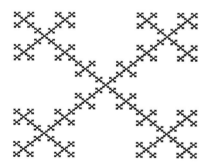

Worksheets

The *Sierpinski Hexagon*

The Sierpinski Hexagon

The **Sierpinski Hexagon** is created by means of the following recursive sequence of steps:

Start. Start with a solid hexagon. The size of the hexagon is not relevant so assume for simplicity that each side of the hexagon has length 1.

Step 1. Replace the solid hexagon with six smaller hexagons each having sides of length 1/3 as shown in the figure below.

Steps 2, 3, ...etc. Replace each solid hexagon with six smaller hexagons each having sides of length 1/3 of the hexagon being replaced.

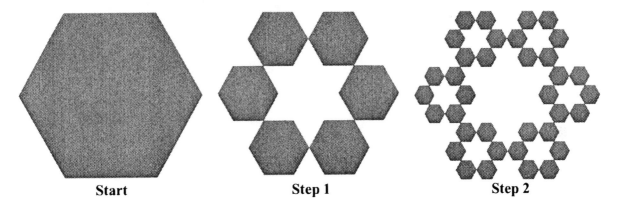

| **Start** | **Step 1** | **Step 2** |

The resulting figure is shown below.

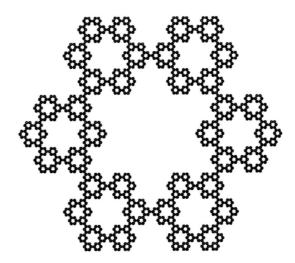

1. Fill in the missing entries in the following table.

	Start	Step 1	Step 2	Step 3	Step 4	...	Step N
Number of sides	6	24					
Length of each side	1	1/3					
Length of the boundary	6	8					

2. Focus now on just the "inner" boundary formed. Fill in the missing entries in the table below.

	Step 1	Step 2	Step 3	Step 4	Step 5	...	Step N
Number of "inner" sides	12	48					
Length of each "inner" side	1/3	1/9					
Length of the "inner" boundary	4	48/9					

3. What is the length of the inner boundary of the Sierpinski Hexagon? What does the shape of this inner boundary remind you of?

4. What is the area of the single large inner region of the Sierpinski Hexagon?

5. Complete the following table.

	Step 1	Step 2	Step 3	Step 4	Step 5	...	Step N
Number of holes	1						

6. [Challenging] Copy the results of the table above to complete this table. Use it to find the total area of the holes that result in the construction of the Sierpinski Hexagon.

	Step 1	Step 2	Step 3	Step 4	Step 5	...	Step N
Number of holes	1						
Area of holes							

7. Play the chaos game on the vertices of a regular hexagon using the applet found at http://math.bu.edu/DYSYS/applets/fractalina.html. Describe the resulting figure.

Chapter 13

Learning Outcomes

Students will

- ➡ identify whether a given survey or poll is biased.

- ➡ list and discuss the quality of several sampling methods.

- ➡ identify components of a well-constructed clinical study.

- ➡ define key terminology in the data collection process.

- ➡ estimate the size of a population using the capture-recapture method.

Skill Objectives

- ➡ Identify the population, sample, and sampling frame.

- ➡ Distinguish between a parameter and a statistic.

- ➡ Identify the sampling method used in a survey or poll.

- ➡ Identify whether sampling error is a result of sampling variability or bias.

- ➡ Estimate the size of a population using capture-recapture.

- ➡ Identify whether a study is blind, double-blind, or neither.

- ➡ List possible confounding variables in an experiment.

- ➡ Discuss elements of poor design.

Ideas for the Classroom

Distinguish between simple random sampling, stratified sampling, quota sampling, and convenience sampling using the following story:

Farmer Bob own a vineyard. Most of his vineyard is located near his winery in the valley, but part of the vineyard is located on a nearby hill. He grows four varieties of grapes – *A*, *B*, *C*, and *D*. He wants to calculate his yield from each variety so during harvest he sends out one of him farmhands to take a survey.
Convenience Sampling – the farmhand selects the first 100 vines that he comes across as he enters the fields. As a result, none of the vines from atop the hill are in his sample. [...and this is a problem since variety *D* grows better in such an environment.]

Quota Sampling – The farmer instructs the farmhand to select 25 vines of each type, but he is free to choose any 25 vines that he wants. [again, the farmhand may be too lazy to walk to the top of the hill to do any sampling so variety *D*, which grows better on the hill, may be shortchanged in the sample.]

Stratified Random Sampling – The farmer knows that his vines are equally distributed among variety *A*, *B*, *C*, and *D*. From each variety, he asks the farmhand to sample 25 vines at random.

Simple Random Sampling – The farmer asks his farmhand to select 100 vines at random from the vineyard.

Describe how it is that simple random sampling is a type of random sampling. Give an example of random sampling that is *not* simple random sampling. Systematic random sampling would be one such example.

Discuss the effect of cell phones on modern public opinion polling. In particular, if cellular phones are not called in public opinion polls discuss any bias introduced.

Discuss validity of online polls and give current examples. Some websites (such as cbs.sportsline.com/fantasy) allow a user to develop their own instant poll. You might try creating a "fun" poll at the beginning of class – one in which the target population (American adults) greatly differs from that of the sampling frame (say, fantasy football fanatics). Then, at the end of class, note the biased results of the poll.

Present various studies and have students responds to the following prompts:
- What is the *target population* under study? What is the *sampling frame*?
- Are there any problems with the sample? If so, what are they?
- What are the *sample statistics* and *population parameters* for the survey/study?

Study 1: You are conducting a poll of 1,500 people to predict the outcome of the next gubernatorial election. You randomly sample from a list of registered voters in the state. 45% say they will vote for _____.

Study 2: In order to estimate how effective Dr. _____ is in his Math ___ class, s/he gives 5 students in each of his/her two sections a survey on which they rate his/her effectiveness on a scale of 1-10. S/he chooses students from each section in the following way: one that is getting an "A", one that is getting a "B", one that is getting a "C", etc…

Study 3: You want to decide if residents of __(your city)__ prefer Coca-cola or Pepsi. You set up a taste test booth at one of the local supermarkets and offer free samples in return for an opinion.

To model capture-recapture, buy two bags of dried beans – one white and one colored (red, green, black, whatever). Put all of the white beans in an ice cream bucket along with 300 of the colored beans. Identify the beans with a deer population (albino deer!). Note that 300 of the deer in the population have been captured and tagged (painted with nontoxic red paint!). Have a pair of students recapture a set of deer from the population by reaching into the bucket to pull out a handful of beans. Based on their sample, ask them to estimate the deer population (i.e. how many beans are in the bucket). Discuss accuracy of this technique. [Thanks go to Ms. Janis Cimperman of St. Cloud State University for this activity.]

Discuss the following experiment: A college student thinks that drinking herbal tea will improve the health of nursing home patients. She and some friends visit a large nursing home regularly and serve herbal tea to the residents in one wing. Residents in the other wing are not visited. After six months, the residents who were served tea had fewer days ill than the second.

Worksheets

Sampling Activity

Sampling Activity

Consider the handout consisting of 100 rectangles. Suppose these represent a *population* of rectangles and we are interested in determining the average (mean) size of all of the rectangles in this population. To do this, you will sample 10 rectangles and calculate the average size of the rectangles in your *sample*. This sample average will be your estimate of the population average of interest.

You will actually take two different samples, one where you are allowed to pick any 10 rectangles you desire (with the goal of selecting a "representative" sample), and the other being a simple random sample based on using a table of random numbers to select the 10 rectangles. Data from the entire class will be consolidated, and the results of each sampling technique will be compared.

On your own…

1. Select 10 rectangles from the population that you think make up a *representative sample* (in terms of the sizes of the rectangles). List the numbers of the rectangles selected under "Rectangle" in the first column of the table below (for the *"Representative"* sample).

2. Using the table on the next page, record the sizes (area) of each of the rectangles in your sample under "Area" in the first column of the table below.

3. Calculate the average (mean) size of the rectangles in your 'representative' sample. Record this in the table below.

Sampling Method I ("Representative")		Sampling Method II (Simple Random)	
Rectangle	Area	Rectangle	Area
1.		1.	
2.		2.	
3.		3.	
4.		4.	
5.		5.	
6.		6.	
7.		7.	
8.		8.	
9.		9.	
10.		10.	
Average =		Average =	

4. Now use the table of random numbers to randomly select 10 rectangles from the population. Your instructor will explain how to use this table. This will give you a *simple random sample* of rectangles. List the numbers of the rectangles selected under "Rectangle" in the second column of the table on the previous page (for the *Simple Random* sample).

5. Using the table below, record the sizes (area) of each of the rectangles in your sample under "Area" in the second column of the table on the previous page.

6. Calculate the average (mean) size of the rectangles in your simple random sample. Record this in the table on the previous page.

As a class…

7. Consolidate the results for the class (your instructor will do this). For each sampling technique, is the overall average for the class close to the true population average? Which is closer? Why?

Rectangle Activity Data (sizes of rectangles)

Rectangle	Area	Rectangle	Area	Rectangle	Area	Rectangle	Area	Rectangle	Area
1	1	21	1	41	16	61	8	81	15
2	1	22	4	42	6	62	3	82	6
3	1	23	10	43	4	63	9	83	2
4	1	24	5	44	1	64	1	84	5
5	1	25	18	45	10	65	5	85	8
6	5	26	12	46	3	66	10	86	5
7	12	27	4	47	16	67	4	87	8
8	1	28	5	48	6	68	12	88	4
9	1	29	10	49	10	69	4	89	12
10	1	30	4	50	1	70	18	90	16
11	1	31	16	51	16	71	4	91	3
12	8	32	5	52	12	72	12	92	5
13	16	33	12	53	6	73	16	93	16
14	4	34	12	54	3	74	10	94	3
15	9	35	4	55	16	75	8	95	6
16	1	36	4	56	4	76	18	96	18
17	9	37	10	57	18	77	3	97	4
18	4	38	9	58	4	78	4	98	6
19	1	39	12	59	8	79	8	99	9
20	1	40	8	60	16	80	2	100	12

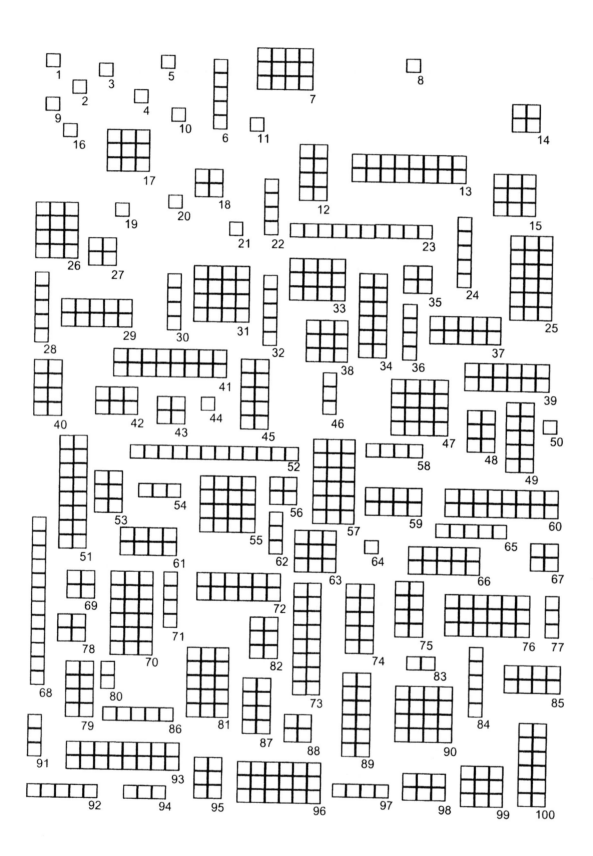

Column

Line	1	2	3	4	5	6	7	8	9	10	11	12	13	14
1	13300	87074	79666	95725	24878	82651	66566	14778	76797	14780	81525	72295	04839	96423
2	92259	57102	80428	25280	46901	20849	89768	81536	86645	12659	29676	20591	68086	26432
3	64760	64585	96096	98253	84673	40027	32832	61362	98947	96067	00742	57392	39064	66432
4	75470	66520	34693	90449	44407	44048	37937	63904	45766	66134	05366	04213	25669	26422
5	91402	42416	07844	69618	26766	25940	39972	22209	71500	64568	91921	26418	64117	94305
6	29080	09250	79656	73211	04024	86385	29880	99730	55536	84855	91567	42595	27958	30134
7	73708	83517	36103	42791	20044	59931	06115	20542	18059	02008	17955	56349	90999	49127
8	56942	53389	20562	87338	02304	51038	20655	58727	28168	15475	46503	18584	18845	49618
9	25555	21246	35509	20468	84610	82834	09922	25417	44137	48413	92157	89634	94824	78171
10	89656	20103	77490	18062	39667	47358	56873	56307	61607	49518	14577	62765	35605	81263
11	31720	57375	56228	41546	65831	38857	50490	83765	55657	14361	90725	52210	83974	29992
12	35931	04110	23726	51900	14883	24413	59744	92351	97473	89286	64364	67412	33339	31926
13	48373	45578	78547	81788	61642	34072	81249	35648	56891	69352	08962	00358	31662	25388
14	28865	14777	62730	92277	10592	04542	76463	54328	02349	17247	95012	68379	93524	70765
15	46751	22923	32261	85653	91132	21999	59516	81652	27195	48223	15664	10493	20492	38391
16	43808	76655	62028	76620	42206	35126	74087	99547	81817	42607	00582	04711	87917	77341
17	76038	65855	77919	88006	86324	88072	76222	36086	84637	93161	00725	69884	62797	56170
18	29841	80150	12777	48501	18988	27354	26575	08625	40801	59920	69011	65795	95876	55293
19	33611	54262	85963	03547	67917	48708	18912	82271	65424	69774	25976	57948	29888	88604
20	34952	37888	38917	88050	30883	18317	28290	35797	05998	41688	09763	83473	73577	12908
21	46565	04102	46880	45709	01638	92477	66969	98420	04880	45585	98427	07523	33362	64270
22	70663	88863	77775	69348	34476	17032	87589	40836	32427	70002	34914	63976	88720	82765
23	19661	72828	00102	66794	23219	53416	94970	25832	69975	94884	70060	28277	39475	46473
24	47363	46634	06541	97809	68350	82948	11398	42878	80287	88267	53976	54914	06990	67245
25	41151	14222	60697	59583	58745	25774	22987	80059	39911	96189	76072	29515	40980	07391
26	10480	15011	01536	02011	81647	91646	69179	14194	62590	36207	20969	99570	91291	90700
27	22368	46573	25595	85393	30995	89198	27982	53402	93965	34095	52666	19174	39615	99505
28	24130	48360	22527	97265	76393	64809	15179	24830	49340	32081	30680	19655	63348	58629
29	42167	93093	06243	61680	07856	16376	39440	53537	71341	57004	00849	74917	97758	16379
30	37570	39975	81837	16656	06121	91782	60468	81305	49684	60672	14110	06927	01263	54613
31	51085	12765	51821	51259	77452	16308	60756	92144	49442	53900	70960	63990	75601	40719
32	02368	21382	52404	60268	89368	19885	55322	44819	01188	65255	64835	44919	05944	55157
33	01011	54092	33362	94904	31273	04146	18594	29852	71585	85030	51132	01915	92747	64951
34	52162	53916	46369	58586	23216	14513	83149	98736	23495	64350	94738	17752	35156	35749
35	07056	97628	33787	09998	42698	06691	76988	13602	51851	46104	88916	19509	25625	58104
36	77921	06907	11008	42751	27756	53498	18602	70659	90655	15053	21916	81825	44394	42880
37	99562	72905	56420	69994	98872	31016	71194	18738	44013	48840	63213	21069	10634	12952
38	96301	91977	05463	07972	18876	20922	94595	56869	69014	60045	18425	84903	42508	32307
39	89579	14342	63661	10281	17453	18103	57740	84378	25331	12566	58678	44947	05585	56941
40	84575	36857	53342	53988	53060	59533	38867	62300	08158	17983	16439	11458	18593	64952
41	48663	91245	85828	14346	09172	30168	90229	04734	59193	22178	30421	61666	99904	32812
42	54164	58492	22421	74103	47070	25306	76468	26384	58151	06646	21524	15227	96909	44592
43	32639	32363	05597	24200	13363	38005	94342	28728	35806	06912	17012	64161	18296	22851
44	29334	27001	87637	87308	58731	00256	45834	15398	46557	41135	10367	07684	36188	18510
45	02488	33062	28834	07351	19731	92420	60952	61280	50001	67658	32586	86679	50720	94953
46	28918	69578	88231	33276	70997	79936	56865	05859	90106	31595	01547	85590	91610	78188
47	63553	40961	48235	03427	49626	69445	18663	72695	52180	20847	12234	90511	33703	90322
48	09429	93969	52636	92737	88974	33488	36320	17617	30015	08272	84115	27156	30613	74952
49	10365	61129	87529	85689	48127	52267	67689	93394	01511	26358	85104	20285	29975	89868
50	07119	97336	71048	08178	77233	13916	47564	81056	97735	85977	29372	74461	28551	90707

Chapter 14

Learning Outcomes

Students will

➡ interpret and produce an effective graphical summary of a data set.

➡ identify various types of numerical variables.

➡ interpret and produce numerical summaries of data including percentiles and five-number summaries.

➡ describe the spread of a data set using range, interquartile range, and standard deviation.

Skill Objectives

➡ Read and produce frequency tables, bar graphs, and pie charts.

➡ Read and interpret histograms.

➡ Compute means and medians.

➡ Compute percentiles (including quartiles).

➡ Compute five-number summaries and produce box plots.

➡ Interpret box plots.

➡ Compute range, interquartile range, and determine the existence of outliers.

➡ Compute standard deviation.

➡ Compute mode.

Ideas for the Classroom

Discuss the difficulties with summarizing a data set with one number – the mean.
- The average 24-hour temperature in both Florida and Arizona may be 70 degrees. However, in Arizona this might represent a temperature of 30 degrees at night and 110 degrees during the day. In Florida, on the other hand, this might represent a temperature of 60 degrees at night and 80 degrees during the day. Measures of spread are critical in summarizing a data set.
- Hall of Fame NBA player David Robinson graduated from the Naval Academy in 1987 with a mathematics major and signed a rookie contract with the San Antonio Spurs for a reported $1,046,000. Each year, roughly 35 math majors graduate from the Naval Academy. In that year, the average starting salary of math majors from the Naval Academy was at least $30,000 (even if 34 of the 35 graduates earned $0 per year fresh out of

school).

Generate a data set from your students by having them each independently guess your age and write it down on a post-it note. Have the students form a bar graph at the blackboard with their guesses. From the bar graph, determine
- a frequency table
- the mean and mode(s) using the frequency table
- the five-number summary and box plot
- any outliers (based on the definition that an outlier is any data value more than 1.5 times the IQR above the third quartile or more than 1.5 times the IQR below the first quartile)

Collect a second data set from the students by having them guess the age of a celebrity (of your choice) that is having a birthday that day. Add your own guess (make it a definite outlier!) to the mix so that the N-value of the data set is different than the previous case. Summarize this data set in a similar manner and compare the two summaries against one another (compare and contrast measures of location and measures of spread).

An interesting data set to summarize consists of tuition data for public and private institutions in your state.

Using Excel, compute the standard deviation of the data set shown in the first column below. Use two different processes. In the first, create the table shown. In the second, use the built-in STDEV function. Discuss why Excel produces two different results (see the STDEVP command for more on this).

Note: The mean is 10, the variance is 25, and the standard deviation is 5.

Data	Deviation from Mean	Squared Deviations
0	-10	100
2	-8	64
3	-7	49
6	-4	16
6	-4	16
8	-2	4
9	-1	1
10	0	0
10	0	0
10	0	0
10	0	0
10	0	0
10	0	0
11	1	1
12	2	4
14	4	16
14	4	16
17	7	49
18	8	64
20	10	100

Chapter 15

Learning Outcomes

Students will

➡ describe an appropriate sample space of a random experiment.

➡ apply the multiplication rule, permutations, and combinations to counting problems.

➡ understand the concept of a probability assignment.

➡ identify independent events and their properties.

➡ use the language of odds in describing probabilities of events.

Skill Objectives

➡ Describe an appropriate sample space for a given random experiment.

➡ Apply the multiplication rule to counting problems.

➡ Compute the value of a given combination or permutation.

➡ Apply combinations or permutations to counting problems.

➡ Construct a probability assignment for a given sample space.

➡ Describe an event using set notation.

➡ Find the probability of a given event.

➡ Write odds as probabilities and vice-versa.

Ideas for the Classroom

In discussing the concept of probability assignment, consider not only assignments made based on geometry (rolling dice, flipping coins, spinning spinners), but also assignments made arbitrarily such as in the (old and new) NBA draft lotteries.

- In 1985, each team not making the playoffs (there were 7) had an equal chance at landing the picks 1 through 7 in the draft.
- In 1990, a weighted lottery system was introduced. Of the 11 non-playoff teams, the worst received 11 balls in an urn, the second worst 10 balls, the third worst 9 balls and so on. The lottery only determined the draft order of the first three teams.
- In 1994, the probability assignment was changed again to the current weighting system (found at nba.com). *Historical note:* The change was made because the Orlando Magic defied the lottery odds by winning the No. 1

pick two years in a row. In 1992, with the second-worst record, they drafted Shaquille O'Neal. O'Neal helped Orlando make a 20-win improvement and the Magic just missed the playoffs the next year. With just one chance out of 66, the Magic won the No. 1 pick yet again in 1993 and drafted Chris Webber.

One approach to help students visualize when to use combinations and permutations involves boxes representing the elements to be selected from and filling the boxes with either checkmarks (order of selection is not relevant…use a combination) or number labels (order of selection is relevant…use a permutation).

Example: How many three-person committees can be selected from a group of 18 people?
Ans. Represent the 18 people with boxes. How many ways are there to "check" three of these boxes?

☐ ☐ ☐ ☐ ☒ ☐ ☐ ☒ ☒ ☐ ☐ ☐ ☐ ☐ ☐ ☐ ☐ ☐

How many committees consisting of a President, a Vice-President, and a Secretary can be selected from a group of 18 people?
Ans. Represent the 18 people with boxes. How many ways are there to place three different numbers in these boxes (1 = President, 2 = VP, 3 = Secretary)?

☐ ☐ ☐ ☐ [2] ☐ ☐ [3] [1] ☐ ☐ ☐ ☐ ☐ ☐ ☐ ☐ ☐

Example: How many five-card *draw* poker hands can be dealt from a standard deck of cards?
Ans. Represent the 52 cards with boxes. How many ways are there to "check" five of these boxes (a check represents that you were dealt the card)?

☐ ☐ ☐ ☐ ☒ ☐ ☐ ☒ ☒ ☐ ☐ ☒ ☐ ☐ ☐ ☒ ☐ ☐ …

How many five-card *stud* poker hands can be dealt from a standard deck of cards?
Ans. Represent the 52 cards with boxes. How many ways are there to place three different numbers in these boxes (1 = 1st card dealt, 2 = 2nd card dealt, etc.)?

☐ ☐ ☐ ☐ [2] ☐ ☐ [3] [1] ☐ ☐ [5] ☐ ☐ ☐ [4] ☐ ☐ …

Consider playing the game of 5-card Tasmanian *stud* poker with a 65-card deck consisting of the standard 52 cards in 4 suits (♠, ♣, ♦, and ♥) and 13 cards of an additional suit ☼.
- Compute various probabilities starting with that of being dealt a royal ☼ flush *in the order* A☼, K☼, Q☼, J☼, and then 10☼.
- Consider also computing probabilities in the game of Tasmanian *draw* poker.

Local state lottery games have websites that list odds of winning. Compare a few of these odds to those computed in class.

Illustrate the connection between combinations and Pascal's triangle. For example, consider building a submarine sandwich having anywhere from 0 to 5 toppings. Count how many such sandwiches can be constructed in two ways. One solution is to argue that one could select exactly 0 of the 5 toppings ($_5C_0$), exactly 1 of the 5 toppings ($_5C_1$), etc. [This gives a total of

$$_5C_0 + {_5C_1} + {_5C_2} + {_5C_3} + {_5C_4} + {_5C_5} = 1 + 5 + 10 + 10 + 5 + 1 = 32 \text{ possible sandwiches.]}$$ A second solution is to

argue that a topping can either be on the sandwich or not. That is, there are five stages of construction in which two choices are made at each stage (yielding $(1+1)^5 = 2^5 = 32$ possible sandwiches).

Bring a die from the game of Scattegories to class. (You may even want to discuss why it has 20 sides rather than 26 as a footnote on geometry.)
- Discuss a sample space for the random experiment in which this die is rolled three times.
- Calculate the probability of rolling the word CAT (rolled in order) in three consecutive rolls.
- Calculate the probability of rolling letters that spell the word CAT when rolling three dice all at once.
- Calculate the probability of rolling a vowel on a single roll of the die.
- Calculate the probability of rolling a total of two consonants and one vowel in three rolls of the die.

Students at your institution likely have ID numbers. Count how many such ID numbers are possible. It may be that all ID numbers at your institution begin with a finite sequence of zeroes. If so, be sure to take that into account. If students have computer generated e-mail addresses, count the number of distinct addresses possible.

Each state has a particular system for license plate numbers. For your state, count the number of distinct plates possible. Compare that to another (larger or smaller) state. Or, compare that number to a previous system in place in your state (in the "pioneer" days of the Model A or Model T). Explain why the system required a change.

Discuss the number of possible outcomes in the game of Clue. Given knowledge of six particular cards, discuss the probability of guessing "whodunit."

Consider a random experiment in which the spinner on the right is spun once.
- Write out a sample space for this experiment.
- Compute Pr(*A*).
- Compute Pr(*C*).
Consider a random experiment in which the spinner is spun twice.
- Write out a sample space for this experiment.
- Compute Pr(*AA*).
- Compute Pr(*CC*).
- Compute Pr(at least one *A* is spun)
- Compute Pr(not spinning an *A*)
- Compute Pr(at least one *C* is spun)
- Compute Pr(not spinning a *C*)
Consider a random experiment in which the spinner is spun eight times.
- Compute Pr(at least one C is spun)
- Compute Pr(exactly seven C's are spun)

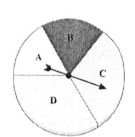

Who Wants To Be a Millionaire? In this game show, contestants answer a series of 15 multiple-choice trivia questions. Describe the rules of the game to students (including the lifelines – phone a friend, 50:50, and ask the audience). Assume Jed has absolutely no knowledge whatsoever, but that Jed has an all-knowing friend and an all-knowing studio audience. If the lifelines are used on three of the 15 questions, what is the probability of Jed winning $1,000,000?

Worksheets

Is it Fair?

Funky Yahtzee

Is It Fair?

Game A. Two players each roll a standard six-sided die. Player 1 will win if the *difference* of the two rolls is 0, 1, or 2. Player 2 will win if the difference of the two rolls is 3, 4, or 5.

1. Is this game fair?

2. What is the probability of each player winning this game?

Game B. Two players each roll a standard six-sided die. Player 1 will win if the difference of the two rolls is even. Player 2 will win if the difference of the two rolls is odd.

3. Is this game fair?

4. What is the probability of each player winning this game?

Game C. Two players each roll a standard six-sided die. Player 1 will win if the difference of the two rolls is 0, 1, or 5. Player 2 will win if the difference of the two rolls is 2, 3, or 4.

5. Is this game fair?

6. What is the probability of each player winning this game?

Game D. A fair coin is flipped nine times. Player 1 will win if it lands heads exactly 4 or 5 times. Otherwise player 2 will win.

7. Is this game fair?

8. What is the probability of each player winning this game?

Game E. Player 1 spins wheel 1, player 2 spins wheel 2, and player 3 spins wheel 3. The player spinning the highest number wins.

9. Is this game fair?

10. What is the probability of each player winning this game?

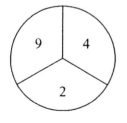

Wheel 1

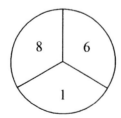

Wheel 2

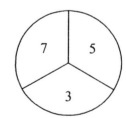

Wheel 3

Funky Yahtzee

Yahtzee is a dice game in which five standard six-sided dice are rolled at one time. In Exercise 85 in the text, you are asked to compute the probability of various outcomes in one roll of the dice (Yahtzee, four of a kind, a large straight, and trips). There are other outcomes (e.g. full house, two pair, one pair, nothing) in Yahtzee that one can compute the probability of too. Two of these calculations follow below.

Full House. Three dice that have the same value, and a pair of dice that have the same value as each other but not the same value as the first three. *Example:* {4, 4, 3, 3, 4}

There are a total of $6^5 = 7,776$ possible (ordered) outcomes when rolling five dice. There are $_5C_3 = 10$ ways to select which 3 of the 5 dice will match. Then, there are $_6P_2 = 30$ ways to select the values for the three of a kind and the other pair. This totals 300 outcomes. So, the probability of rolling a full house in a single roll of five dice is 300/7,776.

Two Pairs. *Example:* {4, 3, 3, 2, 4}

There are $_5C_2 = 10$ ways to select the location of one pair of the dice. Then, there are $_3C_2 = 3$ ways to select the location of the other pair. Next, there are $_6C_2 = 15$ ways to select the values for the pairs. Finally, there are $_4C_1 = 4$ ways to select the value of the remaining die. This totals 1800 outcomes. So, the probability of rolling two pairs in a single roll of five dice is 1800/7,776.

In this activity, we introduce a slight complication. The Yahtzee outcomes you count will come not from an ordinary game of Yahtzee but from a funky game (which we will call *Funky Yahtzee*) where *six 10-sided* dice are used.

If we use *six 10-sided* dice rather than five dice we consider twelve possible *types* of outcomes. These are described and illustrated below.

Yahtzee. This is the same idea as in five-dice Yahtzee; it consists of matching all of the six dice. *Example:* {4, 4, 4, 4, 4, 4}

Five of a Kind. Five dice of the same value, plus one die that doesn't match the other five. *Example:* {4, 4, 4, 3, 4, 4}

Four and a Pair. Four dice that have the same value, and a pair of dice that have the same value as each other but not the same value as the first four. *Example:* {4, 4, 3, 3, 4, 4}

Two Triples. Three dice that have the same value, and another three dice that have the same value as each other but not the same value as the other three. *Example:* {4, 4, 3, 4, 3, 3}

Large Straight. Six dice that are *in sequence*. *Example:* {4, 6, 7, 5, 8, 3}

Four of a Kind. Four dice of the same value, and two other dice that don't match each other or the first four. *Example:* {3, 3, 2, 4, 3, 3}

Three Pairs. Just what you'd expect. *Example:* {4, 3, 3, 2, 4, 2}

Three-Two-One. Three dice that have the same value, two other dice that have the same value as each other but not the same value as the first three, and one die that doesn't match any of the other five. *Example:* {4, 4, 2, 3, 4, 3}

Three of a Kind. Three dice that have the same value, plus three other dice that all have different values and all fail to match the other three. *Example:* {4, 3, 2, 4, 4, 6}

Two Pairs. *Example:* {4, 3, 3, 2, 6, 4}

One Pair. *Example:* {4, 3, 2, 6, 1, 4}

Nothing. Any outcome other than those listed above. That is, six non-matching dice that do not form a large straight. *Example:* {2, 6, 4, 5, 8, 3}

Calculate the probability of each type of outcome in *Funky Yahtzee*. Place your answers in the following table.

Outcome	Probability
Yahtzee	
Five of a Kind	
Four and a Pair	
Two Triples	
Large Straight	
Four of a Kind	
Three Pairs	
Three-Two-One	
Three of a Kind	
Two Pairs	
One Pair	
Nothing	

Chapter 16

Learning Outcomes

Students will

➡ identify and describe an approximately normal distribution.

➡ state properties of a normal distribution.

➡ understand a data set in terms of standardized data values.

➡ state the 68-95-99.7 rule.

➡ apply the honest and dishonest-coin principles to understand the concept of a confidence interval.

Skill Objectives

➡ Find parameters (mean, median, standard deviation, etc.) of a normal distribution given in graphical form.

➡ Find the value of other parameters given two parameters of a normal distribution.

➡ find standardized values given two parameters of a normal distribution.

➡ Use standardized values to determine parameters of a normal distribution.

➡ Determine the percent of data that falls between key values of a normal distribution.

➡ Apply the 68-95-99.7 rule to approximately normal distributions.

➡ Use the (dis)honest-coin principle to understand a random variable X.

Ideas for the Classroom

The properties of the normal curve can be discussed using one of many applets found on the internet. Below are locations for several (among many) that fit well with this chapter.

- http://it.stlawu.edu/~rlock/MooreApplets/applets/normalcurve.html
- http://www.spsu.edu/math/deng/m2260/stat/nd2/SNormal.html
- http://www.stat.berkeley.edu/~stark/Java/Html/NormHiLite.htm
- http://www.stat.sc.edu/~west/javahtml/CLT.html
- http://davidmlane.com/hyperstat/z_table.html
- http://webphysics.davidson.edu/applets/Galton/BallDrop.html (alternatively
http://www.ucs.louisiana.edu/~ras2777/methods/normal.html)

Point out that there are many ways a data set may be approximately distributed (besides normally). Graphically illustrate other (continuous) distributions. These might include a uniform, bimodal, or decreasing (e.g. exponential) distribution. Give examples of data sets that each distribution models.

Simulating an experiment in which a fair coin is tossed 10 times is easy using software such as Excel. The built-in RAND function in Excel will produce a uniformly distributed random number between 0 and 1. So, =ROUNDDOWN(2*RAND(),0) will uniformly produce a 1 or 0 (heads or tails).

Below is the start of an Excel worksheet that simulates several trials of this experiment. To generate it, the formula in cell B2 was copied across row 2. Then, =SUM(B2:K2) was placed in cell M2. Finally, row 2 was copied down the worksheet (generating as many trials as one would like).

To start to "see" the bell-curve being formed, a frequency table can be created. The possible number of heads for each trial are put in column O of the worksheet (place the value 0 in cell O2 and formula =A3 in cell O3 and copy down). To find the frequencies (say for 50 trials), use the formula =COUNTIF($M$2:$M$51,O2) in cell P2 and copy it down column P.

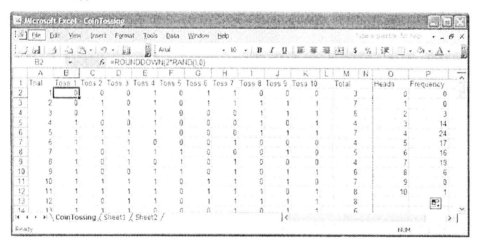

The dishonest-coin principle can also be illustrated with the Excel worksheet generated above. Simply change the coin toss to "selecting a card from a well-shuffled deck and note its suit." The only changes necessary is in are to use the formula =ROUNDDOWN(4*RAND(),0) and to use =COUNTIF(B2:BK2,0) in cell M2.

Worksheets

ACTing Normal

ACTing Normal

In 2005, 1,186,251 (roughly 40% of high school graduates) took the ACT college entrance exam. Composite scores on this exam had mean $\mu = 20.9$ and standard deviation $\sigma = 4.9$. More detailed information can be found in the table below.

ACT Composite Score	Frequency	Percent at or Below
36	193	100.00%
35	1617	99.98%
34	3729	99.85%
33	6752	99.53%
32	10359	98.96%
31	15401	98.09%
30	21725	96.79%
29	27109	94.96%
28	35992	92.68%
27	44428	89.64%
26	52811	85.90%
25	62669	81.44%
24	70594	76.16%
23	77953	70.21%
22	83849	63.64%
21	89908	56.57%
20	91333	48.99%
19	89073	41.29%
18	87315	33.78%
17	79103	26.42%
16	70716	19.75%
15	59275	13.79%
14	45796	8.80%
13	31658	4.94%
12	18095	2.27%
11	6586	0.74%
10	1594	0.19%
9	420	0.05%
8	138	0.02%
7	41	0.01%
6	12	0.00%
5	7	0.00%
4	0	0.00%
3	0	0.00%
2	0	0.00%
1	0	0.00%

A frequency chart of the data indicates that this data is approximately normally distributed with mean $\mu = 20.9$ and standard deviation $\sigma = 4.9$. Use this fact to answer the questions that follow.

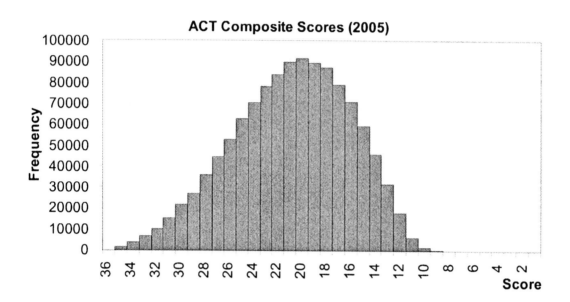

1. Estimate the value of the first quartile Q_1. Compare this value to the data table.

2. Estimate the value of the third quartile Q_3. Compare this value to the data table.

3. Compare the interquartile range of the normal distribution with the data table.

4. If a normal curve were imposed on top of the bar graph, approximate the location of the two inflection points.

5. Estimate the range of scores based on the normal distribution. How does this range match the data given in the table?

6. Estimate the number of students that scored between 11.1 and 30.7 (i.e. between 11 and 31).

7. Estimate the number of students that scored below 25.8 (i.e. below 26).

8. Estimate the number of students that scored above 17.6 (i.e. 18 or more).

9. Locate the average ACT score for entering freshmen at your school. Determine the standardized data value for this value. Then, use the chart given prior to Exercise 67 to estimate the percentile of this value.

Chapter 1

WALKING

A.   Ballots and Preference Schedules

1. (a) There are 12 votes all together. A majority is more than half of the votes, or at least 7.

(b) The Country Cookery has the most first-place votes (6). It is a plurality.

(c)

Number of voters	5	3	1	3
1st choice	*A*	*C*	*B*	*C*
2nd choice	*B*	*B*	*D*	*B*
3rd choice	*C*	*A*	*C*	*D*
4th choice	*D*	*D*	*A*	*A*

2. (a) There are 11 votes altogether, so a majority winner would have to have at least 6 votes.

(b) Arsenio (*A*) with 5 first-place votes—a plurality.

(c)

Number of voters	2	1	3	3	2
1st choice	*A*	*C*	*A*	*C*	*B*
2nd choice	*B*	*A*	*C*	*B*	*C*
3rd choice	*C*	*B*	*B*	*A*	*A*

3. (a) $5 + 3 + 5 + 3 + 2 + 3 = 21$

(b) There are 21 votes all together. A majority is more than half of the votes, or at least 11.

(c) $A \ (5 + 3 = 8)$

(d) $E \ (5 + 3 + 2 = 10)$

4. (a) $55 \ (3 + 4 + 9 + 9 + 2 + 5 + 8 + 3 + 12 = 55)$

(b) 28

(c) C (with 11 first-place votes)

(d) C (with 4 last-place votes)

5. (a) No candidate has a majority of the first-place votes. So all candidates with 20% or less of the 21 first-place votes are eliminated. $0.20(21) = 4.2$, so all candidates with fewer than 4.2 first-place votes (4 votes or fewer) are eliminated. The candidates that are eliminated are *B* (3 first-place votes) and *E* (0 first-place votes).

(b)

Number of voters	5	3	5	3	2	3
1st choice	A	A	C	D	D	A
2nd choice	C	D	D	C	C	C
3rd choice	D	C	A	A	A	D

(c) Candidate *A* now has 11 first-place votes and is the majority winner.

6. (a) *A* and *C* (There are 1240 ballots; 25% of 1240 = 310; *A* has 310 first-place votes and *C* has 270 first place votes; *B* and *D* each have 330 first-place votes.)

(b)

Number of voters	745	495
1st choice	B	D
2nd choice	D	B

(c) *B* (with 745 first-place votes)

7.

Number of voters	255	480	765
1st choice	L	C	M
2nd choice	M	M	L
3rd choice	C	L	C

8.

Number of voters	450	900	225	675
1st choice	A	B	C	C
2nd choice	C	C	B	A
3rd choice	B	A	A	B

9.

Number of voters	47	36	24	13	5
1st choice	B	A	B	E	C
2nd choice	E	B	A	B	E
3rd choice	A	D	D	C	A
4th choice	C	C	E	A	D
5th choice	D	E	C	D	B

10.

Number of voters	47	36	24	13	5
A	1	2	5	2	4
B	3	1	2	4	1
C	2	4	3	1	5
D	5	3	1	5	2
E	4	5	4	3	3

B.   Plurality Method

11. (a) *B* and *D* tie with 330 first-place votes each.
    A has 153 + 102 + 55 = 310 first-place votes.
    B has 202 + 108 + 20 = 330 first-place votes.
    C has 110 + 160 = 270 first-place votes.
    D has 175 + 155 = 330 first-place votes.

(b) *D* wins the election.
    B has 55 + 110 + 175 = 340 last-place votes.
    D has 153 + 20 + 160 = 333 last-place votes.

12. (a) It's a tie between *A* and *B*, each with 16 first-place votes.

(b) *B* (December 20, 9:00 p.m.)
    A has 17 last-place votes and *B* has 15 last-place votes.

13. (a) 23 votes will guarantee *A* at least a tie for first; 24 votes guarantee that *A* is the only winner. (With 23 of the remaining 30 votes *A* has 49 votes. The only candidate with a chance to have that many votes is *C*. Even if *C* gets the other 7 remaining votes, *C* would not have enough votes to beat *A*.)

For another way to compute this answer, suppose that A receives *x* out of the remaining 30 votes and the competitor with the most votes, *C*, receives the remaining 30 - *x* votes. To determine the values of *x* that guarantee a win for *A*, we solve $26 + x \geq 42 + (30 - x)$, i.e. $2x \geq 46$. So $x \geq 23$ votes will guarantee *A* at least a tie for first.

(b) 11 votes will guarantee *C* at least a tie for first; 12 votes guarantee *C* is the only winner. (With 11 of the remaining votes *C* has 53 votes. The only candidate with a chance to have that many votes is *D*. Even if *D* gets the other 19 remaining votes, *D* would not have enough votes to beat *C*.)

For another way to compute this answer, suppose that *C* receives *y* out of the remaining 30 votes and the competitor with the most votes, *D*, receives the remaining 30-*y* votes. To determine the values of *y* that guarantee a win for *C*, we solve $42 + y \geq 34 + (30 - y)$, i.e. $2y \geq 22$. So $y \geq 11$ votes will guarantee *C* at least a tie for first.

14. (a) 27 votes will guarantee *B* at least a tie for first; 28 votes guarantee *B* is the only winner.
    With 27 of the remaining 30 votes *B* has 45 votes. The only candidate with a chance to have that many votes is *C*. Even if *C* gets the other 3 remaining votes, it would not have enough votes to beat *B*.

(b) 19 votes will guarantee *D* at least a tie for first; 20 votes guarantee *D* is the only winner.
    With 19 of the remaining 30 votes *D* has 53 votes. The only candidate with a chance to have that many votes is *C*. Even if *C* gets the other 11 remaining votes, it would not have enough votes to beat *D*.

15. (a) 721/2 = 360.5 so that 361 votes are needed to have a majority.

(b) The winning candidate has the smallest number of votes possible if the votes are distributed as evenly as possible. $\frac{721}{5} = 144.2$, so the smallest number of votes a winning candidate can have is 145. (If this were the case, then four of the candidates each receive 144 votes and one of the candidates, the winning candidate, receives 145 votes.)

(c) The winning candidate has the smallest number of votes possible if the votes are distributed as evenly as possible. $\frac{721}{10} = 72.1$, so the smallest number of votes a winning candidate can have is 73. (If this were the case, then nine of the candidates each receive 72 votes and one of the candidates, the winning candidate, receives 73 votes.)

16. (a) $1025/2 = 512.5$ so that 513 votes are needed to have a majority.

(b) The winning candidate has the smallest number of votes possible if the votes are distributed as evenly as possible. $\frac{1025}{4} = 256.25$, so the smallest number of votes a winning candidate can have is 257. (If this were the case, then three of the candidates each receive 256 votes and one of the candidates, the winning candidate, receives 257 votes.)

(c) The winning candidate has the smallest number of votes possible if the votes are distributed as evenly as possible. $\frac{1025}{8} = 128.125$, so the smallest number of votes a winning candidate can have is 129. (If this were the case, then seven of the candidates each receive 128 votes and one of the candidates, the winning candidate, receives 129 votes.)

C.   Borda Count Method

17. (a) The winner is Professor Chavez.

A has $5 \times (5+3) + 4 \times 0 + 3 \times 3 + 2 \times (5+2) + 1 \times 3 = 66$ points.
B has $5 \times 3 + 4 \times 5 + 3 \times (3+3+2) + 2 \times 0 + 1 \times 5 = 64$ points.
C has $5 \times 5 + 4 \times (3+2) + 3 \times 5 + 2 \times (3+3) + 1 \times 0 = 72$ points.
D has $5 \times (3+2) + 4 \times 3 + 3 \times 5 + 2 \times 5 + 1 \times 3 = 65$ points.
E has $5 \times 0 + 4 \times (5+3) + 3 \times 0 + 2 \times 3 + 1 \times (5+3+2) = 48$ points.

(b)

Number of voters	5	3	5	5	3
1st choice	A	A	C	D	B
2nd choice	B	D	D	C	A
3rd choice	C	B	A	B	C
4th choice	D	C	B	A	D

A has $4 \times (5+3) + 3 \times 3 + 2 \times 5 + 1 \times 5 = 56$ points.
B has $4 \times 3 + 3 \times 5 + 2 \times (3+5) + 1 \times 5 = 48$ points.
C has $4 \times 5 + 3 \times 5 + 2 \times (5+3) + 1 \times 3 = 54$ points.

D has $4 \times 5 + 3 \times (3+5) + 2 \times 0 + 1 \times (5+3) = 52$ points.
The winner is Professor Argand.

(c) Professor Chavez (choice C) was the winner of an election and when an irrelevant alternative (candidate E) is disqualified and the ballots recounted, we find that Professor Argand (choice A) is now the winner of the election.

18. (a) A has $4 \times (153 + 102 + 55) + 3 \times (110 + 175) + 2 \times (202 + 20 + 160) + 1 \times (108 + 155) = 3122$ points.

B has $4 \times (202 + 108 + 20) + 3 \times (102 + 160 + 155) + 2 \times 153 + 1 \times (55 + 110 + 175) = 3217$ points.

C has $4 \times (110 + 160) + 3 \times (153 + 108 + 20) + 2 \times (55 + 175 + 155) + 1 \times (102 + 202) = 2997$ points.

D has $4 \times (175 + 155) + 3 \times (55 + 202) + 2 \times (102 + 108 + 110) + 1 \times (153 + 20 + 160) = 3064$ points.

Brandy is the winner.

(b)

Number of voters	153	102	55	202	108	20	110	160	175	155
1st choice	A	A	A	B	B	B	C	C	A	B
2nd choice	C	B	C	A	C	C	A	B	C	C
3rd choice	B	C	B	C	A	A	B	A	B	A

A has $3 \times (153 + 102 + 55 + 175) + 2 \times (202 + 110) + 1 \times (108 + 20 + 160 + 155) = 2522$ points.

B has $3 \times (202 + 108 + 20 + 155) + 2 \times (102 + 160) + 1 \times (153 + 55 + 110 + 175) = 2472$ points.

C has $3 \times (110 + 160) + 2 \times (153 + 55 + 108 + 20 + 175 + 155) + 1 \times (102 + 202) = 2446$ points.

Alicia is the winner.

(c) Brandy is the winner of the election and, after the irrelevant alternative Dionne is removed, in the reelection Alicia is the winner.

19. (a) The winner is Borrelli.
    A has 79 points. B has 92 points. C has 61 points. D has 88 points. E has 40 points.

(b) Dante has a majority of the first-place votes (13 out of a possible 24 votes) but does not win the election.

(c) Dante, having a majority of the first-place votes, is a Condorcet candidate but does not win the election.

20. (a) The winner is Delgado.

(b) Chou has a majority (14) of the first-place votes but does not win the election.

(c) Chou, having a majority of the first-place votes, is a Condorcet candidate but does not win the election.

21. (a) Column 1: $0.40 \times 200 = 80$ voters; Column 2: $0.25 \times 200 = 50$ voters;
    Column 3: $0.20 \times 200 = 40$ voters; Column 4: $0.15 \times 200 = 30$ voters.
    A has $4 \times 80 + 3 \times 30 + 2 \times 40 + 1 \times 50 = 540$ points.
    B has $4 \times (40 + 30) + 3 \times 50 + 2 \times 80 + 1 \times 0 = 590$ points.

C has $4 \times 50 + 3 \times 0 + 2 \times 0 + 1 \times (80 + 40 + 30) = 350$ points.

D has $4 \times 0 + 3 \times (80 + 40) + 2 \times (50 + 30) + 1 \times 0 = 520$ points.

The winner is B.

(b) The winner is B.

Column 1: $0.40 \times 100N = 40N$ voters; Column 2: $0.25 \times 100N = 25N$ voters;

Column 3: $0.20 \times 100N = 20N$ voters; Column 4: $0.15 \times 100N = 15N$ voters.

A has $4 \times 40N + 3 \times 15N + 2 \times 20N + 1 \times 25N = 270N$ points.

B has $4 \times (20N + 15N) + 3 \times 25N + 2 \times 40N + 1 \times 0N = 295N$ points.

C has $4 \times 25N + 3 \times 0N + 2 \times 0N + 1 \times (40N + 20N + 15N) = 175N$ points.

D has $4 \times 0N + 3 \times (40N + 20N) + 2 \times (25N + 15N) + 1 \times 0N = 260N$ points.

(c) No. The number of points for each candidate is just multiplied by N.

22. **(a)** 36, 18, 12, 9. The winner is A.

(b) $12N$, $6N$, $4N$, $3N$. The winner is A.

(c) No. The number of points for each candidate is just multiplied by N.

23. **(a)** To achieve the maximum number of points possible, a candidate would need to receive all 50 first-place votes. Such a candidate would have $4 \times 50 + 3 \times 0 + 2 \times 0 + 1 \times 0 = 200$ points.

(b) To achieve the minimum number of points possible, a candidate would need to receive all 50 last-place votes. Such a candidate would have $4 \times 0 + 3 \times 0 + 2 \times 0 + 1 \times 50 = 50$ points.

24. **(a)** To achieve the maximum number of points possible, a candidate would need to receive all 100 first-place votes. Such a candidate would have $3 \times 100 + 2 \times 0 + 1 \times 0 = 300$ points.

(b) To achieve the minimum number of points possible, a candidate would need to receive all 100 last-place votes. Such a candidate would have $3 \times 0 + 2 \times 0 + 1 \times 100 = 100$ points.

25. **(a)** $4 + 3 + 2 + 1 = 10$ points

(b) $10 \times 110 = 1100$ points

(c) $1100 - 320 - 290 - 180 = 310$ points

26. E. There is a total of $45 \times 15 = 600$ points given out. Therefore, candidate E has $600 - (139 + 121 + 80 + 113) = 147$ points.

D.   Plurality-with-Elimination Method

27. **(a)** Professor Argand
Round 1:

Candidate	A	B	C	D	E
Number of first-place	8	3	5	5	0

E is eliminated.
Round 2:
Eliminating *E* does not affect the first-place votes of the candidates. Using the table from Round 1, we see that *B* now has the fewest number of first-place votes, so *B* is eliminated.
Round 3:
The three votes originally going to *B* would next go to *E*, but *E* has also been eliminated. So *B*'s three votes go to *A*.

Candidate	*A*	*B*	*C*	*D*	*E*
Number of first-place votes	11		5	5	

Candidate *A* now has a majority of the first-place votes and is declared the winner.

(b) Professor Epstein.
Since Professor Chavez is not under consideration, the resulting preference schedule would contain only four candidates.

Number of voters	5	3	5	3	2	3
1st choice	*A*	*A*	*E*	*D*	*D*	*B*
2nd choice	*B*	*D*	*D*	*B*	*B*	*E*
3rd choice	*D*	*B*	*A*	*E*	*A*	*A*
4th choice	*E*	*E*	*B*	*A*	*E*	*D*

Round 1:

Candidate	*A*	*B*	*D*	*E*
Number of first-place votes	8	3	5	5

B is eliminated.
Round 2: The three votes originally going to *B* go to *E*.

Candidate	*A*	*B*	*D*	*E*
Number of first-place votes	8		5	8

D is eliminated.
Round 3: The 5 votes that D had in round 2 would go to B except that B has been eliminated. Instead, three of these votes go to E and two of these five votes go to A.

Candidate	*A*	*B*	*D*	*E*
Number of first-place votes	10			11

Candidate *E* now has a majority of the first-place votes and is declared the winner.

(c) *A* was the winner of the original election, and, in the re-election without candidate *C* (an irrelevant alternative) it turned out that candidate *E* was declared the winner. This violates the Independence-of-Irrelevant-Alternatives criterion.

28. Brandy is the winner.
Round 1:

Candidate	*A*	*B*	*C*	*D*
Number of first-place	310	330	270	330

C is eliminated.

Round 2:

Candidate	*A*	*B*	*C*	*D*
Number of first-place	420	490		330

D is eliminated.

Round 3:

Candidate	*A*	*B*	*C*	*D*
Number of first-place	595	645		

Brandy now has a majority of the first-place votes and is declared the winner.

29. (a) Dante is the winner.

Round 1:

Candidate	*A*	*B*	*C*	*D*	*E*
Number of first-place	8	0	2	13	1

Candidate *D* has a majority of the first-place votes and is declared the winner.

(b) Since Dante is a majority winner, in this case the winner is determined in the first round.

(c) If there is a choice that has a majority of the first-place votes, then that candidate will be the winner under the plurality-with-elimination method. So, the plurality-with-elimination method satisfies the majority criterion.

30. (a) Chou is the winner.

Round 1:

Candidate	*A*	*B*	*C*	*D*
Number of first-place	12	1	14	0

(b) Chou has a majority (14 of 27) of the first-place votes.

31. Candidate *B* is the winner.

Round 1:

Candidate	*A*	*B*	*C*	*D*
Number of first-place	40	35	25	0

D is eliminated.

Round 2: Eliminating *D* does not affect the first-place votes of the other candidates. Using the table from Round 1, we see that candidate *C* now has the fewest number of first-place votes, so *C* is eliminated.

Round 3: The 25 votes originally going to *C* now go to *B*.

Candidate	*A*	*B*	*C*	*D*
Number of first-place	40	60		

Candidate *B* now has a majority of the first-place votes and is declared the winner.

32. Candidate *B* is the winner.

Round 1:

Candidate	A	B	C	D
Number of first-place	48%	28%	24%	0%

D is eliminated.
Round 2: Eliminating *D* does not affect the first-place votes of the other candidates. Using the table from Round 1, we see that candidate *C* now has the fewest number of first-place votes, so *C* is eliminated.
Round 3:

Candidate	A	B	C	D
Number of first-place	48%	52%		

Candidate *B* now has a majority of the first-place votes and is declared the winner.

33. **(a)** Año Nuevo, California is the winner.
Round 1:

Candidate	A	B	C	D
Number of first-place	10	11	4	2

Candidate *D* is eliminated.
Round 2: The two votes originally going to *D* now go to *C*.

Candidate	A	B	C	D
Number of first-place	10	11	6	

Candidate *C* is eliminated.
Round 3: Of the six votes going to *C* in Round 2, four will go to *A* and two will go to *B*.

Candidate	A	B	C	D
Number of first-place	14	13		

Candidate *A* has a majority of the first-place votes and is declared the winner.

(b) *C* is Condorcet candidate.
In a head-to-head contest, *C* beats *A*, 17 votes to 10 votes.
In a head-to-head contest, *C* beats *B*, 16 votes to 11 votes.
In a head-to-head contest, *C* beats *D*, 19 votes to 8 votes.

(c) Cloudbreak, Fiji, which is the Condorcet candidate, fails to win the election under the plurality-with-elimination method.

34. **(a)** Clinton is the winner.
Round 1:

Candidate	A	B	C	D
Number of first-place	6	5	6	0

Candidate *D* is eliminated.
Round 2:
Eliminating *D* does not affect the first-place votes of the other candidates. Using the table from Round 1, we see that candidate *B* now has the fewest number of first-place votes, so *B* is eliminated.

Round 3:

Candidate	A	B	C	D
Number of first-place	6		11	

Candidate A is eliminated. Clinton is the winner.

(b) Buford is the winner.
Round 1:

Candidate	A	B	C	D
Number of first-place	4	5	8	0

Candidate D is eliminated.
Round 2: Eliminating D does not affect the first-place votes of the other candidates. Using the table from Round 1, we see that candidate A now has the fewest number of first-place votes, so A is eliminated.
Round 3:

Candidate	A	B	C	D
Number of first-place		9	8	

Candidate C is eliminated. Buford is the winner.

(c) The monotonicity criterion.

E.   Pairwise Comparisons Method

35. (a) Chad is the winner.

A versus B: 13 votes to 13 votes (tie). A gets $\frac{1}{2}$ point, B gets $\frac{1}{2}$ point.

A versus C: 8 votes to 18 votes (C wins). C gets 1 point.
A versus D: 14 votes to 12 votes (A wins). A gets 1 point.
A versus E: 21 votes to 5 votes (A wins). A gets 1 point.
B versus C: 8 votes to 18 votes (C wins). C gets 1 point.
B versus D: 8 votes to 18 votes (D wins). D gets 1 point.
B versus E: 8 votes to 18 votes (E wins). E gets 1 point.

C versus D: 13 votes to 13 votes (tie). C gets $\frac{1}{2}$ point, D gets $\frac{1}{2}$ point.

C versus E: 13 votes to 13 votes (tie). C gets $\frac{1}{2}$ point, E gets $\frac{1}{2}$ point.

D versus E: 15 votes to 11 votes. D gets 1 point.

The final tally, is $2\frac{1}{2}$ points for A, $\frac{1}{2}$ point for B, 3 points for C, $2\frac{1}{2}$ points for D, and $1\frac{1}{2}$ points for E. Candidate C, Chad, is the winner.

  (b) The preference schedule without Alberto is shown below.

Number of voters	8	6	5	5	2
1st choice	C	E	E	D	D
2nd choice	B	D	C	C	E
3rd choice	D	B	D	E	B
4th choice	E	C	B	B	C

B versus *C*: 8 votes to 18 votes (*C* wins). *C* gets 1 point.

B versus *D*: 8 votes to 18 votes (*D* wins). *D* gets 1 point.

B versus *E*: 8 votes to 18 votes (*E* wins). *E* gets 1 point.

C versus *D*: 13 votes to 13 votes (tie). *C* gets $\frac{1}{2}$ point, *D* gets $\frac{1}{2}$ point.

C versus *E*: 13 votes to 13 votes (tie). *C* gets $\frac{1}{2}$ point, *E* gets $\frac{1}{2}$ point.

D versus *E*: 15 votes to 11 votes. *D* gets 1 point.

The final tally, is 0 points for *B*, 2 points for *C*, $2\frac{1}{2}$ points for *D*, and $1\frac{1}{2}$ points for *E*. Candidate *D*, Dora, is now the winner.

  (c) *C* was the winner of the original election, and, in the re-election without candidate *A* (an irrelevant alternative) it turned out that candidate *D* was declared the winner. This violates the Independence-of-Irrelevant-Alternatives criterion.

36. Candidate *C* is the winner.
  A versus *B*: 31 votes to 24 votes (*A* wins). *A* gets 1 point.
  A versus *C*: 18 votes to 37 votes (*C* wins). *C* gets 1 point.
  A versus *D*: 26 votes to 29 votes (*D* wins). *D* gets 1 point.
  B versus *C*: 23 votes to 32 votes (*C* wins). *C* gets 1 point.
  B versus *D*: 32 votes to 23 votes (*B* wins). *B* gets 1 point.
  C versus *D*: 39 votes to 16 votes. (*C* wins). *C* gets 1 point.
  The final tally is 1 point for *A*, 1 point for *B*, 3 points for *C*, and 1 point for *D*.

37. Candidate *A* is the winner.
  A versus *B*: 13 votes to 8 votes (*A* wins). *A* gets 1 point.
  A versus *C*: 11 votes to 10 votes (*A* wins). *A* gets 1 point.
  A versus *D*: 11 votes to 10 votes (*A* wins). *A* gets 1 point.
  A versus *E*: 10 votes to 11 votes (*E* wins). *E* gets 1 point.
  B versus *C*: 11 votes to 10 votes (*B* wins). *B* gets 1 point.
  B versus *D*: 8 votes to 13 votes (*D* wins). *D* gets 1 point.
  B versus *E*: 16 votes to 5 votes (*B* wins). *B* gets 1 point.
  C versus *D*: 13 votes to 8 votes (*C* wins). *C* gets 1 point.
  C versus *E*: 18 votes to 3 votes (*C* wins). *C* gets 1 point.
  D versus *E*: 13 votes to 8 votes (*D* wins). *D* gets 1 point.
  The final tally is 3 points for *A*, 2 points for *B*, 2 points for *C*, 2 points for *D*, and 1 point for *E*.

38. Candidate *D* is the winner.
  A versus *B*: 11 votes to 13 votes (*B* wins). *B* gets 1 point.

A versus *C*: 16 votes to 8 votes (*A* wins). *A* gets 1 point.
A versus *D*: 11 votes to 13 votes (*D* wins). *D* gets 1 point.
A versus *E*: 17 votes to 7 votes (*A* wins). *A* gets 1 point.
B versus *C*: 22 votes to 2 votes (*B* wins). *B* gets 1 point.
B versus *D*: 10 votes to 14 votes (*D* wins). *D* gets 1 point.
B versus *E*: 23 votes to 1 vote (*B* wins). *B* gets 1 point.
C versus *D*: 10 votes to 14 votes (*D* wins). *D* gets 1 point.
C versus *E*: 17 votes to 7 votes (*C* wins). *C* gets 1 point.
D versus *E*: 23 votes to 1 vote (*D* wins). *D* gets 1 point.
The final tally is 2 points for *A*, 3 points for *B*, 1 point for *C*, 4 points for *D*, and 0 points for *E*.

39. Candidate *E* is the winner.

With five candidates, there are a total of 10 pairwise comparisons. *E* wins $10 - 2 - 2\frac{1}{2} - 1 - 1\frac{1}{2} = 3$. The

10 points are distributed as follows: *A* gets 2 points, *B* gets $2\frac{1}{2}$ points, *C* gets 1 point, *D* gets $1\frac{1}{2}$

points, and *E* gets the remaining 3 points.

40. (a) *A* and *F* tie for first place.
Since there is a total of $(6 \times 5)/2 = 15$ pairwise comparisons, *F* must have won three of them. This means *A* and *F* tie for first place.

(b) *D* and *E* tie.
They are the only candidates to have received half points.

F.   Ranking Methods

41. (a) Winner *A*: Second place: *C*. Third place: *D*. Last place: *B*.
A has $4 + 8 = 12$ first-place votes.
B has 1 first-place vote.
C has 9 first-place votes.
D has 5 first-place votes.

(b) Winner: *A*. Second place: *C*. Third place: *D*. Last place: *B*.
A has $4 \times (4 + 8) + 3 \times 1 + 2 \times 9 + 1 \times 5 = 74$ points.

B has $4 \times 1 + 3 \times 8 + 2 \times (4 + 5) + 1 \times 9 = 55$ points.

C has $4 \times 9 + 3 \times (4 + 5) + 2 \times 0 + 1 \times (1 + 8) = 72$ points.

D has $4 \times 5 + 3 \times 9 + 2 \times (1 + 8) + 1 \times 4 = 69$ points.

(c) Winner: *C*. Second place: *A*. Third place: *D*. Last place: *B*.
Round 1:

Candidate	*A*	*B*	*C*	*D*
Number of votes	12	1	9	5

B is eliminated.
Round 2: The vote originally going to *B* now goes to *A*.

Candidate	A	B	C	D
Number of votes	13		9	5

D is eliminated.
Round 3: The five votes going to *D* now go to *C*.

Candidate	A	B	C	D
Number of votes	13		14	

A is eliminated, and *C* is declared the winner.

(d) Winner: *D*. Second place: *C*. Third place: *A*. Last place: *B*.
A versus B: 21 votes to 6 votes (*A* wins). *A* gets 1 point.
A versus C: 13 votes to 14 votes (*C* wins). *C* gets 1 point.
A versus D: 13 votes to 14 votes (*D* wins). *D* gets 1 point.
B versus C: 9 votes to 18 votes (*C* wins). *C* gets 1 point.
B versus D: 13 votes to 14 votes (*D* wins). *D* gets 1 point.
C versus D: 13 votes to 14 votes (*D* wins). *D* gets 1 point.
The final tally is 1 point for *A*, 0 points for *B*, 2 points for *C*, and 3 points for *D*.

42. (a) Winner *B*: Second place: *A*. Third place: *C*. Last place: *D*.
A has 10 first-place votes.
B has 11 first-place vote.
C has 4 first-place votes.
D has 2 first-place votes.

(b) Winner: *C*. Second place: *B*. Third place: *A*. Last place: *D*.
A has $4 \times 10 + 3 \times 4 + 2 \times 5 + 1 \times (6 + 2) = 70$ points.

B has $4 \times (6 + 5) + 3 \times 0 + 2 \times (10 + 2) + 1 \times 4 = 72$ points.

C has $4 \times 4 + 3 \times (10 + 5 + 2) + 2 \times 6 + 1 \times 0 = 79$ points.

D has $4 \times 2 + 3 \times 6 + 2 \times 4 + 1 \times (10 + 5) = 49$ points.

(c) Winner: *A*. Second place: *B*. Third place: *C*. Last place: *D*.
Round 1:

Candidate	A	B	C	D
Number of votes	10	11	4	2

D is eliminated.
Round 2: The vote originally going to *D* now goes to *C*.

Candidate	A	B	C	D
Number of votes	10	11	6	

C is eliminated.
Round 3: Four of the votes going to *C* now go to *A*. Two of the votes going to *C* now go to *B*.

Candidate	A	B	C	D
Number of votes	14	13		

B is eliminated, and *A* is declared the winner.

(d) Winner: *C*. Second place: *A*. Third place: *B*. Last place: *D*.
A versus *B*: 14 votes to 13 votes (*A* wins). *A* gets 1 point.
A versus *C*: 10 votes to 17 votes (*C* wins). *C* gets 1 point.
A versus *D*: 19 votes to 8 votes (*A* wins). *A* gets 1 point.
B versus *C*: 11 votes to 16 votes (*C* wins). *C* gets 1 point.
B versus *D*: 21 votes to 6 votes (*D* wins). *B* gets 1 point.
C versus *D*: 19 votes to 8 votes (*C* wins). *C* gets 1 point.
The final tally is 2 points for *A*, 1 point for *B*, 3 points for *C*, and 0 points for *D*.

43. **(a)** *A* has 40% of the first-place votes.
B has 35% of the first-place votes.
C has 25% of the first-place votes.
D has 0% of the first-place votes.
Winner *A*: Second place: *B*. Third place: *C*. Last place: *D*.

(b) We treat each 1% of voters as 1 "block" of votes.
A has $4 \times 40 + 3 \times 15 + 2 \times 20 + 1 \times 25 = 270$ points.
B has $4 \times (20 + 15) + 3 \times 25 + 2 \times 40 + 1 \times 0 = 295$ points.
C has $4 \times 25 + 3 \times 0 + 2 \times 0 + 1 \times (40 + 20 + 15) = 175$ points.
D has $4 \times 0 + 3 \times (40 + 20) + 2 \times (25 + 15) + 1 \times 0 = 260$ points.
Winner: *B*. Second place: *A*. Third place: *D*. Last place: *C*.

(c) Round 1:

Candidate	*A*	*B*	*C*	*D*
Number of votes	40%	35%	25%	0%

D is eliminated.
Round 2: Eliminating *D* does not affect the first-place votes of the other candidates. Using the table from Round 1, we see that candidate *C* now has the fewest number of first-place votes, so *C* is eliminated.
Round 3: The 25% of the votes going to *C* now go to *B*.

Candidate	*A*	*B*	*C*	*D*
Number of votes	40%	60%		

A is eliminated, and *B* is declared the winner.
Winner: *B*. Second place: *A*. Third place: *C*. Last place: *D*.

(d) *A* versus *B*: 40% of the votes to 60% of the votes (*B* wins). *B* gets 1 point.
A versus *C*: 75% of the votes to 25% of the votes (*A* wins). *A* gets 1 point.
A versus *D*: 55% of the votes to 45% of the votes (*A* wins). *A* gets 1 point.
B versus *C*: 75% of the votes to 25% of the votes (*B* wins). *B* gets 1 point.
B versus *D*: 60% of the votes to 40% of the votes (*B* wins). *B* gets 1 point.
C versus *D*: 25% of the votes to 75% of the votes (*D* wins). *D* gets 1 point.
The final tally is 2 points for *A*, 3 points for *B*, 0 points for *C*, and 1 point for *D*.
Winner: *B*. Second place: *A*. Third place: *D*. Last place: *C*.

44. **(a)** Winner *A*: Second place: *B*. Third place: *C*. Last place: *D*.
A has 48% of the first-place votes.
B has 28% of the first-place vote.

C has 24% of the first-place votes.
D has no first-place votes.

(b) Winner: *A*. Second place: *B*. Third place: *D*. Last place: *C*.
   A has $4 \times 48 + 3 \times 12 + 2 \times 16 + 1 \times 24 = 284$ points.
   B has $4 \times (16 + 12) + 3 \times 24 + 2 \times 48 + 1 \times 0 = 280$ points.
   C has $4 \times 24 + 3 \times 0 + 2 \times 0 + 1 \times (48 + 16 + 12) = 172$ points.
   D has $4 \times 0 + 3 \times (48 + 16) + 2 \times (24 + 12) + 1 \times 0 = 264$ points.

(c) Winner: *B*. Second place: *A*. Third place: *C*. Last place: *D*.
   Round 1:

Candidate	*A*	*B*	*C*	*D*
Percent of votes	48%	28%	24%	0%

   D is eliminated.
   Round 2: Eliminating *D* does not affect the first-place votes of the other candidates. Using the table from Round 1, we see that candidate *C* now has the fewest number of first-place votes, so *C* is eliminated.
   Round 3: The 24% of the vote going to *C* now goes to *B*.

Candidate	*A*	*B*	*C*	*D*
Percent of votes	48%	52%		

   A is eliminated, and *B* is declared the winner.

(b) Winner: *B*. Second place: *A*. Third place: *D*. Last place: *C*.
   A versus *B*: 48% to 52% (*B* wins). *B* gets 1 point.
   A versus *C*: 76% to 24% (*A* wins). *A* gets 1 point.
   A versus *D*: 60% to 40% (*A* wins). *A* gets 1 point.
   B versus *C*: 76% to 24% (*B* wins). *B* gets 1 point.
   B versus *D*: 52% to 48% (*B* wins). *B* gets 1 point.
   C versus *D*: 24% to 76% (*D* wins). *D* gets 1 point.
   The final tally is 2 points for *A*, 3 points for *B*, 0 points for *C*, and 1 point for *D*.

45. Step 1: From Example 1.5 we know that the winner using the Borda count method is *B* with 106 points.
   Step 2: Removing *B* gives the following preference schedule.

Number of voters	14	10	8	4	1
1st choice	*A*	*C*	*D*	*D*	*C*
2nd choice	*C*	*D*	*C*	*C*	*D*
3rd choice	*D*	*A*	*A*	*A*	*A*

This preference schedule can be consolidated (simplified) to produce the following schedule.

Number of voters	14	11	12
1st choice	*A*	*C*	*D*
2nd choice	*C*	*D*	*C*
3rd choice	*D*	*A*	*A*

A has $3 \times 14 + 2 \times 0 + 1 \times (11 + 12) = 65$ points;

C has $3 \times 11 + 2 \times (14 + 12) + 1 \times 0 = 85$ points;

D has $3 \times 12 + 2 \times 11 + 1 \times 14 = 72$ points;

In this schedule the winner using the Borda count method is C, with 85 points. Thus, second place goes to C.

Step 3: Removing C gives the following preference schedule.

Number of voters	14	11	12
1st choice	A	D	D
2nd choice	D	A	A

A has $2 \times 14 + 1 \times (11 + 12) = 51$ points;

D has $2 \times (11 + 12) + 1 \times 14 = 60$ points;

In this schedule the winner using the Borda count method is D, with 60 points. Thus, third place goes to D, and last place goes to A.

46.   Step 1: From Example 1.11 we know that the winner using the pairwise comparisons method is C.
      Step 2: Removing C gives the following preference schedule.

Number of voters	14	10	8	4	1
1st choice	A	B	D	B	D
2nd choice	B	D	B	D	B
3rd choice	D	A	A	A	A

A versus B: 14 votes to 23 votes (B wins). B gets 1 point.
A versus D: 14 votes to 23 votes (D wins). D gets 1 point.
B versus D: 28 votes to 9 votes (B wins). B gets 1 point.
The final tally is 0 points for A, 2 points for B, and 1 point for D. Thus, second place goes to B.
Step 3: Removing B gives the following preference schedule.

Number of voters	14	23
1st choice	A	D
2nd choice	D	A

Thus, third place goes to D and last place goes to A.

47.   (a) Step 1: From Exercise 41(a) we know that the winner, using plurality, is A with 12 first-place votes.
      Step 2: Removing A gives the following preference schedule.

Number of voters	4	1	9	8	5
1st choice	C	B	C	B	D
2nd choice	B	D	D	D	C
3rd choice	D	C	B	C	B

In this schedule the winner using plurality is C, with 13 first-place votes. Thus, second place goes to C.
Step 3: Removing C gives the following preference schedule.

Number of voters	4	1	9	8	5
1st choice	B	B	D	B	D
2nd choice	D	D	B	D	B

In this schedule the winner using plurality is D, with 14 first-place votes. Thus, third place goes to D and last place goes to B.

(b) Step 1: From Exercise 41(b) we know that the winner using the Borda count method is A with 74 points.

Step 2: Removing A gives the following preference schedule.

Number of voters	4	1	9	8	5
1st choice	C	B	C	B	D
2nd choice	B	D	D	D	C
3rd choice	D	C	B	C	B

B has $3 \times (1+8) + 2 \times 4 + 1 \times (9+5) = 49$ points;

C has $3 \times (4+9) + 2 \times 5 + 1 \times (1+8) = 58$ points;

D has $3 \times 5 + 2 \times (1+9+8) + 1 \times 4 = 55$ points;

In this schedule the winner using the Borda count method is C, with 58 points. Thus, second place goes to C.

Step 3: Removing C gives the following preference schedule.

Number of voters	4	1	9	8	5
1st choice	B	B	D	B	D
2nd choice	D	D	B	D	B

B has $2 \times 13 + 1 \times 14 = 40$ points;

D has $2 \times 14 + 1 \times 13 = 41$ points;

In this schedule the winner using the Borda count method is D, with 41 points. Thus, third place goes to D, and last place goes to B.

(c) Step 1: From Exercise 41(c) we know that the winner using plurality-with-elimination is C.

Step 2: Removing C gives the following preference schedule.

Number of voters	4	1	9	8	5
1st choice	A	B	D	A	D
2nd choice	B	A	A	B	B
3rd choice	D	D	B	D	A

In this schedule the winner using plurality-with-elimination is D because D has a majority (14) of the first-place votes. Thus, second place goes to D.

Step 3: Removing D gives the following preference schedule.

Number of voters	4	1	9	6	5
1st choice	A	B	A	A	B
2nd choice	B	A	B	B	A

In this schedule the winner using plurality-with-elimination is A because A has a majority (21) of the first-place votes. Thus, third place goes to A, and last place goes to B.

(d) Step 1: From Exercise 41(d) we know that the winner using pairwise comparisons is D.

Step 2: Removing D gives the following preference schedule.

Number of voters	4	1	9	8	5
1st choice	A	B	C	A	C
2nd choice	C	A	A	B	B
3rd choice	B	C	B	C	A

A versus B: 21 votes to 6 votes (A wins). A gets 1 point.
A versus C: 13 votes to 14 votes (C wins). C gets 1 point.
B versus C: 9 votes to 18 votes (C wins). C gets 1 point.
The final tally is 1 point for A, 0 points for B, and 2 points for C. In this schedule the winner using pairwise comparisons is C, with 2 points. Thus, second place goes to C.
Step 3: Removing C gives the following preference schedule.

Number of voters	4	1	9	8	5
1st choice	A	B	A	A	B
2nd choice	B	A	B	B	A

A versus B: 21 votes to 6 votes (A wins). A gets 1 point. The final tally is 1 point for A, 0 points for B. In this schedule the winner using pairwise comparisons is A, with 1 point. Thus, third place goes to A, and last place goes to B.

48. **(a)** Step 1: From Exercise 42(a) we know that the winner, using plurality, is B with 11 first-place votes.
Step 2: Removing B gives the following preference schedule.

Number of voters	10	6	5	4	2
1st choice	A	D	C	C	D
2nd choice	C	C	A	A	C
3rd choice	D	A	D	D	A

In this schedule the winner using plurality is A, with 10 first-place votes. Thus, second place goes to A.
Step 3: Removing A gives the following preference schedule.

Number of voters	10	6	5	4	2
1st choice	C	D	C	C	D
2nd choice	D	C	D	D	C

In this schedule the winner using plurality is C, with 19 first-place votes. Thus, third place goes to C and last place goes to D.

(b) Step 1: From Exercise 42(b) we know that the winner using the Borda count method is C.
Step 2: Removing C gives the following preference schedule.

Number of voters	10	6	5	4	2
1st choice	A	B	B	A	D
2nd choice	B	D	A	D	B
3rd choice	D	A	D	B	A

A has $3 \times (10+4) + 2 \times 5 + 1 \times (6+2) = 60$ points;

B has $3 \times (6+5) + 2 \times (10+2) + 1 \times 4 = 61$ points;

D has $3 \times 2 + 2 \times (6+4) + 1 \times (10+5) = 41$ points;

In this schedule the winner using the Borda count method is B, with 61 points. Thus, second place

goes to *B*.
Step 3: Removing *B* gives the following preference schedule.

Number of voters	10	6	5	4	2
1st choice	*A*	*D*	*A*	*A*	*D*
2nd choice	*D*	*A*	*D*	*D*	*A*

In this schedule the winner using the Borda count method is *A*. Thus, third place goes to *A*, and last place goes to *D*.

(c) Step 1: From Exercise 42(c) we know that the winner using plurality-with-elimination is *A*.
Step 2: Removing *A* gives the following preference schedule.

Number of voters	10	6	5	4	2
1st choice	*C*	*B*	*B*	*C*	*D*
2nd choice	*B*	*D*	*C*	*D*	*C*
3rd choice	*D*	*C*	*D*	*B*	*B*

In this schedule the winner using plurality-with-elimination is *C* because *C* has a majority (14) of the first-place votes. Thus, second place goes to *C*.
Step 3: Removing *C* gives the following preference schedule.

Number of voters	10	6	5	4	2
1st choice	*B*	*B*	*B*	*D*	*D*
2nd choice	*D*	*D*	*D*	*B*	*B*

In this schedule the winner using plurality-with-elimination is *B* because *B* has a majority (21) of the first-place votes. Thus, third place goes to *B*, and last place goes to *D*.

(d) Step 1: From Exercise 42(d) we know that the winner using pairwise comparisons is *C*.
Step 2: Removing *C* gives the following preference schedule.

Number of voters	10	6	5	4	2
1st choice	*A*	*B*	*B*	*A*	*D*
2nd choice	*B*	*D*	*A*	*D*	*B*
3rd choice	*D*	*A*	*D*	*B*	*A*

A versus *B*: 14 votes to 13 votes (*A* wins). *A* gets 1 point.
A versus *D*: 19 votes to 8 votes (*A* wins). *A* gets 1 point.
B versus *D*: 21 votes to 6 votes (*B* wins). *B* gets 1 point.
The final tally is 2 points for *A*, 1 point for *B*, and 0 points for *D*. In this schedule the winner using pairwise comparisons is *A*, with 2 points. Thus, second place goes to *A*.

Step 3: Removing *A* gives the following preference schedule.

Number of voters	10	6	5	4	2
1st choice	*B*	*B*	*B*	*D*	*D*
2nd choice	*D*	*D*	*D*	*B*	*B*

Thus, third place goes to *B*, and last place goes to *D*.

49. (a) Step 1: From Exercise 43(a) we know that the winner, using plurality, is *A* with 40% of the first-place votes.
Step 2: Removing *A* gives the following preference schedule.

Percentage of voters	40%	25%	20%	15%
1st choice	D	C	B	B
2nd choice	B	B	D	D
3rd choice	C	D	C	C

In this schedule the winner using plurality is *D*, with 40% of the first-place votes. Thus, second place goes to *D*.
Step 3: Removing *D* gives the following preference schedule.

Percentage of voters	40%	25%	20%	15%
1st choice	B	C	B	B
2nd choice	C	B	C	C

In this schedule the winner using plurality is *B*, with 75% of the first-place votes. Thus, third place goes to *B* and last place goes to *C*.

(b) Step 1: From Exercise 43(b) we know that the winner using the Borda count method is *B* with 295 Borda points.
Step 2: Removing *B* gives the following preference schedule.

Percentage of voters	40%	25%	20%	15%
1st choice	A	C	D	A
2nd choice	D	D	A	D
3rd choice	C	A	C	C

A has $3 \times (40 + 15) + 2 \times 20 + 1 \times 25 = 230$ points;

C has $3 \times 25 + 2 \times 0 + 1 \times (40 + 20 + 15) = 150$ points;

D has $3 \times 20 + 2 \times (40 + 25 + 15) + 1 \times 0 = 220$ points;

In this schedule the winner using the Borda count method is *A*, with 230 points. Thus, second place goes to *A*.
Step 3: Removing *A* gives the following preference schedule.

Percentage of voters	40%	25%	20%	15%
1st choice	D	C	D	D
2nd choice	C	D	C	C

C has $2 \times 25 + 1 \times (40 + 20 + 15) = 125$ points;

D has $2 \times (40 + 20 + 15) + 1 \times 25 = 175$ points;

In this schedule the winner using the Borda count method is *D*, with 175 points. Thus, third place goes to *D*, and last place goes to *C*.

(c) Step 1: From Exercise 43(c) we know that the winner using plurality-with-elimination is *B*.
Step 2: Removing *B* gives the following preference schedule.

Percentage of voters	40%	25%	20%	15%
1st choice	A	C	D	A
2nd choice	D	D	A	D
3rd choice	C	A	C	C

In this schedule the winner using plurality-with-elimination is *A* because *A* has a majority (55%) of the first-place votes. Thus, second place goes to *A*.
Step 3: Removing *A* gives the following preference schedule.

Percentage of voters	40%	25%	20%	15%
1st choice	*D*	*C*	*D*	*D*
2nd choice	*C*	*D*	*C*	*C*

In this schedule the winner using plurality-with-elimination is *D* because *D* has a majority (75%) of the first-place votes. Thus, third place goes to *D*, and last place goes to *C*.

(d) Step 1: From Exercise 43(d) we know that the winner using pairwise comparisons is *B*.
Step 2: Removing *B* gives the following preference schedule.

Percentage of voters	40%	25%	20%	15%
1st choice	*A*	*C*	*D*	*A*
2nd choice	*D*	*D*	*A*	*D*
3rd choice	*C*	*A*	*C*	*C*

A versus *C*: 75% of the votes to 25% of the votes (*A* wins). *A* gets 1 point.
A versus *D*: 55% of the votes to 45% of the votes (*A* wins). *A* gets 1 point.
C versus *D*: 25% of the votes to 75% of the votes (*D* wins). *D* gets 1 point.
The final tally is 2 points for *A*, 0 points for *C*, and 1 point for *D*. In this schedule the winner using pairwise comparisons is *A*, with 2 points. Thus, second place goes to *A*.
Step 3: Removing *A* gives the following preference schedule.

Percentage of voters	40%	25%	20%	15%
1st choice	*D*	*C*	*D*	*D*
2nd choice	*C*	*D*	*C*	*C*

C versus *D*: 25% of the votes to 75% of the votes (*D* wins). *D* gets 1 point. The final tally is 0 points for *C*, 1 point for *D*. In this schedule the winner using pairwise comparisons is *D*, with 1 point. Thus, third place goes to *D*, and last place goes to *C*.

50. (a) Step 1: From Exercise 44(a) we know that the winner, using plurality, is *A* with 48% of the first-place votes.
Step 2: Removing *A* gives the following preference schedule.

Percentage of voters	48%	24%	16%	12%
1st choice	*D*	*C*	*B*	*B*
2nd choice	*B*	*B*	*D*	*D*
3rd choice	*C*	*D*	*C*	*C*

In this schedule the winner using plurality is *D*, with 48% of the first-place votes. Thus, second place goes to *D*.
Step 3: Removing *D* gives the following preference schedule.

Percentage of voters	48%	24%	16%	12%
1st choice	*B*	*C*	*B*	*B*
2nd choice	*C*	*B*	*C*	*C*

In this schedule the winner using plurality is *B*, with 76% of the first-place votes. Thus, third place goes to *B* and last place goes to *C*.

(b) Step 1: From Exercise 44(b) we know that the winner using the Borda count method is A.

Step 2: Removing A gives the following preference schedule.

Percentage of voters	48%	24%	16%	12%
1st choice	D	C	B	B
2nd choice	B	B	D	D
3rd choice	C	D	C	C

B has $3 \times (16 + 12) + 2 \times (48 + 24) + 1 \times 0 = 228$ points;

C has $3 \times 24 + 2 \times 0 + 1 \times (48 + 16 + 12) = 148$ points;

D has $3 \times 48 + 2 \times (16 + 12) + 1 \times 24 = 224$ points;

In this schedule the winner using the Borda count method is B, with 228 points. Thus, second place goes to B.

Step 3: Removing B gives the following preference schedule.

Percentage of voters	48%	24%	16%	12%
1st choice	D	C	D	D
2nd choice	C	D	C	C

In this schedule the winner using the Borda count method is D. Thus, third place goes to D, and last place goes to C.

(c) Step 1: From Exercise 44(c) we know that the winner using plurality-with-elimination is B.

Step 2: Removing B gives the following preference schedule.

Percentage of voters	48%	24%	16%	12%
1st choice	A	C	D	A
2nd choice	D	D	A	D
3rd choice	C	A	C	C

In this schedule the winner using plurality-with-elimination is A because A has a majority (60%) of the first-place votes. Thus, second place goes to A.

Step 3: Removing A gives the following preference schedule.

Percentage of voters	48%	24%	16%	12%
1st choice	D	C	D	D
2nd choice	C	D	C	C

In this schedule the winner using plurality-with-elimination is D because D has a majority (76%) of the first-place votes. Thus, third place goes to D, and last place goes to C.

(d) Step 1: From Exercise 44(d) we know that the winner using pairwise comparisons is B.

Step 2: Removing B gives the following preference schedule.

Percentage of voters	48%	24%	16%	12%
1st choice	A	C	D	A
2nd choice	D	D	A	D
3rd choice	C	A	C	C

A versus C: 76% of the votes to 24% of the votes (A wins). A gets 1 point.

A versus D: 60% of the votes to 40% of the votes (A wins). A gets 1 point.

C versus *D*: 24% of the votes to 76% of the votes (*D* wins). *D* gets 1 point.
The final tally is 2 points for *A*, 0 points for *C*, and 1 point for *D*. In this schedule the winner using pairwise comparisons is *A*, with 2 points. Thus, second place goes to *A*.
Step 3: Removing *A* gives the following preference schedule.

Percentage of voters	48%	24%	16%	12%
1st choice	*D*	*C*	*D*	*D*
2nd choice	*C*	*D*	*C*	*C*

In this schedule the winner using pairwise comparisons is *D*, with 1 point. Thus, third place goes to *D*, and last place goes to *C*.

G.   Miscellaneous

51. 125,250 $\left(\text{i.e.,}\ \dfrac{500 \times 501}{2} \right)$

52. 5,185,810 $\left(\text{i.e.,}\ \dfrac{3220 \times 3221}{2} \right)$

53. 5,060,560

$$1 + 2 + 3 + \ldots + 3218 + 3219 + 3220 = \frac{3220 \times 3221}{2} = 5,185,810$$

Combining this with the result from Exercise 51, we get
$$501 + 502 + 503 + \ldots + 3218 + 3219 + 3220 = 5,185,810 - 125,250 = 5,060,560.$$

54. 37,500,535

$$\text{i.e.,}\ \left(\frac{8845 \times 8846}{2} \right) - \left(\frac{1800 \times 1801}{2} \right)$$

55. (a) 105

$$1 + 2 + 3 + \ldots + 12 + 13 + 14 = \frac{14 \times 15}{2} = 105$$

(b) 1 hour and 45 minutes

56. (a) 210 matches

$$20 + 19 + 18 + \ldots + 2 + 1 = \frac{20 \times 21}{2} = 210$$

(b) 3 days (A maximum of $6 \times 12 = 72$ matches can be scheduled in one day.)

57. $3! = 6$

58. (a) $4! = 24$

(b) $4 \times 3 = 12$

59. (a) A has a majority of the first-place votes (7), so A is the Condorcet candidate.

(b) A has $4 \times 7 + 3 \times 2 + 2 \times 0 + 1 \times 4 = 38$ points;
B has $4 \times 4 + 3 \times 7 + 2 \times 0 + 1 \times 2 = 39$ points;
C has $4 \times 0 + 3 \times 0 + 2 \times (7 + 4 + 2) + 1 \times 0 = 26$ points;
D has $4 \times 2 + 3 \times 4 + 2 \times 0 + 1 \times 7 = 27$ points;
The winner is B.

(c) Removing C gives the following preference schedule.

Number of voters	7	4	2
1st choice	A	B	D
2nd choice	B	D	A
3rd choice	D	A	B

A has $3 \times 7 + 2 \times 2 + 1 \times 4 = 29$ points;
B has $3 \times 4 + 2 \times 7 + 1 \times 2 = 28$ points;
D has $3 \times 2 + 2 \times 4 + 1 \times 7 = 21$ points;
The winner is A.

(d) Based on (a) and (b), the Condorcet criterion and the majority criterion are violated. Based on (b) and (c), the independence of irrelevant alternatives criterion is violated. Furthermore, based on (b), the Borda count also violates the majority criterion since A has a majority of the first-place votes but does not win the election.

60. (a) C is the Condorcet candidate.
C beats A 17-10, C beats B 16-11, C beats D 19-8.

(b) The winner is A.

(c) **Note: The exercise should state that *B* drops out of the race.** In that case, the winner is C. Removing B gives the following preference schedule.

Number of voters	10	6	5	4	2
1st choice	A	D	C	C	D
2nd choice	C	C	A	A	C
3rd choice	D	A	D	D	A

A has 10 first-place votes, C has 9 first-place votes, D has 8 first-place votes. Candidate D is eliminated.

Number of voters	10	6	5	4	2
1st choice	A	C	C	C	C
2nd choice	C	A	A	A	A

Candidate C has a majority of first-place votes.

(d) From (a) and (b) we conclude that the plurality-with-elimination method violates the Condorcet criterion; from (b) and (c) we conclude that the plurality-with-elimination method violates the Independence of Irrelevant Alternatives Criterion.

JOGGING

61. Suppose the two candidates are A and B and that A gets a first-place votes and B gets b first-place votes and suppose that $a > b$. Then A has a majority of the votes and the preference schedule is

Number of voters	a	b
1st choice	A	B
2nd choice	B	A

It is clear that candidate A wins the election under the plurality method, the plurality-with-elimination method, and the method of pairwise comparisons. Under the Borda count method, A gets $2a + b$ points while B gets $2b + a$ points. Since $a > b$, $2a + b > 2b + a$ and so again A wins the election.

62. One possible example is the following.

Number of voters	8	4	3	2
1st choice	A	B	B	D
2nd choice	C	D	C	C
3rd choice	B	C	D	B
4th choice	D	A	A	A

i. There are 17 voters, so 9 votes are required for a majority. No candidate has 9 or more first-place votes.

ii. C beats every other candidate in a head-to-head contest, so C is a Condorcet candidate, but C has no first-place votes.

iii. Under the Borda count method,
A has $4 \times 8 + 3 \times 0 + 2 \times 0 + 1 \times (4 + 3 + 2) = 41$ points;
B has $4 \times (4 + 3) + 3 \times 0 + 2 \times (8 + 2) + 1 \times 0 = 48$ points;
C has $4 \times 0 + 3 \times (8 + 3 + 2) + 2 \times 4 + 1 \times 0 = 47$ points;
D has $4 \times 2 + 3 \times 4 + 2 \times 3 + 1 \times 8 = 34$ points;
The winner is B.

iv. A has 8 first-place votes; B has $4 + 3 = 7$ first-place votes;
C has 0 first-place votes; D has 2 first-place votes.
So A is the winner under the plurality method.

63. If X is the winner of an election using the plurality method and, in a reelection, the only changes in the ballots are changes that only favor X, then no candidate other than X can increase his/her first-place votes and so X is still the winner of the election.

64. If X is the winner of an election using the Borda count method and, in a reelection, the only changes in the ballots are changes that *only* favor X, then no candidate other than X can increase his/her Borda count and so X is still the winner of the election.

65. (a) If X is the winner of an election using the method of pairwise comparisons and, in a reelection, the only changes in the ballots are changes that favor X and only favor X, then candidate X will still win every pairwise comparison that he/she won in the original election and possibly even some new ones — while no other candidate will win any new pairwise comparisons (since there were no changes favorable to any other candidate). That is, if X has A wins in the original election and A' wins in the reelection, then $A' \geq A$. Consequently, X is also the winner of the reelection.

(b) Since the only changes are changes that favor X and not Y, it must be that $B' \leq B$. That is, $B' - B \leq 0$. So, we have $A' - A \geq 0 \geq B' - B$ by part (a).

(c) Suppose that X is the winner of an election and the only changes in ballots are changes that favor X and only X. By part (b), X will gain more points than any other candidate will gain and hence will remain the winner of the election.

66. (a) In this variation, each candidate gets 1 point less on each ballot. Thus, if there are k voters, each candidate gets a total of k fewer points, i.e., $q = p - k$.

(b) Since each candidate's total is decreased by the same amount k, using this variation of the Borda count method the extended ranking of the candidates is the same. (If $a < b$ then $a - k < b - k$.)

67. (a) Suppose a candidate, C, gets v_1 first-place votes, v_2 second-place votes, v_3 third-place votes, ..., v_N Nth-place votes. For this candidate $p = v_1 N + v_2(N-1) + v_3(N-2) + \ldots + v_{N-1} \cdot 2 + v_N \cdot 1$, and $r = v_1 \cdot 1 + v_2 \cdot 2 + v_3 \cdot 3 + \ldots + v_{N-1}(N-1) + v_N N$.

So, $p + r = v_1(N+1) + v_2(N+1) + v_3(N+1) + \ldots + v_{N-1}(N+1) + v_N(N+1)$
$$= (v_1 + v_2 + \ldots + v_N)(N+1)$$
$$= k(N+1)$$

(b) Suppose candidates C_1 and C_2 receive p_1 and p_2 points respectively using the Borda count as originally described in the chaper and r_1 and r_2 points under the variation described in this exercise. Then if $p_1 < p_2$, we have $-p_1 > -p_2$ and so $k(N+1) - p_1 > k(N+1) - p_2$ which implies [using part (a)], $r_1 > r_2$. Consequently the relative ranking of the candidates is not changed.

68. The count would be the same as the method described in Exercise 67 only each candidates Borda count is divided by the number of ballots. Since each total is divided by the fixed number of ballots, the ranking remains the same.

69. (a) This follows since $1610 + 1540 + 1530 = 65 \times (25 + 24 + 23)$. That is, these three teams combined received as many first, second, and third-place votes as possible.

(b) USC: Let x = the number of second-place votes. Then $1610 = 25 \times 52 + 24 \times x + 23 \times (65 - 52 - x)$ and so $x = 11$. This leaves $65 - 52 - 11 = 2$ third-place votes.
Oklahoma: Let y = the number of second-place votes. Then $1540 = 25 \times 7 + 24 \times y + 23 \times (65 - 7 - y)$ and so $y = 31$. This leaves $65 - 7 - 31 = 27$ third-place votes.
Auburn: Let z = the number of second-place votes. Then $1530 = 25 \times 6 + 24 \times z + 23 \times (65 - 6 - z)$ and so $z = 23$. This leaves $65 - 6 - 23 = 36$ third-place votes.

70. (a) By looking at Alana Beard's vote totals, it is clear that 5 points are awarded for each first-place vote. Let x = points awarded for each second-place vote. Then, $2x + 45 \times 5 = 231$ gives $x = 3$.
Next, let y = points awarded for each third-place vote. Looking at Nicole Ohlde's votes, we see that

$3y + 8 \times 3 + 36 \times 5 = 207$. Solving this equation gives $y = 1$.

5 points for each first-place vote; 3 points for each second-place vote; 1 point for each third-place vote.

(b) 43 second-place votes; 4 third-place votes.
Let x = the number of second-place ballots that Nicole received. Then, solve
$25 \times 5 + x \times 3 + (47 - 25 - x) \times 1 = 183$ for x.

71. By looking at Dwayne Wade's vote totals, it is clear that 1 point is awarded for each third-place vote.
Let x = points awarded for each second-place vote. Then, $3x + 108 = 117$ gives $x = 3$.
Next, let y = points awarded for each third-place vote. Looking at LeBron James' votes, we see that
$78y + 39 \times 3 + 1 \times 1 = 508$. Solving this equation gives $y = 5$.
5 points for each first-place vote; 3 points for each second-place vote; 1 point for each third-place vote.

Note: The results of this election would never be different if standard Borda points were used. The following argument explains why. Suppose that candidate X beats candidate Y by a score of p_1 to q_1 points using the standard Borda count points (3 points per first-place vote, 2 points per second-place vote, 1 point per third-place vote). Then, candidate X will also beat candidate Y by a score of p_2 to q_2 points using an equivalent Borda count method in which each candidate receives 2 points per first-place vote, 1 point per second-place vote, and 0 point per third-place vote (see Exercise 66). Using a scoring system of 5 points per first-place vote, 3 points per second-place vote, and 1 point per third-place vote, candidate X would still beat candidate Y by a score of $p_1 + p_2$ to $q_1 + q_2$ points.

72. (a) Using plurality with a runoff in the Math Appreciation Society election results in B and D being eliminated first and then C winning (over A) the election. Recall that D was the winner using the plurality-with-elimination method.

(b) Example 1.10 in the text (used to demonstrate that the plurality-with-elimination method violates the monotonicity criterion) also demonstrates that plurality with a runoff violates the monotonicity criterion.

(c) Consider an election with 3 alternatives (A, B, and C) and preference schedule as follows.

Number of voters	10	8	6
1st choice	A	C	B
2nd choice	B	B	C
3rd choice	C	A	A

In this election B is a Condorcet candidate (since B beats A 14 to 10 and B beats C 16 to 8) and yet, B is eliminated first using plurality with a runoff (and C is the winner).

73. (a) C . A is eliminated first, D is eliminated next, and then C beats B.

(b) A is a Condorcet candidate but is eliminated in the first round.

Number of voters	10	6	6	3	3
1st choice	B	A	A	D	C
2nd choice	C	B	C	A	A
3rd choice	D	D	B	C	B
4th choice	A	C	D	B	D

(c) *B* wins under the Coombs method. However, if 8 voters move *B* from their 3rd choice to their 2nd choice, then *C* wins.

Number of voters	10	8	7	4
1st choice	B	C	C	A
2nd choice	A	A	B	B
3rd choice	C	B	A	C

RUNNING

74. (a) The Math Club election of Example 1.2 violates this criterion. Candidate *A* has a majority of last-place votes and yet wins the election.

    (b) Consider an election with the following preference schedule:

Number of voters	2	2	3
1st choice	A	B	C
2nd choice	B	A	A
3rd choice	C	C	B

   In this election, *C* is the winner under the plurality method (in the case of the tie in round 1, eliminate all candidates with the fewest number of votes). However, a majority of the voters (4 out of 7) prefer both *A* and *B* over *C*.

    (c) Under the method of pairwise comparisons, if a majority of voters have candidate *X* ranked last on their ballot, then candidate *X* will never win a head-to-head comparison (since any other candidate *Y* is preferred to *X* by a majority of voters). Thus, *X* will end up with 0 points under the method and cannot win the election.

    (d) Suppose there are *N* candidates, *x* is the number of voters placing *X* last, and *y* is the remaining number of voters. Since a majority of the voters place *X* last, $x > y$. The *maximum* number of points that *X* can receive using a Borda count is $x + Ny$. (One point for each of the *x* last place votes and assuming all other voters place *X* in first-place, *N* points for each of the other *y* voters.) The total number of points given out by each voter is $1 + 2 + 3 + \ldots + N = N(N + 1)/2$ and so the total number of points given out by all $x + y$ voters is $N(N + 1)(x + y)/2$. Since some candidate must receive at least $1/N$ of the total points, some candidate must receive at least $(N + 1)(x + y)/2$ points. A little algebraic mumbo jumbo can be used to show that $x > y$ implies $(N + 1)(x + y)/2 > x + Ny$. and consequently, *X* cannot be the winner of the election using the Borda count method.

75. Consider an election with the following preference schedule:

Number of voters	8	5	3	2	4
1st choice	A	C	C	C	B
2nd choice	B	D	B	B	D
3rd choice	C	A	D	A	A
4th choice	D	B	A	D	C

In this election, D is preferred over A by a majority of the voters (12 to 10) and yet all four extended ranking methods discussed in the chapter rank A above D —

Extended ranking method	Winner	2nd place	3rd place	Last place
Plurality	C	A	B	D
Plurality with elimination	A	C	B	D
Borda count	C,B (tied)		A	D
Pairwise comparison	A,B (tied)		C,D (tied)	

76. **(a)** Under the Borda count method, each voter gives X more points than Y. Hence, the Borda count for X will be greater than the Borda count for Y and so X will rank above Y.

     (b) Since every voter prefers candidate X to candidate Y, a pairwise comparison between X and Y results in a win for X. If Y wins a pairwise comparison against Z, then X must also win against Z (by transitivity – since X is above Y on each ballot, when Y is above Z it must be that X is also above Z). Therefore X will have at least one more point than Y (from the head-to-head between X and Y). Thus, X will rank above Y under extended pairwise comparisons.

77. We will assume that each election has N candidates so that N-1 preference schedules are used to determine the recursive rankings.

     The recursive plurality ranking method satisfies the Pareto criterion since if every voter prefers candidate X to candidate Y, then candidate Y will not have a plurality at the kth stage of the ranking process unless candidate X has already been ranked. Candidate Y need not be ranked last, but it will certainly be ranked below X since whenever X and Y appear together in a preference schedule, only X could possibly have a plurality of votes.

     The recursive plurality-with-elimination ranking method satisfies the Pareto criterion since if every voter prefers candidate X to candidate Y, and Y is the winner at the kth stage of the ranking process, then X must have been a winner in a previous stage. This is because Y is eliminated in any preference schedule in which X and Y both appear.

     The recursive Borda count ranking method satisfies the Pareto criterion since if every voter prefers candidate X to candidate Y, then in any preference schedule containing candidates X and Y, X will have a larger Borda count than Y. So, X will be a winner of an election at some stage before Y will.

     The recursive pairwise comparisons ranking method satisfies the Pareto criterion since if every voter prefers candidate X to candidate Y, then in any preference schedule containing candidates X and Y, X will have at least one more point than Y. So, X will be a winner of an election at some stage before Y will.

78. (a) Consider an election with the following preference schedule:

Number of voters	2	2	3
1st choice	*A*	*B*	*C*
2nd choice	*B*	*A*	*A*
3rd choice	*C*	*C*	*B*

In this election, *C* is the winner under the plurality method yet a majority of the voters (4 out of 7) prefer both *A* and *B* over *C*.

(b) Same example as in part (a). Both *A* and *B* are eliminated in the first round and so *C* is the winner under the plurality-with-elimination method.

(c) Suppose there are k voters and N candidates. Under the Borda count method, the total number of points for all the candidates is $\dfrac{kN(N+1)}{2}$ (each voter contributes $1+2+\cdots+N = \dfrac{N(N+1)}{2}$ points to the total), so the average number of points per candidate is $\dfrac{k(N+1)}{2}$. Now suppose that *X* is a candidate that loses to every other candidate in a one-to-one comparison. The claim is that under the Borda count method, *X* will receive less than the average $\dfrac{k(N+1)}{2}$ points and therefore cannot be the winner. (One way to see this is as follows: Suppose that the N candidates are presented to the voters one at a time, with each voter keeping an updated partial ranking of the candidates as they are being presented. Suppose, moreover, that *X* is the first candidate to be presented. When this happens, *X* starts with kN points (*X* is the only candidate in every voter's ballot and therefore has all the first-place votes.) As soon as the next candidate (say *Y*) is presented, *X*'s points will drop by more than $k/2$ (*X* loses to *Y* in a one-to-one comparison means that more than $k/2$ of the voters have ranked *Y* above *X*.) By the same argument each time one of the subsequent candidates is presented *X*'s points drop by more than $k/2$. By the time we are done, *X* must have less than $kN - \frac{k}{2}(N-1) = \frac{k}{2}(N+1)$ points.)

79. Suppose there are k voters and N candidates.

Case 1. k is odd, say $k = 2t + 1$. Suppose the candidate with a majority of the first-place votes is *X*. The fewest possible Borda points *X* can have is $F(t + 1) + t$ [when there are $(t + 1)$ votes that place *X* first and the remaining votes place *X* last]. The most Borda points that any other candidate can have is $(N - 1)(t + 1) + Ft$ [when there are $(t + 1)$ voters that place the candidate second and the remaining voters place that candidate first]. Thus, the majority criterion will be satisfied when $F(t+ 1) + t > (N - 1)(t + 1) + Ft$, which after simplification implies $F > N(t + 1) - (2t + 1)$, or $F > N\left(\frac{k+1}{2}\right) - k$.

Case 2. k is even, say $k = 2t$. An argument similar to the one given in Case 1 gives the inequality $F(t + 1) + (t - 1) > (N - 1)(t + 1) + F(t - 1)$ which after simplification implies $F > [N(t + 1) - 2t]/2$, or $F > \left[N\left(\frac{k}{2}+1\right) - k\right]/2$.

80. Consider an election with N candidates. Each pairwise comparison results in 1 point being given to one of the candidates. (Since there are an odd number of voters, no one-to-one comparison can result in a tie.) Consequently, a candidate can end up with 0 points (winning no pairwise comparison), 1 point (winning one pairwise comparison), 2 points (winning two pairwise comparisons), ..., $N-1$ points (winning every pairwise comparison). Since there are N possible point values (0, 1, 2, 3, ..., $N-1$) and there are N voters, there will be no ties if and only if each of the possible point values is received by exactly one candidate, in which case, some candidate must receive $N-1$ points and be a Condorcet candidate. If there are an even number of voters, one-to-one comparisons can end up in a tie and so there are many more possible point values.

Chapter 2

WALKING

A. **Weighted Voting Systems**

1. **(a)** There are 6 players.

   (b) $7 + 4 + 3 + 3 + 2 + 1 = 20$ votes.

   (c) 4

   (d) 65% (13/20)

2. **(a)** There are 15 players.

   (b) $10 + 10 + 10 + 10 + 8 + 5 + 5 + 5 + 5 + 4 + 4 + 3 + 3 + 3 + 2 = 87$ votes.

   (c) 5

   (d) 72% (62/87)

3. **(a)** The quota must be more than half of the total votes. This system has $10 + 6 + 5 + 4 + 2 = 27$ total votes. $\frac{1}{2} \times 27 = 13.5$, so the smallest value q can take is 14.

   (b) The largest value q can take is 27, the total number of votes.

   (c) $\frac{2}{3} \times 27 = 18$, so the value of the quota q would be 18.

   (d) 19

4. **(a)** The quota must be more than half of the total votes. This system has 20 total votes. $\frac{1}{2} \times 20 = 10$, so the smallest value q can take is 11.

   (b) The largest value q can take is 20, the total number of votes.

   (c) $\frac{3}{4} \times 20 = 15$.

   (d) 16.

5. To determine the number of votes each player has, let P_4 have 1 vote. Then P_3 has $2 \times 1 = 2$ votes; P_2 has $2 \times 2 = 4$ votes; P_1 has $2 \times 4 = 8$ votes. The parts of the problem then require determining the quotas for various scenarios when there are $1 + 2 + 4 + 8 = 15$ total votes.

(a) $\dfrac{2}{3} \times 15 = 10$

[10: 8, 4, 2, 1]

(b) [11: 8, 4, 2, 1]

(c) $0.80 \times 15 = 12$

[12: 8, 4, 2, 1]

(d) [13: 8, 4, 2, 1]

6. (a) [11: 8, 4, 4, 2, 1, 1]

(b) [15: 8, 4, 4, 2, 1, 1]

(c) [16: 8, 4, 4, 2, 1, 1]

(d) [14: 8, 4, 4, 2, 1, 1]

(e) [14: 8, 4, 4, 2, 1, 1]

7. (a) There is no dictator; P_1 and P_2 have veto power; P_3 is a dummy.

(b) P_1 is a dictator; P_2 and P_3 are dummies.

(b) There is no dictator, no one has veto power, and no one is a dummy.

8. (a) P_1 is a dictator; P_2, P_3 and P_4 are dummies.

(b) P_1 has veto power; P_4 is a dummy.

(c) P_1 and P_2 have veto power; P_3, P_4, P_5 and P_6 are dummies.

9. (a) There is no dictator; P_1 and P_2 have veto power; P_5 is a dummy.

(b) P_1 is a dictator; P_2, P_3, and P_4 are dummies.

(c) There is no dictator; P_1 and P_2 have veto power; P_3 and P_4 are dummies.

(c) There is no dictator; all 4 players have veto power.

10. (a) All 4 players have veto power.

(b) P_1, P_2 and P_3 have veto power; P_4 and P_5 are dummies.

(c) P_1 is a dictator; P_2, P_3, and P_4 are dummies.

(d) P_1 and P_2 have veto power; P_3 and P_4 are dummies.

B.   Banzhaf Power

11. (a) $6 + 4 = 10$

(b) $\{P_1, P_2\}$, $\{P_1, P_3\}$, $\{P_1, P_2, P_3\}$, $\{P_1, P_2, P_4\}$, $\{P_1, P_3, P_4\}$, $\{P_2, P_3, P_4\}$, $\{P_1, P_2, P_3, P_4\}$

(c) P_1 only

(d) $P_1 : \dfrac{5}{12} = 41\dfrac{2}{3}\%$; $P_2 : \dfrac{3}{12} = 25\%$; $P_3 : \dfrac{3}{12} = 25\%$; $P_4 : \dfrac{1}{12} = 8\dfrac{1}{3}\%$.

The winning coalitions (with critical players underlined) are: $\{\underline{P_1}, \underline{P_2}\}$, $\{\underline{P_1}, \underline{P_3}\}$, $\{\underline{P_1}, P_2, P_3\}$, $\{\underline{P_1}, \underline{P_2}, P_4\}$, $\{\underline{P_1}, \underline{P_3}, P_4\}$, $\{\underline{P_2}, \underline{P_3}, \underline{P_4}\}$, $\{P_1, P_2, P_3, P_4\}$.

12. (a) $3 + 1 = 4$

(b) P_1 and P_2

(c) P_1, P_3, and P_4

(d) $\{P_1, P_2\}$, $\{P_1, P_2, P_3\}$, $\{P_1, P_2, P_4\}$, $\{P_1, P_3, P_4\}$, $\{P_1, P_2, P_3, P_4\}$

(e) $P_1 : \dfrac{1}{2}$; $P_2 : \dfrac{3}{10}$; $P_3 : \dfrac{1}{10}$; $P_4 : \dfrac{1}{10}$.

The winning coalitions (with critical players underlined) are: $\{\underline{P_1}, \underline{P_2}\}$, $\{\underline{P_1}, \underline{P_2}, P_3\}$, $\{\underline{P_1}, \underline{P_2}, P_4\}$, $\{\underline{P_1}, \underline{P_3}, \underline{P_4}\}$, $\{\underline{P_1}, P_2, P_3, P_4\}$.

13. (a) $P_1 : \dfrac{3}{5} = 60\%$; $P_2 : \dfrac{1}{5} = 20\%$; $P_3 : \dfrac{1}{5} = 20\%$.

The winning coalitions (with critical players underlined) are: $\{\underline{P_1}, \underline{P_2}\}$, $\{\underline{P_1}, \underline{P_3}\}$, $\{\underline{P_1}, P_2, P_3\}$.

(b) $P_1 : \dfrac{3}{5} = 60\%$; $P_2 : \dfrac{1}{5} = 20\%$; $P_3 : \dfrac{1}{5} = 20\%$.

The winning coalitions and critical players are exactly the same as in part (a). The weighted voting systems in (a) and (b) are equivalent weighted voting systems.

14. (a) $P_1 : \dfrac{1}{2} = 50\%$; $P_2 : \dfrac{1}{2} = 50\%$; $P_3 : 0$.

The winning coalitions (with critical players underlined) are: $\{\underline{P_1}, \underline{P_2}\}$, $\{\underline{P_1}, \underline{P_2}, P_3\}$.

(b) $P_1: \frac{1}{2} = 50\%$; $P_2: \frac{1}{2} = 50\%$; $P_3: 0$.

The winning coalitions and critical players are exactly the same as in part (a). The weighted voting systems in (a) and (b) are equivalent weighted voting systems.

15. (a) $P_1: \frac{8}{24}$; $P_2: \frac{6}{24}$; $P_3: \frac{4}{24}$; $P_4: \frac{4}{24}$; $P_5: \frac{2}{24}$.

The winning coalitions (with critical players underlined) are: $\{\underline{P_1}, \underline{P_2}, \underline{P_3}\}$, $\{\underline{P_1}, \underline{P_2}, \underline{P_4}\}$, $\{\underline{P_1}, \underline{P_2}, \underline{P_5}\}$,

$\{\underline{P_1}, \underline{P_3}, \underline{P_4}\}$, $\{\underline{P_1}, P_2, P_3, P_4\}$, $\{\underline{P_1}, \underline{P_2}, P_3, P_5\}$, $\{\underline{P_1}, \underline{P_2}, P_4, P_5\}$, $\{\underline{P_1}, \underline{P_3}, \underline{P_4}, P_5\}$, $\{\underline{P_2}, \underline{P_3}, \underline{P_4}, \underline{P_5}\}$,

$\{P_1, P_2, P_3, P_4, P_5\}$.

(b) $P_1: \frac{7}{19}$; $P_2: \frac{5}{19}$; $P_3: \frac{3}{19}$; $P_4: \frac{3}{19}$; $P_5: \frac{1}{19}$.

The quota is one more than in (a), so some winning coalitions may now be losing coalitions. For the ones that are still winning, any players that were critical in (a) will still be critical, and there may be additional critical players. A quick check shows that $\{P_1, P_2, P_5\}$, $\{P_1, P_3, P_4\}$, and $\{P_2, P_3, P_4, P_5\}$ are now losing coalitions (they all have exactly 10 votes). The winning coalitions (with critical players underlined) are: $\{\underline{P_1}, \underline{P_2}, \underline{P_3}\}$, $\{\underline{P_1}, \underline{P_2}, \underline{P_4}\}$, $\{\underline{P_1}, \underline{P_2}, P_3, P_4\}$, $\{\underline{P_1}, \underline{P_2}, P_3, P_5\}$,

$\{\underline{P_1}, \underline{P_2}, \underline{P_4}, P_5\}$, $\{\underline{P_1}, \underline{P_3}, \underline{P_4}, \underline{P_5}\}$, $\{\underline{P_1}, P_2, P_3, P_4, P_5\}$.

16. (a) $P_1: \frac{8}{24}$; $P_2: \frac{8}{24}$; $P_3: \frac{8}{24}$; $P_4: 0$; $P_5: 0$.

The winning coalitions (with critical players underlined) are: $A: \frac{1}{3}$; $B: \frac{1}{3}$; $C: \frac{1}{3}$; $D: 0$. $\{\underline{P_1}, \underline{P_3}\}$,

$\{\underline{P_2}, \underline{P_3}\}$, $\{P_1, P_2, P_3\}$ $\{P_1, P_2, P_3\}$, $\{\underline{P_1}, \underline{P_2}, P_4\}$, $\{\underline{P_1}, \underline{P_2}, P_5\}$, $\{\underline{P_1}, \underline{P_3}, P_4\}$, $\{\underline{P_1}, \underline{P_3}, P_5\}$, $\{\underline{P_2}, \underline{P_3}, P_4\}$,

$\{\underline{P_2}, \underline{P_3}, P_5\}$, $\{P_1, P_2, P_3, P_4\}$, $\{P_1, P_2, P_3, P_5\}$, $\{\underline{P_1}, \underline{P_2}, P_4, P_5\}$, $\{\underline{P_1}, \underline{P_3}, P_4, P_5\}$, $\{\underline{P_2}, \underline{P_3}, P_4, P_5\}$,

$\{P_1, P_2, P_3, P_4, P_5\}$.

(b) $P_1: \frac{4}{13}$; $P_2: \frac{4}{13}$; $P_3: \frac{3}{13}$; $P_4: \frac{1}{13}$; $P_5: \frac{1}{13}$.

The winning coalitions (with critical players underlined) are: $\{\underline{P_1}, \underline{P_2}\}$, $\{\underline{P_1}, \underline{P_2}, P_3\}$, $\{\underline{P_1}, \underline{P_2}, P_4\}$,

$\{\underline{P_1}, \underline{P_2}, P_5\}$, $\{\underline{P_1}, \underline{P_3}, \underline{P_4}\}$, $\{\underline{P_1}, \underline{P_3}, \underline{P_5}\}$, $\{\underline{P_2}, \underline{P_3}, \underline{P_4}\}$, $\{\underline{P_2}, \underline{P_3}, \underline{P_5}\}$, $\{\underline{P_1}, P_2, P_3, P_4\}$, $\{P_1, P_2, P_3, P_5\}$,

$\{\underline{P_1}, \underline{P_2}, P_4, P_5\}$, $\{\underline{P_1}, \underline{P_3}, P_4, P_5\}$, $\{\underline{P_2}, \underline{P_3}, P_4, P_5\}$, $\{\underline{P_1}, P_2, P_3, P_4, P_5\}$.

17. (a) $A: \frac{12}{24}$; $B: \frac{4}{24}$; $C: \frac{4}{24}$; $D: \frac{4}{24}$. 1; $P_2: 0$; $P_3: 0$; $P_4: 0$. P_1 is a dictator and the other players are dummies. Thus P_1 is the only critical player in each winning coalition.

(b) $P_1 : \frac{7}{10}$; $P_2 : \frac{1}{10}$; $P_3 : \frac{1}{10}$; $P_4 : \frac{1}{10}$.

The winning coalitions (with critical players underlined) are: $\{\underline{P_1}, \underline{P_2}\}$, $\{\underline{P_1}, \underline{P_3}\}$, $\{\underline{P_1}, \underline{P_4}\}$, $\{\underline{P_1}, P_2, P_3\}$, $\{\underline{P_1}, P_2, P_4\}$, $\{\underline{P_1}, P_3, P_4\}$, $\{\underline{P_1}, P_2, P_3, P_4\}$.

(c) $P_1 : \frac{6}{10}$; $P_2 : \frac{2}{10}$; $P_3 : \frac{2}{10}$; $P_4 : 0$.

The winning coalitions (with critical players underlined) are: $\{\underline{P_1}, \underline{P_2}\}$, $\{\underline{P_1}, \underline{P_3}\}$, $\{\underline{P_1}, P_2, P_3\}$, $\{\underline{P_1}, \underline{P_2}, P_4\}$, $\{\underline{P_1}, \underline{P_3}, P_4\}$, $\{\underline{P_1}, P_2, P_3, P_4\}$.

(d) $P_1 : \frac{4}{8}$; $P_2 : \frac{4}{8}$; $P_3 : 0$; $P_4 : 0$.

The winning coalitions (with critical players underlined) are: $\{\underline{P_1}, \underline{P_2}\}$, $\{\underline{P_1}, \underline{P_3}\}$, $\{\underline{P_1}, P_2, P_3\}$, $\{\underline{P_1}, \underline{P_2}, P_4\}$, $\{\underline{P_1}, \underline{P_3}, P_4\}$, $\{\underline{P_1}, P_2, P_3, P_4\}$.

(e) $P_1 : \frac{1}{3}$; $P_2 : \frac{1}{3}$; $P_3 : \frac{1}{3}$; $P_4 : 0$.

The winning coalitions (with critical players underlined) are: $\{\underline{P_1}, \underline{P_2}, \underline{P_3}\}$, $\{\underline{P_1}, \underline{P_2}, \underline{P_3}, P_4\}$.

18. (a) $P_1 : 1$; $P_2 : 0$; $P_3 : 0$.

The winning coalitions (with critical players underlined) are: $\{\underline{P_1}\}$, $\{\underline{P_1}, P_2\}$, $\{\underline{P_1}, P_3\}$, $\{\underline{P_1}, P_2, P_3\}$.

(b) $P_1 : \frac{3}{5}$; $P_2 : \frac{1}{5}$; $P_3 : \frac{1}{5}$.

The winning coalitions (with critical players underlined) are: $\{\underline{P_1}, \underline{P_2}\}$, $\{\underline{P_1}, \underline{P_3}\}$, $\{\underline{P_1}, P_2, P_3\}$.

(c) $P_1 : \frac{2}{4}$; $P_2 : \frac{2}{4}$; $P_3 : 0$.

The winning coalitions (with critical players underlined) are: $\{\underline{P_1}, \underline{P_2}\}$, $\{\underline{P_1}, \underline{P_2}, P_3\}$.

(d) $P_1 : \frac{2}{4}$; $P_2 : \frac{2}{4}$; $P_3 : 0$.

The winning coalitions (with critical players underlined) are: $\{\underline{P_1}, \underline{P_2}\}$, $\{\underline{P_1}, \underline{P_2}, P_3\}$. Note that (c) and (d) are equivalent.

(e) $P_1 : \frac{1}{3}$; $P_2 : \frac{1}{3}$; $P_3 : \frac{1}{3}$.

The only winning coalitions is the grand coalition: $\{\underline{P_1}, \underline{P_2}, \underline{P_3}\}$.

19. $A : \frac{1}{3};\ B : \frac{1}{3};\ C : \frac{1}{3};\ D: 0.$

D is never a critical player, and the other three have equal power.

20. (a) The winning coalitions (with critical players underlined) are: $\{\underline{P_1}, \underline{P_2}\}$, $\{\underline{P_1}, \underline{P_2}, P_3\}$, $\{\underline{P_1}, \underline{P_2}, P_4\}$, $\{\underline{P_1}, \underline{P_2}, P_5\}$, $\{\underline{P_1}, \underline{P_2}, P_3, P_4\}$, $\{\underline{P_1}, \underline{P_2}, P_3, P_5\}$, $\{\underline{P_1}, \underline{P_2}, P_4, P_5\}$, $\{\underline{P_1}, P_3, \underline{P_4}, \underline{P_5}\}$, $\{\underline{P_1}, P_2, P_3, P_4, P_5\}$.

(b) $P_1 : \frac{9}{19};\ P_2 : \frac{7}{19};\ P_3 : \frac{1}{19};\ P_4 : \frac{1}{19};\ P_5 : \frac{1}{19}.$

(c) $P_1 : \frac{8}{16};\ P_2 : \frac{8}{16};\ P_3 : 0;\ P_4 : 0;\ P_5 : 0.$

In the system [8: 4, 4, 1, 1, 1], the winning coalitions (with critical players underlined) are:
$\{\underline{P_1}, \underline{P_2}\}$, $\{\underline{P_1}, \underline{P_2}, P_3\}$, $\{\underline{P_1}, \underline{P_2}, P_4\}$, $\{\underline{P_1}, \underline{P_2}, P_5\}$, $\{\underline{P_1}, \underline{P_2}, P_3, P_4\}$, $\{\underline{P_1}, \underline{P_2}, P_3, P_5\}$, $\{\underline{P_1}, \underline{P_2}, P_4, P_5\}$,
$\{\underline{P_1}, \underline{P_2}, P_3, P_4, P_5\}$.

(d) P_1 has more power after selling one of her votes.

21. (a) $\{P_1, P_2\}$, $\{P_1, P_3\}$, $\{P_2, P_3\}$, $\{P_1, P_2, P_3\}$

(b) $\{P_1, P_2, P_4\}$, $\{P_1, P_3, P_4\}$, $\{P_2, P_3, P_4\}$, $\{P_1, P_2, P_3, P_4\}$, $\{P_1, P_2, P_4, P_5\}$, $\{P_1, P_2, P_4, P_6\}$, $\{P_1, P_3, P_4, P_5\}$, $\{P_1, P_3, P_4, P_6\}$, $\{P_2, P_3, P_4, P_5\}$, $\{P_2, P_3, P_4, P_6\}$, $\{P_1, P_2, P_3, P_4, P_5\}$, $\{P_1, P_2, P_3, P_4, P_6\}$, $\{P_1, P_2, P_3, P_4, P_5, P_6\}$

(c) P_4 is never a critical player since every time it is part of a winning coalition, that coalition is a winning coalition without P_4 as well.

(d) A similar argument to that used in part (c) shows that P_5 and P_6 are also dummies. One could also argue that any player with fewer votes than P_4, a dummy, will also be a dummy. So, P_4, P_5, and P_6 will never be critical -- they all have zero power.

The only winning coalitions with only 2 players are $\{P_1, P_2\}$, $\{P_1, P_3\}$, and $\{P_2, P_3\}$; and both players are critical in each of those coalitions. All other winning coalitions consist of one of these coalitions plus additional players, and the only critical players will be the ones from the two-player coalition. So P_1, P_2, and P_3 will be critical in every winning coalition they are in, and they will all be in the same number of winning coalitions, so they all have the same power. Thus, the Banzhaf power distribution is $P_1 : \frac{1}{3} = 33\frac{1}{3}\%$; $P_2 : \frac{1}{3} = 33\frac{1}{3}\%$; $P_3 : \frac{1}{3} = 33\frac{1}{3}\%$; $P_4 : 0$; $P_5 : 0$; $P_6 : 0$.

22. (a) Three-player winning coalitions (with critical players underlined): $\{\underline{P_1}, \underline{P_2}, \underline{P_3}\}$, $\{\underline{P_1}, \underline{P_2}, \underline{P_4}\}$, $\{\underline{P_1}, \underline{P_2}, \underline{P_5}\}$, $\{\underline{P_1}, \underline{P_3}, \underline{P_4}\}$, $\{\underline{P_2}, \underline{P_3}, \underline{P_4}\}$.

(b) Four-player winning coalitions (with critical players underlined): $\{P_1, P_2, P_3, P_4\}$, $\{\underline{P_1}, \underline{P_2}, P_3, P_5\}$, $\{\underline{P_1}, \underline{P_2}, \underline{P_3}, P_6\}$, $\{\underline{P_1}, \underline{P_2}, P_4, P_5\}$, $\{\underline{P_1}, \underline{P_2}, \underline{P_4}, P_6\}$, $\{\underline{P_1}, \underline{P_2}, \underline{P_5}, \underline{P_6}\}$, $\{\underline{P_1}, \underline{P_3}, \underline{P_4}, P_5\}$, $\{\underline{P_1}, \underline{P_3}, \underline{P_4}, \underline{P_6}\}$, $\{\underline{P_1}, \underline{P_3}, \underline{P_5}, \underline{P_6}\}$, $\{\underline{P_2}, \underline{P_3}, \underline{P_4}, P_5\}$, $\{\underline{P_2}, \underline{P_3}, \underline{P_4}, \underline{P_6}\}$.

(c) Five-player winning coalitions (with critical players underlined): $\{P_1, P_2, P_3, P_4, P_5\}$, $\{P_1, P_2, P_3, P_4, P_6\}$, $\{\underline{P_1}, P_2, P_3, P_5, P_6\}$, $\{\underline{P_1}, \underline{P_2}, P_4, P_5, P_6\}$, $\{\underline{P_1}, \underline{P_3}, P_4, P_5, P_6\}$, $\{\underline{P_2}, \underline{P_3}, \underline{P_4}, P_5, P_6\}$.

(d) $P_1 : \dfrac{15}{52}$; $P_2 : \dfrac{13}{52}$; $P_3 : \dfrac{11}{52}$; $P_4 : \dfrac{9}{52}$; $P_5 : \dfrac{3}{52}$; $P_6 : \dfrac{1}{52}$. Note: The grand coalition is also a winning coalition. However, it has no critical players.

C. Shapley-Shubik Power

23. (a) There are 3! = 6 sequential coalitions of the three players.

$< P_1, P_2, P_3 >, < P_1, P_3, P_2 >, < P_2, P_1, P_3 >, < P_2, P_3, P_1 >, < P_3, P_1, P_2 >, < P_3, P_2, P_1 >$

(b) $< P_1, \underline{P_2}, P_3 >, < P_1, \underline{P_3}, P_2 >, < P_2, \underline{P_1}, P_3 >, < P_2, P_3, \underline{P_1} >, < P_3, \underline{P_1}, P_2 >, < P_3, P_2, \underline{P_1} >$

(c) $P_1 : \dfrac{4}{6}$; $P_2 : \dfrac{1}{6}$; $P_3 : \dfrac{1}{6}$.

24. (a) There are 3! = 6 sequential coalitions of the three players.

$< P_1, P_2, P_3 >, < P_1, P_3, P_2 >, < P_2, P_1, P_3 >, < P_2, P_3, P_1 >, < P_3, P_1, P_2 >, < P_3, P_2, P_1 >$

(b) $< P_1, \underline{P_2}, P_3 >, < P_1, \underline{P_3}, P_2 >, < P_2, \underline{P_1}, P_3 >, < P_2, \underline{P_3}, P_1 >, < P_3, \underline{P_1}, P_2 >, < P_3, \underline{P_2}, P_1 >$

(c) $P_1 : \dfrac{2}{6}$; $P_2 : \dfrac{2}{6}$; $P_3 : \dfrac{2}{6}$.

25. $P_1 : \dfrac{14}{24}$; $P_2 : \dfrac{6}{24}$; $P_3 : \dfrac{2}{24}$; $P_4 : \dfrac{2}{24}$.

There are 4! = 24 sequential coalitions of the four players. The pivotal player in each coalition is underlined.

$< P_1, \underline{P_2}, P_3, P_4 >, < P_1, \underline{P_2}, P_4, P_3 >, < P_1, P_3, \underline{P_2}, P_4 >, < P_1, P_3, \underline{P_4}, P_2 >,$

$< P_1, P_4, \underline{P_2}, P_3 >, < P_1, P_4, \underline{P_3}, P_2 >, < P_2, \underline{P_1}, P_3, P_4 >, < P_2, \underline{P_1}, P_4, P_3 >,$

$< P_2, P_3, \underline{P_1}, P_4 >, < P_2, P_3, P_4, \underline{P_1} >, < P_2, P_4, \underline{P_1}, P_3 >, < P_2, P_4, P_3, \underline{P_1} >,$

$< P_3, P_1, \underline{P_2}, P_4 >, < P_3, P_1, \underline{P_4}, P_2 >, < P_3, P_2, \underline{P_1}, P_4 >, < P_3, P_2, P_4, \underline{P_1} >,$

$< P_3, P_4, \underline{P_1}, P_2 >, < P_3, P_4, P_2, \underline{P_1} >, < P_4, P_1, \underline{P_2}, P_3 >, < P_4, P_1, \underline{P_3}, P_2 >,$

$< P_4, P_2, \underline{P_1}, P_3 >, < P_4, P_2, P_3, \underline{P_1} >, < P_4, P_3, \underline{P_1}, P_2 >, < P_4, P_3, P_2, \underline{P_1} >$

26. $P_1 : \dfrac{10}{24}; \ P_2 : \dfrac{6}{24}; \ P_3 : \dfrac{6}{24}; \ P_4 : \dfrac{2}{24}.$

There are 4! = 24 sequential coalitions of the four players. The pivotal player in each coalition is underlined.

$< P_1, \underline{P_2}, P_3, P_4 >, \ < P_1, \underline{P_2}, P_4, P_3 >, \ < P_1, \underline{P_3}, P_2, P_4 >, \ < P_1, \underline{P_3}, P_4, P_2 >,$

$< P_1, P_4, \underline{P_2}, P_3 >, \ < P_1, P_4, \underline{P_3}, P_2 >, \ < P_2, \underline{P_1}, P_3, P_4 >, \ < P_2, \underline{P_1}, P_4, P_3 >,$

$< P_2, P_3, \underline{P_1}, P_4 >, \ < P_2, P_3, \underline{P_4}, P_1 >, \ < P_2, P_4, \underline{P_1}, P_3 >, \ < P_2, P_4, \underline{P_3}, P_1 >,$

$< P_3, \underline{P_1}, P_2, P_4 >, \ < P_3, \underline{P_1}, P_4, P_2 >, \ < P_3, P_2, \underline{P_1}, P_4 >, \ < P_3, P_2, \underline{P_4}, P_1 >,$

$< P_3, P_4, \underline{P_1}, P_2 >, \ < P_3, P_4, \underline{P_2}, P_1 >, \ < P_4, P_1, \underline{P_2}, P_3 >, \ < P_4, P_1, \underline{P_3}, P_2 >,$

$< P_4, P_2, \underline{P_1}, P_3 >, \ < P_4, P_2, \underline{P_3}, P_1 >, \ < P_4, P_3, \underline{P_1}, P_2 >, \ < P_4, P_3, \underline{P_2}, P_1 >$

27. (a) $P_1 : 1; \ P_2 : 0; \ P_3 : 0.$

$< \underline{P_1}, P_2, P_3 >, \ < \underline{P_1}, P_3, P_2 >, \ < P_2, \underline{P_1}, P_3 >, \ < P_2, P_3, \underline{P_1} >, \ < P_3, \underline{P_1}, P_2 >, \ < P_3, P_2, \underline{P_1} >$

(b) $P_1 : \dfrac{4}{6}; \ P_2 : \dfrac{1}{6}; \ P_3 : \dfrac{1}{6}.$

$< P_1, \underline{P_2}, P_3 >, \ < P_1, \underline{P_3}, P_2 >, \ < P_2, \underline{P_1}, P_3 >, \ < P_2, P_3, \underline{P_1} >, \ < P_3, \underline{P_1}, P_2 >, \ < P_3, P_2, \underline{P_1} >$

(c) $P_1 : \dfrac{4}{6}; \ P_2 : \dfrac{1}{6}; \ P_3 : \dfrac{1}{6}.$

$< P_1, \underline{P_2}, P_3 >, \ < P_1, \underline{P_3}, P_2 >, \ < P_2, \underline{P_1}, P_3 >, \ < P_2, P_3, \underline{P_1} >, \ < P_3, \underline{P_1}, P_2 >, \ < P_3, P_2, \underline{P_1} >$

(This is effectively the same as in (b).)

(d) $P_1 : \dfrac{3}{6}; \ P_2 : \dfrac{3}{6}; \ P_3 : 0.$

$< P_1, \underline{P_2}, P_3 >, \ < P_1, P_3, \underline{P_2} >, \ < P_2, \underline{P_1}, P_3 >, \ < P_2, P_3, \underline{P_1} >, \ < P_3, P_1, \underline{P_2} >, \ < P_3, P_2, \underline{P_1} >$

(e) $P_1 : \dfrac{1}{3}; \ P_2 : \dfrac{1}{3}; \ P_3 : \dfrac{1}{3}.$

$< P_1, \underline{P_2}, P_3 >, \ < P_1, \underline{P_3}, P_2 >, \ < P_2, \underline{P_1}, P_3 >, \ < P_2, \underline{P_3}, P_1 >, \ < P_3, \underline{P_1}, P_2 >, \ < P_3, \underline{P_2}, P_1 >$

28. (a) $P_1 : \dfrac{10}{24}; \ P_2 : \dfrac{6}{24}; \ P_3 : \dfrac{6}{24}; \ P_4 : \dfrac{2}{24}.$

The sequential coalitions (with pivotal player in each coalition underlined) are:

$< P_1, \underline{P_2}, P_3, P_4 >, \ < P_1, \underline{P_2}, P_4, P_3 >, \ < P_1, \underline{P_3}, P_2, P_4 >, \ < P_1, \underline{P_3}, P_4, P_2 >,$

$< P_1, P_4, \underline{P_2}, P_3 >, \ < P_1, P_4, \underline{P_3}, P_2 >, \ < P_2, \underline{P_1}, P_3, P_4 >, \ < P_2, \underline{P_1}, P_4, P_3 >,$

$< P_2, P_3, \underline{P_1}, P_4 >, \ < P_2, P_3, \underline{P_4}, P_1 >, \ < P_2, P_4, \underline{P_1}, P_3 >, \ < P_2, P_4, \underline{P_3}, P_1 >,$

$< P_3, \underline{P_1}, P_2, P_4 >, \ < P_3, \underline{P_1}, P_4, P_2 >, \ < P_3, P_2, \underline{P_1}, P_4 >, \ < P_3, P_2, \underline{P_4}, P_1 >,$

$< P_3, P_4, \underline{P_1}, P_2 >, < P_3, P_4, \underline{P_2}, P_1 >, < P_4, P_1, \underline{P_2}, P_3 >, < P_4, P_1, \underline{P_3}, P_2 >,$

$< P_4, P_2, \underline{P_1}, P_3 >, < P_4, P_2, \underline{P_3}, P_1 >, < P_4, P_3, \underline{P_1}, P_2 >, < P_4, P_3, \underline{P_2}, P_1 >$

(b) $P_1 : \dfrac{14}{24}; \quad P_2 : \dfrac{6}{24}; \quad P_3 : \dfrac{2}{24}; \quad P_4 : \dfrac{2}{24}.$

The sequential coalitions (with pivotal player in each coalition underlined) are:

$< P_1, \underline{P_2}, P_3, P_4 >, < P_1, \underline{P_2}, P_4, P_3 >, < P_1, P_3, \underline{P_2}, P_4 >, < P_1, P_3, \underline{P_4}, P_2 >,$

$< P_1, P_4, \underline{P_2}, P_3 >, < P_1, P_4, \underline{P_3}, P_2 >, < P_2, \underline{P_1}, P_3, P_4 >, < P_2, \underline{P_1}, P_4, P_3 >,$

$< P_2, P_3, \underline{P_1}, P_4 >, < P_2, P_3, P_4, \underline{P_1} >, < P_2, P_4, \underline{P_1}, P_3 >, < P_2, P_4, P_3, \underline{P_1} >,$

$< P_3, P_1, \underline{P_2}, P_4 >, < P_3, P_1, \underline{P_4}, P_2 >, < P_3, P_2, \underline{P_1}, P_4 >, < P_3, P_2, P_4, \underline{P_1} >,$

$< P_3, P_4, \underline{P_1}, P_2 >, < P_3, P_4, P_2, \underline{P_1} >, < P_4, P_1, \underline{P_2}, P_3 >, < P_4, P_1, \underline{P_3}, P_2 >,$

$< P_4, P_2, \underline{P_1}, P_3 >, < P_4, P_2, P_3, \underline{P_1} >, < P_4, P_3, \underline{P_1}, P_2 >, < P_4, P_3, P_2, \underline{P_1} >$

(c) $P_1 : \dfrac{10}{24}; \quad P_2 : \dfrac{10}{24}; \quad P_3 : \dfrac{2}{24}; \quad P_4 : \dfrac{2}{24}.$

The sequential coalitions (with pivotal player in each coalition underlined) are:

$< P_1, P_2, \underline{P_3}, P_4 >, < P_1, P_2, \underline{P_4}, P_3 >, < P_1, P_3, \underline{P_2}, P_4 >, < P_1, P_3, P_4, \underline{P_2} >,$

$< P_1, P_4, \underline{P_2}, P_3 >, < P_1, P_4, P_3, \underline{P_2} >, < P_2, P_1, \underline{P_3}, P_4 >, < P_2, P_1, \underline{P_4}, P_3 >,$

$< P_2, P_3, \underline{P_1}, P_4 >, < P_2, P_3, P_4, \underline{P_1} >, < P_2, P_4, \underline{P_1}, P_3 >, < P_2, P_4, P_3, \underline{P_1} >,$

$< P_3, P_1, \underline{P_2}, P_4 >, < P_3, P_1, P_4, \underline{P_2} >, < P_3, P_2, \underline{P_1}, P_4 >, < P_3, P_2, P_4, \underline{P_1} >,$

$< P_3, P_4, P_1, \underline{P_2} >, < P_3, P_4, P_2, \underline{P_1} >, < P_4, P_1, \underline{P_2}, P_3 >, < P_4, P_1, P_3, \underline{P_2} >,$

$< P_4, P_2, \underline{P_1}, P_3 >, < P_4, P_2, P_3, \underline{P_1} >, < P_4, P_3, P_1, \underline{P_2} >, < P_4, P_3, P_2, \underline{P_1} >$

(d) $P_1 : \dfrac{8}{24}; \quad P_2 : \dfrac{8}{24}; \quad P_3 : \dfrac{8}{24}; \quad P_4 : 0.$

The sequential coalitions (with pivotal player in each coalition underlined) are:

$< P_1, P_2, \underline{P_3}, P_4 >, < P_1, P_2, P_4, \underline{P_3} >, < P_1, P_3, \underline{P_2}, P_4 >, < P_1, P_3, P_4, \underline{P_2} >,$

$< P_1, P_4, P_2, \underline{P_3} >, < P_1, P_4, P_3, \underline{P_2} >, < P_2, P_1, \underline{P_3}, P_4 >, < P_2, P_1, P_4, \underline{P_3} >,$

$< P_2, P_3, \underline{P_1}, P_4 >, < P_2, P_3, P_4, \underline{P_1} >, < P_2, P_4, P_1, \underline{P_3} >, < P_2, P_4, P_3, \underline{P_1} >,$

$< P_3, P_1, \underline{P_2}, P_4 >, < P_3, P_1, P_4, \underline{P_2} >, < P_3, P_2, \underline{P_1}, P_4 >, < P_3, P_2, P_4, \underline{P_1} >,$

$< P_3, P_4, P_1, \underline{P_2} >, < P_3, P_4, P_2, \underline{P_1} >, < P_4, P_1, P_2, \underline{P_3} >, < P_4, P_1, P_3, \underline{P_2} >,$

$< P_4, P_2, P_1, \underline{P_3} >, < P_4, P_2, P_3, \underline{P_1} >, < P_4, P_3, P_1, \underline{P_2} >, < P_4, P_3, P_2, \underline{P_1} >$

(e) $P_1 : \dfrac{6}{24}; \quad P_2 : \dfrac{6}{24}; \quad P_3 : \dfrac{6}{24}; \quad P_4 : \dfrac{6}{24}.$

The sequential coalitions (with pivotal player in each coalition underlined) are:

$< P_1, P_2, P_3, \underline{P_4} >, < P_1, P_2, P_4, \underline{P_3} >, < P_1, P_3, P_2, \underline{P_4} >, < P_1, P_3, P_4, \underline{P_2} >,$

$< P_1, P_4, P_2, \underline{P_3} >, < P_1, P_4, P_3, \underline{P_2} >, < P_2, P_1, P_3, \underline{P_4} >, < P_2, P_1, P_4, \underline{P_3} >,$

$< P_2, P_3, P_1, \underline{P_4} >, < P_2, P_3, P_4, \underline{P_1} >, < P_2, P_4, P_1, \underline{P_3} >, < P_2, P_4, P_3, \underline{P_1} >,$

$< P_3, P_1, P_2, \underline{P_4} >, < P_3, P_1, P_4, \underline{P_2} >, < P_3, P_2, P_1, \underline{P_4} >, < P_3, P_2, P_4, \underline{P_1} >,$

$< P_3, P_4, P_1, \underline{P_2} >, < P_3, P_4, P_2, \underline{P_1} >, < P_4, P_1, P_2, \underline{P_3} >, < P_4, P_1, P_3, \underline{P_2} >,$

$< P_4, P_2, P_1, \underline{P_3} >, < P_4, P_2, P_3, \underline{P_1} >, < P_4, P_3, P_1, \underline{P_2} >, < P_4, P_3, P_2, \underline{P_1} >$

29. (a) $P_1 : 1; P_2 : 0; P_3 : 0.$

The sequential coalitions (with pivotal player in each coalition underlined) are:

$< \underline{P_1}, P_2, P_3 >, < \underline{P_1}, P_3, P_2 >, < P_2, \underline{P_1}, P_3 >, < P_2, P_3, \underline{P_1} >, < P_3, \underline{P_1}, P_2 >, < P_3, P_2, \underline{P_1} >$

(b) $P_1 : \dfrac{4}{6}; P_2 : \dfrac{1}{6}; P_3 : \dfrac{1}{6}.$

$< P_1, \underline{P_2}, P_3 >, < P_1, \underline{P_3}, P_2 >, < P_2, \underline{P_1}, P_3 >, < P_2, P_3, \underline{P_1} >, < P_3, \underline{P_1}, P_2 >, < P_3, P_2, \underline{P_1} >$

(c) $P_1 : \dfrac{3}{6}; P_2 : \dfrac{3}{6}; P_3 : 0.$

$< P_1, \underline{P_2}, P_3 >, < P_1, \underline{P_3}, P_2 >, < P_2, \underline{P_1}, P_3 >, < P_2, P_3, \underline{P_1} >, < P_3, P_1, \underline{P_2} >, < P_3, P_2, \underline{P_1} >$

(d) $P_1 : \dfrac{3}{6}; P_2 : \dfrac{3}{6}; P_3 : 0.$

This is effectively the same system as in (c).

(e) $P_1 : \dfrac{2}{6}; P_2 : \dfrac{2}{6}; P_3 : \dfrac{2}{6}.$

In this system, the last player in the coalition will always be the pivotal player. Since every player is last in the same number of sequential coalitions, the players all have the same power.

30. (a) $P_1 : \dfrac{2}{6}; P_2 : \dfrac{2}{6}; P_3 : \dfrac{2}{6}.$

The sequential coalitions (with pivotal player in each coalition underlined) are:

$< P_1, \underline{P_2}, P_3 >, < P_1, \underline{P_3}, P_2 >, < P_2, \underline{P_1}, P_3 >, < P_2, P_3, \underline{P_1} >, < P_3, \underline{P_1}, P_2 >, < P_3, P_2, \underline{P_1} >$

(b) $P_1 : \dfrac{4}{6}; P_2 : \dfrac{1}{6}; P_3 : \dfrac{1}{6}.$

The sequential coalitions (with pivotal player in each coalition underlined) are:

$< P_1, \underline{P_2}, P_3 >, < P_1, \underline{P_3}, P_2 >, < P_2, \underline{P_1}, P_3 >, < P_2, P_3, \underline{P_1} >, < P_3, \underline{P_1}, P_2 >, < P_3, P_2, \underline{P_1} >$

(c) $P_1 : \dfrac{3}{6}; P_2 : \dfrac{3}{6}; P_3 : 0.$

The sequential coalitions (with pivotal player in each coalition underlined) are:

$< P_1, \underline{P_2}, P_3 >, < P_1, P_3, \underline{P_2} >, < P_2, \underline{P_1}, P_3 >, < P_2, P_3, \underline{P_1} >, < P_3, P_1, \underline{P_2} >, < P_3, P_2, \underline{P_1} >$

(d) $P_1 : \dfrac{2}{6}; P_2 : \dfrac{2}{6}; P_3 : \dfrac{2}{6}.$

The sequential coalitions (with pivotal player in each coalition underlined) are:

$< P_1, P_2, \underline{P_3} >, < P_1, P_3, \underline{P_2} >, < P_2, P_1, \underline{P_3} >, < P_2, P_3, \underline{P_1} >, < P_3, P_1, \underline{P_2} >, < P_3, P_2, \underline{P_1} >$

(e) $P_1 : \dfrac{2}{6}; P_2 : \dfrac{2}{6}; P_3 : \dfrac{2}{6}.$

The sequential coalitions (with pivotal player in each coalition underlined) are:

$< P_1, P_2, \underline{P_3} >, < P_1, P_3, \underline{P_2} >, < P_2, P_1, \underline{P_3} >, < P_2, P_3, \underline{P_1} >, < P_3, P_1, \underline{P_2} >, < P_3, P_2, \underline{P_1} >$

31. (a) $P_1 : \dfrac{10}{24}; P_2 : \dfrac{6}{24}; P_3 : \dfrac{6}{24}; P_4 : \dfrac{2}{24}.$

The sequential coalitions (with pivotal player in each coalition underlined) are:

$< P_1, \underline{P_2}, P_3, P_4 >, < P_1, \underline{P_2}, P_4, P_3 >, < P_1, \underline{P_3}, P_2, P_4 >, < P_1, \underline{P_3}, P_4, P_2 >,$

$< P_1, P_4, \underline{P_2}, P_3 >, < P_1, P_4, \underline{P_3}, P_2 >, < P_2, \underline{P_1}, P_3, P_4 >, < P_2, \underline{P_1}, P_4, P_3 >,$

$< P_2, P_3, \underline{P_1}, P_4 >, < P_2, P_3, \underline{P_4}, P_1 >, < P_2, P_4, \underline{P_1}, P_3 >, < P_2, P_4, \underline{P_3}, P_1 >,$

$< P_3, \underline{P_1}, P_2, P_4 >, < P_3, \underline{P_1}, P_4, P_2 >, < P_3, P_2, \underline{P_1}, P_4 >, < P_3, P_2, \underline{P_4}, P_1 >,$

$< P_3, P_4, \underline{P_1}, P_2 >, < P_3, P_4, \underline{P_2}, P_1 >, < P_4, P_1, \underline{P_2}, P_3 >, < P_4, P_1, \underline{P_3}, P_2 >,$

$< P_4, P_2, \underline{P_1}, P_3 >, < P_4, P_2, \underline{P_3}, P_1 >, < P_4, P_3, \underline{P_1}, P_2 >, < P_4, P_3, \underline{P_2}, P_1 >$

(b) $P_1 : \dfrac{10}{24}; P_2 : \dfrac{6}{24}; P_3 : \dfrac{6}{24}; P_4 : \dfrac{2}{24}.$

This is the same situation as in (a) – there is essentially no difference between 51 and 59 because the players' votes are all multiples of 10.

(c) $P_1 : \dfrac{10}{24}; P_2 : \dfrac{6}{24}; P_3 : \dfrac{6}{24}; P_4 : \dfrac{2}{24}.$

This is also the same situation as in (a) – any time a group of players has 51 votes, they must have 60 votes.

32. (a) $P_1 : \dfrac{18}{24}; P_2 : \dfrac{2}{24}; P_3 : \dfrac{2}{24}; P_4 : \dfrac{2}{24}.$

The sequential coalitions (with pivotal player in each coalition underlined) are:

$< P_1, \underline{P_2}, P_3, P_4 >, < P_1, \underline{P_2}, P_4, P_3 >, < P_1, \underline{P_3}, P_2, P_4 >, < P_1, \underline{P_3}, P_4, P_2 >,$

$< P_1, \underline{P_4}, P_2, P_3 >, < P_1, \underline{P_4}, P_3, P_2 >, < P_2, \underline{P_1}, P_3, P_4 >, < P_2, \underline{P_1}, P_4, P_3 >,$

$< P_2, P_3, \underline{P_1}, P_4 >, < P_2, P_3, P_4, \underline{P_1} >, < P_2, P_4, \underline{P_1}, P_3 >, < P_2, P_4, P_3, \underline{P_1} >,$

$< P_3, \underline{P_1}, P_2, P_4 >, < P_3, \underline{P_1}, P_4, P_2 >, < P_3, P_2, \underline{P_1}, P_4 >, < P_3, P_2, P_4, \underline{P_1} >,$

$< P_3, P_4, \underline{P_1}, P_2 >, < P_3, P_4, P_2, \underline{P_1} >, < P_4, \underline{P_1}, P_2, P_3 >, < P_4, \underline{P_1}, P_3, P_2 >,$

$< P_4, P_2, \underline{P_1}, P_3 >, < P_4, P_2, P_3, \underline{P_1} >, < P_4, P_3, \underline{P_1}, P_2 >, < P_4, P_3, P_2, \underline{P_1} >$

(b) $P_1 : \dfrac{18}{24}; P_2 : \dfrac{2}{24}; P_3 : \dfrac{2}{24}; P_4 \dfrac{2}{24}.$

This is the same situation as in (a).

(c) $P_1 : \dfrac{12}{24} =; P_2 : \dfrac{4}{24}; P_3 : \dfrac{4}{24}; P_4 : \dfrac{4}{24}.$

The sequential coalitions (with pivotal player in each coalition underlined) are:

$< P_1, P_2, \underline{P_3}, P_4 >, < P_1, P_2, \underline{P_4}, P_3 >, < P_1, P_3, \underline{P_2}, P_4 >, < P_1, P_3, \underline{P_4}, P_2 >,$

$< P_1, P_4, \underline{P_2}, P_3 >, < P_1, P_4, \underline{P_3}, P_2 >, < P_2, P_1, \underline{P_3}, P_4 >, < P_2, P_1, \underline{P_4}, P_3 >,$

$< P_2, P_3, \underline{P_1}, P_4 >, < P_2, P_3, P_4, \underline{P_1} >, < P_2, P_4, \underline{P_1}, P_3 >, < P_2, P_4, P_3, \underline{P_1} >,$

$< P_3, P_1, \underline{P_2}, P_4 >, < P_3, P_1, \underline{P_4}, P_2 >, < P_3, P_2, \underline{P_1}, P_4 >, < P_3, P_2, P_4, \underline{P_1} >,$

$< P_3, P_4, \underline{P_1}, P_2 >, < P_3, P_4, P_2, \underline{P_1} >, < P_4, P_1, \underline{P_2}, P_3 >, < P_4, P_1, \underline{P_3}, P_2 >,$

$< P_4, P_2, \underline{P_1}, P_3 >, < P_4, P_2, P_3, \underline{P_1} >, < P_4, P_3, \underline{P_1}, P_2 >, < P_4, P_3, P_2, \underline{P_1} >$

33. $A : \dfrac{1}{3}; B : \dfrac{1}{3}; C : \dfrac{1}{3}; D : 0.$

D will never be pivotal and has no power. Each of the other players will be pivotal in the same number of coalitions, so they will all have equal power.

34. $A : \dfrac{12}{24}; B : \dfrac{4}{24}; C : \dfrac{4}{24}; D : \dfrac{4}{24}.$

The sequential coalitions (with pivotal player in each coalition underlined) are:

$< A, \underline{B}, C, D >, < A, \underline{B}, D, C >, < A, \underline{C}, B, D >, < A, \underline{C}, D, B >,$

$< A, \underline{D}, B, C >, < A, \underline{D}, C, B >, < B, \underline{A}, C, D >, < B, \underline{A}, D, C >,$

$< B, C, \underline{A}, D >, < B, C, \underline{D}, A >, < B, D, \underline{A}, C >, < B, D, \underline{C}, A >,$

$< C, \underline{A}, B, D >, < C, \underline{A}, D, B >, < C, B, \underline{A}, D >, < C, B, \underline{D}, A >,$

$< C, D, \underline{A}, B >, < C, D, \underline{B}, A >, < D, \underline{A}, B, C >, < D, \underline{A}, C, B >,$

$< D, B, \underline{A}, C >, < D, B, \underline{C}, A >, < D, C, \underline{A}, B >, < D, C, \underline{B}, A >.$

D.   Miscellaneous

35. (a) $13! = 6,227,020,800$

(b) $18! = 6,402,373,705,728,000 \approx 6.402374 \times 10^{15}$

(c) $25! = 15,511,210,043,330,985,984,000,000 \approx 1.551121 \times 10^{25}$

(d) There are 25! sequential coalitions of 25 players.

25! sequential coaltions $\times \dfrac{1 \text{ second}}{1,000,000 \text{ sequential coalitions}} \times \dfrac{1 \text{ hour}}{3600 \text{ seconds}} \times \dfrac{1 \text{ day}}{24 \text{ hours}} \times \dfrac{1 \text{ year}}{365 \text{ days}}$

$\approx 4.92 \times 10^{11}$ years

This is roughly 500 billion years.

36. (a) $12! = 479,001,600$

   (b) $15! \approx 1.307674 \times 10^{12}$

   (c) $20! = 2,432,902,008,176,640,000 \approx 2.432902 \times 10^{18}$

   (d) There are 20! sequential coalitions of 20 players.

   $20!$ sequential coaltions $\times \dfrac{1 \text{ second}}{10,000 \text{ sequential coalitions}} \times \dfrac{1 \text{ hour}}{3600 \text{ seconds}} \times \dfrac{1 \text{ day}}{24 \text{ hours}} \times \dfrac{1 \text{ year}}{365 \text{ days}}$

   $\approx 7.71 \times 10^{6}$ years

   This is roughly 8 million years.

37. (a) $10! = 10 \times 9 \times 8 \times \ldots \times 3 \times 2 \times 1$

   $\qquad = 10 \times 9!$

   So, $9! = \dfrac{10!}{10} = \dfrac{3,628,800}{10} = 362,880$.

   (b) $11! = 11 \times 10 \times 9 \times \ldots \times 3 \times 2 \times 1 = 11 \times 10!$

   So, $\dfrac{11!}{10!} = \dfrac{11 \times 10!}{10!} = 11$.

   (c) $11! = 11 \times 10 \times (9 \times \ldots \times 3 \times 2 \times 1) = 11 \times 10 \times 9!$

   So, $\dfrac{11!}{9!} = \dfrac{11 \times 10 \times 9!}{9!} = 11 \times 10 = 110$.

   (d) $\dfrac{9!}{6!} = \dfrac{9 \times 8 \times 7 \times 6!}{6!} = 9 \times 8 \times 7 = 504$

   (e) $\dfrac{101!}{99!} = \dfrac{101 \times 100 \times 99!}{99!} = 101 \times 100 = 10,100$

38. (a) $20! = 20 \times 19!$ so $19! = \dfrac{20!}{20} = \dfrac{2,432,902,008,176,640,000}{20} = 121,645,100,408,832,000$

   (b) 20

   (c) $\dfrac{201!}{199!} = \dfrac{201 \times 200 \times 199!}{199!} = 201 \times 200 = 40,200$

   (d) 990

   $11!/8! = (11 \times 10 \times 9 \times 8!)/8! = 11 \times 10 \times 9 = 990$

39. (a) $\dfrac{9! + 11!}{10!} = \dfrac{9!}{10!} + \dfrac{11!}{10!} = \dfrac{9!}{10 \times 9!} + \dfrac{11 \times 10!}{10!} = \dfrac{1}{10} + 11 = 11.1$

146

(b) $\dfrac{101!+99!}{100!}=\dfrac{101!}{100!}+\dfrac{99!}{100!}=\dfrac{101\times100!}{100!}+\dfrac{99!}{100\times99!}=101+\dfrac{1}{100}=101.01$

40. (a) $\dfrac{19!+21!}{20!}=\dfrac{19!}{20!}+\dfrac{21!}{20!}=\dfrac{19!}{20\times19!}+\dfrac{21\times20!}{20!}=\dfrac{1}{20}+21=21.05$

    (b) $\dfrac{201!+199!}{200!}=\dfrac{201!}{200!}+\dfrac{199!}{200!}=\dfrac{201\times200!}{200!}+\dfrac{199!}{200\times199!}=201+\dfrac{1}{200}=201.005$

41. (a) $2^6-1=63$ coalitions

    (b) There are $2^5-1=31$ coalitions of the remaining five players $P_1,P_2,P_3,P_4,$ and P_5. These are exactly those coalitions that do not include P_6.

    (c) There are $2^4-1=15$ coalitions of the remaining four players P_1,P_2,P_3,P_4. These are exactly those coalitions that do not include P_5 or P_6.

    (d) $63-15=48$ coalitions include P_5 and P_6.

42. (a) $2^7-1=127$ coalitions

    (b) There are $2^6-1=63$ coalitions of the remaining six players $P_1,P_2,P_3,P_4,$ P_5 and P_6. These are exactly those coalitions that do not include P_7.

    (c) There are $2^5-1=31$ coalitions of the remaining five players P_1,P_2,P_3,P_4,P_5. These are exactly those coalitions that do not include P_6 or P_7.

    (d) $127-31=96$ coalitions include both P_6 and P_7.

43. (a) $6!=720$ sequential coalitions

    (b) There are $5!=120$ sequential coalitions of the remaining five players P_2,P_3,P_4,P_5 and P_6. These are exactly those coalitions that have P_1 as the last player.

    (c) $720-120=600$ sequential coalitions do not have P_1 as the last player.

44. (a) $7!=5040$ sequential coalitions

    (b) There are $6!=720$ sequential coalitions of the remaining six players P_1,P_2,P_3,P_4,P_5 and P_6. These are exactly those coalitions that have P_7 as the first player.

    (c) $5040-720=4320$ sequential coalitions do not have P_7 as the first player.

45. (a) There are $6 + 5 + 4 + 4 + 3 + 2 = 24$ votes in this system. The smallest value of the quota q is more than half of this or 13. No player has veto power when $q = 13$. The strongest player (P_1 having 6 votes) gains veto power if the sum of the votes of the other players is less than the quota q. This happens if $q > 18$. Thus, no player has veto power when $q = 13, 14, 15, 16, 17,$ or 18 (i.e., $13 \le q \le 18$).

(b) When $q = 19$, P_1 has veto power. However, when $q = 20$, P_2 will also gain veto power. So the only value of q for which P_1 is the only player with veto power is $q = 19$.

(c) Clearly, every player has veto power when $q = 24$. However, every player also has veto power when $q = 23$. Also P_6, the weakest player, does not have veto power when $q = 22$. It follows that every player has veto power when $23 \le q \le 24$.

(d) The only values of q for which the only winning coalition is the grand coalition are the same as those in part (c), namely $q = 23$ and $q = 24$.

(e) The answers to (c) and (d) are the same. The only winning coalition is the grand coalition if and only if every player has veto power.

46. (a) There are $10 + 8 + 7 + 5 + 4 + 4 + 3 = 41$ votes in this system. The smallest value of the quota q is more than half of this or 21. No player has veto power when $q = 21$. The strongest player (P_1 having 10 votes) gains veto power if the sum of the votes of the other players is less than the quota q. This happens if $q > 31$. Thus, no player has veto power when $q = 21, 22, 23, \ldots, 31$ (i.e., $21 \le q \le 31$).

(b) When $q = 32$ or $q = 33$, P_1 has veto power. However, when $q = 34$, P_2 will also gain veto power. So the only values of q for which P_1 is the only player with veto power are $q = 32$ and $q = 33$.

(c) Clearly, every player has veto power when $q = 41$. However, every player also has veto power when $q = 40$ or $q = 39$. Also P_7, the weakest player, does not have veto power when $q = 38$. It follows that every player has veto power when $39 \le q \le 41$.

(d) The only values of q for which the only winning coalition is the grand coalition are the same as those in part (c), namely $q = 39, 40,$ and 41.

(e) The answers to (c) and (d) are the same. The only winning coalition is the grand coalition if and only if every player has veto power.

JOGGING

47.

Winning Coalitions	Critical players
$\{P_1, P_2, P_3\}$	P_1, P_2, P_3
$\{P_1, P_2, P_4\}$	P_1, P_2, P_4
$\{P_1, P_2, P_3, P_4\}$	P_1, P_2
$\{P_1, P_2, P_3, P_5\}$	P_1, P_2, P_3
$\{P_1, P_2, P_4, P_5\}$	P_1, P_2, P_4
$\{P_1, P_2, P_3, P_4, P_5\}$	P_1, P_2

Finding the critical players in the above table can be done as follows. Since there are no two-player coalitions, every player in a three-player coalition is critical. To decide if a given player in a four-player coalition is critical, one need only look for the remaining players to appear as a winning three-player coalition. If the remaining players are a winning coalition, then that given player is not critical. Similarly in the grand (five-player) coalition, one need only look at the winning four-player coalitions to decide which players are critical. According to the table, the Banzhaf power distribution is

$$P_1 : \frac{6}{16} = 37.5\%; \quad P_2 : \frac{6}{16} = 37.5\%; \quad P_3 : \frac{2}{16} = 12.5\%; \quad P_4 : \frac{2}{16} = 12.5\%; \quad P_5 : 0.$$

48. **(a)** $\{\underline{P_1}, \underline{P_2}, \underline{P_3}, \underline{P_4}, \underline{P_5}, \underline{P_6}\}$

The only winning coalition is the one with all the players (the grand coalition) and every player is critical in this coalition.

(b) The Banzhaf power index of each player is 1/6.

(c) If the quota equals the sum of all the weights $\left(q = w_1 + w_2 + \ldots + w_N\right)$ then the only winning coalition is the grand coalition and every player in it is critical. It follows that each of the N players is critical once and so the Banzhaf power index of each player is $1/N$.

49. **(a)** $6! = 720$ sequential coalitions

(b) 120

When P_6 is in the last position, there are 5! ways to arrange the other five players. So P_6 is pivotal in $5! = 120$ sequential coalitions.

(c) $\dfrac{120}{720} = \dfrac{1}{6}$

(d) $\dfrac{1}{6}$ (Each player is the last player in 120 of the 720 sequential coalitions.)

(e) If the quota equals the sum of all the weights, then the only way a player can be pivotal is for the player to be the last player in the sequential coalition. Since every player will be the last player in the same number of sequential coalitions, all players must have the same Shapley-Shubik power index. It follows that each of the N players has a Shapley-Shubik power index of $1/N$.

50. (a) $f_1 : \dfrac{7}{29}; f_2 : \dfrac{7}{29}; s_1 : \dfrac{5}{29}; s_2 : \dfrac{5}{29}; s_3 : \dfrac{5}{29}.$

The winning coalitions (with critical players underlined) are: $\{\underline{f_1}, \underline{s_1}, \underline{s_2}\}$, $\{\underline{f_1}, \underline{s_1}, \underline{s_3}\}$, $\{\underline{f_1}, \underline{s_2}, \underline{s_3}\}$,

$\{\underline{f_2}, \underline{s_1}, \underline{s_2}\}$, $\{\underline{f_2}, \underline{s_1}, \underline{s_3}\}$, $\{\underline{f_2}, \underline{s_2}, \underline{s_3}\}$, $\{\underline{f_1}, \underline{f_2}, \underline{s_1}\}$, $\{\underline{f_1}, \underline{f_2}, \underline{s_2}\}$, $\{\underline{f_1}, \underline{f_2}, \underline{s_3}\}$, $\{\underline{f_1}, s_1, s_2, s_3\}$,

$\{\underline{f_2}, s_1, s_2, s_3\}$, $\{f_1, f_2, s_1, s_2\}$, $\{f_1, f_2, s_1, s_3\}$, $\{f_1, f_2, s_2, s_3\}$, $\{f_1, f_2, s_1, s_2, s_3\}$.

(b) [7: 3, 3, 2, 2, 2] is one possibility.

51. (a) [4: 2, 1, 1, 1] or [9: 5, 2, 2, 2] are among the possible answers.

(b) $H : \dfrac{12}{24}; A_1 : \dfrac{4}{24}; A_2 : \dfrac{4}{24}; A_3 : \dfrac{4}{24}.$

The sequential coalitions (with pivotal players underlined) are:

$< H, A_1, \underline{A_2}, A_3 >, < H, A_1, \underline{A_3}, A_2 >, < H, A_2, \underline{A_1}, A_3 >, < H, A_2, \underline{A_3}, A_1 >,$

$< H, A_3, \underline{A_1}, A_2 >, < H, A_3, \underline{A_2}, A_1 >, < A_1, H, \underline{A_2}, A_3 >, < A_1, H, \underline{A_3}, A_2 >,$

$< A_1, A_2, \underline{H}, A_3 >, < A_1, A_2, A_3, \underline{H} >, < A_1, A_3, \underline{H}, A_2 >, < A_1, A_3, A_2, \underline{H} >,$

$< A_2, H, \underline{A_1}, A_3 >, < A_2, H, \underline{A_3}, A_1 >, < A_2, A_1, \underline{H}, A_3 >, < A_2, A_1, A_3, \underline{H} >,$

$< A_2, A_3, \underline{H}, A_1 >, < A_2, A_3, A_1, \underline{H} >, < A_3, H, \underline{A_1}, A_2 >, < A_3, H, \underline{A_2}, A_1 >,$

$< A_3, A_1, \underline{H}, A_2 >, < A_3, A_1, A_2, \underline{H} >, < A_3, A_2, \underline{H}, A_1 >, < A_3, A_2, A_1, \underline{H} > .$

52. (a) Suppose that P has veto power. Further, suppose that W is a winning coalition. If W did not contain P, then it would be a losing coalition since even the (possibly larger) coalition consisting of all players other than P is a losing one. So, W contains P.

(b) Suppose that P is a critical member of every winning coalition. Consider the coalition formed by all the other players. Such a coalition must be losing since it does not contain P. Thus, P has veto power.

53. (a) Suppose that a winning coalition that contains P is not a winning coalition without P. Then, by definition, P would be a critical player in that coalition.

(b) Suppose that P is a member of every winning coalition. Then removing P from any winning coalition cannot result in another winning coalition. So P is critical in every winning coalition. Since there is at least one winning coalition (the grand coalition), P is not a dummy.

(c) Suppose that P is a pivotal member of some sequential coalition. Let's say that P is the kth player listed. Then, consider the k-player coalition consisting of the previous $k-1$ players listed in that sequential coalition and P. P would be a critical player in that coalition and is therefore not a dummy.

(d) Suppose that P is never a pivotal member in a sequential coalition. If P were ever critical in some coalition S, then a sequential coalition that lists the members of S other than P, then P, and then the voters not in S would have P as its pivotal player.

54. (a) P_5 is a dummy. It takes (at least) three of the first four players to pass a motion. P_5's vote doesn't make any difference.

(b) In both cases, $P_1 : \dfrac{1}{4};\ P_2 : \dfrac{1}{4};\ P_3 : \dfrac{1}{4};\ P_4 : \dfrac{1}{4};\ P_5 : 0$.

(b) $q = 21, q = 31, q = 41$.

(d) Since we assume that the weights are listed in nonincreasing order, P_5 is a dummy if $w = 1, 2, 3$.

55. (a) $7 \le q \le 13$.
The quota must be at least half of the total number of votes and not more than the total number of votes.

(b) For $q = 7$ or $q = 8$, P_1 is a dictator because $\{P_1\}$ is a winning coalition.

(c) For $q = 9$, only P_1 has veto power since P_2 and P_3 together have just 5 votes.

(c) For $10 \le q \le 12$, both P_1 and P_2 have veto power since no motion can pass without both of their votes. For $q = 13$, all three players have veto power.

(e) For $q = 7$ or $q = 8$, both P_2 and P_3 are dummies because P_1 is a dictator. For $10 \le q \le 12$, P_3 is a dummy since all winning coalitions contain $\{P_1, P_2\}$ which is itself a winning coalition.

56. (a) $5 \le w \le 9$.
Since we assume that the weights are listed in nonincreasing order, we have $5 \le w$. In addition, we have $\dfrac{w + 5 + 2 + 1}{2} < 9 \le w + 5 + 2 + 1$, i.e., $w + 8 < 18$ and $9 \le w + 8$. Since w is a whole number, this gives $5 \le w \le 9$.

(b) P_1 is a dictator if $w = 9$.

(c) For $w = 5$, P_1 and P_2 have veto power. If $6 \le w \le 8$, then P_1 alone has veto power.

(d) If $w = 5$, all winning coalitions contain $\{P_1, P_2\}$ which is itself a winning coalition and so both P_3 and P_4 are dummies. If $w = 9$, P_2, P_3, and P_4 are all dummies since P_1 is a dictator.

57. (a) Both have Banzhaf power distribution $P_1 : \dfrac{2}{5};\ P_2 : \dfrac{1}{5};\ P_3 : \dfrac{1}{5};\ P_4 : \dfrac{1}{5}$.
[24: 14, 8, 6, 4] is just [12: 7, 4, 3, 2] with each value multiplied by 2.

(b) In the weighted voting system $[q : w_1, w_2, \ldots, w_N]$, if P_k is critical in a coalition then the sum of the weights of all the players in that coalition (including P_k) is at least q, but the sum of the weights of all the players in the coalition except P_k is less than q. Consequently, if the weights of all the players in that coalition are multiplied by $c > 0$ ($c = 0$ would make no sense), then the sum of the weights of all the players in the coalition (including P_k) is at least cq but the sum of the weights of all the players in the coalition except P_k is less than cq. Therefore P_k is critical in the same coalition in the weighted voting system $[cq : cw_1, cw_2, \ldots, cw_N]$. Since the critical players are the same in both weighted voting systems, the Banzhaf power distributions will be the same.

58. (a) Both have Shapley-Shubik power distribution $P_1 : \dfrac{1}{2}; \; P_2 : \dfrac{1}{6}; \; P_3 : \dfrac{1}{6}; \; P_4 : \dfrac{1}{6}.$

(b) In the weighted voting system $[q : w_1, w_2, \ldots, w_N]$, P_k is pivotal in the sequential coalition $\langle P_1, P_2, \ldots, P_k, \ldots, P_N \rangle$ means $w_1 + w_2 + \ldots + w_k \geq q$ but $w_1 + w_2 + \ldots + w_{k-1} < q$. In the weighted voting system $[cq : cw_1, cw_2, \ldots, cw_N]$, P_k is pivotal in the sequential coalition $\langle P_1, P_2, \ldots, P_k, \ldots, P_N \rangle$ means $cw_1 + cw_2 + \ldots + cw_k \geq cq$ but $cw_1 + cw_2 + \ldots + cw_{k-1} < cq$. These two statements are equivalent since $cw_1 + cw_2 + \ldots + cw_k = c(w_1 + w_2 + \ldots + w_k) \geq cq$ if and only if $w_1 + w_2 + \ldots + w_k \geq q$, and $cw_1 + cw_2 + \ldots + cw_{k-1} = c(w_1 + w_2 + \ldots + w_{k-1}) < cq$ if and only if $w_1 + w_2 + \ldots + w_{k-1} < q$. This same reasoning applies to any sequential coalition and so the pivotal players are exactly the same.

59. (a) There are $5! = 120$ ways that P_1 can be the last player in a sequential coalition (this is the number of sequential coalitions consisting of the other 5 players).

(b) There are $5! = 120$ ways that P_1 can be the fifth player in a sequential coalition (the other players can be ordered this many ways).

(c) P_1 is not pivotal as the fourth, third, second, or first player in a sequential coalition. It follows that P_1 is pivotal in $120 + 120 = 240$ of the 720 sequential coalitions. So, the Shapley-Shubik power index of P_1 is $\dfrac{240}{720} = \dfrac{1}{3} = 33\dfrac{1}{3}\%.$

(d) Since all of the other players in the system have same weight, it follows that they will share the remaining power equally. That is, these five players share $1 - \dfrac{240}{720} = \dfrac{480}{720}$ of the power. Since $\dfrac{1}{5}\left(\dfrac{480}{720}\right) = \dfrac{96}{720} = \dfrac{2}{15}$, it follows that the Shapley-Shibik power distribution is given by

$$P_1 : \dfrac{1}{3} = 33\dfrac{1}{3}\%; \; P_2 : \dfrac{2}{15} = 13\dfrac{1}{3}\%; \; P_3 : \dfrac{2}{15} = 13\dfrac{1}{3}\%; \; P_4 : \dfrac{2}{15} = 13\dfrac{1}{3}\%; \; P_5 : \dfrac{2}{15} = 13\dfrac{1}{3}\%; \; P_6 : \dfrac{2}{15} = 13\dfrac{1}{3}\%.$$

60. (a) $\dfrac{w_1 + w_2 + \ldots + w_N}{2} < q \leq w_2 + w_3 + \ldots + w_N$

In this case, even the strongest player, w_1, does not have veto power.

(b) $w_1 + w_2 + \ldots + w_{N-1} + 1 \le q \le w_1 + w_2 + \ldots + w_N$

In this case, even the weakest player, w_N, has veto power.

61. You should buy your vote from P_1. The following table explains why.

Buying a vote from	Resulting weighted voting system	Resulting Banzhaf power distribution	Your power
P_1	$[6: 3, 2, 2, 2, 2]$	$P_1 : \frac{1}{5}; P_2 : \frac{1}{5}; P_3 : \frac{1}{5}; P_4 : \frac{1}{5}; P_5 : \frac{1}{5}$	$\frac{1}{5}$
P_2	$[6: 4, 1, 2, 2, 2]$	$P_1 : \frac{1}{2}; P_2 : 0; P_3 : \frac{1}{6}; P_4 : \frac{1}{6}; P_5 : \frac{1}{6}$	$\frac{1}{6}$
P_3	$[6: 4, 2, 1, 2, 2]$	$P_1 : \frac{1}{2}; P_2 : \frac{1}{6}; P_3 : 0; P_4 : \frac{1}{6}; P_5 : \frac{1}{6}$	$\frac{1}{6}$
P_4	$[6: 4, 2, 2, 1, 2]$	$P_1 : \frac{1}{2}; P_2 : \frac{1}{6}; P_3 : \frac{1}{6}; P_4 : 0; P_5 : \frac{1}{6}$	$\frac{1}{6}$

62. You should buy your vote from P_4. The following table explains why.

Buying a vote from	Resulting weighted voting system	Resulting Banzhaf power distribution	Your power
P_1	$[27: 9, 8, 6, 4, 3]$	$P_1 : \frac{1}{4}, P_2 : \frac{1}{4}; P_3 : \frac{1}{4}; P_4 : \frac{1}{4}; P_5 : 0$	0
P_2	$[27: 10, 7, 6, 4, 3]$	$P_1 : \frac{1}{4}; P_2 : \frac{1}{4}; P_3 : \frac{1}{4}; P_4 : \frac{1}{4}; P_5 : 0$	0
P_3	$[27: 10, 8, 5, 4, 3]$	$P_1 : \frac{1}{4}; P_2 : \frac{1}{4}; P_3 : \frac{1}{4}; P_4 : \frac{1}{4}; P_5 : 0$	0
P_4	$[27: 10, 8, 6, 3, 3]$	$P_1 : \frac{3}{11}; P_2 : \frac{3}{11}; P_3 : \frac{3}{11}; P_4 : \frac{1}{11}; P_5 : \frac{1}{11}$	$\frac{1}{11}$

63. (a) You should buy your vote from P_2. The following table explains why.

Buying a vote from	Resulting weighted voting system	Resulting Banzhaf power distribution	Your power
P_1	$[18: 9, 8, 6, 4, 3]$	$P_1 : \frac{4}{13}; P_2 : \frac{3}{13}; P_3 : \frac{3}{13}; P_4 : \frac{2}{13}; P_5 : \frac{1}{13}$	$\frac{1}{13}$
P_2	$[18: 10, 7, 6, 4, 3]$	$P_1 : \frac{9}{25}; P_2 : \frac{1}{5}; P_3 : \frac{1}{5}; P_4 : \frac{3}{25}; P_5 : \frac{3}{25}$	$\frac{3}{25}$
P_3	$[18: 10, 8, 5, 4, 3]$	$P_1 : \frac{5}{12}; P_2 : \frac{1}{4}; P_3 : \frac{1}{6}; P_4 : \frac{1}{12}; P_5 : \frac{1}{12}$	$\frac{1}{12}$
P_4	$[18: 10, 8, 6, 3, 3]$	$P_1 : \frac{5}{12}; P_2 : \frac{1}{4}; P_3 : \frac{1}{6}; P_4 : \frac{1}{12}; P_5 : \frac{1}{12}$	$\frac{1}{12}$

(b) You should buy 2 votes from P_2. The following table explains why.

Buying a vote from	Resulting weighted voting system	Resulting Banzhaf power distribution	Your power
P_1	[18: 8, 8, 6, 4, 4]	$P_1: \frac{7}{27}; P_2: \frac{7}{27}; P_3: \frac{7}{27}; P_4: \frac{1}{9}; P_5: \frac{1}{9}$	$\frac{1}{9}$
P_2	[18: 10, 6, 6, 4, 4]	$P_1: \frac{5}{13}; P_2: \frac{2}{13}; P_3: \frac{2}{13}; P_4: \frac{2}{13}; P_5: \frac{2}{13}$	$\frac{2}{13}$
P_3	[18: 10, 8, 4, 4, 4]	$P_1: \frac{11}{25}; P_2: \frac{1}{5}; P_3: \frac{3}{25}; P_4: \frac{3}{25}; P_5: \frac{3}{25}$	$\frac{3}{25}$
P_4	[18: 10, 8, 6, 2, 4]	$P_1: \frac{9}{25}; P_2: \frac{7}{25}; P_3: \frac{1}{5}; P_4: \frac{1}{25}; P_5: \frac{3}{25}$	$\frac{3}{25}$

(c) Buying a single vote from P_2 raises your power from $\frac{1}{25} = 4\%$ to $\frac{3}{25} = 12\%$. Buying a second vote from P_2 raises your power to $\frac{2}{13} \approx 15.4\%$. The increase in power is less with the second vote, but if you value power over money, it might still be worth it to you to buy that second vote.

64. (a) Before the merger: $P_1: \frac{3}{5}; P_2: \frac{1}{5}; P_3: \frac{1}{5}$; after the merger $P_1: \frac{1}{2}; P*: \frac{1}{2}$.

   (b) Before the merger: $P_1: \frac{1}{2}; P_2: \frac{1}{2}; P_3: 0$; after the merger $P_1: \frac{1}{2}; P*: \frac{1}{2}$.

   (c) Before the merger: $P_1: \frac{1}{3}; P_2: \frac{1}{3}; P_3: \frac{1}{3}$; after the merger $P_1: \frac{1}{2}; P*: \frac{1}{2}$.

   (d) The Banzhaf power index of the merger of two players can be greater than, equal to, or less than the sum of Banzhaf power indices of the individual players.

65. (a) The losing coalitions are $\{P_1\}, \{P_2\}$, and $\{P_3\}$. The complements of these coalitions are $\{P_2, P_3\}$, $\{P_1, P_3\}$, and $\{P_1, P_2\}$ respectively, all of which are winning coalitions.

   (b) The losing coalitions are $\{P_1\}, \{P_2\}, \{P_3\}, \{P_4\}, \{P_2, P_3\}, \{P_2, P_4\}$, and $\{P_3, P_4\}$. The complements of these coalitions are $\{P_2, P_3, P_4\}, \{P_1, P_3, P_4\}, \{P_1, P_2, P_4\}, \{P_1, P_2, P_3\}, \{P_1, P_4\}, \{P_1, P_3\}$, and $\{P_1, P_2\}$ respectively, all of which are winning coalitions.

   (c) If P is a dictator, the losing coalitions are all the coalitions without P; the winning coalitions are all the coalitions that include P. The complement of any coalition without P (losing) is a coalition with P (winning).

   (d) Take the grand coalition out of the picture for a moment. Of the remaining $2^N - 2$ coalitions, half are losing coalitions and half are winning coalitions, since each losing coalition pairs up with a winning coalition (its complement). Half of $2^N - 2$ is $2^{N-1} - 1$. In addition, we have the grand coalition (always a winning coalition). Thus, the total number of winning coalitions is 2^{N-1}.

66. (a) The winning coalitions for both weighted voting systems [8: 5, 3, 2] and [2: 1, 1, 0] are $\{P_1, P_2\}$ and $\{P_1, P_2, P_3\}$.

(b) The winning coalitions for both weighted voting systems [7: 4, 3, 2, 1] and [5: 3, 2, 1, 1] are $\{P_1, P_2\}$, $\{P_1, P_2, P_3\}$, $\{P_1, P_2, P_4\}$, $\{P_1, P_3, P_4\}$, and $\{P_1, P_2, P_3, P_4\}$.

(c) The winning coalitions for both weighted voting systems are those consisting of any three of the five players, any four of the five players, and the grand coalition.

(d) If a player is critical in a winning coalition, then that coalition is no longer winning if the player is removed. An equivalent system (with the same winning coalitions) will find that player critical in the same coalitions. When calculating the Banzhaf power indexes in two equivalent systems, the same players will be critical in the same coalitions. Thus, the numerators and denominators in each player's Banzhaf power index will be the same.

(e) If a player, P, is pivotal in a sequential coalition, then the players to P's left in the sequential coalition do not form a winning coalition, but including P does make it a winning coalition. An equivalent system (with the same winning coalitions) will find the player P pivotal in that same sequential coalition. When calculating the Shapley-Shubik indexes in two equivalent systems, the same players will be pivotal in the same sequential coalitions. Thus, the numerators and denominators in each Shapley-Shubik index will be the same.

67. (a) In each nine-member winning coalition, every member is critical. In each coalition having 10 or more members, only the five permanent members are critical.

(b) At least nine members are needed to form a winning coalition. So, there are $210 + 638 = 848$ winning coalitions. Since every member is critical in each nine-member coalition, the nine-member coalitions yield a total of $210 \times 9 = 1890$ critical players. Since only the permanent members are critical in coalitions having 10 or more members, there are $638 \times 5 = 3190$ critical players in these coalitions. Thus, the total number of critical players in all winning coalitions is 5080.

(c) Each permanent member is critical in each of the 848 winning coalitions. Thus, the Banzhaf Power Index of a permanent member is 848/5080.

(d) The 5 permanent members together have $5 \times 848/5080 = 4240/5080$ of the power. The remaining 840/5080 of the power is shared equally among the 10 nonpermanent members, giving each a Banzhaf power index of 84/5080.

(e) In the given weighted voting system, the quota is 39, each permanent member has 7 votes, and each nonpermanent member has 1 vote. The total number of votes is 45 and so if any one of the permanent members does not vote for a measure there would be at most $45 - 7 = 38$ votes and the measure would not pass. Thus all permanent members have veto power. On the other hand, all 5 permanent members votes only add up to 35 and so at least 4 nonpermanent members votes are needed for a measure to pass.

RUNNING

68. (a) There are $(N-1)!$ sequential coalitions in which P is in the first place. There are $(N-1)!$ sequential coalitions in which P is in the second place. There are also $(N-1)!$ sequential coalitions in which P is in the last place.

(b) There are $(N-2)!$ sequential coalitions in which P is in the first place and Q is in the second place. There are $(N-2)!$ sequential coalitions in which P is in the last place and Q is in the first place. There are also $(N-2)!$ sequential coalitions in which P is in the jth place and Q is in the kth place.

(c) There are $(N-3)!$ sequential coalitions in which P is in the jth place, Q is in the kth place, and R is in the mth place.

(d) There are $(N-k)!$ sequential coalitions in which k players can be placed in k distinct, but fixed, positions in a system having N players.

69. (a) In the weighted voting system [3: 2, 1, 1] there are no dummies, so any equivalent weighted voting system will have 3 players each with positive weight. The smallest such weight is 1. P_1 has veto power, so P_1 has a greater weight. The quota must be greater than 4/2, so it cannot be less than 3.

(b) The weighted voting system [4: 2, 1, 1] has only one winning coalition (the grand coalition) as does the weighted voting system [3: 1, 1, 1].

(c) The weighted voting system [8: 5, 3, 1] has winning coalitions $\{P_1, P_2\}$ and $\{P_1, P_2, P_3\}$ as does the minimal weighted voting system [2: 1, 1, 0].

(d) [1: 1, 0, 0, ..., 0] (All players are dummies except for the dictator.)

70. (a) The winning coalitions in the 1994 Nassau County Board weighted voting system [65: 30, 28, 22, 15, 7, 6] (with critical players underlined) are: $\{\underline{P_1}, \underline{P_2}, \underline{P_3}\}$, $\{\underline{P_1}, \underline{P_2}, \underline{P_4}\}$, $\{\underline{P_1}, \underline{P_2}, \underline{P_5}\}$, $\{\underline{P_1}, \underline{P_3}, \underline{P_4}\}$, $\{\underline{P_2}, \underline{P_3}, \underline{P_4}\}$, $\{P_1, P_2, P_3, P_4\}$, $\{\underline{P_1}, \underline{P_2}, P_3, P_5\}$, $\{\underline{P_1}, \underline{P_2}, \underline{P_3}, P_6\}$, $\{\underline{P_1}, \underline{P_2}, \underline{P_4}, P_5\}$, $\{\underline{P_1}, \underline{P_2}, \underline{P_4}, P_6\}$, $\{\underline{P_1}, \underline{P_2}, \underline{P_5}, P_6\}$, $\{\underline{P_1}, \underline{P_3}, \underline{P_4}, P_5\}$, $\{\underline{P_1}, \underline{P_3}, \underline{P_4}, P_6\}$, $\{\underline{P_1}, \underline{P_3}, \underline{P_5}, P_6\}$, $\{\underline{P_2}, \underline{P_3}, \underline{P_4}, P_5\}$, $\{\underline{P_2}, \underline{P_3}, \underline{P_4}, P_6\}$, $\{P_1, P_2, P_3, P_4, P_5\}$, $\{P_1, P_2, P_3, P_4, P_6\}$, $\{\underline{P_1}, P_2, P_3, P_5, P_6\}$, $\{\underline{P_1}, \underline{P_2}, P_4, P_5, P_6\}$, $\{\underline{P_1}, \underline{P_3}, P_4, P_5, P_6\}$, $\{\underline{P_2}, \underline{P_3}, \underline{P_4}, P_5, P_6\}$, $\{P_1, P_2, P_3, P_4, P_5, P_6\}$.

These are exactly the same winning coalitions as for the weighted voting system [15: 7, 6, 5, 4, 2, 1].

(b) The Banzhaf power distribution of the weighted voting system [65: 30, 28, 22, 15, 7, 6] is $P_1 : \dfrac{15}{52}$, $P_2 : \dfrac{13}{52}$, $P_3 : \dfrac{11}{52}$, $P_4 : \dfrac{9}{52}$, $P_5 : \dfrac{11}{52}$, $P_6 : \dfrac{1}{52}$ [see Exercise 22(b)]. Since the Banzhaf power indexes of the players are all different and decreasing the weights of the players must also be different and decreasing. Thus, the smallest conceivable values they could have are $w_1 = 6$, $w_2 = 5$, $w_3 = 4$, $w_4 = 3$, $w_5 = 2$, and $w_6 = 1$. Since $\{P_1, P_2, P_6\}$ is not a winning coalition, $q > w_1 + w_2 + w_6 \geq 6 + 5 + 1 = 12$ and so the quota must be at least 13. But $\{P_2, P_3, P_4\}$ is also a winning coalition and hence $w_2 + w_3 + w_4 \geq 13$. This means that $w_2 = 5$, $w_3 = 4$, and $w_4 = 3$ is impossible and hence at least one of them is larger which forces w_2 to be at least 6 and so w_1 must be at least 7. Now since $\{P_1, P_2, P_6\}$ is not a winning coalition, $q > w_1 + w_2 + w_6 \geq 7 + 6 + 1 = 14$ and so the quota must be at least 15. Again, since $\{P_2, P_3, P_4\}$ is a winning coalition, $w_2 + w_3 + w_4 \geq 15$. Consequently, either $w_2 = 6$, $w_3 = 5$, and $w_4 = 4$ or else $w_2 > 6$. The sum $7 + 6 + 5 + 4 + 2 + 1$ is a smaller total weight than $8 + 7 + 5 + 3 + 2 + 1$, and thus $[15: 7, 6, 5, 4, 2, 1]$ is minimal.

71. The mayor has power index 5/13 and each of the four other council members has a power index of 2/13. The winning coalitions (with critical players underlined) are: $\{\underline{M}, \underline{P_2}, \underline{P_3}\}$, $\{\underline{M}, \underline{P_2}, \underline{P_4}\}$, $\{\underline{M}, \underline{P_2}, \underline{P_5}\}$, $\{\underline{M}, \underline{P_3}, \underline{P_4}\}$, $\{\underline{M}, \underline{P_3}, \underline{P_5}\}$, $\{\underline{M}, \underline{P_4}, \underline{P_5}\}$, $\{\underline{M}, P_2, P_3, P_4\}$, $\{\underline{M}, P_2, P_3, P_5\}$, $\{\underline{M}, P_2, P_4, P_5\}$, $\{\underline{M}, P_3, P_4, P_5\}$, $\{\underline{P_2}, \underline{P_3}, \underline{P_4}, \underline{P_5}\}$, $\{M, P_2, P_3, P_4, P_5\}$.

72. (a) $[5: 2,1,1,1,1,1,1]$

(b) The mayor has a Shapley-Shubik power index of 2/7. (Of the 7! sequential coalitions, the mayor is pivotal anytime he/she is in the 4th slot or in the 5th slot, and there are 6! of each kind.) Each of the council members has a Shapley-Shubik power index of $\frac{1}{5}\left(1 - \frac{2}{7}\right) = \frac{5}{42}$.

73. (a) The possible coalitions are all coalitions with A but not P in them or with P but not A in them. If we call B and C the players with 4 and 3 votes respectively, the possible coalitions are: $\{A\}, \{A, B\}, \{A, C\}, \{A, B, C\}$ and $\{P\}, \{P, B\}, \{P, C\}, \{P, B, C\}$. The winning coalitions (with critical players underlined) are: $\{\underline{A}, \underline{B}\}, \{\underline{A}, \underline{C}\}, \{\underline{A}, B, C\}, \{\underline{P}, \underline{B}, \underline{C}\}$. The Banzhaf power distribution in this case is $A: \frac{3}{8}; B: \frac{2}{8}; C: \frac{2}{8}; P: \frac{1}{8}$.

(b) The possible coalitions under these circumstances are all subsets of the players that contain either A or P but not both. There are 2^{N-2} subsets that contain neither A nor P (all possible subsets of the $N - 2$ other players). If we throw A into each of these subsets, we get all the coalitions that have A but not P in them—a total of 2^{N-2} coalitions. If we throw P into each of the 2^{N-2} subsets we get all the coalitions that have P but not A in them. Adding these two lists gives $2 \cdot 2^{N-2} = 2^{N-1}$ coalitions.

(c) Consider the same weighted voting system discussed in part (a) but without restrictions. The Banzhaf power distribution in this case is $A: \frac{5}{12}; B: \frac{3}{12}; C: \frac{3}{12}; P: \frac{1}{12}$. When A becomes the antagonist of P, A's Banzhaf power index goes down (to 3/8) and P's Banzhaf power index goes up (to 1/8). If we reverse the roles of A and P (A becomes the "player" and P his "antagonist", the Banzhaf power index calculations remain the same, and in this case it is the antagonist's (P) power index that goes up and the player's (A) power that goes down.

(d) Once P realizes that A will always vote against him, he can vote exactly the opposite way of his true opinion. This puts A's votes behind P's true opinion. If A has more votes than P, this strategy essentially increases P's power at the expense of A.

74. (a) $[4: 3,1,1,1]$
Player 1 is pivotal in every sequential coalition except the 6 sequential coalitions in which player 1

is the first member. So, the Shapley-Shubik power index of player 1 is (24 – 6)/24 = 18/24 = 3/4. P_2, P_3, and P_4 have Shapley-Shubik power index of 1/12.

(b) In a weighted voting system with 4 players there are 24 sequential coalitions — each player is the first member in exactly 6 sequential coalitions. The only way the first member of a coalition can be pivotal is if he or she is a dictator. Consequently, if a player is not a dictator, he or she can be pivotal in at most 24 – 6 = 18 sequential coalitions and so that player's Shapley-Shubik power index can be at most 18/24 = 3/4.

(c) In a weighted voting system with N players there are $N!$ sequential coalitions — each player is the first member in exactly $(N-1)!$ sequential coalitions. The only way the first member of a coalition can be pivotal is if he or she is a dictator. Consequently, if a player is not a dictator, he or she can be pivotal in at most $N! - (N-1)! = (N-1)!(N-1)$ sequential coalitions and so that player's Shapley-Shubik power index can be at most $(N-1)!(N-1)/N! = (N-1)/N$.

(d) [N: $N-1$, 1, 1, 1,…, 1]
Here N is the number of players as well as the quota. Player 1 is pivotal in every sequential coalition except for the $(N-1)!$ sequential coalitions in which player 1 is the first member. So the Shapley-Shubik power index of player 1 is [$N! - (N-1)!$]/$N! = (N-1)/N$.

75. (a) [3: 2, 1, 1]
There are 6 sequential coalitions and player 3 is pivotal only in the sequential coalition $\langle P_1, P_2, P_3 \rangle$. So the Shapley-Shubik power index of player 3 is 1/6.

(b) If a player is not a dummy, then that player must be pivotal in at least one sequential coalition. Since there are only 6 sequential coalitions altogether, the player's smallest possible Shapley-Shubik power index is 1/6.

(c) [4: 3,1,1,1]. See 67(a).

(d) Take any sequential coalition, say $\langle A, B, C, D \rangle$. If A is pivotal, then A has to be pivotal at least six times ($\langle A, B, C, D \rangle, \langle A, B, D, C \rangle, \langle A, C, B, D \rangle, \langle A, C, D, B \rangle, \langle A, D, B, C \rangle, \langle A, D, C, B \rangle$). If B is pivotal, then B has to be pivotal at least twice ($\langle A, B, C, D \rangle, \langle A, B, D, C \rangle$). If C is pivotal then C has to be pivotal at least twice ($\langle A, B, C, D \rangle, \langle B, A, C, D \rangle$). If D is pivotal, then D has to be pivotal at least six times ($\langle A, B, C, D \rangle, \langle A, C, B, D \rangle, \langle B, A, C, D \rangle, \langle B, C, A, D \rangle, \langle C, A, B, D \rangle, \langle C, B, A, D \rangle$). In no case can a player be pivotal only once.

76. (a) [N: 1,1,…,1]
All players have veto power and all have equal power, so each has Shapley-Shubik power index 1/N.

(b) A player with veto power is pivotal in every sequential coalition in which that player is the last player. There are $(N-1)!$ such sequential coalitions. Consequently, the player must have Shapley-Shubik power index of at least $(N-1)!/N! = 1/N$.

77. (a) [N: 1,1,…,1]
All players have veto power and all have equal power, so each has Banzhaf power index 1/N.

(b) A player with veto power is critical in *every* winning coalition. Therefore that player must have Banzhaf power index of *at least* as much as any other player. Since the total Banzhaf power indexes of all N players is 1, they cannot all be less than $1/N$.

78. We instead argue that $W - W_p = W_p - B$ which, when solved for B, gives $B = 2W_p - W$. Now $W - W_p$ is the number of winning coalitions that do not contain P. Consider adding the player P to each of the coalitions. The result will remain a winning coalition (now containing P). However, P is clearly not a critical player. The number of coalitions can thus also be represented as $W_p - B$.

Chapter 3

WALKING

A. Fair Division Concepts

1. (a) $9.00

$C = 3S$; $12 = C + S = 3S + S$; $4S = 12; $S = 3; $C = $12 - $3 = 9.

(b) $3.00

(c) $3.00

$$\frac{60°}{180°} \times (\$3) + \frac{40°}{180°} \times (\$9) = \frac{1}{3} \times (\$3) + \frac{2}{9} \times (\$9) = \$3.00$$

2. (a) $2.70

$S = 4C$; $13.50 = C + S = C + 4C$; $5C = 13.50; $C = 2.70; $S = $13.50 - $2.70 = 10.80.

(b) $10.80

(c) $4.20

$$\left(\frac{60°}{180°} \times \$10.80\right) + \left(\frac{40°}{180°} \times \$2.70\right) = \$3.60 + \$.60 = \$4.20$$

3. (a) $6.00

It is known that $S = 2V$, $C = 3V$, and $C + S + V = 12. So that $V = 2, $S = 4, and $C = 6.

(b) $4.00

(c) $2.00

(d)

piece 1: $\dfrac{60°}{120°} \times (\$2) = \$1.00$;

piece 2: $\dfrac{30°}{120°} \times (\$2) + \dfrac{30°}{120°} \times (\$4) = \$0.50 + \$1.00 = \$1.50$;

piece 3: $\dfrac{60°}{120°} \times (\$4) = \$2.00$;

piece 4: $\dfrac{30°}{120°} \times (\$4) + \dfrac{30°}{120°} \times (\$6) = \$1.00 + \$1.50 = \$2.50$;

piece 5: $\dfrac{60°}{120°} \times (\$6) = \$3.00$;

piece 6: $\dfrac{30°}{120°} \times (\$6) + \dfrac{30°}{120°} \times (\$2) = \$1.50 + \$0.50 = \$2.00$

4. **(a)** $3.20

    $S = 2C; C = 2V; \$11.20 = S + C + V = 4V + 2V + V = 7V; V = \$1.60, S = \$6.40, C = \$3.20.$

  (b) $6.40

  (c) $1.60

  (d)

    piece 1: $\dfrac{60°}{120°} \times \$1.60 = \$.80$;

    piece 2: $\dfrac{30°}{120°} \times (\$1.60) + \dfrac{30°}{120°} \times (\$6.40) = \$0.40 + \$1.60 = \$2.00$;

    piece 3: $\dfrac{60°}{120°} \times (\$6.40) = \$3.20$;

    piece 4: $\dfrac{30°}{120°} \times (\$6.40) + \dfrac{30°}{120°} \times (\$3.20) = \$1.60 + \$0.80 = \$2.40$;

    piece 5: $\dfrac{60°}{120°} \times (\$3.20) = \$1.60$;

    piece 6: $\dfrac{30°}{120°} \times (\$3.20) + \dfrac{30°}{120°} \times (\$1.60) = \$0.80 + \$0.40 = \$1.20$

5. **(a)** Ana: s_2, s_3

    $\dfrac{1}{3} \times (\$12.00) = \$4.00$

    Any slice worth at least $4.00 is a fair share to Ana.

  (b) Ben: s_3

    $\dfrac{1}{3} \times (\$15.00) = \$5.00$

    Any slice worth at least $5.00 is a fair share to Ben.

  (c) Cara: s_1, s_2, s_3

    $\dfrac{1}{3} \times (\$13.50) = \$4.50$

    Any slice worth at least $4.50 is a fair share to Cara.

  (d) Ben must receive s_3 ; So, Ana must receive s_2 and then Cara is left with s_1 .

6. **(a)** Alex: s_2

    Any slice worth at least 1/3 is a fair share to Alex.

  (b) Betty: s_1, s_3

    Any slice worth at least 1/3 is a fair share to Betty.

(c) Cindy: s_1, s_2

Any slice worth at least 1/3 is a fair share to Cindy.

(d) Alex receives s_2 ; Cindy receives s_1 ; Betty receives s_3 .

7. Any parcel worth at least 25% is a fair share.

(a) Adams: s_1, s_4

(b) Benson: s_1, s_2

(c) Cagle: s_1, s_3

(d) Duncan: s_4

(e) Adams: s_1 ; Benson: s_2 ; Cagle: s_3 ; Duncan: s_4

8. **(a)** Abe: s_2, s_3

$$\frac{1}{4} \times (\$15.00) = \$3.75$$

Any slice worth at least \$3.75 is a fair share to Abe.

(b) Betty: s_1, s_2, s_3, s_4

$$\frac{1}{4} \times (\$18.00) = \$4.50$$

Any slice worth at least \$4.50 is a fair share to Betty.

(c) Cory: s_1, s_2, s_4

$$\frac{1}{4} \times (\$12.00) = \$3.00$$

Any slice worth at least \$3.00 is a fair share to Cory.

(d) Dana: s_1

$$\frac{1}{4} \times (\$10.00) = \$2.50$$

Any slice worth at least \$2.50 is a fair share to Dana.

(e) Abe: s_2 , Betty: s_3 , Cory: s_4 , Dana: s_1

9. **(a)** Fair shares to Abe: s_2 and s_3

Let x denote the value of slices s_2 and s_3 to Abe. Then, $2x + 6.50 = 15.00$ and so $x = \$4.25$. Since Abe values a fair share at $\$15.00 / 4 = \$3.75$, he considers slices s_2 and s_3 to be fair shares.

(b) Betty considers each share to be fair.

(c) Fair shares to Cory: s_3

Let x denote the value (as a percentage of the whole cake) of slices s_1, s_2 and s_4 to Cory. Then, $x + x + 3x + x = 1$. So $x = 0.20$. The only share worth 25% of the cake is slice s_3 which is worth 60% of the cake to him.

(d) Fair shares to Dana: s_1

Let x denote the value of slices s_2, s_3 and s_4 to Dana. Then, s_1 has a value of $x + \$2.00$. Also, $(x + \$2.00) + x + x + x = \$18.00$ and so $x = \$4$. Since Dana values a fair share at $\$18.00 / 4 = \$4.50$, she only considers slice s_1 to be a fair share.

(e) Abe: s_2; Betty: s_4; Cory: s_3; Dana: s_1

10. (a) Fair shares to Adams: s_1 and s_4

Let x denote the value of slices s_2 and s_3 to Adams. Then, $(x + \$40,000) + x + x + (x + \$60,000) = \$400,000$ and so $x = \$75,000$. Since a fair share is $\$100,000$, Adams considers slices s_1 ($\$115,000$) and s_4 ($\$135,000$) to be fair shares.

(b) Fair shares to Benson: s_1 and s_2

Let x denote the value of slice s_3 to Benson. Then, since s_4 is worth $8000 more than that and the sum of these two is worth $(0.40)\$400,000 = \$160,000$, it follows that $x + (x + \$8,000) = \$160,000$ and so $x = \$76,000$. So, s_3 is worth $\$76,000$ and s_4 is worth $\$84,000$. Now let y denote the value of slice s_2 to Benson. The value of s_1 is then $y + \$40,000$. So, $(y + \$40,000) + y + \$76,000 + \$84,000 = \$400,000$ and $y = \$150,000$. Since a fair share is $\$100,000$, Benson considers slices s_1 ($\$190,000$) and s_2 ($\$150,000$) to be fair shares.

(c) Fair shares to Cagle: s_1 and s_3

Let x denote the value of slice s_4 to Cagle. Then, s_3 is worth $2x$. So, s_1 is worth $x + \$20,000$. Since s_2 is worth $40,000 less than s_1, the value of s_2 is $x - \$20,000$. Hence, $(x + \$20,000) + (x - \$20,000) + 2x + x = \$400,000$ and $x = \$80,000$. Since a fair share is $\$100,000$, Cagle considers slices s_1 ($\$100,000$) and s_3 ($\$160,000$) to be fair shares.

(d) Fair shares to Duncan: s_4

Let x denote the value of slices s_2 and s_3 to Duncan. Then, $(x + \$4,000) + x + x = \$280,000$ so that $x = \$92,000$. Since a fair share is $\$100,000$, Duncan only considers slice s_4 ($\$120,000$) to be a fair share.

(e) Adams: s_1; Benson: s_2; Cagle: s_3; Duncan: s_4

B.   The Divider–Chooser Method

11. **(a)** Jared would divide the sandwich in two differently sized pieces – one piece would be all of the vegetarian part and 1/3 of the meatball part. The other would consist of 2/3 of the meatball part of the sandwich.

    (b) Karla would divide the sandwich into one piece consisting of half of the vegetarian part (1/4 of the entire size of the sandwich) and another piece consisting of half of the vegetarian part and the entire meatball part (3/4 of the entire size of the sandwich).

    (c) If Jared is the divider then he will cut the sandwich as described in part (a). Karla will obviously choose the vegetarian part. To her, that part is worth $8.00 (the meatball part of the sandwich is worthless to her). To Jared, the meatball part that he ends up with is worth $4.00 (exactly half the value of the sandwich).

    (d) If Karla is the divider then she will cut the sandwich halfway down the vegetarian part (see part (b)). Jared will obviously choose the larger piece containing the entire meatball part (3/4 of the size of the sandwich) for himself. To him, that share is worth $7.00 (the meatball half is worth $6.00 and he also gets half of the $2.00 vegetarian part). To Karla, the vegetarian part that she ends up with is worth $4.00 (exactly half the value of the sandwich).

12. **(a)** Martha's cut: One piece would consist of 8 inches of Ham and 2 inches of Turkey. The other piece would consist of 10 inches of Turkey and 8 inches of Roast Beef.

    (b) Nick's cut: One piece would consist of 8 inches of Ham and 10 inches of Turkey. The other piece would consist of 2 inches of Turkey and 8 inches of Roast Beef.

    (c) Martha values the Ham part at $4, the Turkey part at $3, and the Roast Beef part at $2. Nick values the Ham part at $2, the Turkey part at $3, and the Roast Beef part at $4. If Martha is the divider, Nick will select the piece consisting of 10 inches of Turkey and 8 inches of Roast Beef. So, Martha's piece would consist of 8 inches of Ham and 2 inches of Turkey and be worth

    $\$4 + \dfrac{2}{12}(\$3) = \$4.50$ to her. Nick's piece would be worth $\$4 + \dfrac{10}{12}(\$3) = \$6.50$ in his eyes.

    (d) Martha values the Ham part at $6, the Turkey part at $4.50, and the Roast Beef part at $3. Nick values the Ham part at $3, the Turkey part at $4.50, and the Roast Beef part at $6. If Nick is the divider, Martha will select the piece consisting of 10 inches of Turkey and 8 inches of Ham. So, Nick's piece would consist of 8 inches of Roast Beef and 2 inches of Turkey and be worth

    $\$6 + \dfrac{2}{12}(\$4.50) = \$6.75$ to him. Martha's piece would be worth $\$6 + \dfrac{10}{12}(\$4.50) = \$9.75$ in her eyes.

13. **(a)** According to David, **(iii)** is the only one that shows a division of the pizza into fair shares because it is the only one in which the total amount of pepperoni, sausage, and mushroom is the same in each piece.

    (b) Paul could choose either of the pieces in **(iii)** because the total amount of anchovies, mushroom, and pepperoni is the same in each piece.

14. (a) Cut 1, Cut 3, and Cut 5.
Raul: $C = 3S$; $100\% = C + S = 3S + S = 4S$; $S = 25\%$, $C = 75\%$.
Cut 1: Consistent with any value system.
Cut 2: Chocolate part worth 75% and strawberry part worth 25%.
Cut 3: A chocolate slice of 120° is worth $\frac{120°}{180°} \times 75\% = 50\%$ of the total value of the cake and so the other piece is also worth 50% of the value of the cake.
Cut 4: A chocolate slice of 60° is worth $\frac{60°}{180°} \times 75\% = 25\%$ of the value of the total value of the cake and a strawberry slice of 72° is worth $\frac{72°}{180°} \times 25\% = 10\%$ of the value of the cake making the left piece worth only 35% of the value of the cake.
Cut 5: A chocolate slice of 96° is worth $\frac{96°}{180°} \times 75\% = 40\%$ of the total value of the cake, and a strawberry slice of 72° is worth $\frac{72°}{180°} \times 25\% = 10\%$ making the left piece worth 50% of the value of the cake.

(b) Cut 1: either piece. Cut 2: the top half. Cut 3: the larger piece. Cut 4: the piece to the right. Cut 5: the piece to the right.
Karli: $C = 2S$; $100\% = C + S = 2S + S = 3S$; $S = 33\frac{1}{3}\%$, $C = 66\frac{2}{3}\%$.
Cut 1: Consistent with any value system.
Cut 2: Chocolate part worth $66\frac{2}{3}\%$ and strawberry part worth $33\frac{1}{3}\%$.
Cut 3: A chocolate slice of 120° is worth $\frac{120°}{180°} \times 66\frac{2}{3}\% = 44\frac{4}{9}\%$ of the total value of the cake and so the larger piece is worth $55\frac{5}{9}\%$ of the value of the cake.
Cut 4: A chocolate slice of 60° is worth $\frac{60°}{180°} \times 66\frac{2}{3}\% = 22\frac{2}{9}\%$ of the value of the total value of the cake and a strawberry slice of 72° is worth $\frac{72°}{180°} \times 33\frac{1}{3}\% = 13\frac{1}{3}\%$ of the value of the cake making the left piece worth only $35\frac{5}{9}\%$ of the value of the cake.
Cut 5: A chocolate slice of 96° is worth $\frac{96°}{180°} \times 66\frac{2}{3}\% = 35\frac{5}{9}\%$ of the total value of the cake, and a strawberry slice of 72° is worth $\frac{72°}{180°} \times 33\frac{1}{3}\% = 13\frac{1}{3}\%$ making the left piece worth $48\frac{8}{9}\%$ of the value of the cake.

15. (a) Answers may vary. For example,

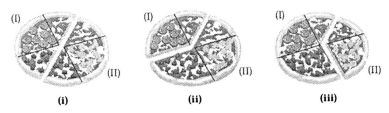

(i)   (ii)   (iii)

(b) David will choose the piece with the greatest total amount of pepperoni, sausage, and mushroom.
(i) either piece; (ii) II; (iii) I

16. (a) Answers may vary. For example,

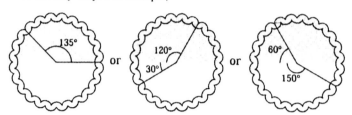

A chocolate slice of 135° is worth $\frac{135°}{180°} \times 66\frac{2}{3}\% = 50\%$.

A chocolate slice of 120° is worth $\frac{120°}{180°} \times 66\frac{2}{3}\% = 44\frac{4}{9}\%$ and a strawberry slice of 30° is worth

$\frac{30°}{180°} \times 33\frac{1}{3}\% = 5\frac{5}{9}\%$ making a total of 50%.

A chocolate slice of 60° is worth $\frac{60°}{180°} \times 66\frac{2}{3}\% = 22\frac{2}{9}\%$ and a strawberry slice of 150° is worth

$\frac{150°}{180°} \times 33\frac{1}{3}\% = 27\frac{7}{9}\%$ making a total of 50%.

(b) Cut 1: either piece. Cut 2: the top half. Cut 3: the larger piece. Cut 4: the piece to the right. Cut 5: the piece to the right.

17. (a) 50%
Since the two pieces are exact opposites, Mo must value pineapple and orange equally. Thus, the pineapple half is 50%.

(b) left piece: 40%; right piece: 60%
Let P = the value of the pineapple half (in Jamie's eyes)
   O = the value of the orange half (in Jamie's eyes)
It is known that $O = 4P$ and $O + P = 100\%$.
$4P + P = 100\%$

$\quad 5P = 100\%$

$\quad\ P = 20\%$

$\quad\ O = 4 \times 20\% = 80\%$

left piece: $\dfrac{60°}{180°} \times 80\% + \dfrac{120°}{180°} \times 20\% = \dfrac{1}{3} \times 80\% + \dfrac{2}{3} \times 20\% = 40\%$

right piece: $\dfrac{120°}{180°} \times 80\% + \dfrac{60°}{180°} \times 20\% = \dfrac{2}{3} \times 80\% + \dfrac{1}{3} \times 20\% = 60\%$

(c) Jamie takes the right piece; Mo gets the left piece.

18. (a) 75%
$(2/3)P = 50\%$ so $P = 75\%$.

(b) the smaller piece: $13\frac{1}{3}\%$; the larger piece: $86\frac{2}{3}\%$
Let P = the value of the pineapple half (in Susan's eyes)
   O = the value of the orange half (in Susan's eyes)

It is known that $O = 4P$ and $O + P = 100\%$.
$$4P + P = 100\%$$
$$5P = 100\%$$
$$P = 20\%$$
$$O = 4 \times 20\% = 80\%$$

smaller piece: $\dfrac{120°}{180°} \times 20\% = 13\dfrac{1}{3}\%$

larger piece: $\dfrac{60°}{180°} \times 20\% + 80\% = 86\dfrac{2}{3}\%$

    (c) Susan takes the larger piece; Veronica gets the smaller piece.

C.   **The Lone-Divider Method**

19. (a) If Divine is to receive s_1, then Chandra must receive s_3. So, Chase's fair share is s_2.

    (b) If Divine is to receive s_2, then Chase must receive s_3. So, Chandra's fair share is s_1.

    (c) If Divine is to receive s_3, then Chase must receive s_2 and Chandra must receive s_1.

20. (a) Divine: s_2; Chase: s_3; Chandra: s_1.

    (b) Divine: s_3; Chase: s_2; Chandra: s_1.

21. (a) DiPalma: s_1; Chou: s_4; Choate: s_3; Childs: s_2.

    (b) DiPalma: s_2; Childs: s_3; Choate: s_4; Chou: s_1.

    (c) DiPalma: s_3; Choate: s_4; Chou: s_1; Childs: s_2.

    (d) DiPalma: s_4; Choate: s_3; Childs: s_2; Chou: s_1.

22. (a) DiPalma: s_1; Chou: s_4; Choate: s_3; Childs: s_2.

    (b) Clearly s_4 must go to Chou. This forces s_3 to go to Choate, which then forces s_2 to go to Childs. This leaves only s_1 for DiPalma.

23. (a) Desi: s_4; Cher: s_2; Cheech: s_3; Chong: s_1.

    (b) Desi: s_4; Cher: s_3; Cheech: s_1; Chong: s_2.

    (c) None of the choosers chose s_4, which can only be given to the divider.

24. Since Cher, Cheech, and Chong covet two of the four slices (s_1 and s_2), we give Desi either s_3 or s_4. Take the remaining three slices and reconstitute them into a new cake to be divided among the Cher, Cheech, and Chong using the lone-divider method for three players.

25. (a) If C_1 is to receive s_2, then C_2 must receive s_4. So, C_3 must receive s_3. It follows that C_4 must receive s_5. This leaves D with s_1.

    (b) If C_1 is to receive s_4, then C_2 must receive s_2. So, C_3 must receive s_3. It follows that C_4 must receive s_5. This leaves D with s_1.

    (c) There are only two possible cases: C_1 receives s_2 or C_1 receives s_4 (since those were the slices in C_1's bid list). The outcome of both cases appear in (a) and (b).

26. (a) $C_1 : s_5 ; C_2 : s_2 ; C_3 : s_4 ; C_4 : s_1 ; \; D: s_3$.

    (b) $C_1 : s_2 ; C_2 : s_1 ; C_3 : s_4 ; C_4 : s_5 ; \; D: s_3$.

    (c) If C_3 receives s_1 then C_2 would get s_2 and C_4 would get s_5 leaving no fair share for C_1. If C_3 receives s_5 then C_1 would get s_2 and C_4 would get s_1 leaving no fair share for C_2.

27. (a) A fair division of the cake is

C_1	C_2	C_3	C_4	C_5	D
s_5	s_1	s_6	s_2	s_3	s_4

    (b) C_5 must get s_3 which forces C_4 to get s_2. This leaves only s_5 for C_1 which in turn leaves only s_6 for C_3. Consequently only s_1 is left for C_2 and the divider D must get s_4.

28. Answers can vary. For example, it is possible to give s_2 to C_2, s_4 to C_3, s_5 to C_4, and s_6 to the divider D. Since C_1 and C_5 both covet slice s_1, take slices s_1 and s_3 and reconstitute them into a new cake to be divided between C_1 and C_5 using the divider-chooser method.

29. (a) The Divider was Gong since that is the only player that could possibly value each piece equally.

    (b) Use the fact that each chooser's bid list must add up to $480,000 to complete the table.

	s_1	s_2	s_3	s_4
Egan	$80,000	$85,000	$120,000	$195,000
Fine	$125,000	$100,000	$135,000	$120,000
Gong	$120,000	$120,000	$120,000	$120,000
Hart	$95,000	$100,000	$175,000	$110,000

Based on this table, the choosers would make the following declarations: Egan: $\{s_3,s_4\}$; Fine: $\{s_1,s_3,s_4\}$; Hart: $\{s_3\}$.

(c) One possible fair division of the land is

Egan	Fine	Gong	Hart
s_4	s_1	s_2	s_3

(d) This is the only possible division of the land since Hart must receive s_3 , so that Egan in turn must receive s_4 . It follows that Fine must receive s_1 so that Gong (the divider) winds up with s_2 .

30. (a) The Divider was Hart since that is the only player that could possibly value each piece equally.

(b) Use the fact that each chooser's bid list must add up to 100% to complete the table.

	s_1	s_2	s_3	s_4
Egan	27%	30%	21%	22%
Fine	35%	20%	25%	20%
Gong	25%	26%	28%	21%
Hart	25%	25%	25%	25%

Based on this table, the choosers would make the following declarations: Egan: $\{s_1,s_2\}$; Fine: $\{s_1,s_3\}$; Gong: $\{s_1,s_2,s_3\}$.

(c) A fair division of the land where Gong's fair share is s_2 : Egan: s_1 ; Fine: s_3 ; Gong: s_2 ; Hart: s_4 .

D.　The Lone-Chooser Method

31. (a) Angela sees the left half of the cake as being worth $18. In her second division, she will create three $6 pieces.

$$\frac{x}{90°} \times \$13.50 = \$6.00$$

$$x = 40°$$

So Angela cuts two 40° pieces from the strawberry, and the remaining strawberry plus the vanilla makes up the third piece.

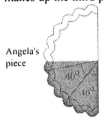

Angela's piece

(b) Boris sees the right half of the cake as being worth \$15. In his second division, he will create three \$5 pieces.

$$\frac{x}{90°} \times \$9.00 = \$5.00$$

$$x = 50°$$

So Boris cuts one 50° piece from the strawberry part of the cake. Also,

$$\frac{x}{90°} \times \$6.00 = \$5.00$$

$$x = 75°$$

So, Boris cuts one 75° piece from the vanilla part of the cake. The remaining 15° piece of vanilla plus the 40° piece of strawberry makes up the third piece.

Boris's pieces

(c) Since Carlos values vanilla twice as much as strawberry, Carlos would clearly take the vanilla part of Angela's division. He would also want to take the most vanilla that he could from Boris. One possible fair division is

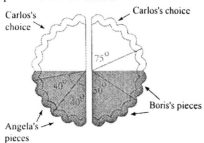

Carlos's choice

Carlos's choice

Boris's pieces

Angela's pieces

(d) Since she receives two of her \$6.00 pieces, the value of Angela's final share (in Angela's eyes) is \$12.00. Similarly, the value of Boris' final share (in Boris' eyes) is \$10.00. The value of Carlos' final share (in Carlos' eyes) is

$$\frac{90°}{90°} \times \$12 + \frac{10°}{90°} \times \$6 + \frac{75°}{90°} \times \$12$$

$$= \$22.67.$$

32. (a) One possible second division by Carlos is

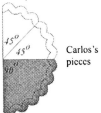

Carlos's
pieces

(b) One possible second division by Angela is

Angela's
piece

(c) One possible fair division is

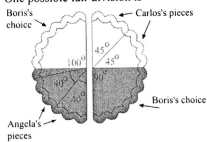

Boris's
choice

Carlos's pieces

Boris's choice

Angela's
pieces

(d) The value of Angela's final share (in Angela's eyes) is $\frac{8}{9} \times \$13.50 = \$12.00$. The value of Boris'

final share (in Boris' eyes) is $\$6 + \frac{1}{9} \times \$9 + \$9 = \$16.00$. The value of Carlos' final share (in Carlos'

eyes) is $\$12.00$.

33. The value of the strawberry piece (in Angela's eyes) is $\frac{120°}{180°} \times \$9 = \$6.00$. The value of the other piece

is, of course, also $\$6.00$. Boris chooses the piece with all of the vanilla because he views it as being
worth $\$12.00 + \$6.00 = \$18.00$.

(a) One possible second division by Boris is

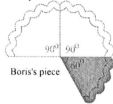

Boris's piece

Boris views his portion of the cake as being worth $\$12 + \dfrac{60°}{180°} \times \$18 \approx \$18.00$.

So he will divide the cake into 3 pieces each worth $6.00.

(b) The second division by Angela is

Angela's piece

She divides the piece evenly.

(c) Carlos will select any one of Angela's pieces since they are identical in value to him. He will also select one of Boris's vanilla wedges since he values vanilla twice as much as he values strawberry. One possible fair division is

Carlos's
choice

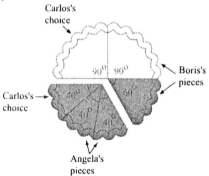

Boris's
pieces

Carlos's →
choice

Angela's
pieces

(d) Angela thinks her share is worth $\dfrac{80°}{180°} \times \$27 = \$12.00$.

Boris thinks his share is worth $\dfrac{90°}{180°} \times \$12 + \dfrac{60°}{180°} \times \$18 = \$12.00$.

Carlos thinks his share is worth $\dfrac{40°}{180°} \times \$12 + \dfrac{90°}{180°} \times \$24 = \$14.67$.

34. (a) Angela's choice of the first division and one possible second division by Angela:

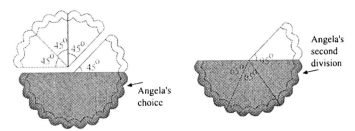

(b) One possible second division by Carlos is

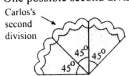

(c) One possible fair division is

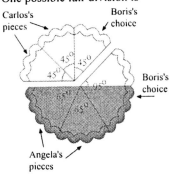

(d) Angela thinks her share is worth $\dfrac{130°}{180°} \times \$27.00 = \$19.50$. Boris thinks his share is worth

$\dfrac{45°}{180°} \times \$12.00 + \dfrac{45°}{180°} \times \$12.00 + \dfrac{50°}{180°} \times \$18.00 = \$11.00$. Carlos thinks his share is worth

$\dfrac{90°}{180°} \times \$24.00 = \$12.00$.

35. After Arthur makes the first cut, Brian chooses the piece with the chocolate and strawberry, worth (to him) 100% of the cake.

(a) One possible second division by Brian is

Brian likes chocolate and strawberry equally well, so he divides the piece evenly.

(b) The second division by Arthur is

Arthur places all of the value on the orange half of the piece, so he divides the orange evenly.

(c) Since Carl likes chocolate and vanilla, one possible fair division is

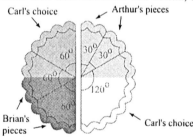

(d) Arthur thinks his share is worth $33\frac{1}{3}$%. Brian thinks his share is worth $66\frac{2}{3}$%. Carl thinks his share is worth $\frac{60°}{90°} \times 50\% + 50\% = 83\frac{1}{3}\%$.

36. (a) Arthurs's choice of the first division and one possible second division by Arthur:

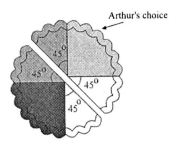

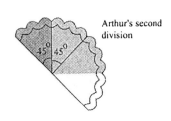

(b) One possible second division by Carl is

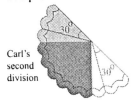

(c) One possible fair division is

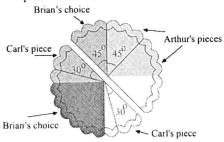

(d) Arthur thinks his share is worth $\frac{45°}{180°} \times 100\% + \frac{45°}{180°} \times 100\% = 50\%$ of the cake. Brian thinks his

share is worth $\frac{45°}{180°} \times 100\% + \frac{15°}{180°} \times 100\% + \frac{90°}{180°} \times 100\% = 83\frac{1}{3}\%$ of the cake. Carl thinks his share

is worth $\frac{30°}{180°} \times 100\% + \frac{30°}{180°} \times 100\% = 33\frac{1}{3}\%$ of the cake.

37. Suppose that Carl chooses the top half, worth (to him) 50% of the cake.
(Carl could also have chosen the bottom half.)

(a) A second division by Carl is

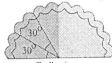

Carl places all of the value on the chocolate half of the piece, so he divides the chocolate evenly.

(b) A second division by Brian is

Brian places all of the value on the strawberry half of the piece, so he divides the strawberry evenly.

(c) One possible fair division is

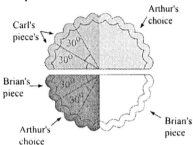

(d) Arthur thinks his share is worth
$$50\% + \frac{30°}{90°} \times 50\% = 66\frac{2}{3}\%.$$
Brian thinks his share is worth $33\frac{1}{3}\%$. Carl thinks his share is worth $33\frac{1}{3}\%$.

38. Note that both halves are of equal value to Carl and so he can choose either half. Suppose that Carl chooses the left half.

    (a) One possible second division by Carl is

    (b) One possible second division by Arthur is

(c) One possible fair division is

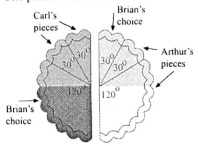

(d) Arthur thinks his share is worth $\frac{30°}{90°} \times 50\% + \frac{30°}{90°} \times 50\% + 0\% = 33\frac{1}{3}\%$ of the cake. Brian thinks his

share is worth $50\% + \frac{30°}{90°} \times 50\% = 66\frac{2}{3}\%$ of the cake. Carl thinks his share is worth

$\frac{30°}{90°} \times 50\% + \frac{30°}{90°} \times 50\% = 33\frac{1}{3}\%$ of the cake.

39. (a) Karla would divide the sandwich into one piece consisting of half of the vegetarian part (1/4 of the entire size of the sandwich) and another piece consisting of half of the vegetarian part and the entire meatball part (3/4 of the entire size of the sandwich). Jared would choose the larger slice containing the meatball part and half of the vegetarian part.

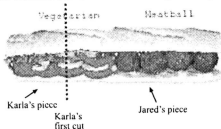

(b) Jared would divide his piece in three equally sized pieces – two pieces would be all meat (each 1/4 of the total sandwich) and the other would be all vegetarian (1/4 of the total sandwich).

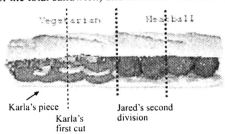

(c) Karla would divide her piece in three equally sized pieces – each piece would be all vegetarian (each 1/3 of 1/4 of the total sandwich).

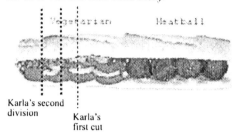

Karla's second division
Karla's first cut

(d) Since Lori, the chooser, likes the meatball part twice as much as the vegetarian part, she will select one of Jared's meatball parts and one of Karla's vegetarian parts.

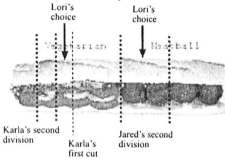

Lori's choice   Lori's choice

Karla's second division
Karla's first cut
Jared's second division

Jared will receive 1/2 of the total sandwich (part meatball and part vegetarian) which, since he views each part equally, he values at 1/2 of the total sandwich. Karla will receive 2/3 of 1/2 (that is, 1/3) of the vegetarian part. She values this as worth 1/3 of the sandwich. Lori will receive 1/2 of the meatball part and 1/3 of 1/2 (that is 1/6) of the vegetarian part. Since she views the meatball half of

the sandwich as being worth 2/3 of the entire sandwich, she values her piece as $\dfrac{1}{2} \times \dfrac{2}{3} + \dfrac{1}{6} \times \dfrac{1}{3} = \dfrac{7}{18}$ of

the entire sandwich.

40. (a) Lori would divide the sandwich into one piece consisting of the entire vegetarian part and 1/4 of the meatball part and another piece consisting of 3/4 of the meatball part. Karla would choose the piece containing the entire vegetarian part.

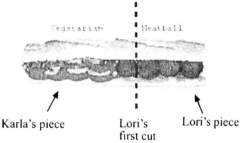

Karla's piece   Lori's first cut   Lori's piece

(b) Karla would divide her piece by separating the meatball part and dividing the vegetarian part in equal halves – two pieces would be all vegetarian (each 1/4 of the total sandwich) and the other would be all meatball (1/8 of the total sandwich).

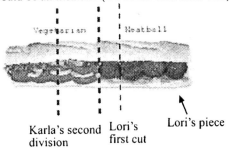

Karla's second division   Lori's first cut   Lori's piece

(c) Lori would divide her piece in three equally sized pieces – each piece would be all meatball.

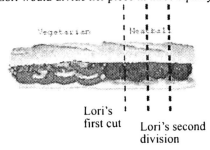

Lori's first cut   Lori's second division

(d) Since Jared, the chooser, likes the meatball part and the vegetarian part the same, he will select the largest pieces that he can.

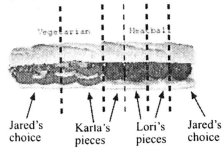

Jared's choice   Karla's pieces   Lori's pieces   Jared's choice

Jared will receive 1/2 of the vegetarian part of the sandwich and 1/4 of the meatball part of the sandwich. He values this as 3/8 of the total value of the sandwich. Lori will receive 1/2 of the meatball part of the sandwich. She values this as 1/2 of 2/3 (i.e. 1/3) of the total sandwich. Karla will receive 1/2 of the vegetarian part of the sandwich and 1/4 of the meatball part of the sandwich. Despite not valuing the meatball part at all, she values her pieces as being worth 1/2 of the total sandwich.

E.   The Last-Diminisher Method

41. (a) P_4 ; P_2 and P_4 are both diminishers since they value the piece when it is their turn as worth more than $6.00. However, P_4 is the last diminisher.

(b) $6.00; While P_4 values the piece as being worth $6.50 when it is their turn to play, they diminish its value to $6.00 when they make a claim.

(c) P_1 ; The remaining players are everyone except for P_4 . They divide what remains into quarters.

42. (a) P_3 ; P_2 and P_3 are both diminishers since they value the piece when it is their turn as worth more than $7.50. However, P_3 is the last diminisher.

(b) $7.50; While P_3 values the piece as being worth $8.50 when it is their turn to play, they diminish its value to $7.50 when they make a claim.

(c) P_1

43. (a) P_5 ; P_4 and P_5 are both diminishers since they value the piece when it is their turn as worth more than $6.00. P_5 is the last diminisher.

(b) $7.00; Since P_5 is the last player to play, they diminish the piece by 0%.

(c) P_1

44. (a) P_4 ; P_3 and P_4 are both diminishers since they value the piece when it is their turn as worth more than $7.50. P_4 is the last diminisher.

(b) $8.00; Since P_4 is the last player to play, they diminish the piece by 0%.

(c) P_1

45. (a) P_9 (the last diminisher)

(b) P_1

(c) P_5 (the last diminisher)

(d) P_1 ; There are no diminishers.

(e) P_2 ; P_1 already has a piece.

46. (a) P_6 (P_6 was the last diminisher.)

(b) P_1 (P_1 continues to cut the first piece in each round until she gets a piece.)

(c) P_1 (P_1 cuts in round 2 and there are no diminishers.)

(d) P_5

(e) P_2

47. **(a)** Arthur's claim is a $45°$ wedge. He views the chocolate $90°$ wedge of the cake as being worth ½ of the total value of the cake. So ½ of that is worth ¼ of the value of the entire cake.

Arthur's claim

    (b) No players are diminishers in round 1. Brian and Carl both view Arthur's claim as being worth exactly 1/4 of the cake. Damian only views Arthur's claim as being worth 1/8 of the cake.

    (c) Since there were no diminishers, Arthur receives his original claim at the end of round 1.

    (d) Brian could stake two different types of claims at the beginning of round 2. He could either claim the remaining $45°$ wedge of chocolate or he could claim a $45°$ wedge of strawberry (he views both as worth 1/3 of what remains of the cake). Neither Carl nor Damian will view such a piece as being worth more than 1/3 of the remaining cake (at best, Carl views a $45°$ wedge of chocolate as being worth 1/3 of what remains). So, Brian will receive his share at the end of round 2.

    (e) There are two possibilities for what remains of the cake after round 2.
Case I: All of the chocolate has been removed. In this case, Carl makes a claim on a $45°$ wedge of vanilla. Damian is happy to pass. So Carl will receive his share at the end of round 3.
Case II: A $45°$ wedge of chocolate and a $45°$ wedge of strawberry have been removed. In this case, Carl makes a claim on a $67.5°$ wedge of vanilla. Damian is happy to pass and Carl will again receive his share at the end of round 3.

48. **(a)** Dale claims the entire vanilla half of the cake.

    (b) Carlos and Boris are both diminishers. Carlos cuts the C-piece in half. Boris then cuts that C-piece in half. In doing so, Boris claims a $45°$ wedge of vanilla.

    (c) Boris is the last diminisher in round 1 and receives a $45°$ wedge of vanilla.

    (d) At the start of round 2, Dale values the strawberry four times more than he values the vanilla (since Boris received a $45°$ wedge of vanilla in round 1). That is, the strawberry is worth 4/5 of the entire cake to Dale at this point. Since Dale will cut a wedge made up entirely of strawberry, the size of that slice is determined by $\dfrac{x°}{180°}\left(\dfrac{4}{5}\right) = \dfrac{1}{3}$ so that $x = 75°$. Dale claims a $75°$ wedge of strawberry as the *C*-piece at the beginning of round 2. Since neither Angela nor Carlos values strawberry as much as Dale they will not diminish his *C*-piece in round 2.

(e) Dale receives a 75° wedge of strawberry at the end of round 2.

49. (a) Lori values the vegetarian part three times as much as she values the meatball part. Assume, for example, that she values the vegetarian part as being worth $3 and the meatball part as being worth $1. Then, she will cut a share worth 1/3 of the entire $4 sub. She will claim some fraction *x* of the $3 vegetarian part of the sandwich. Thus, $x(\$3) = \dfrac{1}{3}(\$4)$ making $x = \dfrac{4}{9}$. So, 4/9 of the vegetarian half of the sandwich will make up the *C*-piece.

(b) Karla will diminish the *C*-piece cut by Lori from 4/9 to 1/3 of the vegetarian part of the sandwich. Jared will pass and Karla is the last diminisher in round 1.

(c) Karla will receive 1/3 of the vegetarian part of the sandwich.

(d) At the end of round 1, 2/3 of the vegetarian part and the entire meatball part are left. Lori would value the vegetarian part at $2 and the meatball part at $1. She will claim some fraction *x* of the $2 vegetarian part of the remaining $3 sandwich. Thus, $x(\$2) = \dfrac{1}{2}(\$3)$ so that $x = \dfrac{3}{4}$. So, 3/4 of 2/3 of the vegetarian part of the sandwich will make up her *C*-piece. Jared will pass. Lori will receive a 1/2 of the vegetarian part of the sandwich (that is 1/4 of the entire sandwich).

(e) Jared will receive the entire meatball part of the sandwich and part of the vegetarian part of the sandwich. Since Karla receives 1/3 of the vegetarian part and Lori receives 1/2 of the vegetarian part, Jared will receive 1-1/3-1/2 = 1/6 of the vegetarian part in addition to the entire meatball part of the sandwich.

50. (a) Jared's *C*-piece will consist of 2/3 of the vegetarian part of the sandwich (1/3 of the total sandwich). Lori will then diminish that piece and so will Karla. Karla will be the last diminisher in round 1.

(b) Karla will receive 1/3 of the vegetarian part of the sandwich.

(c) Jared will cut what remains of the sandwich exactly in half at the beginning of round 2. If Jared's *C*-piece is all meatball, Lori will pass and end up with the other part (1/6 of the meatball half and 2/3 of the vegetarian half). If, on the other hand, Jared's *C*-piece is 1/6 of the meatball half and 2/3 of the vegetarian half, Lori will claim it and diminish it by 0%. Either way, Lori ends up with the same piece – one that is 1/6 of the meatball half and 2/3 of the vegetarian half.

(d) Jared will end up with a piece that is 5/6 of the meatball part of the sandwich.

F.   The Method of Sealed Bids

51. (a) In the first settlement, Ana gets the desk and receives $120 in cash; Belle gets the; Chloe gets the vanity and the tapestry and pays $360.

Item	Ana	Belle	Chloe	
Dresser	150	**300**	275	
Desk	**180**	150	165	
Vanity	170	200	**260**	
Tapestry	400	250	**500**	
Total Bids	900	900	1200	
Fair share	300	300	400	Total
Value of items received	180	300	760	Surplus
Prelim cash settlement	120	0	−360	240

(b) Ana, Belle, and Chloe split the $240 surplus cash three ways. This adds $80 cash to the first settlement. In the final settlement, Ana gets the desk and receives $200 in cash; Belle gets the dresser and receives $80; Chloe gets the vanity and the tapestry and pays $280.

Item	Ana	Belle	Chloe	Surplus
Prelim cash settlement	120	0	−360	240
Share of surplus	80	80	80	
Final cash settlement	200	80	−280	

52. (a) In the first settlement, Peter gets both the car and the cabin and pays $49,250 to the estate. Robert's fair share of the estate is $45,050.

Item	Robert	Peter	
Car	29200	**33200**	
Cabin	60900	**65300**	
Total Bids	90100	98500	
Fair share	45050	49250	Total
Value of items received	0	98500	Surplus
Prelim cash settlement	45050	−49250	4200

(b) In the final settlement, Peter and Robert split the $4,200 surplus evenly. So Peter winds up with the car, the cabin, and pays the estate $47,150. Robert receives $47,150 cash from the estate.

53. Bob gets the business and pays $155,000. Jane gets $80,000 and Ann gets $75,000.

Item	Bob	Ann	Jane	
Partnership	240000	210000	225000	
Total Bids	240000	210000	225000	
Fair Share	80000	70000	75000	Total
Value of items received	240000	0	0	Surplus
Prelim. cash settlement	−160000	70000	75000	15000
Share of surplus	5000	5000	50000	
Final cash settlement	−155000	75000	80000	

54. (a) In the first settlement, Andre gets the farm and pays $220,000; Bea gets the painting and $151,000; Chad gets the house and $45,000.

Item	Andre	Bea	Chad	
House	150000	146000	**175000**	
Farm	**430000**	425000	428000	
Painting	50000	**59000**	57000	
Total Bids	630000	630000	660000	
Fair Share	210000	210000	220000	Total
Value of items received	430000	59000	175000	Surplus
Prelim. cash settlement	−220000	151000	45000	24000

(b) In the final settlement, Andre, Bea, and Chad split the $24,000 surplus evenly. Andre gets the farm and pays $212,000; Bea gets the painting and $159,000; Chad gets the house and $53,000.

55. (a) There is a surplus of $130 after the first settlement in which A ends up with items 4 and 5, C ends up with items 1 and 3, and E ends up with items 2 and 6.

Item	*A*	*B*	*C*	*D*	*E*	
Item 1	352	295	**395**	368	324	
Item 2	98	102	98	95	**105**	
Item 3	460	449	**510**	501	476	
Item 4	**852**	825	832	817	843	
Item 5	**513**	501	505	505	491	
Item 6	725	738	750	744	**761**	
Total Bids	3000	2910	3090	3030	3000	
Fair Share	600	582	618	606	600	Total
Value of items rec'd	1365	0	905	0	866	Surplus
Prelim. cash	–765	582	–287	606	–266	130

(b) *A, B, C, D,* and *E* split the $130 surplus 5 ways ($26 each). *A* ends up with items 4 and 5 and pays $739; *B* ends up with $608; *C* ends up with items 1 and 3 and pays $261; *D* ends up with $632; *E* ends up with items 2 and 6 and pays $240.

56. (a) There is a surplus of $21,666.67 after the first settlement in which Alan receives $29,333.33, Bly receives items 3 and 5 and pays $13,666.67, and Claire ends up with items 1, 2 and 4 and pays the estate $37,333.33.

Item	Alan	Bly	Claire	
Item 1	$14,000	$12,000	**$22,000**	
Item 2	$24,000	$15,000	**$33,000**	
Item 3	$16,000	**$18,000**	$14,000	
Item 4	$16,000	$16,000	**$18,000**	
Item 5	$18,000	**$24,000**	$20,000	
Total Bids	$88,000	$85,000	$107,000	
Fair Share	29,333.33	$28,333.33	$35,666.67	Total
Value of items rec'd	0	$42,000	$73,000	Surplus
Prelim. cash	$29,333.33	-$13,666.67	-$37,333.33	$21,666.67

(b) Alan, Bly, and Claire split the $21,666.67 surplus 3 ways ($7,222.22 each). Alan ends up with $36,555.55; Bly ends up with items 3 and 5 and pays the estate $6,444.45; Claire ends up with items 1, 2 and 4 and pays $30,111.10.

57. Suppose that Angelina bid x on the laptop. Then, she values the entire estate at $x+\$2900$. Brad, on the other hand, values the entire estate at $4640. The rest of the story is given in the table below.

	Angelina	Brad
Fair Share	(x+$2900)/2	$2320
Value of items rec'd	x+$300	$2780
Prelim. cash	(x+$2900)/2-(x+$300)	-$460
Share of surplus	$105	$105
Final cash	$355	-$355

To determine the value of x, it must be that $\dfrac{\$2300-x}{2}+\$105=\$355$. This leads to $\$2300-x=\$500$ and $x=\$1800$. Angelina bid $1800 on the laptop.

58. Suppose that Claire bid $x on the item 2. Then, she values the entire estate at $x+$5100. Alan values the entire estate at $5700. Bly values the estate at $6180. The rest of the story is given in the table below.

	Alan	Bly	Claire
Fair Share	$1900	$2060	($x+$5100)/3
Value of items rec'd	$1800	$4000	$x
Prelim. cash	$100	-$1940	-(2/3)$x+$1700
Share of surplus			$140/3 + (2/9)$x
Final cash			$1480

To determine the value of x, it must be that $\$1700-\dfrac{2}{3}\$x+\dfrac{\$140}{3}+\dfrac{2}{9}\$x=\$1480$. This leads to $x=\$600$. Claire bid $600 on item 2.

G.   The Method of Markers

59. (a) First *B* gets items 1, 2, 3; Then, *C* gets items 5, 6, 7; Finally, *A* gets items 10, 11, 12, 13.

   (b) Items 4, 8, and 9 are left over.

60. (a) *A* gets items 4, 5, 6, 7, 8; *B* gets items 10, 11, 12, 13; *C* gets items 1, 2.

   (b) Items 3 and 9 are left over.

61. (a) First *A* gets items 1, 2; Then, *C* gets items 4, 5, 6, 7; Finally, *B* gets items 10, 11, 12.

   (b) Items 3, 8, and 9 are left over.

62. (a) *A* gets items 3, 4, 5, 6, 7; *B* gets items 10, 11, and 12; *C* gets item 1.

   (b) Items 2, 8 and 9 are left over.

63. (a) First C gets items 1, 2, 3; Then, E gets items 5, 6, 7, 8; Then, D gets items 11, 12, 13; Then, B gets items 15, 16, 17; Finally, A gets items 19, 20.

(b) Items 4, 9, 10, 14, and 18 are left over.

64. (a) A gets item 7; B gets item 15; C gets items 1, 2, and 3; D gets item 11.

(b) Items 4, 5, 6, 8, 9, 10, 12, 13, and 14 are left over.

65. (a) Quintin thinks the total value is $3 \times \$12 + 6 \times \$7 + 6 \times \$4 + 3 \times \$6 = \$120$, so to him a fair share is worth \$30. Ramon thinks the total value is $3 \times \$9 + 6 \times \$5 + 6 \times \$5 + 3 \times \$11 = \$120$, so to him a fair share is worth \$30. Stephone thinks the total value is $3 \times \$8 + 6 \times \$7 + 6 \times \$6 + 3 \times \$14 = \$144$, so to him a fair share is worth \$36. Tim thinks the total value is $3 \times \$5 + 6 \times \$4 + 6 \times \$4 + 3 \times \$7 = \$84$, so to him a fair share is worth \$21. They would place their markers as shown below.

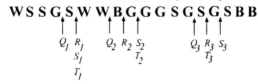

(b)

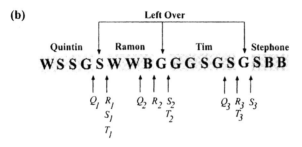

(c) A coin toss would be needed to decide if Quentin or Stephone should receive S. If Stephone were to receive S, then Stephone would receive S and both G's and would pay \$13.32. In that case, Quentin and Ramon would receive \$4.69 and Tim would receive \$3.94.

66. (a) Each player places markers as shown below.

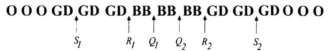

(b) Two Greatful Dead and two Beach Boys CDs are leftover.

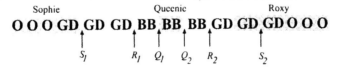

(c) Queenie would pick a Beach Boys CD, Sophie would pick a Greatful Dead CD, and Roxy would pick either of the remaining Beach Boys or Greatful Dead CD.

67. (a) Ana places her markers between the different types of candy bars. Belle places her markers between each of the Nestle Crunch bars. Chloe places her markers thinking that each Snickers and Nestle Crunch bar is worth $1 and each Reese's is worth $2. Since Chloe would then value the bars to be worth $12 in total, she would place markers after each $4 worth of bars.

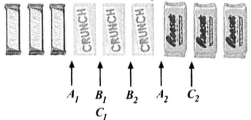

(b) Two Nestle Crunch bars and one Reese's Peanut Butter Cup is left over.

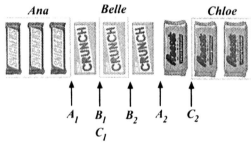

(c) Belle would select one of the Nestle Crunch bars, Chloe would then select the Reese's Peanut Butter Cup, and then Ana would be left with the last Nestle Crunch bar.

68. (a) The players would place their markers as shown below.

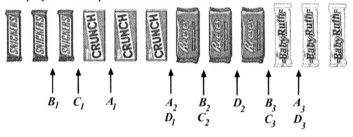

(b) One Snickers, one Nestle Crunch, one Reese's Peanut Butter Cup and one Baby Ruth bar are left over.

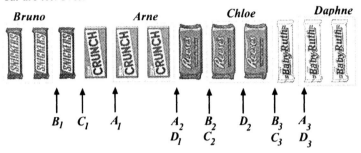

(c) Chloe would choose a Reese's Peanut Butter Cup. Daphne picks up the Baby Ruth. After that Bruno would choose the Snickers. Finally, Arne will choose the Nestle Crunch bar. The final division: Arne – 3 Nestle Crunch, Bruno – 3 Snickers, Chole – 3 Reese's, Daphne – 3 Baby Ruth.

JOGGING

69. (a) Two divisions are possible.

Abe	Babe	Cassie
P, S	Q	R
P, S	R	Q

(b) Four divisions are possible.

Abe	Babe	Cassie
R, S	Q	P
P, R	Q	S
Q, S	R	P
P, Q	R	S

(c) Out of P, Q, and S, Abe gets two of the three. Combine the left over one with R. Since Babe and Cassie each consider Abe's pieces to be worth less than \$1.50 each, they much think the rest is worth more than \$3.00, and thus, they can divide it fairly using the divider-chooser method.

70. (a) Dandy: s_4 ; Burly: s_1 ; Curly: s_2 ; Greedy: s_3 .

(b) If Greedy only bids on s_1, then the bid lists are as follows: Dandy: $\{s_1, s_2, s_3, s_4\}$; Burly: $\{s_1\}$; Curly: $\{s_1, s_2\}$; Greedy: $\{s_1\}$. Suppose that Curly is given s_2 and Dandy is given s_3 . The parcels s_1 and s_4 would then be joined together and split by Burly and Greedy. But a parcel consisting of s_1 and s_4 is only worth \$440,000 to Greedy so half of that is only worth \$220,000.

71. (a) The total area is $30,000\, m^2$ and the area of C is only $8000\, m^2$. Since P_2 and P_3 value the land uniformly, each thinks that a fair share must have an area of at least $10,000\, m^2$.

(b) Since there are $22,000\, m^2$ left, any cut that divides the remaining property in parts of $11,000\, m^2$ will work. For example,

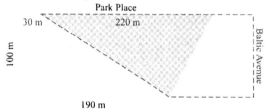

(c) The cut parallel to Park Place which divides the parcel in half is illustrated below. The cut is made x meters from the bottom. We know that $\dfrac{y}{x} = \dfrac{60}{100}$ so that $y = \dfrac{3}{5}x$. The bottom trapezoid is to have area of $11,000\, m^2$. So, $\dfrac{\left(190 + (3/5)x\right) + 190}{2} \times x = 11,000$ or $3x^2 + 1900x - 110,000 = 0$. By the quadratic formula, the value of x is $\dfrac{-950 + 50\sqrt{493}}{3} \approx 53.4$ m.

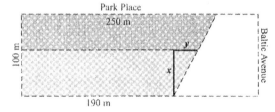

(d) The cut parallel to Baltic Avenue which divides the parcel in half is

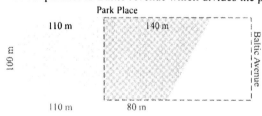

72. (a) The total area is $30,000\, m^2$ and the area of C is only $9,000\, m^2$. Since P_2 and P_3 value the land uniformly, each thinks that a fair share must have an area of at least $10,000\, m^2$.

(b) Since there are 21,000 m^2 left, any cut that divides the remaining property in parts of 10,500 m^2 will work.

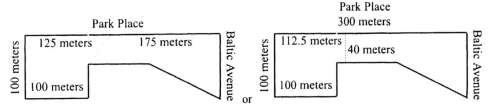

(c) A possible cut is

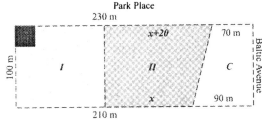

73. (a) If P_2 and P_3 each value the land (except for the 20m by 20m plot in the upper left corner) at v dollars per square meter, then the total value of the land to each of them is $(300)(100)v - 2(20)(20)v = 29,200v$. Thus a fair share to each of them would have value at least $9,733.33v$. But the value of piece C to each of them is $100\left(\dfrac{70+90}{2}\right)v = 8000v$ and so they would both pass and P_1 would end up with piece C.

(b) Since the value of the remaining land to each of P_2 and P_3 is $29,200v - 8000v = 21,200v$, the divider in round 2 wants to make the cut so that each piece is worth $\dfrac{21,200}{2}v = 10,600v$. Letting x denote the length of the shorter base of the trapezoid II as shown in the figure,

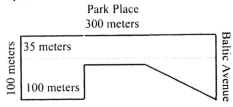

the value of piece II to each of them is $100\left(\dfrac{x+(x+20)}{2}\right)v = 100(x+10)v$ and consequently x must satisfy the equation $100(x+10)v = 10,600v$ which gives $x = 96$.

74. (a) In the first settlement A receives $\$x/2$; B receives the partnership and pays $\$y/2$.

(b) The surplus is $\dfrac{y}{2} - \dfrac{x}{2} = \dfrac{y-x}{2}$ dollars.

(c) *B* must pay *A*'s original fair share plus half of the surplus, or (in dollars)

$$\frac{x}{2} + \frac{1}{2}x\left(\frac{y-x}{2}\right) = \frac{x}{2} + \left(\frac{y-x}{4}\right)$$
$$= \frac{x}{2} + \frac{y}{4} - \frac{x}{4}$$
$$= \frac{x}{4} + \frac{y}{4}$$
$$= \frac{x+y}{4}.$$

75. (a) No. The chooser is not assured a fair share in her own value system.

(b) The divider.
The divider has the advantage that he can assure himself a fair share of the cake if he divides it appropriately. The chooser is essentially at the mercy of the laws of chance.

76. (a) In the first settlement *A* receives $\$x/3$; *B* receives $\$y/3$; *C* receives the business and pays $\$2z/3$.

(b) The surplus is $\dfrac{2z}{3} - \dfrac{x}{3} - \dfrac{y}{3} = \dfrac{2z-x-y}{3}$ dollars.

(c) *A* will receive $\dfrac{x}{3} + \dfrac{2z-x-y}{9}$ dollars. *B* will receive $\dfrac{y}{3} + \dfrac{2z-x-y}{9}$ dollars. *C* receives the business and pays $\dfrac{x}{3} + \dfrac{y}{3} + 2 \times \dfrac{2z-x-y}{9}$ dollars.

77. (a) *A*-Allen, Bryant; *B*-Evans, Francis; *C*-Carter, Duncan
First pick: *A*-Allen; Second pick: *B*-Evans; Third pick: *C*-Carter; Fourth pick: *A*-Bryant; Fifth pick: *B*-Francis; Sixth pick: *C*-Duncan

(b) *A*-Allen, Duncan; *B*-Evans, Bryant; *C*-Carter, Francis
First pick: *A*-Allen; Second pick: *B*-Evans; Third pick: *C*-Carter; Fourth pick: *C*-Francis; Fifth pick: *B*-Bryant; Sixth pick: *A*-Duncan

(c) No. In (a), *A* and *B* do as well as they can. In (b), *C* does as well as they can and cannot be improved. This means that *B* cannot be improved since Francis must go to *C*.

RUNNING

78. Ruth cleans bathrooms and pays $11.67 per month; Sarah cooks and pays $11.67 per month; Tamara washes dishes, vacuums, mows the lawn and receives $23.34 per month.

Item	Ruth	Sarah	Tamara	
Clean bathrooms	**-20**	-30	-40	
Do cooking	-50	**-10**	-25	
Wash dishes	-30	-20	**-15**	
Mow the lawn	-30	-20	**-10**	
Vacuum and dust	-20	-40	**-15**	
Total Bids	-150	-120	-105	
Fair Share	-50	-40	-35	Total
Value of items received	-20	-10	-40	Surplus
Prelim. cash settlement	-30	-30	5	55
Share of surplus	18.33	18.33	18.34	
Final cash settlement	-11.67	-11.67	23.34	

79. Quintin ends up with the stereo and the table and pays $298.75; Ramon patches the nail holes, repairs the window and gets $6.25 and the couch; Stephone ends up with $251.25; Tim cleans the rugs and gets the desk and $41.25.

Item	Quintin	Ramon	Stephone	Tim	
Stereo	**300**	250	200	280	
Couch	200	**350**	300	100	
Table	**250**	200	240	80	
Desk	150	150	200	**220**	
Cleaning rugs	-80	-70	-100	**-60**	
Patching holes	-60	**-30**	-60	-40	
Repairing window	-60	**-50**	-80	-80	
Total Bids	700	800	700	500	
Fair Share	175	200	175	125	Total
Value of items received	550	270	0	160	Surplus
Prelim. cash settlement	-375	-70	175	-35	305
Share of surplus	76.25	76.25	76.25	76.25	
Final cash settlement	-298.75	6.25	251.25	41.25	

193

80. *B* receives the piece they valued at 50%. *C* will receive 5/6 of the piece they valued at 60%. *A* receives the piece they valued at 47% and 1/6 of the piece they valued at 18%.

81. (a) We begin with the fact that the three dividers D_1, D_2, and D_3 can divide the cake so that each has (in their own opinion) 1/3 of the cake. At the next step of the lone-chooser method, each of these three dividers divides their 1/3 of the cake into four equal pieces. Thus, in each divider's eyes, each of the four equal pieces is worth 1/4 of 1/3 (or 1/12) of the cake. Since in the end each divider keeps three of these pieces, they end up with 3/12 (or 1/4) of the cake. The chooser then chooses one piece from each of the dividers. Now it could be that the divider does not value each of the original "thirds" equally. Say, for example, the chooser thinks that D_1's piece is worth $x_1\%$, D_2's piece is worth $x_2\%$, and D_3's piece is worth $x_3\%$ of the total. Note that $x_1 + x_2 + x_3 = 100$. From D_1 the chooser picks a piece worth at least 1/4 of $x_1\%$ of the cake. From D_2 the chooser picks a piece again worth at least 1/4 of $x_2\%$ of the cake. Similarly, they choose from D_3. The pieces that the chooser picks are thus worth at least $1/4(x_1 + x_2 + x_3)\% = 1/4(100\%) = 25\%$ of the cake.

(b) The reasoning is that same as in part (a) except that each divider starts by dividing the cake into $1/(N-1)$ of the cake. Each divider then cuts each piece into N smaller pieces and keeps $N-1$ of these. That is, a total of $N-1$ pieces worth $1/(N-1)$ of $1/N$ of the cake (i.e. $1/N$ of the cake). If the chooser values each of D_i's part of the cake as worth $x_i\%$, then the process has the chooser picking pieces worth at least $1/N(x_1 + x_2 + x_3 + ... + x_{N-1})\% = 1/N(100\%) = 1/N$ of the cake. Thus, each player is guaranteed a fair share.

82. (a) Boris. His share looks like

(b) Angela. Her share looks like

(c) Carlos gets the remaining part of the cake. The value of Boris's piece in his eyes is $4. The value of Angela's piece in her eyes is $5. The value of Carlos's piece in his eyes is $5.25.

83. (a) Boris. His share will be a $\frac{3}{4}(90°) = 67.5°$ wedge of vanilla.

(b) First, determine the value of the remainder of the cake in the eyes of each of the remaining players:

Angela: $\$8 + \dfrac{112.5°}{180°}(\$4) = \$10.50$

Carlos: $\$6 + \dfrac{112.5°}{180°}(\$6) = \$9.75$

Dale: $\$9 + \dfrac{112.5°}{180°}(\$3) = \$10.88$

The next piece would contain a 22.5° wedge of vanilla and a wedge of x degrees of strawberry. In order for each player to yell "Stop!" the following would need to be true:

Angela: $\dfrac{22.5°}{180°}(\$4) + \dfrac{x°}{180°}(\$8) = \dfrac{\$10.50}{3}$; $x = 67.5°$

Carlos: $\dfrac{22.5°}{180°}(\$6) + \dfrac{x°}{180°}\$6 = \dfrac{\$9.75}{3}$; $x = 65°$

Dale: $\dfrac{22.5°}{180°}(\$3) + \dfrac{x°}{180°}\$9 = \dfrac{\$10.88}{3}$; $x = 75°$

So, Carlos would be the second player to yell "Stop!" after the knife has moved another $x = 22.5° + 65° = 87.5°$.

Carlos's piece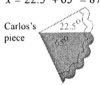

(c) Once again, determine the value of the remainder of the cake in the eyes of each of the remaining players:

Angela: $\dfrac{115°}{180°}(\$8) + \dfrac{90°}{180°}(\$4) = \$7.11$

Dale: $\dfrac{115°}{180°}(\$9) + \dfrac{90°}{180°}(\$3) = \$7.25$

The next piece will clearly be all strawberry. Suppose that it is a wedge of x degrees of strawberry. In order for each player to yell "Stop!" the following would need to be true:

Angela: $\dfrac{x°}{180°}(\$8) = \dfrac{\$7.11}{2}$; $x = 80°$

Dale: $\dfrac{x°}{180°}(\$9) = \dfrac{\$7.25}{2}$; $x = 72.5°$

So, Dale would be the third player to yell "Stop!" after the knife has moved another $x = 72.5°$.

 Dale's share

84. (a) For simplicity, we first illustrate the argument in the case of two players and two items.

	Player 1	**Player 2**
Item 1	x_1	x_2
Item 2	y_1	y_2

$$\text{Surplus} = -\left(\frac{x_1 + y_1}{2}\right) - \left(\frac{x_2 + y_2}{2}\right) + \max\{x_1, x_2\} + \max\{y_1, y_2\}.$$

After some rearranging of terms,

$$\text{Surplus} = \max\{x_1, x_2\} - \left(\frac{x_1 + x_2}{2}\right) + \max\{y_1, y_2\} - \left(\frac{y_1 + y_2}{2}\right).$$

Now, $\max\{x_1, x_2\} \geq \left(\frac{x_1 + x_2}{2}\right)$ with equality if and only if $x_1 = x_2$.

Likewise, $\max\{y_1, y_2\} \geq \left(\frac{y_1 + y_2}{2}\right)$ with equality if and only if $y_1 = y_2$.

If follows that Surplus ≥ 0 with equality if and only if $x_1 = x_2$ and $y_1 = y_2$.

The argument can be generalized to any number of players (N) and items (M), although the notation can get cumbersome. The critical observation is that after a little algebraic manipulation we can write

Surplus = (maximum entry in row 1 – average of entries in row 1) +
       (maximum entry in row 2 – average of entries in row 2) +
       …+
       (maximum entry in last row – average of entries in last row).

Each of the terms in the above sum is greater than or equal to zero, with equality if and only if in each row the entries are equal

(b) See part (a).

Chapter 4

WALKING

A. Standard Divisors and Quotas

1. (a) Standard divisor $= \dfrac{3,310,000 + 2,670,000 + 1,330,000 + 690,000}{160} = 50,000$

(b) Apure: $\dfrac{3,310,000}{50,000} = 66.2$; Barinas: $\dfrac{2,670,000}{50,000} = 53.4$; Carabobo: $\dfrac{1,330,000}{50,000} = 26.6$;

Dolores: $\dfrac{690,000}{50,000} = 13.8$

(c)

State	Apure	Barinas	Carabobo	Dolores
Upper Quota	67	54	27	14
Lower Quota	66	53	26	13

2. (a) Standard divisor $= \dfrac{3,310,000 + 2,670,000 + 1,330,000 + 690,000}{200} = 40,000$

(b) Apure: $\dfrac{3,310,000}{40,000} = 82.75$; Barinas: $\dfrac{2,670,000}{40,000} = 66.75$; Carabobo: $\dfrac{1,330,000}{40,000} = 33.25$;

Dolores: $\dfrac{690,000}{40,000} = 17.25$

(c)

State	Apure	Barinas	Carabobo	Dolores
Upper Quota	83	67	34	18
Lower Quota	82	66	33	17

3. (a) The "states" in any apportionment problem are the entities that will have "seats" assigned to them according to a share rule. In this case, the states are the 6 bus routes and the seats are the 130 buses.

(b) Standard divisor $= \dfrac{45,300 + 31,070 + 20,490 + 14,160 + 10,260 + 8,720}{130} = 1000$

The standard divisor represents the average number of passengers per bus per day.

(c) A: $\dfrac{45,300}{1000} = 45.30$; B: $\dfrac{31,070}{1000} = 31.07$; C: $\dfrac{20,490}{1000} = 20.49$;

D: $\dfrac{14,160}{1000} = 14.16$; E: $\dfrac{10,260}{1000} = 10.26$; F: $\dfrac{8,720}{1000} = 8.72$

4. (a) The "states" in any apportionment problem are the entities that will have "seats" assigned to them according to a share rule. In this case, the states are the 4 shifts and the seats are the 225 nurses.

   (b) Standard divisor $= \dfrac{871 + 1029 + 610 + 190}{225} = 12$

   The standard divisor represents the average number of patients per nurse.

   (c) A: $\dfrac{871}{12} = 72.583$; B: $\dfrac{1029}{12} = 85.75$; C: $\dfrac{610}{12} = 50.833$; D: $\dfrac{190}{12} = 15.833$

5. (a) Number of seats $= 40.50 + 29.70 + 23.65 + 14.60 + 10.55 = 119$

   (b) Standard divisor $= \dfrac{23,800,000}{119} = 200,000$

   (c) Population = standard quota × standard divisor, so
   A: $40.5 \times 200,000 = 8,100,000$; B: $29.7 \times 200,000 = 5,940,000$; C: $23.65 \times 200,000 = 4,730,000$; D: $14.60 \times 200,000 = 2,920,000$; E: $10.55 \times 200,000 = 2,110,000$

6. (a) Number of faculty positions $= 32.92 + 15.24 + 41.62 + 21.32 + 138.90 = 250$

   (b) 50. The standard divisor (SD = 12,500/250 = 50) represents the average number of students per faculty position.

   (c) Agriculture: $32.92 \times 50 = 1646$; Business: $15.24 \times 50 = 762$; Education: $41.62 \times 50 = 2081$; Humanities: $21.32 \times 50 = 1066$; Science: $138.90 \times 50 = 6945$

7. Standard quota of Texas = 32.32.
   With 7.43% of the U.S. population, Texas should receive 7.43% of the number of seats available in the House of Representatives. So, the standard quota for Texas is $0.0743 \times 435 = 32.3205$.

8. Percent of U.S. population that lives in California = 12.06%.

9. (a) Standard divisor $= \dfrac{100\%}{200} = 0.5\%$

   (b)

State	A	B	C	D	E	F
Standard Quota	22.74	16.14	77.24	29.96	20.84	33.08

10. **(a)** Standard divisor $= \dfrac{6.24 + 26.16 + 28.48 + 39.12}{125} = \dfrac{100}{125} = 0.8\%$

   (b) Aleta: $\dfrac{6.24}{.8} = 7.8$; Bonita: $\dfrac{26.16}{.8} = 32.7$; Corona: $\dfrac{28.48}{.8} = 35.6$; Doritos: $\dfrac{39.12}{.8} = 48.9$

B. **Hamilton's Method**

11. A: 66; B: 53; C: 27; D: 14.
   Lower Quotas are:
   A : 66; B : 53; C : 26; D : 13
   Sum is 158. So we have 160–158 = 2 seats remaining to allocate. These are given to D and C, since they have the largest fractional parts of the standard quota.

12. A: 83; B: 67; C: 33; D: 17.

13. A: 45; B: 31; C: 21; D: 14; E: 10; F: 9.
   Lower Quotas are:
   A: 45; B: 31; C: 20; D: 14; E: 10; F: 8, and the sum is 128. So we have 130–128 = 2 buses remaining to allocate. These are given to F and C, since they have the largest fractional parts of the standard quota.

14. A: 72; B: 86; C: 51; D: 16.

15. A: 40; B: 30; C: 24; D: 15; E: 10.
   Lower Quotas are:
   A: 40; B: 29; C: 23; D: 14; E: 10, and the sum is 116. So we have 119–116 = 3 seats remaining to allocate. These are given to B, C and D, since they have the largest fractional parts of the standard quota.

16. Agriculture: 33; Business: 15; Education: 42; Humanities: 21; Science: 139.

17. A: 23; B: 16; C: 77; D: 30; E: 21; F: 33.
   Lower Quotas are:
   A: 22; B: 16; C: 77; D: 29; E: 20, F: 33, and the sum is 197. So we have 200–197 = 3 seats remaining to allocate. These are given to A, D and E, since they have the largest fractional parts of the standard quota.

18. A: 8; B: 33; C: 35; D: 49.
   Lower Quotas are A: 7; B: 32; C: 35; and D: 48, and the sum is 122. So we have 125–122 = 3 seats remaining to allocate. These are given to D, A, and B, since they have the largest fractional parts of the standard quota.

19. **(a)** Bob: 0; Peter: 3; Ron: 8.

Child	Bob	Peter	Ron
Standard quota	0.594	2.673	7.733
Lower quota	0	2	7

Note: standard divisor: $= \dfrac{54 + 243 + 703}{11} = 90.\overline{90}$

The sum of lower quotas is 9, so there are 2 remaining pieces of candy to allocate. These are given to Ron and Peter, since they have the largest fractional parts of the standard quota.

(b) Bob: 1; Peter: 2; Ron: 8.

Child	Bob	Peter	Ron
Study time	56	255	789
Standard quota	0.56	2.55	7.89
Lower quota	0	2	7

Note: standard divisor $= \dfrac{56 + 255 + 789}{11} = 100$

The sum of the lower quotas is 9, so there are 2 remaining pieces of candy to allocate. These are given to Ron and Bob, since they have the largest fractional parts of the standard quota.

(c) Yes. For studying an extra 2 minutes (an increase of 3.70%), Bob gets a piece of candy. However, Peter, who studies an extra 12 minutes (an increase of 4.94%), has to give up a piece. This is an example of the population paradox.

20. (a) Bob: 1; Peter: 2; Ron: 7.

(b) Bob: 0; Peter: 3; Ron: 8.

(c) Yes. When 10 pieces of candy are divided, Bob is to get one piece, but when 11 pieces are divided, Bob ends up with none. This is an example of the Alabama paradox.

21. (a) Bob: 0; Peter: 3; Ron: 8.

Child	Bob	Peter	Ron
Standard quota	0.594	2.673	7.733
Lower quota	0	2	7

Note: standard divisor: $= \dfrac{54 + 243 + 703}{11} = 90.\overline{90}$

The sum of lower quotas is 9, so there are 2 remaining pieces of candy to allocate. These are given to Ron and Peter, since they have the largest fractional parts of the standard quota.

(b) Bob: 1; Peter: 3; Ron: 7; Jim: 6.

Child	Bob	Peter	Ron	Jim
Study time	54	243	703	580
Standard quota	0.58	2.61	7.56	6.24
Lower quota	0	2	7	6

Note: standard divisor $= \dfrac{54 + 243 + 703 + 580}{17} \approx 92.94$

The sum of the lower quotas is 15, so there are 2 remaining pieces of candy to allocate. These are given to Peter and Bob, since they have the largest fractional parts of the standard quota.

(c) Ron loses a piece of candy to Bob when Jim enters the discussion and is given his fair share (6 pieces) of candy. This is an example of the new-states paradox.

22. (a) It is impossible for all three daughters to end up with 5 pieces of candy each since Hamilton's method will always satisfy the quota rule. Hence, Katie will receive either 6 or 7 pieces of candy.

(b) Same reason as in (a).

(c) Lily's standard quota must be less than or equal to 8.47. If her standard quota is between 8 and 8.47, Lily will only receive 8 pieces under Hamilton's method since her decimal part is less than Katie's. If Lily's standard quota is less than 8, she will not receive 9 pieces because Hamilton's method satisfies the quota rule.

C.   Jefferson's Method

23. *A*: 67; *B*: 54; *C*: 26; *D*: 13
Any modified divisor between approximately 49,285.72 and 49,402.98 can be used for this problem. Using $D = 49,300$ we obtain:

State	*A*	*B*	*C*	*D*
Modified Quota	67.14	54.16	26.98	13.996
Modified Lower Quota	67	54	26	13

24. *A*: 83; *B*: 67; *C*: 33; *D*: 17
Any divisor between 39,405 and 39,850 will work for this problem.

25. *A*: 46; *B*: 31; *C*: 21; *D*: 14; *E*: 10; *F*: 8
Any divisor between 971 and 975 will work for this problem. Using $D = 975$ we obtain:

Route	*A*	*B*	*C*	*D*	*E*	*F*
Modified Quota	46.46	31.87	21.02	14.52	10.52	8.94
Modified Lower Quota	46	31	21	14	10	8

26. *A*: 73; *B*: 86; *C*: 51; *D*: 15
    Any divisor between 11.876 and 11.931 will work for this problem.

27. *A*: 41; *B*: 30; *C*: 24; *D*: 14; *E*: 10
    Any modified divisor between approximately 194,666.67 and 197,083.33 can be used for this problem. Using *D* = 195,000 we obtain:

State	*A*	*B*	*C*	*D*	*E*
Modified Quota	41.54	30.46	24.26	14.97	10.82
Modified Lower Quota	41	30	24	14	10

28. Agriculture: 33; Business: 15; Education: 41; Humanities: 21; Science: 140.
    Any divisor between 49.55 and 49.60 will work for this problem.

29. Any modified divisor between approximately 0.4944% and 0.4951 can be used for this problem. Using *D* = 0.495% we obtain:

State	*A*	*B*	*C*	*D*	*E*	*F*
Modified Quota	22.9697	16.3030	78.0202	30.2626	21.0505	33.4141
Modified Lower Quota	22	16	78	30	21	33

    The final apportionment is the modified lower quota value in the table.

30. Aleta: 7; Bonita: 33; Corona: 36; Doritos: 49

31. From Exercise 7, the standard quota of Texas was 32.32 for the 2000 Census. However, Jefferson's method only allows for violations of the upper quota. This means that Texas could not receive fewer than 32 seats under Jefferson's method.

32. This fact illustrates that Jefferson's method violates the quota rule.
    The difference between 55 (the number of seats that California would receive under Jefferson's method) and 52.45 (California's standard quota) is greater than 1.

D. **Adams' Method**

33. *A*: 66; *B*: 53; *C*: 27; *D*: 14
    Any modified divisor between approximately 50,377.4 and 50,923 can be used for this problem. Using *D* = 50,500 we obtain:

State	A	B	C	D
Modified Quota	65.54	52.87	26.34	13.66
Modified Upper Quota	66	53	27	14

34. *A:* 82; *B:* 67; *C:* 33; *D:* 18.
Any divisor between 40,366 and 40,454 will work for this problem.

35. *A:* 45; *B:* 31; *C:* 20; *D:* 14; *E:* 11; *F:* 9
Any modified divisor between approximately 1024.6 and 1026 can be used for this problem. Using $D = 1025$ we obtain:

Route	A	B	C	D	E	F
Modified Quota	44.20	30.31	19.99	13.81	10.01	8.51
Modified Upper Quota	45	31	20	14	11	9

36. *A:* 72; *B:* 86; *C:* 51; *D:* 16
Any divisor between 12.098 and 12.105 will work for this problem.

37. *A:* 40; *B:* 29; *C:* 24; *D:* 15; *E:* 11
Any modified divisor between approximately 204,828 and 205,652 can be used for this problem. Using $D = 205,000$ we obtain:

State	A	B	C	D	E
Modified Quota	39.51	28.98	23.07	14.24	10.29
Modified Upper Quota	40	29	24	15	11

38. Agriculture: 33; Business: 16; Education: 42; Humanities: 22; Science: 137.
Any divisor between 50.694 and 50.756 will work for this problem.

39. Any modified divisor between approximately 0.5044% and 0.5081% can be used for this problem. Using $D = 0.505\%$ we obtain:

State	A	B	C	D	E	F
Modified Quota	22.5149	15.9802	76.4752	29.6633	20.6337	32.7525
Modified Upper Quota	23	16	77	30	21	33

The final apportionment is the modified upper quota value in the table.

40. Aleta: 8; Bonita: 33; Corona: 35; Doritos: 49

41. This fact illustrates that Adams's method violates the quota rule. The difference between 50 (the number of seats that California would receive under Adams's method) and 52.45 (California's standard quota) is greater than 1.

42. From Exercise 7, the standard quota of Texas was 32.32 for the 2000 Census. However, Adams's method only allows for violations of the lower quota. This means that Texas could not receive more than 33 seats under Adams's method.

E.   Webster's Method

43. *A*: 66; *B*: 53; *C*: 27; *D*: 14.
Any modified divisor between approximately 49,907 and 50,188 can be used for this problem. Using $D = 50,000$ we obtain:

State	*A*	*B*	*C*	*D*
Modified Quota	66.2	53.4	26.6	13.8
Rounded Quota	66	53	27	14

44. *A*: 83; *B*: 67; *C*: 33; *D*: 17.
Any divisor between 39,702 and 40,121 will work for this problem.

45. *A*: 45; *B*: 31; *C*: 21; *D*: 14; *E*: 10; *F*: 9.
Any modified divisor between approximately 995.61 and 999.51 can be used for this problem. Using $D = 996$ we obtain:

Route	*A*	*B*	*C*	*D*	*E*	*F*
Modified Quota	45.48	31.19	20.57	14.22	10.30	8.76
Rounded Quota	45	31	21	14	10	9

46. *A*: 72; *B*: 86; *C*: 51; *D*: 16.
Any divisor between 12.014 and 12.035 will work for this problem.

47. *A*: 40; *B*: 30; *C*: 24; *D*: 15; *E*: 10.
Any modified divisor between approximately 200,953 and 201,276 can be used for this problem. Using $D = 201,000$ we obtain:

State	*A*	*B*	*C*	*D*	*E*
Modified Quota	40.30	29.55	23.53	14.53	10.498
Rounded Quota	40	30	24	15	10

48. Agriculture: 33; Business: 15; Education: 42; Humanities: 21; Science: 139.
Any divisor between 49.79 and 50.14 will work for this problem.

49. Any modified divisor between approximately 0.499% and 0.504% can be used for this problem. Using $D = 0.5\%$ we obtain:

State	A	B	C	D	E	F
Modified Quota	22.74	16.14	77.24	29.96	20.84	33.08
Rounded Quota	23	16	77	30	21	33

The final apportionment is the rounded quota value in the table.

50. Aleta: 8; Bonita: 33; Corona: 35; Doritos: 49

JOGGING

51. (a) $q_1 + q_2 + \ldots + q_N$ represents the total number of seats available.

(b) $\dfrac{P_1 + P_2 + \ldots + P_N}{q_1 + q_2 + \ldots + q_N}$ represents the total population divided by the total number of seats available which also happens to be the standard divisor.

(c) $\dfrac{P_N}{P_1 + P_2 + \ldots + P_N}$ represents the percentage of the total population in the Nth state.

52. (a) A: 33; B: 138; C: 4; D: 41; E: 14; F: 20

(b) State D is apportioned 41 seats under Lowndes' method while all of the methods shown in Table 4-21 apportion 42 seats to state D. States C and E do better under Lowndes' method than under Hamilton's method.

53. (a) Take for example $q_1 = 3.9$ and $q_2 = 10.1$ (with $m = 14$). Under both Hamilton's method and Lowndes' method, A gets 4 seats and B gets 10 seats.

(b) Take for example $q_1 = 3.4$ and $q_2 = 10.6$ (with $m = 14$). Under Hamilton's method, A gets 3 seats and B gets 11 seats. Under Lowndes' method, A gets 4 seats and B gets 10 seats.

(c) Assume that $f_1 > f_2$, so under Hamilton's method the surplus seat goes to A. Under Lowndes' method, the surplus seat would go to B if

$$\frac{f_2}{q_2 - f_2} > \frac{f_1}{q_1 - f_1}$$

which can be simplified to

$$f_2(q_1 - f_1) > f_1(q_2 - f_2)$$
$$f_2 q_1 - f_2 f_1 > f_1 q_2 - f_1 f_2$$
$$f_2 q_1 > f_1 q_2$$
$$\frac{q_1}{q_2} > \frac{f_1}{f_2} \text{ since all values are} > 0.$$

54. (a) Since the quotas are not whole numbers the two fractional parts must add up to 1. It follows that, either they are both 0.5, or one is more than 0.5 and the other is less than 0.5.

(b) Since the two fractional parts add up to 1, the surplus to be allocated using Hamilton's method is 1, and it will go to the state with larger fractional part, that is, the state with fractional part more than 0.5. This is the same result that is obtained by just rounding off in the conventional way, which in this case happens to be the result given by Webster's method. (Anytime that rounding off the quotas the conventional way produces integers that add up to *M*, Webster's method reduces to rounding off the standard quotas in the conventional way.)

(c) When there are only 2 states, Hamilton's and Webster's methods agree and Webster's method can never suffer from the Alabama or population paradox, hence neither will Hamilton's method.

(d) When there are only 2 states, Webster's and Hamilton's methods agree and Hamilton's method can never violate the quota rule, hence neither will Webster's method.

55. (a) In Jefferson's method the modified quotas are larger than the standard quotas and so rounding downward will give each state at least the integer part of the standard quota for that state.

(b) In Adam's method the modified quotas are smaller than the standard quota and so rounding upward will give each state at most one more than the integer part of the standard quota for that state.

(c) If there are only two states, an upper quota violation for one state results in a lower quota violation for the other state (and vice versa). Since neither Jefferson's nor Adams' method can have both upper and lower violations of the quota rule, neither can violate the quota rule when there are only two states.

56. (a) State X has received at least one more seat than the standard quota suggested; an upper quota violation.

(b) State X has received at least one fewer seat than the standard quota suggested; a lower quota violation.

(c) The number of seats that state X has received is within 0.5 of its standard quota. Except for the case in which the standard quota has 0.5 as it's decimal part, then number of seats that state X receives is the same as that found by using conventional rounding of the standard quota.

(d) The number of seats that state X has received satisfies the quota rule, but is not the result of conventional rounding of the standard quota.

57. (a) 49,374,462

The standard divisor is given by $\frac{1,262,505}{7.671} \approx 164,581.54$. This means each representative represents (roughly) 164,582 people. Since the number of seats is M = 300, the U.S. population can be estimated as $300 \times 164,581.54 \approx 49,374,462$.

(b) 1,591,833

Since the standard quota for Texas is defined as the population of Texas divided by the standard divisor, it follows that the population of Texas is the product of its standard quota (9.672) and the standard divisor (164,581.54). That is, the population of Texas is $9.672 \times 164,581.54 \approx 1,591,833$.

58. (a) A: 5; B: 10; C: 15; D: 19.

(b) For $D = 100$, the modified quotas are A: 5, B: 10, C: 15, D: 20 which sum to 50 seats. For $D < 100$, each of the modified quotas will increase, so rounding downward will give at least A: 5, B: 10, C: 15, D: 20 for a total of at least 50 seats. But for $D > 100$, each of the modified quotas will decrease, and so rounding downward will give at most A: 4, B: 9, C: 14, D: 19 for a total of 46 at most.

(c) From part (b), we see that there is no divisor such that the sum of the modified upper quotas will be 49.

59. (a) A: 5; B: 10; C: 15; D: 21.
Any modified divisor between approximately 93.8 and 95.2 can be used for this problem. Using $D = 95$ we obtain:

State	A	B	C	D
Modified Quota	5.26	10.53	15.79	21.05
Modified Lower Quota	5	10	15	21

(b) For $D = 100$, the modified quotas are A: 5, B: 10, C: 15, D: 20; which sums to 50 seats. For $D < 100$, each of the modified quotas will increase, so rounding upward will give at least A: 6, B: 11, C: 16, D: 21 for a total of at least 54 seats. But for $D > 100$, each of the modified quotas will decrease, and so rounding upward will give at most A: 5, B: 10, C: 15, D: 20 for a total of 50 at most.

(c) From part (b), we see that there is no divisor such that the sum of the modified upper quotas will be 51.

60. Each state will either receive its upper quota, its lower quota, or, when the standard quota is an integer, its standard quota. Of those states for which the standard quota is not an integer, there are K that receive their lower quota. The remaining states (those with the largest fractional parts) receive their upper quota of seats. The states receiving their upper and lower quotas are the same under Hamilton's method or this alternate version of Hamilton's method.

61. Apportionment #1: Webster's method; Apportionment #2: Adams' method; Apportionment #3: Jefferson's method.
Adams' method favors small states and Jefferson's method favors large states.

RUNNING

62. (a) We use a standard divisor of $D = \dfrac{200,000}{22} \approx 9090.91$. The standard quotas are given below.

State	A	B	C	D
Population	18,000	18,179	40,950	122,871
Standard Quota	1.98	1.9997	4.5045	13.5158

Each state would then receive its lower quota: A: 1; B: 1; C: 4; D: 13. This leads to 3 surplus seats to be divided among the four states. To apportion these surplus seats, we use Jefferson's method. A modified divisor of $D = 40,955$ works to apportion these three surplus seats.

State	A	B	C	D
Population	18,000	18,179	40,950	122,871
Modified Quota $D = 40,955$	0.4395	0.4439	0.9999	3.0001
Lower Quota	0	0	0	3

The final apportionment would have state D receiving the 3 surplus seats: A: 1; B: 1; C: 4; D: 16.

(b) The Hamilton-Jefferson hybrid method can produce apportionments different from Hamilton's method because, as is clear from (a), the quota rule can be violated in the hybrid method.
For the example in (a), the apportionment due to Jefferson's method is: A: 2; B: 2; C: 4; D: 14. This example shows that the Hamilton-Jefferson hybrid method can produce apportionments different from Jefferson's method. The bias towards large states present in Hamilton's method and in Jefferson's method are both being exploited to make this method even more biased towards large states.

(c) The hybrid method can violate the quota rule since more than one surplus seat can be handed out in the second step of the method (the Jefferson step).

63. (a) The standard quotas for the Parador Congress apportionment are given below.

State	A	B	C	D	E	F
Population	1,646,000	6,936,000	154,000	2,091,000	685,000	988,000
Standard Quota	32.92	138.72	3.08	41.82	13.70	19.76

A lottery for the 4 surplus seats would then be held among the 6 states. The number of tickets that each state would have is shown in the table below. To make the number of tickets as small as possible (200), we have divided the decimal parts by 2.

State	A	B	C	D	E	F
Lottery Tickets	46	36	4	41	35	38

(b) The following example shows that the "Hamilton lottery" method and Adams's method can produce different apportionments regardless of the results of the lottery. It consists of a small country having 3 states and 9 seats in the legislature. The standard divisor is then $D = \dfrac{1000}{9} \approx 111.11$.

State	A	B	C
Population	900	50	50
Standard Quota	8.1	0.45	0.45

Using Adams's method gives the following apportionment: A: 7; B: 1; C: 1. It is clear that this is not a possible result regardless of the results of the lottery since A would have at least 8 seats.

(c) The "Hamilton lottery" method can violate the quota rule. However, it will only produce upper quota violations since each state is guaranteed at least its lower quota.

64. (a) The smallest possible value of k is $k=0$. An example is a country having 3 states and 10 seats in the legislature.

State	A	B	C
Population	500	300	200
Standard Quota	5	3	2

(b) The largest possible value of k is $k=N-1$. An example is a country having $N=3$ states and 10 seats in the legislature. There are at most $N-1=2$ surplus seats.

State	A	B	C
Population	300	300	200
Standard Quota	3.75	3.75	2.5

We must have $k<N$ since the number of surplus seats k is the sum of the decimal parts of the standard quotas. Since there are N states and each decimal part must be less than 1, we must have $k<N$.

65. (a) Under Jefferson's method, an increase in the total number of seats to be apportioned results in a decrease in the modified divisor which will result in some of the states gaining seats, but none will lose seats (since all modified quotas will increase).

(b) Under Jefferson's method, the addition of a new state with its fair share of seats may require a new modified divisor. If the modified divisor is increased, some original states may lose seats, but none will gain seats; if the modified divisor is decreased, some original states may gain seats, but none will lose seats.

66. (a) Under Adams' method, an increase in the total number of seats to be apportioned results in a decrease in the modified divisor which will result in some of the states gaining seats, but none will lose seats (since all modified quotas will increase).

(b) Under Adams' method, the addition of a new state with its fair share of seats may require a new modified divisor. If the modified divisor is increased, some original states may lose seats, but none will gain seats; if the modified divisor is decreased, some original states may gain seats, but none will lose seats.

67. (a) Under Webster's method, an increase in the total number of seats to be apportioned results in a decrease in the modified divisor which will result in some of the states gaining seats, but none will lose seats (since all modified quotas will increase).

(b) Under Webster's method, the addition of a new state with its fair share of seats may require a new modified divisor. If the modified divisor is increased, some original states may lose seats, but none will gain seats; if the modified divisor is decreased, some original states may gain seats, but none will lose seats.

Mini-Excursion 1

A.   The Geometric Mean

1. (a) $G = \sqrt{10 \times 100} = \sqrt{1000} = 100$

   (b) $G = \sqrt{20 \times 2000} = \sqrt{40,000} = 200$

   (c) $G = \sqrt{\dfrac{1}{20} \times \dfrac{1}{2000}} = \sqrt{\dfrac{1}{40,000}} = \dfrac{1}{\sqrt{40,000}} = \dfrac{1}{200}$

2. (a) $G = \sqrt{2 \times 8} = \sqrt{16} = 4$

   (b) $G = \sqrt{20 \times 80} = \sqrt{1600} = 40$

   (c) $G = \sqrt{\dfrac{1}{20} \times \dfrac{1}{80}} = \sqrt{\dfrac{1}{1600}} = \dfrac{1}{\sqrt{1600}} = \dfrac{1}{40}$

3. $G = \sqrt{2 \cdot 3^4 \cdot 7^3 \cdot 11 \cdot 2^7 \cdot 7^5 \cdot 11} = \sqrt{2^8 \cdot 3^4 \cdot 7^8 \cdot 11^2} = 2^4 \cdot 3^2 \cdot 7^4 \cdot 11$

4. $G = \sqrt{11^5 \cdot 13^8 \cdot 17^3 \cdot 19 \cdot 11^7 \cdot 17^5 \cdot 19} = \sqrt{11^{12} \cdot 13^8 \cdot 17^8 \cdot 19^2} = 11^6 \cdot 13^4 \cdot 17^4 \cdot 19$

5.   Approximately 18.6%
    To compute the average annual increase in home prices, we first find the geometric mean of 1.117 and 1.259. This is given by $G = \sqrt{1.117 \times 1.259} = \sqrt{1.406303} \approx 1.186$. So, the average annual increase in home prices is approximately 18.6%.

6.   Approximately 9.3%
    To compute the average annual increase in share prices, we first find the geometric mean of 1.0725 and 1.1145. This is given by $G = \sqrt{1.0725 \times 1.1145} = \sqrt{1.19530125} \approx 1.0933$. So, the average annual increase in the shares is approximately 9.3%.

7.

Consecutive integers	Geometric mean (G)	Arithmetic mean (A)	Difference (A-G)
15,16	15.492	15.5	0.008
16,17	16.492	16.5	0.008
17,18	17.493	17.5	0.007
18,19	18.493	18.5	0.007
19,20	19.494	19.5	0.006
29,30	29.496	29.5	0.004
39,40	39.497	39.5	0.003
49,50	49.497	49.5	0.003

8. **(a)** $3.75G$

   If $G = \sqrt{a \cdot b}$, then the geometric mean of $3.75a$ and $3.75b$ is

   $\sqrt{3.75a \cdot 3.75b} = \sqrt{3.75^2 \cdot a \cdot b} = 3.75\sqrt{a \cdot b}$.

   (b) $100G$

   If $G = \sqrt{a \cdot b}$, then the geometric mean of $10a$ and $1000b$ is

   $\sqrt{10a \cdot 1000b} = \sqrt{10000 \cdot a \cdot b} = 100\sqrt{a \cdot b}$.

   (c) $\dfrac{1}{G}$

   If $G = \sqrt{a \cdot b}$, then the geometric mean of $\dfrac{1}{a}$ and $\dfrac{1}{b}$ is $\sqrt{\dfrac{1}{a} \cdot \dfrac{1}{b}} = \sqrt{\dfrac{1}{a \cdot b}} = \dfrac{1}{\sqrt{a \cdot b}}$.

   (d) G^2

   If $G = \sqrt{a \cdot b}$, then the geometric mean of a^2 and b^2 is $\sqrt{a^2 \cdot b^2} = \left(\sqrt{a \cdot b}\right)^2$.

9. **(a)** Since $G = \sqrt{a \cdot b}$, the geometric mean of $k \cdot a$ and $k \cdot b$ is $\sqrt{ka \cdot kb} = k\sqrt{a \cdot b} = kG$.

   (b) Since $G = \sqrt{a \cdot b}$, the geometric mean of $\dfrac{k}{a}$ and $\dfrac{k}{b}$ is $\sqrt{\dfrac{k}{a} \cdot \dfrac{k}{b}} = k\dfrac{1}{\sqrt{a \cdot b}} = \dfrac{k}{G}$.

10. **(a)** If $b = a$, then $A = \dfrac{a+b}{2} = \dfrac{2a}{2} = a$ and $G = \sqrt{a \cdot b} = \sqrt{a \cdot a} = a$ so that $A = a = G$.

(b) We show $G = \sqrt{ab} < \dfrac{a+b}{2} = A$. But, $(a-b)^2 \geq 0$

$\Rightarrow a^2 - 2ab + b^2 \geq 0$

$\Rightarrow a^2 + b^2 \geq 2ab$

$\Rightarrow \dfrac{a^2 + b^2}{4} \geq \dfrac{ab}{2}$

$\Rightarrow \dfrac{a^2 + 2ab + b^2}{4} \geq ab$

$\Rightarrow \left(\dfrac{a+b}{2}\right)^2 \geq ab$

Since a and b are both positive, taking square roots of both sides gives the desired result.

11. **(a)** Since $b > a$ and

$$|AC|^2 - |AB|^2 = \left(\frac{b+a}{2}\right)^2 - \left(\frac{b-a}{2}\right)^2$$

$$= \frac{b^2 + 2ab + a^2 - b^2 + 2ab - a^2}{4}$$

$$= ab$$

the length of BC is given by $\sqrt{ab}$.

(b) Since the length of the legs of a right triangle are always strictly less than the length of the hypotenuse, it follows that $\sqrt{ab} < \dfrac{a+b}{2}$.

B.   The Huntington-Hill Method

12. **(a)** 4

In this case, the cutoff for rounding is given by $G = \sqrt{4 \times 5} = \sqrt{20} \approx 4.472$. Since $q < G$, q is rounded down.

(b) 5

Once again the cutoff for rounding is given by $G = \sqrt{4 \times 5} = \sqrt{20} \approx 4.472$. Since $q > G$, q is rounded up.

(c) 51

The cutoff for rounding is given by $G = \sqrt{50 \times 51} = \sqrt{2550} \approx 50.4975$. Since $q > G$, q is rounded up.

(d) 4

Since $3 < \sqrt{12} < 4$, the cutoff for rounding is given by $G = \sqrt{3 \times 4} = \sqrt{12}$. Since $q > G$, q is rounded up.

13. In this example the Huntington-Hill method produces the same apportionment as Webster's method and in fact, the standard divisor can be used as an appropriate divisor.

State	A	B	C	D	E	Total
Std. Quota	25.26	18.32	2.58	37.16	40.68	124
Geo. Mean (cutoff)	$\sqrt{25 \times 26} \approx$ 25.4951	$\sqrt{18 \times 19} \approx$ 18.4932	$\sqrt{2 \times 3} \approx$ 2.4495	$\sqrt{37 \times 38} \approx$ 37.4967	$\sqrt{40 \times 41} \approx$ 40.4969	
Apportionment	25	18	3	37	41	124

14. (a) *A*: 33; *B*: 138; *C*: 3; *D*: 42; *E*: 14; *F*: 20

   (b) The Huntington-Hill method produces the same apportionments as Webster's method for Parador's Congress.

15. (a) Under Webster's method the standard divisor $D = 10,000$ works!

State	A	B	C	D	E	F	Total
Population	344,970	408,700	219,200	587,210	154,920	285,000	2,000,000
Standard Quota	34.497	40.87	21.92	58.721	15.492	28.5	
Apportionment	34	41	22	59	15	29	200

   (b) Under the Huntington-Hill method the standard divisor does not work! However, a modified divisor of $D = 10,001$ does work.

State	A	B	C	D	E	F	Total
Population	344,970	408,700	219,200	587,210	154,920	285,000	2,000,000
Mod. Quota ($D = 10,001$)	34.494	40.866	21.918	58.715	15.490	28.497	
Geo. Mean	34.496	40.497	21.494	58.498	15.492	28.496	
Apportionment	34	41	22	59	15	29	200

   (c) The apportionments came out the same for both methods.

16. (a) Under Webster's method: The standard divisor (10,000) is too large, but a modified divisor of 9,999 works.

State	A	B	C	D	E	F	Total
Population	344,970	204,950	515,100	84,860	154,960	695,160	2,000,000
Mod. Quota ($D = 9,999$)	34.5005	20.4970	51.5152	8.4868	15.4976	69.5230	
Apportionment	35	20	52	8	15	70	200

(b) Under Huntington-Hill: A modified divisor of 10,001 works.

State	A	B	C	D	E	F	Total
Population	344,970	204,950	515,100	84,860	154,960	695,160	2,000,000
Mod. Quota ($D = 10,001$)	34.494	20.4930	51.5048	8.4852	15.4945	69.5090	
Geo. Mean	34.496	20.4939	51.4976	8.4853	15.4919	69.4982	
Apportionment	34	20	52	8	16	70	200

(c) The apportionments came out different.

17. (a) Under the Huntington-Hill method the standard divisor does not work but a modified divisor of $D = 990$ works!

State	Aleta	Bonita	Corona	Doritos	Total
Population	86,915	4,325	5,400	3,360	100,000
Modified Quota ($D = 990$)	87.793	4.369	5.455	3.394	
Geo. Mean	87.4986	4.4721	5.4772	3.4641	
Apportionment	88	4	5	3	100

(b) The apportionment using the Huntington-Hill method violates the quota rule (an upper quota violation). Aleta has a standard quota of 86.915 and yet receives 88 representatives in the final apportionment.

214

RUNNING

18. Suppose that N is any positive integer. Since the square roots increase at a decreasing rate, we know that $\sqrt{N+1} - \sqrt{N} > \sqrt{N+2} - \sqrt{N+1}$. Squaring both sides tells us that

$$\left(\sqrt{N+1} - \sqrt{N}\right)^2 > \left(\sqrt{N+2} - \sqrt{N+1}\right)^2$$

$$\Rightarrow N+1 - 2\sqrt{N(N+1)} + N > N+2 - 2\sqrt{(N+1)(N+2)} + N+1$$

$$\Rightarrow \frac{(N+1)+N}{2} - \sqrt{N(N+1)} > \frac{(N+2)+(N+1)}{2} - \sqrt{(N+1)(N+2)}$$

That is, the difference between the arithmetic and geometric means of N and $N+1$ is greater than the difference between the arithmetic and geometric means of $N+1$ and $N+2$.

19. If $a < b$, then $\sqrt{a} < \sqrt{b}$. It follows that $-\sqrt{a} > -\sqrt{b}$ and hence $\sqrt{c} - \sqrt{a} > \sqrt{c} - \sqrt{b}$. Squaring both sides yields $\left(\sqrt{c} - \sqrt{a}\right)^2 > \left(\sqrt{c} - \sqrt{b}\right)^2$. Multiplying this out gives $c - 2\sqrt{ac} + a > c - 2\sqrt{bc} + b$. Dividing both sides by 2 and rearranging terms produces the inequality we are seeking: $\frac{a+c}{2} - \sqrt{ac} > \frac{b+c}{2} - \sqrt{bc}$.

20. **(a)** Under the Huntington-Hill method the standard divisor $D = \frac{1215}{\sqrt{2}}$ does not work. The divisor is too small since two of the standard quotas are exactly at the geometric mean (cutoff) and are rounded up.

State	A	B	C	Total
Population	7,290	1,495	1,215	10,000
Standard Quota $\left(D = \frac{1215}{\sqrt{2}}\right)$	$6\sqrt{2}$	$\frac{299}{243}\sqrt{2}$	$\sqrt{2}$	
Geo. Mean	$6\sqrt{2}$	$\sqrt{2}$	$\sqrt{2}$	
Apportionment	9	2	2	13

(b) For any divisor $D > \frac{1215}{\sqrt{2}}$, the divisor is too large since two of the modified quotas are then certainly less than the geometric mean and are rounded down.

State	A	B	C	Total
Population	7,290	1,495	1,215	10,000
Modified Quota $\left(D > \dfrac{1215}{\sqrt{2}}\right)$	$< 6\sqrt{2}$	$< \dfrac{1495}{1215}\sqrt{2}$	$< \sqrt{2}$	
Geo. Mean	$6\sqrt{2}$	$\sqrt{2}$	$\sqrt{2}$	
Apportionment	8	2	1	11

(c) Part (a) shows that any modified divisor $D \leq \dfrac{1215}{\sqrt{2}}$ will not work because it is too small. Part (b) shows that any modified divisor $D > \dfrac{1215}{\sqrt{2}}$ will not work because it would be too large. Hence, the Huntington-Hill method will not work on this problem.

21. (a)

a	b	Q	a	b	Q
1	2	1.581	9	10	9.513
2	3	2.550	19	20	19.506
3	4	3.536	29	30	29.504
4	5	4.528	99	100	99.501
5	6	5.523	10	20	15.811
6	7	6.519	10	90	64.031
7	8	7.517	10	190	134.536
8	9	8.515	10	990	700.071

(b) Since $a < b$, and both a and b are positive, it follows that $a^2 = \dfrac{a^2 + a^2}{2} < \dfrac{a^2 + b^2}{2} < \dfrac{b^2 + b^2}{2} = b^2$.

Thus, taking square roots and using the fact that a and b are positive, $a < \sqrt{\dfrac{a^2 + b^2}{2}} < b$.

(c) $Q = \sqrt{\dfrac{a^2+b^2}{2}} = \sqrt{\left(\dfrac{b-a}{2}\right)^2 + \left(\dfrac{b+a}{2}\right)^2} \geq \sqrt{\left(\dfrac{b+a}{2}\right)^2} = \dfrac{b+a}{2}$ since $a < b$, and both a and b are positive.

22. (a)

a	b	H	a	b	H
1	2	1.333	9	10	9.474
2	3	2.400	19	20	19.487
3	4	3.429	29	30	29.492
4	5	4.444	99	100	99.497
5	6	5.455	10	20	13.333
6	7	6.462	10	90	18.000
7	8	7.467	10	190	19.000
8	9	8.471	10	990	19.800

(b) Since $a < b$, we have $2a < a+b < 2b$. Thus, $\dfrac{1}{b} = \dfrac{2a}{2ab} < \dfrac{a+b}{2ab} < \dfrac{2b}{2ab} = \dfrac{1}{a}$. That is, $\dfrac{1}{b} < \dfrac{1}{H} < \dfrac{1}{a}$. It then follows that $b > H > a$.

(c) First, note that $H = \dfrac{G^2}{A}$ where H is the harmonic mean, G is the geometric mean, and A is the arithmetic mean. From Exercise 10, $A > G$ so that $\dfrac{G}{A} < 1$. Hence, $H = \dfrac{G}{A} \cdot G < G$.

Chapter 5

WALKING

A. Graphs: Basic Concepts

1. (a) Vertex set: V = {A, B, C, X, Y, Z};
Edge set: E = {AX, AY, AZ, BX, BY, BZ, CX, CY, CZ};
deg(A) = 3, deg(B) = 3, deg(C) = 3,
deg(X) = 3, deg(Y) = 3, deg(Z) = 3.

(b) Vertex set: V = {A, B, C};
Edge set: E = { };
deg(A) = 0, deg(B) = 0, deg(C) = 0.

(c) Vertex set: V = {V, W, X, Y, Z};
Edge set: E = {XX, XY, XZ, XV, XW, WY, YZ};
deg (V) = 1, deg (W) = 2, deg(X) = 6,
deg(Y) = 3, deg(Z) = 2.

2. (a) Vertex set: V = {A, B, C, D, E};
Edge set: E = {AB, AC, AD, AE, BC, BD, BE, CD, CE, DE};
deg(A) = 4, deg(B) = 4, deg(C) = 4,
deg(D) = 4, deg(E) = 4.

(b) Vertex set: V = {A, B, C, D, E};
Edge set: E = { };
deg(A) = 0, deg(B) = 0, deg(C) = 0.

(c) Vertex set: V = {G, H, S, T, V, K};
Edge set: E = {GG, GH, HV, HV, SV, SK, KV, TV};
deg (G) = 3, deg (H) = 3, deg(S) = 2,
deg(T) = 1, deg(V) = 5, deg(K) = 2.

3. (a)

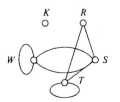

(b)

4. (a)

(b)

5. (a) Both graphs have four vertices A, B, C, and D and (the same) edges AB, AC, AD, BD.

(b)

6. (a) Both graphs have 5 vertices A, B, C, D, E and the same five edges AB, AC, AD, AE, BC.

(b)

7. (a)

(b)

(c)

8. (a)

(b)

(c)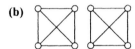

9. (a)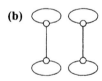

(b)

(c)

(d)

10. (a)

(b)

(c)

(d)

11. (a) *C, B, A, H, F*

    (b) *C, B, D, A, H, F*

    (c) *C, B, A, H, F*

    (d) *C, D, B, A, H, G, G, F*

    (e) 4 (*C, B, A*; *C, D, A*; *C, B, D A*; *C, D, B, A*)

    (f) 3 (*H, F*; *H, G, F*; *H, G, G, F*)

    (g) 12 (Any one of the paths in (e) followed by any one of the paths in (f).)

12. (a) *D, A, H, G, F, E*

    (b) *D, B, A, H, G, G, F, E*

    (c) *D, A, H, F, E*

    (d) *D, C, B, A, H, G, G, F, E*

    (e) 5 (*D, A*; *D, B, A*; *D, B, C, D, A*; *D, C, B, A*; *D, C, B, D, A*)

    (f) 3 (*H, F, E*; *H, G, F, E*; *H, G, G, F, E*)

    (g) 15 (Any one of the paths in (e) followed by *AH* followed by any one of the paths in (f).)

13. Circuits of length 1: *E, E*
    Circuits of length 2: *B*, C, *B*

Circuits of length 3: *A, B, C, A;*
                     A, B, C, A
[There are two edges between *B* and *C*.]
Circuits of length 4: *A, B, E, D, A*
Circuits of length 5: *A, B, E, E, D, A;*
                     A, C, B, E, D, A;
                     A, C, B, E, D, A;
Circuits of length 6: *A, C, B, E, E, D, A;*
                     A, C, B, E, E, D, A;
                     A, B, C, B, E, D, A
Circuits of length 7: *A, B, C, B, E, E, D, A*

14. Circuits of length 2: *A, R, A;*
                     A, L, A;
Circuits of length 3: *A, D, L, A;*
                     A, D, L, A;
                     A, D, R, A;
                     A, D, R, A;
Circuits of length 4: *A, R, A, L, A;*
                     A, R, A, L, A;
                     A, R, A, L, A;
                     A, R, A, L, A;
                     A, R, D, L, A;
                     A, R, D, L, A;
                     A, R, D, L, A;
                     A, R, D, L, A;
Circuits of length 5: *A, R, D, A, L, A;*
                     A, R, D, A, L, A;
                     A, L, D, A, R, A;
                     A, L, D, A, R, A;

B.   Graph Models

15.

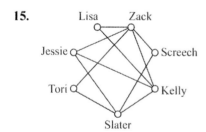

16. (a)

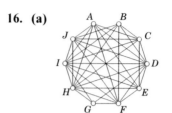

(b)

17.

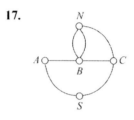

18.

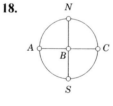

19.

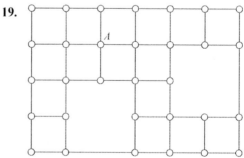

20.

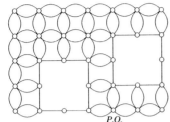

P.O.

C.   Euler's Theorems

21. (a) Has an Euler circuit because all vertices have even degree.

   (b) Has neither an Euler circuit nor an Euler path because there are four vertices of odd degree.

22. (a) Has no Euler circuit, but has an Euler path because there are exactly two vertices of odd degree.

   (b) Has no Euler circuit, but has an Euler path because there are exactly two vertices of odd degree.

23. (a) Has neither an Euler circuit nor an Euler path because there are more than two (10 in fact) vertices of odd degree.

   (b) Has no Euler circuit, but has an Euler path because there are exactly two vertices of odd degree.

   (c) Has neither an Euler circuit nor an Euler path because the graph is not connected.

24. (a) Has an Euler circuit because all vertices have even degree.

   (b) Has no Euler circuit, but has an Euler path because there are exactly two vertices of odd degree.

   (c) Has neither an Euler circuit nor an Euler path because the graph is not connected.

25. (a) Has neither an Euler circuit nor an Euler path because there are eight vertices of odd degree.

   (b) Has no Euler circuit, but has an Euler path because there are exactly two vertices of odd degree.

   (c) Has no Euler circuit, but has an Euler path because there are exactly two vertices of odd degree.

26. (a) Has an Euler circuit because all vertices have even degree.

   (b) Has no Euler circuit, but has an Euler path because there are exactly two vertices of odd degree.

   (c) Has neither an Euler circuit nor an Euler path because there are four vertices of odd degree.

D.   Finding Euler Circuits and Euler Paths

27.

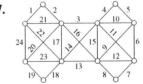

28.

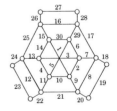

29. There are many possible Euler circuits. One possible circuit is given by:
M, N, G, F, N, K, A, B, C, D, E, F, G, H, I, J, A, J, K, O, D, E, O, L, H, I, L, M, C, B, M

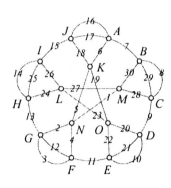

30. There are many possible Euler circuits. One possible circuit is given below.

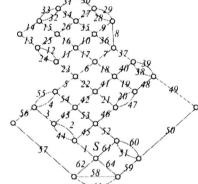

31.

32.

33.

Note that the starting and ending vertices of the Euler path are shown in black.

34.

Note that the starting and ending vertices of the Euler path are shown in black.

35.

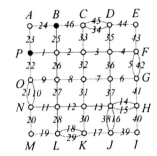

36.

Note that the starting and ending vertices of the Euler path are shown in black.

E.   Unicursal Tracings

37. (a) The drawing has neither because there are more than two vertices of odd degree.

(b) The drawing has an open unicursal tracing. For example,

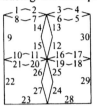

(c) The drawing has an open unicursal tracing. For example,

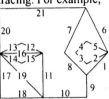

38. (a) There is a closed unicursal tracing. For example,

(b) There is an open unicursal tracing. For example,

39. (a) The drawing has an open unicursal tracing. For example,

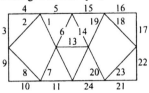

(b) The drawing has an open unicursal tracing. For example,

(c) The drawing has neither an open unicursal tracing nor a closed unicursal tracing because there are more than two vertices of odd degree.

40. (a) There is an open unicursal tracing. For example,

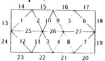

(b) There are no unicursal tracings because there are more than two vertices of odd degree.

(c) There is a closed unicursal tracing. For example,

F.   Eulerizations and Semi-Eulerizations

41. (a)

(b)

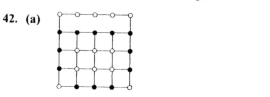

42. (a)

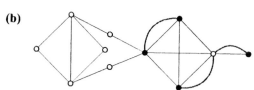

(b)

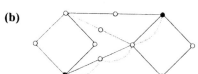

43. (a)

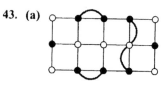

(b)

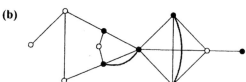

44. (a)

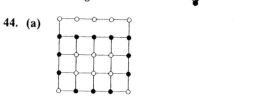

(b)

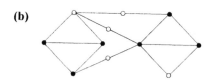

G. Miscellaneous

45. (a) o——o——o——o——o——o

(b)

(c)

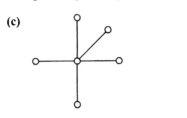

46. None. If a vertex had degree 1, then the edge incident to that vertex would be a bridge.

47. (a)

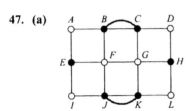

(b) Edges *BC* and *JK* will need to be retraced.

48. One possible optimal semi-eulerization of the graph is

Using this semi-eulerization, edges *CD*, *DH*, *EI*, and *IJ* would be retraced.

49. You would need to lift your pencil 4 times. There are 10 vertices of odd degree. Two can be used as the starting and ending vertices. The remaining eight odd degree vertices can be paired so that each pair forces one lifting of the pencil.

50. (a) Yes. Since each vertex is adjacent to every other vertex, the degree of each vertex is four. By Euler's Circuit Theorem, *G* has an Euler circuit.

(b) No. In this case, the degree of each vertex would be odd (9).

(c) Yes. Each vertex has even degree (998).

51.

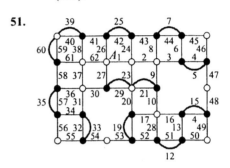

52.

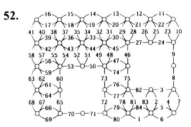

JOGGING

53. (a) An edge *XY* contributes 2 to the sum of the degrees of all vertices (1 to the degree of *X*, and 1 to the degree of *Y*).

(b) If there were an odd number of vertices, the sum of the degrees of all the vertices would be odd.

54. $(k - 2)/2$. Two of the vertices of odd degree can be used as the starting and ending vertices. For the remaining vertices of odd degree the pencil will have to be lifted at least once for every two vertices of odd degree.

55. (a) If each vertex were of odd degree, then the graph has an odd number of odd vertices. This is not possible! So, it must be that each vertex is in fact of even degree. By Euler's Circuit

Theorem, the graph would have an Euler circuit.

(b) The following graph is regular (all vertices are of degree 2) and it has an Euler circuit.

The graph below is also regular (all vertices have degree 3) but it does not have an Euler circuit.

56. (a) If *m* is even, then each of the vertices in the set *B* has even degree. If *n* is even, each vertex in set *A* has even degree. So, if *m* and *n* are both even, every vertex will have even degree and the graph will have an Euler circuit.

(b) In this case, the graph has exactly two odd vertices (those in set *A*). So, the graph will have an Euler path.

57. Recall that in a connected graph, a bridge is an edge such that if we were to erase it, the graph would become disconnected. Also, remember that a connected graph having all even vertices must have an Euler circuit. But if a graph has an Euler circuit, it cannot have a bridge (because then it would be impossible to get from one component of the graph to another and back).

58. The graph model for this problem is shown in the figure, where *N* is the North Bank, *S* is the South Bank, and *A*, *B*, and *C* are the three islands.

Since *N* and *C* are the only vertices of odd degree, this graph has an Euler path (but no

Euler circuit). Thus, it is possible to take a walk and cross each bridge exactly once as long as you start at either *N* or *C* and end at the other one. One possible walking tour (costing $35) is shown in the figure.

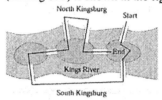

59. (a) 12 (See edges that have been added in part (b).)

(b)

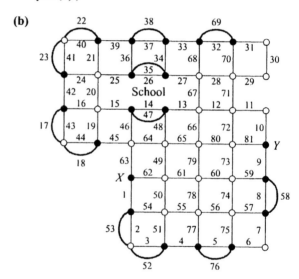

60. (a) Keep adding edges as long as you can without creating any circuits.

(b) *N* – 1 dollars.

61. (a) Make a complete graph with *N* – 1 of the vertices and leave the other vertex as an isolated vertex.

(b) $(N-1)(N-2)/2$ dollars

62. (a) Since vertices *R*, *B*, *D*, and *L* are all odd, two bridges must be crossed twice. For example, crossing the Adams

Bridge twice and the Lincoln Bridge twice produces an optimal route: *D, L, R, L, C, A, R, B, R, B, D, C, L, D.*
Listing the bridges in the order they are crossed: Adams, Washington, Jefferson, Grant, Truman, Lincoln, Lincoln, Hoover, Kennedy, Monroe, Roosevelt, Adams.

(b) In this case, the route must start and end at *L.* One possible optimal route would cross the Lincoln Bridge twice and the Adams Bridge twice: *L, D, L, C, D, B, R, B, R, L, R, A, C, L.*
Listing the bridges in the order they are crossed: Adams, Adams, Roosevelt, Monroe, Kennedy, Hoover, Lincoln, Lincoln, Washington, Jefferson, Truman, Wilson, Grant.

63. (a) Since vertices *R, B, D,* and *L* are all odd, the starting and ending vertices must be selected from this list. Moreover, a route will be optimal if only one bridge needs to be crossed twice. There are many ways to do that. For example, starting at *R* and ending at *B* and crossing the Adams Bridge twice produces an optimal route: *R, L, R, A, C, L, C, D, L, D, B, R, B.*
Listing the bridges in the order they are crossed: Washington, Jefferson, Truman, Wilson, Grant, Roosevelt, Monroe, Adams, Adams, Kennedy, Hoover, Lincoln.

(b) If the route must start at *B* and end at *L,* then one possible optimal route would cross the Lincoln Bridge twice and the Kennedy Bridge twice: *B, R, B, R, L, R, A, C, L, C, D, B, D, L.*
Listing the bridges in the order they are crossed: Hoover, Lincoln, Lincoln, Washington, Jefferson, Truman, Wilson, Grant, Roosevelt, Monroe, Kennedy, Kennedy, Adams.

64. The answer to Euler's question is yes. One of the many possible journeys is given by

crossing the bridges in the following order: *a, b, c, d, e, f, g, h, i, l, m, n, o, p, k.* Note that this journey starts at *E* and ends at *D* which is OK since Euler did not ask that the journey start and end at the same place.

RUNNING

65. The only possible value of *k* is 0. The graph *G* must have an Euler circuit since it is connected and every vertex is even. In a circuit it is possible to get from any vertex to any other vertex two different ways — traveling the circuit forward and backward. Consequently, the removal of a single edge will not disconnect the graph.

66. The possible values of *k* are *k* = 0, 1, 2, 3, ..., *N*-3, and *N*-1. To have *k* = 0 bridges in *G*, place the *N* vertices at the corners of a polygon, connect adjacent corners with an edge and connect one pair of nonadjacent corners.

To have *k* = 1 bridge, attach a single vertex to a graph formed by putting vertices at the corners of a regular *N*-1 polygon.

To have *k* = 2 bridges, consider the following graph formed by attaching two vertices to a graph formed by putting vertices at the corners of a regular *N*-2 polygon. Adding more "single" vertices to the left also explains how to get *k* = 3, 4, ..., *N*-3 bridges.

To get *k* = *N*-1 bridges, consider the following example:

67. **(a)** The following is one possible example.

(b) If a graph has no circuits, then the number of edges (M) is less than the number of vertices (N) (i.e., $M < N$). On the other hand, if the degree of each vertex of a graph is at least 2 then the sum of the degrees of all the vertices is at least $2N$. Since the sum of the degrees of all the vertices equals $2M$, $M = N$. It follows that the graph must have at least one circuit.

If a graph has exactly one circuit, then the number of edges (M) is the same as the number of vertices (N) (i.e., $M = N$). If the degree of each vertex of a graph is at least 2 (with one of them being of degree 3 or higher) then the sum of the degrees of all the vertices is at least $2N+2$. Since the sum of the degrees of all the vertices equals $2M$, $2M \geq 2N+2$ and so $M \geq N+1$. So, the graph cannot have exactly one circuit and must have two or more.

68. Suppose J consists of the graphs G, H, and the additional edge AB joining vertex A of graph G and vertex B of graph H. Since G and H have Euler circuits, all the vertices of G and H have even degree. But in J, since an additional edge joining A and B has been added, A and B will have odd degree. (All the other vertices will remain unchanged and have even degree). Thus J has an Euler path, but no Euler circuit.

69. Each component of the graph is a graph in its own right and so, according to Euler's Theorem 3, the number of vertices of odd degree (in each component) must be even. Therefore the 2 vertices of odd degree must be in the same component.

70. Suppose the graph has N vertices. Since there are no multiple edges or loops, the

maximum degree a vertex can have is $N - 1$. If the degrees of the N vertices are all different, they must be 0, 1, 2, ..., $N - 1$, but this is impossible because the vertex of degree $N - 1$ would have to be adjacent to all the other vertices and then we couldn't have a vertex of degree 0.

71. **(a)** Since N is even, in the complement each vertex will have odd degree. So, the complement cannot have an Euler circuit.

(b) If the graph G is a complete graph, the it will clearly have an Euler circuit (since N is odd so that every vertex has even degree). However, the complement will not since it has no edges.

The following example illustrates how such a graph G and its complement may both have an Euler circuit.

72. **(a)** The circuit kissing A, D, C, A is A, B, D, F, C, E, A. Two circuits that kiss A, B, D, A are C, D, F, C and A, C, E, A.

(b) Consider the complement of C in G. If C is an Euler circuit then the complement is empty. So when C is not an Euler circuit, the complement must contain an edge leading to a vertex in C for otherwise G is not connected. Also, the complement of C has all even vertices. So, the complement has an Euler circuit and that circuit will be one that kisses C.

73. **(a)** There are many ways to implement this algorithm. The following two figures illustrate one possibility.

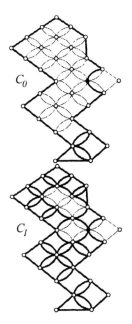

The final circuit would add one more (easy to spot) kissing circuit.

(b) **Step 1:** Find a path C_0 between the two vertices v and w of odd degree.
Step 2: Find a circuit $C_0^{\bullet}$ that kisses C_0 at any vertex that is on C_0. The path and the circuit can be combined into a larger path C_1 between the two odd vertices. If there are no kissing circuits to the larger path, we are done.
Step 3: Repeat Step 2 until an Euler path is found.

Chapter 6

WALKING

A.   Hamilton Circuits and Hamilton Paths

1. **(a)** 1. *A, B, D, C, E, F, G, A*;
            2. *A, D, C, E, B, G, F, A*;
            3. *A, D, B, E, C, F, G, A*

    (b) *A, G, F, E, C, D, B*

    (c) *D, A, G, B, C, E, F*

2. **(a)** 1. *A, F, E, D, C, H, I, J, G, B, A*;
            2. *A, F, E, I, J, G, H, D, C, B, A*;
            3. *A, F, E, I, H, D, C, B, G, J, A*

    (b) *A, F, E, D, C, H, I, J, G, B*

    (c) *F, J, A, B, G, H, C, D, E, I*

3. 1. *A, B, C, D, E, F, G, A*
    2. *A, B, E, D, C, F, G, A*
    3. *A, F, C, D, E, B, G, A*
    4. *A, F, E, D, C, B, G, A*

    Mirror-image circuits:
    5. *A, G, F, E, D, C, B, A*
    6. *A, G, F, C, D, E, B, A*
    7. *A, G, B, E, D, C, F, A*
    8. *A, G, B, C, D, E, F, A*

    The reasons that the above are the only
    Hamilton circuits are as follows. First note
    that edges *CD* and *DE* must be a part of
    every Hamilton circuit and that *CE* cannot
    be a part of any Hamilton circuit.

    There are 2 possibilities at vertex *C*: edge
    BC or edge *CF*. Edge *BC* forces edge *FE*

(otherwise there would be a circuit *E, B, C,
D, E*) and edge *CF* forces edge *EB*.

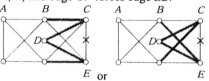

The first of these can be completed in 2
ways giving Hamilton circuits *A, B, C, D, E,
F, G, A* and *A, F, E, D, C, B, G, A* along
with their mirror-image circuits *A, G, F, E,
D, C, B, A* and *A, G, B, C, D, E, F, A*.

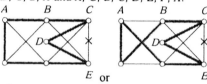

The second of these can also be completed
in 2 ways giving Hamilton circuits *A, B, E,
D, C, F, G, A* and *A, F, C, D, E, B, G, A*
along with their mirror-image circuits *A, G,
B, E, D, C, F, A* and *A, G, F, C, D, E, B, A*.

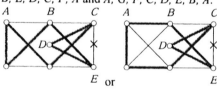

4. 1. *A, B, C, D, E, F, G, A*;
    2. *A, B, E, D, C, F, G, A*;

    Mirror-image circuits:
    3. *A, G, F, E, D, C, B, A*;
    4. *A, G, F, C, D, E, B, A*

    The reasons that the above are the only
    Hamilton circuits are as follows. First note
    that edges *AB* and *BC* must be a part of
    every Hamilton circuit and that *AC* cannot
    be a part of any Hamilton circuit.

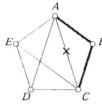

There are 2 possibilities at vertex *A*: edge *AE* or edge *AD*. Each of these alternatives can be completed in only one way.

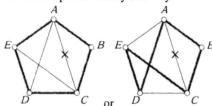

or

5. (a) *A, F, B, C, G, D, E*

   (b) *A, F, B, C, G, D, E, A*

   (c) *A, F, B, E, D, G, C*

   (d) *F, A, B, E, D, C, G*

6. (a) *A, D, G, C, F, B, E*

   (b) *A, D, G, C, F, B, E, A*

   (c) *A, D, E, B, F, C, G*

   (d) *F, B, E, A, D, C, G*

7. (a) 1. *A, B, C, D, E, F, A*
              2. *A, B, E, D, C, F, A*

   Mirror-image circuits:
   3. *A, F, E, D, C, B, A*
   4. *A, F, C, D, E, B, A*

   (b) 1. *D, E, F, A, B, C, D*
              2. *D, C, F, A, B, E, D*

   Mirror-image circuits:
   3. *D, C, B, A, F, E, D*
   4. *D, E, B, A, F, C, D*

(c) The circuits in (b) are the same as the circuits in (a), just rewritten with a different starting vertex.

8. (a) 1. *A, B, C, F, E, D, A;*
              2. *A, D, F, E, B, C, A;*
              3. *A, B, E, D, F, C, A;*

   Mirror-image circuits:
   4. *A, D, E, F, C, B, A;*
   5. *A, C, B, E, F, D, A;*
   6. *A, C, F, D, E, B, A*

   There are 3 possible situations as shown in the following figures.

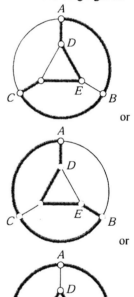

or

or

(b) 1. *D, A, B, C, F, E, D;*
         2. *D, F, E, B, C, A, D;*
         3. *D, F, C, A, B, E, D*
         along with their mirror-images.

(c) The circuits in (b) are the same as the circuits in (a), just rewritten with a different starting vertex.

9. The degree of every vertex in a graph with a Hamilton circuit must be at least 2 since the circuit must "pass through" every vertex. This graph has 2 vertices of degree 1. Any Hamilton path passing through vertex A must contain edge AB. Any path passing through vertex E must contain edge BE. And, any path passing through vertex C must contain edge BC. Consequently, any path passing through vertices A, C, and E must contain at least three edges meeting at B and hence would pass through vertex B more than once. So, this graph does not have any Hamilton paths.

10. The degree of every vertex in a graph with a Hamilton circuit must be at least 2 since the circuit must "pass through" every vertex. This graph does, however, have a Hamilton path. For example, F, B, A, E, C, D, G.

11. (a) $A, I, J, H, B, C, F, E, G, D$

   (b) $G, D, E, F, C, B, A, I, J, H$

   (c) If such a path were to start by heading left, it would not contain C, D, E, F, or G since it would need to pass through B again in order to do so. On the other hand, if a path were to start by heading right, it could not contain $A, I H$, or J.

   (d) Any circuit would need to cross the bridge BC twice (in order to return to where it started). But then B and C would be included twice.

12. (a) D, A, G, F, E, C, B

   (b) B, A, G, F, E, C, D

   (c) Any path passing through vertex B must contain edge AB. Any path passing through vertex D must contain edge AD. Any path passing through vertex G must contain edge AG. Consequently,

any path passing through vertices B, D, and G must contain at least three edges meeting at A and hence would pass through vertex A more than once. So, the path must end at two of these three vertices (since it starts at A) and that is not possible. By symmetry it is clear that there is no Hamilton path that starts at C.

   (d) Any circuit passing through vertex B must contain edge AB. Any circuit passing through vertex D must contain edge AD. Any circuit passing through vertex G must contain edge AG. Consequently, any circuit passing through vertices B, D, and G must contain at least three edges meeting at A and hence would pass through vertex A more than once.

13. (a) 6

   (b) B, D, A, E, C, B
      Weight $= 6 + 1 + 9 + 4 + 7 = 27$

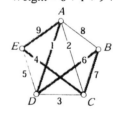

   (c) The mirror image B, C, E, A, D, B
      Weight $= 7 + 4 + 9 + 1 + 6 = 27$

14. (a) 8

   (b) One possible answer: A, D, C, B, E, A
      Weight $= 8 + 1 + 6 + 4 + 3 = 22$

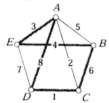

(c) The mirror image *A, E, B, C, D, A*
Weight = 8 + 1 + 6 + 4 + 3 = 22

15. (a) *A, D, F, E, B, C*
Weight = 2 + 7 + 5 + 4 + 11 = 29

(b) *A, B, E, D, F, C*
Weight = 10 + 4 + 3 + 7 + 6 = 30

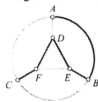

(c) There are only two Hamilton paths that start at *A* and end at *C*. The path *A, D, F, E, B, C* found in part (a) is the optimal such path. It has weight 29.

16. (a) *B, A, E, C, D*
Weight = 3 + 5 + 7 + 4 = 19

(b) *B, A, C, E, D*
Weight = 3 + 9 + 7 + 6 = 25

(c) There are only two Hamilton paths that start at *B* and end at *D*. The path *B, A, E, C, D* found in part (a) is the optimal such path. It has weight 19.

B. Factorials and Complete Graphs

17. (a) $10! = 3,628,800$

(b) $20! = 2,432,902,008,176,640,000$

(c) $\dfrac{20!}{10!} = 670,442,572,800$

18. (a) $15! = 1.307674 \times 10^{12}$

(b) $30! = 2.652528 \times 10^{32}$

(c) $\dfrac{30!}{15!} = 2.028432 \times 10^{20}$

19. (a) $20! = 2,432,902,008,176,640,000$
$\approx 2.43 \times 10^{18}$

(b) $40! \approx 8.16 \times 10^{47}$

(c) $(40-1)! = 39! \approx 2.04 \times 10^{46}$

20. (a) $25! \approx 1.551121 \times 10^{25}$

(b) $50! \approx 3.041409 \times 10^{64}$

(c) $24! \approx 6.204484 \times 10^{23}$

21. (a) $10! = 10 \times 9 \times 8 \times \ldots \times 3 \times 2 \times 1$
$= 10 \times 9!$
So, $9! = \dfrac{10!}{10} = \dfrac{3,628,800}{10} = 362,880$.

(b) $11! = 11 \times 10 \times 9 \times \ldots \times 3 \times 2 \times 1 = 11 \times 10!$
So, $\dfrac{11!}{10!} = \dfrac{11 \times 10!}{10!} = 11$.

(c) $11! = 11 \times 10 \times (9 \times \ldots \times 3 \times 2 \times 1)$
$= 11 \times 10 \times 9!$
So, $\dfrac{11!}{9!} = \dfrac{11 \times 10 \times 9!}{9!} = 11 \times 10 = 110$.

(d) $\dfrac{101!}{99!} = \dfrac{101 \times 100 \times 99!}{99!}$
$= 101 \times 100$
$= 10,100$

22. (a) $20! = 20 \times 19!$ so
$19! = \dfrac{20!}{20}$
$= \dfrac{2,432,902,008,176,640,000}{20}$
$= 121,645,100,408,832,000$

(b) 20

(c) $\dfrac{201!}{199!} = \dfrac{201 \times 200 \times 199!}{199!}$

$= 201 \times 200$

$= 40,200$

23. (a) $\dfrac{9!+11!}{10!} = \dfrac{9!}{10!} + \dfrac{11!}{10!}$

$= \dfrac{9!}{10 \times 9!} + \dfrac{11 \times 10!}{10!}$

$= \dfrac{1}{10} + 11$

$= 11.1$

(b) $\dfrac{101!+99!}{100!} = \dfrac{101!}{100!} + \dfrac{99!}{100!}$

$= \dfrac{101 \times 100!}{100!} + \dfrac{99!}{100 \times 99!}$

$= 101 + \dfrac{1}{100}$

$= 101.01$

24. (a) $\dfrac{19!+21!}{20!} = \dfrac{19!}{20!} + \dfrac{21!}{20!}$

$= \dfrac{19!}{20 \times 19!} + \dfrac{21 \times 20!}{20!}$

$= \dfrac{1}{20} + 21$

$= 21.05$

(b) $\dfrac{201!+199!}{200!} = \dfrac{201!}{200!} + \dfrac{199!}{200!}$

$= \dfrac{201 \times 200!}{200!} + \dfrac{199!}{200 \times 199!}$

$= 201 + \dfrac{1}{200}$

$= 201.005$

25. (a) $\dfrac{20 \times 19}{2} = 190$

(b) K_{21} has 20 more edges than K_{20}.

$\dfrac{21 \times 20}{2} = 210$

(c) If one vertex is added to K_{50} (making for 51 vertices), the new complete graph K_{51} has 50 additional edges (one to each old vertex). In short, K_{51} has 50 more edges than K_{50}. That is, $y - x = 50$.

26. (a) $\dfrac{200 \times 199}{2} = 19,900$

(b) K_{201} has 200 more edges than K_{200}.

$\dfrac{201 \times 200}{2} = 20,100$

(c) 500

27. (a) $120 = 5!$, so $N = 6$.

(b) $45 = \dfrac{9 \times 10}{2}$, so $N = 10$.

(c) $20,100 = \dfrac{200 \times 201}{2}$, so $N = 201$.

28. (a) $720 = 6!$, so $N = 7$.

(b) $66 = \dfrac{11 \times 12}{2}$, so $N = 12$.

(c) $80,200 = \dfrac{400 \times 401}{2}$, so $N = 401$.

C.   Brute Force and Nearest Neighbor Algorithms

29. (a)

Hamilton Circuit (Mirror Image)	Weight
A, B, C, D, A (A, D, C, B, A)	$38 + 22 + 8 + 12 = 80$
A, B, D, C, A (A, C, D, B, A)	$38 + 10 + 8 + 18 = 74$
A, C, B, D, A (A, D, B, C, A)	$18 + 22 + 10 + 12 = 62$

Optimal Hamilton circuit: A, C, B, D, A with cost 62.

(b) A, D, C, B, A; Cost $= 12 + 8 + 22 + 38 + = 80$

(c) B, D, C, A, B; Cost $= 10 + 8 + 18 + 38 = 74$

(d) C, D, B, A, C; Cost $= 8 + 10 + 38 + 18 = 74$

30. (a)

Hamilton Circuit	Weight	Mirror-image Circuit
A, B, C, D, A	$20 + 15 + 50 + 30 = 115$	A, D, C, B, A
A, B, D, C, A	$20 + 10 + 50 + 70 = 150$	A, C, D, B, A
A, C, B, D, A	$70 + 15 + 10 + 30 = 125$	A, D, B, C, A

Optimal Hamilton circuit: A, B, C, D, A with weight $20 + 15 + 50 + 30 = 115$.

(b) A, B, D, C, A
Cost $= 20 + 10 + 50 + 70 = 150$

(c) C, B, D, A, C
Cost $= 15 + 10 + 30 + 70 = 125$

(d) D, B, C, A, D
Cost $= 10 + 15 + 70 + 30 = 125$

31. (a) B, C, A, E, D, B; Cost $= \$121 + \$119 + \$133 + \$199 + \$150 = \$722$

(b) C, A, E, D, B, C; Cost $= \$119 + \$133 + \$199 + \$150 + \$121 = \$722$

(c) D, B, C, A, E, D; Cost $= \$150 + \$121 + \$119 + \$133 + \$199 = \$722$

(d) E, C, A, D, B, E; Cost $= \$120 + \$119 + \$152 + \$150 + \$200 = \$741$

32. (a) A, E, B, C, D, A; Total travel time $= 11 + 13 + 14 + 13 + 12 = 63$ minutes

(b) A, E, B, C, D, A; Total travel time $= 63$ minutes

(c)

Hamilton Circuit	Total Travel Time
A, B, C, E, D, A	$15 + 14 + 23 + 22 + 12 = 86$
A, B, E, C, D, A	$15 + 13 + 23 + 13 + 12 = 76$
A, C, B, E, D, A	$30 + 14 + 13 + 22 + 12 = 91$
A, C, E, B, D, A	$30 + 23 + 13 + 40 + 12 = 118$
A, E, C, B, D, A	$11 + 23 + 14 + 40 + 12 = 100$
A, E, B, C, D, A	$11 + 13 + 14 + 13 + 12 = 63$

Optimal Hamilton circuit: *A, E, B, C, D, A* with total travel time 63.

33. (a) *A, D, E, C, B, A*
Cost of bus trip = $\$8 \times (185 + 302 + 165 + 305 + 500) = \$11{,}656$

(b) *A, D, B, C, E, A*
Cost of bus trip = $\$8 \times (185 + 360 + 305 + 165 + 205) = \$9{,}760$

(c) There are only 6 possible circuits that make *B* the first stop after *A*.

Hamilton Circuit	Cost
A, B, C, D, E, A	$\$8 \times (500 + 305 + 320 + 302 + 205) = \$13{,}056$
A, B, C, E, D, A	$\$8 \times (500 + 305 + 165 + 302 + 185) = \$11{,}656$
A, B, D, C, E, A	$\$8 \times (500 + 360 + 320 + 165 + 205) = \$12{,}400$
A, B, D, E, C, A	$\$8 \times (500 + 360 + 302 + 165 + 200) = \$12{,}216$
A, B, E, C, D, A	$\$8 \times (500 + 340 + 165 + 320 + 185) = \$12{,}080$
A, B, E, D, C, A	$\$8 \times (500 + 340 + 302 + 320 + 200) = \$13{,}296$

Optimal Hamilton circuit starting with *A* and then *B*: *A, B, C, E, D, A*
Cost of bus trip = $\$8 \times (500 + 305 + 165 + 302 + 185) = \$11{,}656$

34. (a) *E, C, I G, M, T, E*
Total Travel Time = $3.1 + 0.8 + 1.1 + 5.7 + 0.6 + 8.1 = 19.4$ years

(b) *T, M, I, C, G, E, T*
Total Travel Time = $8.1 + 0.6 + 4.7 + 0.8 + 1.5 + 3.2 = 18.9$ years
Written with starting vertex *E*, this is *E, T, M, I, C, G, E.*

(c)	**Hamilton Circuit**	**Total Travel Time**
	E, G, I, M, C, T, E	3.2 + 1.1 + 4.7 + 5.2 + 5.6 + 8.1 = 27.9
	E, G, I, M, T, C, E	3.2 + 1.1 + 4.7 + 0.6 + 5.6 + 3.1 = 18.3
	E, G, M, I, C, T, E	3.2 + 5.7 + 4.7 + 0.8 + 5.6 + 8.1 = 28.1
	E, G, M, I, T, C, E	3.2 + 5.7 + 4.7 + 5.1 + 5.6 + 3.1 = 27.4
	E, I, G, M, C, T, E	3.6 + 1.1 + 5.7 + 5.2 + 5.6 + 8.1 = 29.3
	E, I, G, M, T, C, E	3.6 + 1.1 + 5.7 + 0.6 + 5.6 + 3.1 = 19.7
	E, I, M, G, C, T, E	3.6 + 4.7 + 5.7 + 1.5 + 5.6 + 8.1 = 29.2
	E, I, M, G, T, C, E	3.6 + 4.7 + 5.7 + 5.9 + 5.6 + 3.1 = 28.6
	E, M, G, I, C, T, E	8.2 + 5.7 + 1.1 + 0.8 + 5.6 + 8.1 = 29.5
	E, M, G, I, T, C, E	8.2 + 5.7 + 1.1 + 5.1 + 5.6 + 3.1 = 28.8
	E, M, I, G, C, T, E	8.2 + 4.7 + 1.1 + 1.5 + 5.6 + 8.1 = 29.2
	E, M, I, G, T, C, E	8.2 + 4.7 + 1.1 + 5.9 + 5.6 + 3.1 = 28.6

Optimal Hamilton circuit: *E, G, I, M, T, C, E* with total travel time 18.3 years.

35. **(a)** Atlanta, Columbus, Kansas City, Tulsa, Minneapolis, Pierre, Atlanta
Cost of this trip = $0.75 × (533 + 656 + 248 + 695 + 394 + 1361) = $2915.25

   (b) The nearest-neighbor circuit with Kansas City as the starting vertex is Kansas City, Tulsa, Minneapolis, Pierre, Columbus, Atlanta, Kansas City
   Written with starting city Atlanta, the circuit is Atlanta, Kansas City, Tulsa, Minneapolis, Pierre, Columbus, Atlanta
   Cost of this trip = $0.75 × (798 + 248 + 695 + 394 + 1071 + 533) = $2804.25

36. **(a)** Nashville, Louisville, St. Louis, Pittsburgh, Boston, Dallas, Houston, Nashville
Total length = 168 + 263 + 588 + 561 + 1748 + 243 + 769 = 4340 miles

   (b) St. Louis, Houston, Dallas, Boston, Pittsburgh, Nashville, Louisville, St. Louis
   Written with starting city Nashville, this is Nashville, Louisville, St. Louis, Houston, Dallas, Boston, Pittsburgh, Nashville
   Total length = 779 + 243 + 1748 + 561 + 553 + 168 + 263 = 4315 miles

D.   Repetitive Nearest-Neighbor Algorithm

37.

Starting Vertex	Hamilton Circuit	Weight of Circuit
A	A, D, E, B, C, A	2.1 + 1.2 + 2.8 + 2.6 + 2.3 = 11
B	B, A, D, E, C, B	2.2 + 2.1 + 1.2 + 3.1 + 2.6 = 11.2
C	C, D, E, A, B, C	1.4 + 1.2 + 2.4 + 2.2 + 2.6 = 9.8
D	D, E, A, B, C, D	1.2 + 2.4 + 2.2 + 2.6 + 1.4 = 9.8
E	E, D, C, A, B, E	1.2 + 1.4 + 2.3 + 2.2 + 2.8 = 9.9

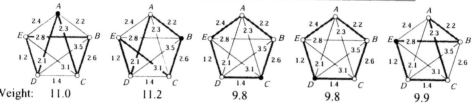

Weight: 11.0   11.2   9.8   9.8   9.9

Starting with vertex *B*, the shortest circuit is *B, C, D, E, A, B* or *B, C, D, E, A, B* with weight 9.8.

38.

Starting Vertex	Hamilton Circuit	Length of Circuit
A	A, F, E, B, D, C, A	8 + 12 + 10 + 18 + 19 + 13 = 80
B	B, E, F, A, C, D, B	10 + 12 + 8 + 13 + 19 + 18 = 80
C	C, A, F, E, B, D, C	13 + 8 + 12 + 10 + 18 + 19 = 80
D	D, A, F, E, B, C, D	17 + 8 + 12 + 10 + 14 + 19 = 80
E	E, F, A, C, B, D, E	12 + 8 + 13 + 14 + 18 + 32 = 80
F	F, A, C, B, E, D, F	8 + 13 + 14 + 10 + 32 + 21 = 98

Any of the first five Hamilton circuits above are the shortest circuit that can be found using the repetitive nearest-neighbor algorithm.

39.

Starting Vertex	Hamilton Circuit	Length of Circuit (Miles)
A	A, D, B, C, E, A	185 + 360 + 305 + 165 + 205 = 1220
B	B, C, E, A, D, B	305 + 165 + 205 + 185 + 360 = 1220
C	C, E, A, D, B, C	165 + 205 + 185 + 360 + 305 = 1220
D	D, A, C, E, B, D	185 + 200 + 165 + 340 + 360 = 1250
E	E, C, A, D, B, E	165 + 200 + 185 + 360 + 340 = 1250

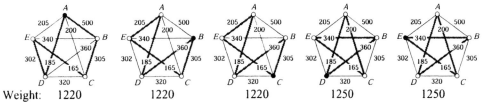

Weight: 1220   1220   1220   1250   1250

The shortest circuit (written as starting and ending at *A*) is *A, D, B, C, E, A* with length 1220. The cost of this bus trip is $8 × 1220 = $9,760.

40.

Starting Vertex	Hamilton Circuit	Length of Circuit (Years)
E	E, C, I, G, M, T, E	3.1 + 0.8 + 1.1 + 5.7 + 0.6 + 8.1 = 19.4
G	G, I, C, E, T, M, G	1.1 + 0.8 + 3.1 + 8.1 + 0.6 + 5.7 = 19.4
C	C, I, G, E, T, M, C	0.8 + 1.1 + 3.2 + 8.1 + 0.6 + 5.2 = 19
I	I, C, G, E, T, M, I	0.8 + 1.5 + 3.2 + 8.1 + 0.6 + 4.7 = 18.9
M	M, T, I, C, G, E, M	0.6 + 5.1 + 0.8 + 1.5 + 3.2 + 8.2 = 19.4
T	T, M, I, C, G, E, T	0.6 + 4.7 + 0.8 + 1.5 + 3.2 + 8.1 = 18.9

The shortest circuit is *I, C, G, E, T, M, I* or *T, M, I, C, G, E, T*. Written starting with Earth, this circuit is *E, T, M, I, C, G, E* and has a length of 18.9 years.

41.

Starting Vertex	Hamilton Circuit	Length of Circuit (Miles)
A	A, C, K, T, M, P, A	533 + 656 + 248 + 695 + 394 + 1361 = 3887
C	C, A, T, K, M, P, C	533 + 772 + 248 + 447 + 394 + 1071 = 3465
K	K, T, M, P, C, A, K	248 + 695 + 394 + 1071 + 533 + 798 = 3739
M	M, P, K, T, A, C, M	394 + 592 + 248 + 772 + 533 + 713 = 3252
P	P, M, K, T, A, C, P	394 + 447 + 248 + 772 + 533 + 1071 = 3465
T	T, K, M, P, C, A, T	248 + 447 + 394 + 1071 + 533 + 772 = 3465

The shortest circuit is *M, P, K, T, A, C, M*. Written starting from Atlanta, this is Atlanta, Columbus, Minneapolis, Pierre, Kansas City, Tulsa, Atlanta and has a length of 3252 miles.

42.	Starting Vertex	Hamilton Circuit	Length of Circuit (Miles)
	B	*B, P, L, N, S, D, H, B*	4093
	P	*P, L, N, S, D, H, B, P*	4093
	L	*L, N, S, P, B, D, H, L*	4535
	N	*N, L, S, P, B, D, H, N*	4340
	S	*S, L, N, P, B, D, H, S*	4315
	D	*D, H, N, L, S, P, B, D*	4340
	H	*H, D, S, L, N, P, B, H*	4222

The shortest circuit is *B, P, L, N, S, D, H, B*. Written starting from Nashville, this is Nashville, St. Louis, Dallas, Houston, Boston, Pittsburgh, Louisville, Nashville and has a length of 4093 miles.

E.   Cheapest-Link Algorithm

43. The successive steps are shown in the following figures.

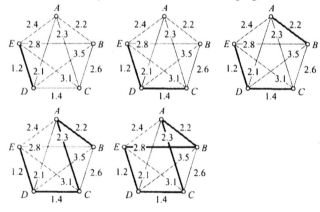

After the fourth step, the next cheapest edge is 2.4. Since this edge makes a circuit, we skip this edge and try the next cheapest edge. The next cheapest edge is 2.6 but that makes three edges come together at vertex *C* so we skip this edge and choose the next cheapest edge which is 2.8. This edge completes the Hamilton circuit. The shortest Hamilton circuit found using this algorithm is *B, E, D, C, A, B*. The weight of this circuit is 1.2 + 1.4 + 2.2 + 2.3 + 2.8 = 9.9.

44. The successive steps are shown in the following figures. The Hamilton circuit obtained by the cheapest-link algorithm is *B, D, C, A,* F, *E, B.*

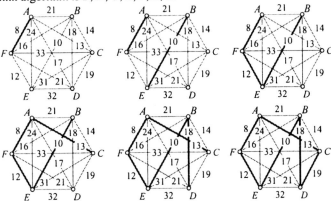

45. The successive steps are shown in the following figures. The shortest Hamilton circuit found using this algorithm is *B, E, C, A, D, B.* The cost of this bus trip is $8 × (165 + 185 + 200 + 340 + 360) = $10,000.

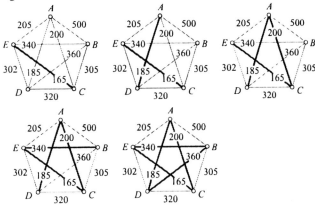

46. The successive steps are shown in the following figures. The shortest Hamilton circuit found using this algorithm is *E, C, I, G, M, T, E* . Total Travel Time = 3.1 + 0.8 + 1.1 + 5.7 + 0.6 + 8.1 = 19.4 years.

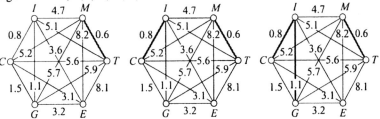

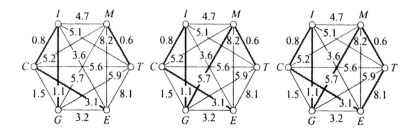

47.

Link Added to Circuit	Cost of Link (Miles)
Kansas City - Tulsa	248
Pierre - Minneapolis	394
Minneapolis - Kansas City	447
Atlanta - Columbus	533
Atlanta - Tulsa	772
Columbus - Pierre	1071

The circuit is Atlanta, Columbus, Pierre, Minneapolis, Kansas City, Tulsa, Atlanta.
Total mileage = 248 + 394 + 447 + 533 + 772 + 1071 = 3465 miles.

48.

Link Added to Circuit	Cost of Link (Miles)
Nashville - Louisville	168
Dallas - Houston	243
Louisville – St. Louis	263
Pittsburgh - Nashville	553
Boston - Pittsburgh	561
St. Louis - Dallas	630
Houston - Boston	1804

The circuit is Nashville, Louisville, St. Louis, Dallas, Houston, Boston, Pittsburgh, Nashville.
Total mileage = 168 + 243 + 263 + 553 + 561 + 630 + 1804 = 4222 miles.

F. Miscellaneous

49. (a) *A, B, C, D, E, A*; Weight = 1 + 1 + 1 + 1 + 100 = 104

(b) *A, B, C, D, E, A*; Weight = 1 + 1 + 1 + 1 + 100 = 104

(c) *A, C, D, E, B, A*; Weight = 2 + 1 + 1 + 2 + 1 = 7

50. (a) Joe needs to find $\frac{30 \times 29}{2} = 435$ fares. This will take 4,350 minutes or 72.5 hours.

(b) Even using the SUPERHERO computer, it will take 284 million years to find the cheapest possible tour.

51. (a)

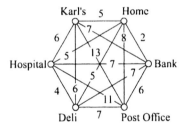

(b) Just "eyeballing it" will give the optimal circuit in this case. It is: Home, Bank, Post Office, Deli, Hospital, Karl's , Home. The total length of the trip is 2 + 6 + 7 + 4 + 6 + 5 = 30 miles.

52. (a)

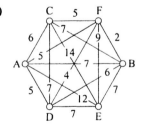

(b) *F, B, E, D, A, C, F*. The total length of the trip is 32 miles.

53. (a)

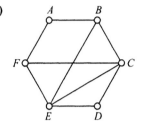

(b) Any Hamilton circuit gives a possible seating arrangement. One possibility is *A, B, C, D, E, F*.

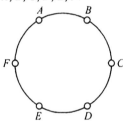

Seating Arrangement

(c) Yes, there is. It corresponds to the Hamilton circuit *A, B, E, D, C, F, A*.

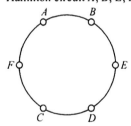

Seating Arrangement

54. (a)

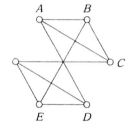

(b) One possibility based on the Hamilton circuit *A, B, C, F, E, D, A* is shown below.

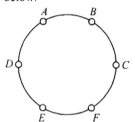

Seating Arrangement

(c) Yes, there is.

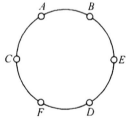

Seating Arrangement

55. If we draw the graph describing the friendships among the guests (see figure) we can see that the graph does not have a Hamilton circuit, which means it is impossible to seat everyone around the table

with friends on both sides.

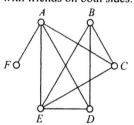

56. The graph describing the friendships among the guests (see figure) does not have a Hamilton circuit. This follows from the observation that the three people with just 2 friends (*B, D,* and *E*) all share one friend (*C*). Thus, it is impossible to seat everyone around the table with friends on both sides.

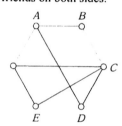

JOGGING

57.

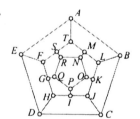

58.

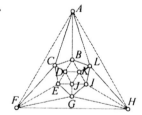

59. *A, B, C, D, J, I, F, G, E, H*

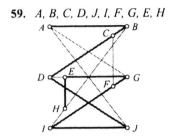

60. (a) One example is:
$I, B_1, C_2, B_2, C_3, B_3, C_4, B_4, C_1$.

(b) One example is:
$C_1, B_1, C_2, B_2, I, B_4, C_4, B_3, C_3$.

(c) One example is:
$C_1, B_4, C_4, B_3, C_3, B_2, C_2, B_1, I$.

(d) Suppose we color the vertices of the grid graph with two colors [say black (B) and white (W)] with adjacent vertices having different colors (see figure). Since there are 5 black vertices and 4 white vertices and in any Hamilton path the vertices must alternate color, the only possible Hamilton paths are of the form $B, W, B, W, B, W, B, W, B$. Since every boundary vertex is white, it is impossible to end a Hamilton path on a boundary vertex.

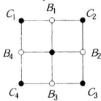

61. The 2 by 2 grid graph cannot have a Hamilton circuit because each of the 4 corner vertices as well as the interior vertex I must be preceded and followed by a boundary vertex. But there are only 4 boundary vertices–not enough to go around.

62. (a) $C_1, B_8, B_7, C_4, B_6, I_3, I_1, I_2, I_4,$
$B_5, C_3, B_4, B_3, C_2, B_2, B_1, C_1$

(b) $C_1, B_8, B_7, C_4, B_6, I_3, I_1, B_1,$
$B_2, I_2, I_4, B_5, C_3, B_4, B_3, C_2$

(c) $C_1, B_8, B_7, C_4, B_6, I_3, I_4, B_5,$
$C_3, B_4, B_3, C_2, B_2, B_1, I_1, I_2$

(d) Suppose that X and Y are any 2 adjacent vertices of the 3-by-3 grid graph. If we pick a Hamilton circuit that contains the edge XY and remove that edge we get a Hamilton path that has X and Y as its endpoints. The fact that such a Hamilton circuit exists follows from the figures below, since the two Hamilton circuits shown cover between them every edge of the graph at least once.

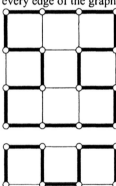

63. (a)

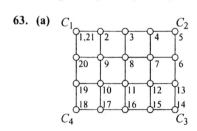

(b)

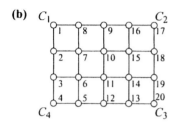

(c) Think of the vertices of the graph as being colored like a checker board with C_1 being a red vertex. Then each time we move from one vertex to the next we must move from a red vertex to a black vertex or from a black vertex to a red vertex. Since there are 10 red vertices and 10 black vertices and we are starting with a red vertex, we must end at a black vertex. But C_2 is a red vertex. Therefore, no such Hamilton path is possible.

64. Suppose the cheapest edge in a graph is the edge joining vertices X and Y. Using the nearest neighbor algorithm we will eventually visit one of these vertices— suppose the first one of these vertices we visit is X. Then, since edge XY is the cheapest edge in the graph and since we have not yet visited vertex Y, the nearest neighbor algorithm will take us to Y.

65.

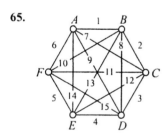

The optimal Hamilton circuit is A, B, C, D, E, F, A. The edges in this circuit are the edges with the 6 lowest weights.

66. (a)

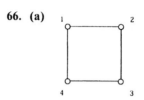

(b)

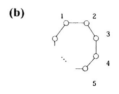

67. (a) Any circuit would need to cross the bridge twice (in order to return to where it started). But then each vertex at the end of the bridge would be included twice.

(b)

$$A \!\!\!\!\! \begin{array}{ccc} & B & C & D \\ & & & \\ E & & & H \\ & F & G & \end{array}$$

68. $21! = 21 \times 20 \times 19 \times \ldots \times 11 \times 10!$
$> 10 \times 10 \times 10 \times \ldots \times 10!$
$= 10^{11} \times 10!$

69. Dallas, Houston, Memphis, Louisville, Columbus, Chicago, Kansas City, Denver, Atlanta, Buffalo, Boston, Dallas.

The process starts by finding the smallest number in the Dallas row. This is 243 miles to Houston. We cross out the Dallas column and proceed by finding the smallest number in the Houston row (other than that representing Dallas which has been crossed out). This is 561 miles to Memphis. We now cross out the Houston column and continue by finding the smallest number in the Memphis row (other than those representing Dallas and Houston which have been crossed out). The process continues in this fashion until all cities have been reached.

70. Dallas, Houston, Denver, Boston, Buffalo, Columbus, Louisville, Chicago, Atlanta, Memphis, Kansas City, Dallas.

71. **(a)** Julie should fly to Detroit. The optimal route will then be to drive $68 + 56 + 68 + 233 + 78 + 164 + 67 + 55 = 789$ miles: Detroit-Flint-Lansing-Grand Rapids-Cheboygan-Sault Ste. Marie-Marquette-Escanaba-Menominee for a total cost of $789 \times (\$0.39) + \$2.50 = \$310.21$. Since Julie can drive from Menominee back to Detroit (via Sault Ste. Marie) in a matter of $227 + 78 + 280 = 585$ miles at a cost of $585 \times (\$0.39) + \$2.50 = \$230.65$, she should do so and drop the rental car back in Detroit (assuming she need not pay extra for gas!). The total cost of her trip would then be $\$310.21 + \$230.65 = \$540.86$.

(b) The optimal route would be for Julie to fly to Detroit and drive $68 + 56 + 68 + 233 + 78 + 164 + 67 + 55 = 789$ miles along the Hamilton path Detroit-Flint-Lansing-Grand Rapids-Cheboygan-Sault Ste. Marie-Marquette-Escanaba-Menominee for a total cost of $789 \times (\$0.49) + \$2.50 = \$389.11$.

RUNNING

72. **(a)** The complete graph on N vertices consists of $N(N-1)/2$ edges. If G has k edges, the number of edges in the complement is $N(N-1)/2 - k$.

(b) For $N = 4$, a Hamilton circuit would need 4 edges. By part (a), the complement would then have $6 - 4 = 2$ edges. So, the complement cannot have a Hamilton circuit.

(c) If $N \geq 5$, then $(N-1)/2 \geq 2$ so that $N(N-1)/2 \geq 2N$ so that both the graph and the complement of the graph could potentially have Hamilton circuits. Define a graph G with vertex set V =

$\{a_1, a_2, a_3, \ldots a_n\}$ and edge set E = $\{a_1 a_2, a_2 a_3, a_3 a_4, \ldots, a_{n-1} a_n, a_n a_1\}$. Then G clearly has a Hamilton circuit. If N is odd, the complement clearly has a Hamilton circuit $a_1 a_3, a_2 a_4, a_3 a_5, \ldots, a_{n-3} a_n, a_{n-2} a_1, a_{n-1} a_2$. If N is even, the complement also has a Hamilton circuit by Dirac's theorem.

73. **(a)** If $a_1, a_2, a_3, \ldots a_n$ are the vertices in set A and $b_1, b_2, b_3, \ldots b_n$ are the vertices in set B, then one possible Hamilton circuit is $a_1, b_1, a_2, b_2, \ldots a_n, b_n, a_1$.

(b) Suppose $a_1, a_2, a_3, \ldots a_n$ are the vertices in set A and $b_1, b_2, b_3, \ldots b_{n+1}$ are the vertices in set B, then one possible Hamilton path is $b_1, a_1, b_2, a_2, \ldots b_n, a_n, b_{n+1}$.

(c) If $a_1, a_2, a_3, \ldots a_m$ are the vertices in set A and $b_1, b_2, b_3, \ldots b_n$ are the vertices in set B, then in any Hamilton path the a's and b's must alternate. This implies that either (i) there is the same number of a's and b's ($m = n$); (ii) there is one more of the a's than there is of the b's ($m = n + 1$); or (iii) there is one more of the b's than there is of the a's ($n = m + 1$). There are no other possibilities.

74. **(a) & (b)**

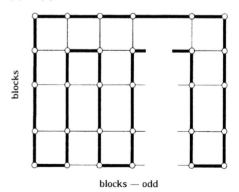

blocks — odd

(c) Using the ideas of Exercise 60(d), we can color the vertices of the grid graph with two colors (black and white) so that adjacent vertices have different colors. This implies that any circuit in this graph must consist of vertices of alternating colors and have the same number of vertices of each color. This, of course, implies that the circuits in this graph must have an even number of vertices. An m-by-n grid graph has a total of $(m+1) \times (n+1)$ vertices. If m and n are both even then the number of vertices in the graph is odd and it follows that the graph cannot have a Hamilton circuit.

75. (a) *A, E, D, C, B, G, I, F, H, J*

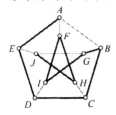

(b) Suppose $\mathcal{H}$ is a Hamilton circuit in the Petersen graph. At least one of the edges of the outside pentagon *ABCDE* must be "out" (by that we mean it cannot be in $\mathcal{H}$).

Let's suppose *AB* is "out". (It is clear by the symmetry of the graph that we could have picked *BC, CD, DE,* or *EA* just as well.) If *AB* is "out", then *EA* and *AF* must be "in" (they are the only two other ways to get in and out of *A*). Likewise, *CB* and *GB* must be "in". Now either *DC* or *DE* (or both) must be be "in"). Suppose *DE* is "in".

Then *GI* must be "out" and we must have *DI* and *IF* "in". This is impossible since then $\mathcal{H}$ would have the subcircuit *A, E, D, I, F, A.*

Mini-Excursion 2

WALKING

A.   Graph Colorings and Chromatic Numbers

1. **(a)**   Many answers are possible.

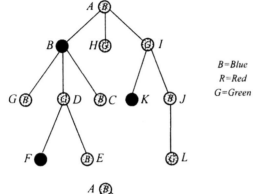

B=Blue
R=Red
G=Green

(b)

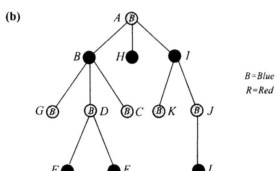

B=Blue
R=Red

(c) $\chi(G) = 2$.   At least 2 colors are needed and (b) shows that G can be colored with 2 colors.

2. **(a)**   Many answers are possible.

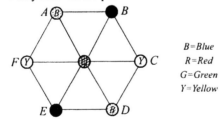

B=Blue
R=Red
G=Green
Y=Yellow

(b)

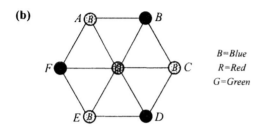

B=Blue
R=Red
G=Green

(c) $\chi(G) = 3$. At least 3 colors are needed because the graph has triangles, and (b) shows that G can be colored with 3 colors.

3. (a) Many answers are possible.

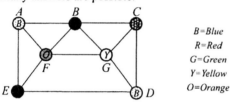

B=Blue
R=Red
G=Green
Y=Yellow
O=Orange

(b)

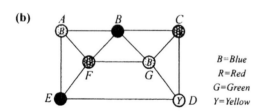

B=Blue
R=Red
G=Green
Y=Yellow

(c) $\chi(G) = 4$. The graph cannot be colored with 3 colors. If we try to color G with 3 colors and start with a triangle, say *AEF*, and color it blue, red, green, then B is forced to be red, G is forced to be blue, C is forced to be green, and then D will require a fourth color.

4. (a)

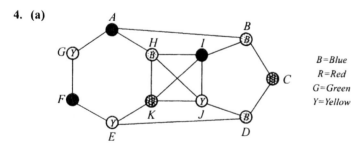

B=Blue
R=Red
G=Green
Y=Yellow

(b) $\chi(G) = 4$. Four colors are needed to color the vertices H, I, J, and K because they are adjacent to each other.

5. (a)

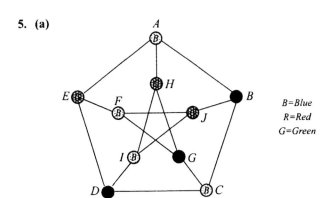

B=Blue
R=Red
G=Green

(b) $\chi(G) = 3$. Three colors are needed because A, B, C, D, and E form a circuit of length 5.

6. (a)

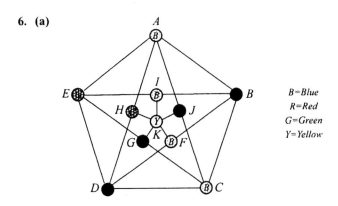

B=Blue
R=Red
G=Green
Y=Yellow

(b) $\chi(G) = 4$. First color A, B, C, D, and E. Three colors are needed. Say A is blue, B red, C blue, D red and E green. This forces G to be red, H to be green, I to be blue. This forces K (the center of the spokes) to be a fourth color.

7. (a) Every vertex of K_n is adjacent to every other vertex, so every vertex has to be colored with a different color.

(b) $\chi(G) = n-1$. If we remove one edge from K_n, then there are two vertices that are not adjacent. They can be colored with the same color (say blue). The remaining vertices have to be colored with different colors other than blue.

8. If a graph has an edge, then two colors are needed just to color the two vertices joined by the edge. It follows that if $\chi(G) = 1$ then G has no edges.

9. (a) Adjacent vertices around the circuit can alternate colors (blue, red, blue, red, …).

(b) To color an odd circuit we start by alternating two colors (blue, red, blue, red,…), but when we get to the last vertex, it is adjacent to both a blue and a red vertex, so a third color is needed.

10. If n is even ($n \geq 4$) then $\chi(W_n) = 4$; if n is odd ($n \geq 5$) then $\chi(W_n) = 3$.

If n is even ($n \geq 4$), the "outer circuit" $v_1 v_2 v_3, ..., v_{n-1}$ is an odd circuit and it will require a minimum of 3 colors. The "center" of the wheel (v_0) is adjacent to all the other vertices, so it will require a fourth color. If n is odd ($n \geq 5$), then $v_1 v_2 v_3, ..., v_{n-1}$ is an even circuit and can be colored with just 2 colors. The center v_0 will require a third color.

11. $\chi(G) = 2$.

Since a tree has no circuits, we can start with any vertex v, color it blue and alternate blue, red, blue, red, blue, ... along any path of the tree. Every vertex of the tree is in a unique path joining it to v and can be colored either red or blue.

12. Start with triangle *AGF* (a similar explanation would work if you start with any other triangle). Use any three colors to color *A*, *F*, and *G*. Let's say we choose red (*A*), blue (*F*), and green (*G*). This coloring forces the color of all the other vertices of the graph: first *E* has to be red, then *C* has to be blue, then *D* has to be green, then *B* has to be red, and finally *H* has to be green. This means that any other coloring will have to be equivalent (same pattern, different colors) to the one shown in the figure below.

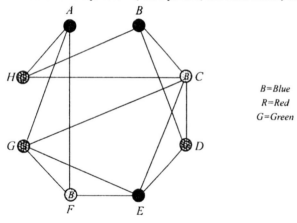

B=Blue
R=Red
G=Green

B. Map Coloring

13. Answers may vary. One possible answer is shown below.

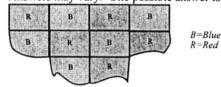

B=Blue
R=Red

14. Many answers are possible. One possible answer is shown below.

B=Blue
R=Red
G=Green
Y=Yellow

15. (a) & (b)

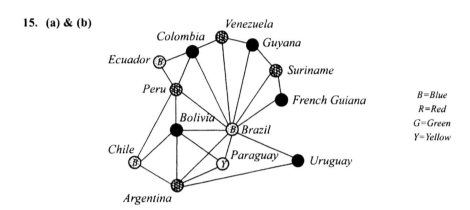

B=Blue
R=Red
G=Green
Y=Yellow

List of vertices (by decreasing order of degrees): Brazil (10), Bolivia (5), Argentina (5), Peru (5), Columbia (4), Chile (3), Paraguay (3), Venezuela (3), Guyana (3), Suriname (3), Ecuador (2), French Guiana (2), Uruguay (2).

Priority list of colors: Blue, Red, Green, Yellow.

(c) The chromatic number is 4 since Brazil, Bolivia, Argentina and Paraguay are all adjacent to each other.

16. Many maps are available showing the lower 48 states colored with 4 colors.

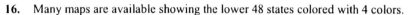

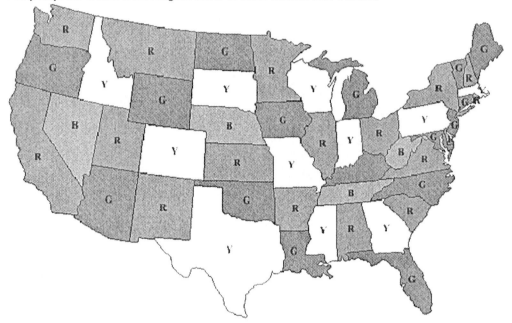

To show that it cannot be done with 3 colors, consider the subgraph of the dual graph formed by California, Oregon, Idaho, Utah, Arizona, and Nevada (see below). This graph is W_6, the "wheel" with 6 vertices (see Exercise 10), and requires 4 colors.

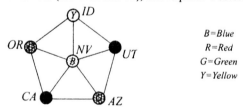

B=Blue
R=Red
G=Green
Y=Yellow

C.   Miscellaneous

17. (a) All the vertices in A can be colored with the same color, and all of the vertices in B can be colored with a second color.

(b) Suppose G has $\chi(G) = 2$. Say the vertices are colored blue and red. Then let A denote the set of blue vertices and B the set of red vertices.

(c) If G had a circuit with an odd number of vertices then that circuit alone would require 3 color (see Exercise 9). But from (a) we know that $\chi(G) = 2$.

18. **(a)** The sum of the degrees of all the vertices in a graph must be even (see Euler's Sum of Degrees theorem in Chapter 5), so if every vertex has degree 3, n must be even. If $n = 2$, it is impossible for a vertex to have degree 3 unless there are multiple edges.

    (b) From Brook's theorem, $\chi(G) \leq 4$.

    (c) From the strong version of Brook's theorem $\chi(G) = 4$ if G is complete (in which case $G = K_4$) or if G is disconnected (in which case it consists of several copies of K_4). The figure shows an example of a 3-regular graph G having $\chi(G) = 4$.

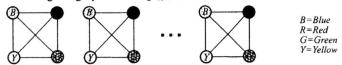

$$B = Blue$$
$$R = Red$$
$$G = Green$$
$$Y = Yellow$$

19. **(a)** Since the sum of the degrees of all the vertices must be even (see Euler's Sum of Degrees theorem in Chapter 5), it follows that the number of vertices of degree 3 must be even, and thus, n must be odd. If $n = 3$, there can be no vertices of degree 3 unless there are multiple edges.

    (b) From the strong version of Brook's theorem we have $\chi(G) \leq 3$. We know $\chi(G)$ cannot be 1 (see Exercise 8). Moreover, G cannot be a bipartite graph (see next paragraph), so $\chi(G)$ cannot be 2 (see Exercise 17). It follows that $\chi(G) = 3$.

    A graph with n-1 vertices of degree 3 and one vertex of degree 2 cannot be bipartite because the vertex of degree 2 must be in one of the two parts, say A. Then the number of edges coming out of A is 2 plus a multiple of 3. On the other hand, the number of edges coming out of B is a multiple of 3. But in a bipartite graph the number of edges coming out of part A must equal the number of edges coming out of part B (they are both equal to the total number of edges in the graph).

20. The vertices listed in decreasing order of degrees are $H(4)$, $G(4)$, $C(3)$, $I(3)$, $D(2)$, $E(2)$, $A(2)$, $F(2)$, $B(2)$, $J(2)$. (There are many other ways to order the vertices by decreasing order of degrees, but a similar explanation will apply in all cases.) Using the greedy algorithm, H is colored with Color 1 and then G must be colored with Color 2. After that, C gets Color 1, I gets Color 2, D gets Color 1, E gets Color 2, A gets Color 2, F gets Color 1, B gets Color 1, J gets Color 2.

21. Suppose that the graph G is colored with $\chi(G)$ colors: Color 1, Color 2, ..., Color K (for simplicity we will use K for $\chi(G)$). Now make a list $v_1, v_2, \ldots, v_n$ of the vertices of the graph as follows: All the vertices of Color 1 (in any order) are listed first (call these vertices Group 1), the vertices of Color 2 are listed next (call these vertices Group 2), and so on, with the vertices of Color K listed last (Group K). Now when we apply the greedy algorithm to this particular list, the vertices in Group 1 get Color 1, the vertices in Group 2 get either Color 1 or Color 2, the vertices in Group 3 get either Color 1, or Color 2, or at worst, Color 3, and so on. The vertices in Group K get Color 1, or 2, ..., or at worst, Color K. It follows that the greedy algorithm gives us an optimal coloring of the graph.

22. Each cell in a Sudoku grid shares a row with 8 other cells, a column with an additional 8 cells, and a box with 8 cells, but 2 of these are in the same row (so we already counted them), and 2 more are in the same column. Thus, there are only 4 additional cells in the box that do not share a row or a column with our

cell. This means that the degree of every vertex of the Sudoku graph is $8 + 8 + 4 = 20$. The graph has 81 vertices of degree 20, giving a total of $81 \times 20 / 2 = 810$ edges.

23. The solution appears in Mini-Excursion 2 after the References and Further Readings.

Chapter 7

A.   Trees

1. **(a)** Is a tree.

    (b) Is not a tree (is not connected).

    (c) Is not a tree (has a circuit).

    (d) Is a tree.

2. **(a)** Is not a tree (is not connected).

    (b) Is a tree.

    (c) Is a tree.

    (d) Is not a tree (has a circuit).

3. **(a)** (II) A tree with 8 vertices must have 7 edges.

    (b) (III)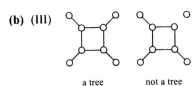

    a tree   not a tree

    (c) (I) If every edge of a graph is a bridge, then the graph must be a tree (Property 2).

4. **(a)** (II) A tree with 10 vertices must have 9 edges.

    (b) (III)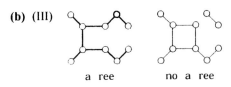

    a ree   no a ree

    (c) (I) A connected graph with 10 vertices and 9 edges must be a tree.

5. **(a)** (I) If there is exactly one path joining any two vertices of a graph, the graph must be a tree.

    (b) (II) A tree with 8 vertices must have 7 edges and every edge must be a bridge.

    (c) (I) If every edge is a bridge, then the graph has no circuits. Since the graph is also connected, it must be a tree.

6. **(a)** (III)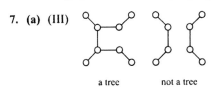

    a ree   no a ree

    (b) (II) In a tree, there is exactly one path joining any two vertices of the graph.

    (c) (I) If every edge of a graph is a bridge, then the graph must be a tree (Property 2).

7. **(a)** (III)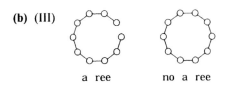

    a tree   not a tree

    (b) (II) A tree has no circuits.

    (c) (I) A graph with 8 vertices, 7 edges, and no circuits, must also be connected and hence must be a tree.

8. **(a)** (II) A tree has no circuits.

    (b) (III)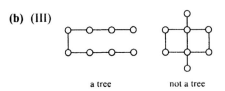

    a ree   no a ree

    (c) (I) A graph with a Hamilton path is connected and hence G is a connected graph with no circuits—a tree.

9. **(a)** (II) Since the degree of each vertex is even, it must be at least 2. Thus, the sum of the degrees of all 8 vertices must be at least 16. But, a tree with 8 vertices must have 7 edges, and the sum of the degrees of all the vertices would have to be 14.

    (b) (III)

    a tree   not a tree

(c) (III)

a tree   not a tree

10. (a) (II) Since the degree of each vertex is 9, the sum of the degrees of all 10 vertices must be 90. But, a tree with 10 vertices must have 9 edges, and the sum of the degrees of all the vertices would have to be 18.

(b) (III)

a ree   no a ree

(c) (II) Since the degree of each vertex is 2, the sum of the degrees of all 10 vertices must be 20. But, a tree with 10 vertices must have 9 edges, and the sum of the degrees of all the vertices would have to be 18.

B.   Spanning Trees

11. (a) One possible spanning tree is

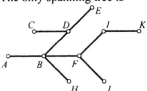

(b) The only spanning tree is

(c) One possible spanning tree is

12. (a) One possible spanning tree is

(b) One possible spanning tree is

(c) The only spanning tree is

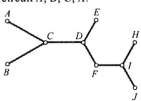

13. (a) There are three ways to eliminate the only circuit *A, B, C, A.*

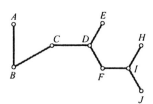

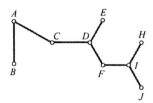

(b) There are five ways to eliminate the only circuit *B, C, D, E, F, B*.

(b) There are five ways to eliminate the only circuit *B, C, D, E, L, B*.

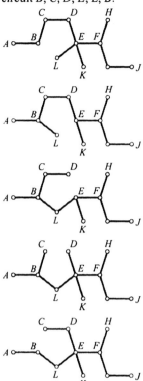

15. (a) Each spanning tree excludes one of the edges *AB, BC, CA* and one of the edges *DE, EI, IF, FD* so there are $3 \times 4 = 12$ different spanning trees.

(b) Each spanning tree excludes one of the edges *EJ, JK, KE* and one of the edges *BC, CD, DE, EF, FB* so there are $3 \times 5 = 15$ different spanning trees.

16. (a) $3 \times 4 = 12$

(b) $3 \times 5 = 15$

14. (a) There are three ways to eliminate the only circuit *D, E, F, D*.

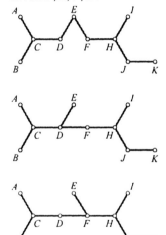

17. (a) Each spanning tree excludes one of the edges *AB, BC, CA*, one of the edges *DE, EI, IF, FD*, and one of the edges *HI, IJ, JH*, so there are $3 \times 4 \times 3 = 36$ different spanning trees.

(b) Each spanning tree excludes one of the edges *AB, BL, LA*, one of the edges *BC, CD, DE, EF, FB*, and one of the edges *EJ, JK, KE*, so there are $3 \times 5 \times 3 = 45$ different spanning trees.

18. (a) $3 \times 3 \times 4 = 36$

(b) $5 \times 3 \times 4 = 60$

C.   Minimum Spanning Trees and Kruskal's Algorithm

19. (a) Add edges to the tree in the following order: *EC, AD, AC, BC*.

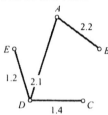

(b) The total weight is $165 + 185 + 200 + 305 = 855$.

20. (a) Add edges to the tree in the following order: *DE, CD, AD, AB*.

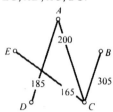

(b) The total weight is $1.2 + 1.4 + 2.1 + 2.2 = 6.9$.

21. (a) Add edges to the tree in the following order: *DC, EF, EC, AB, AC*.

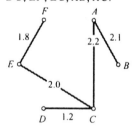

(b) The total weight is $1.2 + 1.8 + 2.0 + 2.1 + 2.2 = 9.3$.

22. (a) Add edges to the tree in the following order: *IJ, AB, BH, EJ, HI, CD, DJ, GH, FH*.

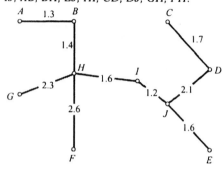

(b) The total weight is $1.3 + 1.4 + 1.6 + 1.6 + 1.7 + 2.1 + 2.3 + 2.6 = 15.8$.

23. Add edges to the tree in the following order: Kansas City – Tulsa (248), Pierre – Minneapolis (394), Minneapolis – Kansas City (447), Atlanta – Columbus (533), Columbus – Kansas City (656).

24. Add edges to the tree in the following order: Louisville – Nashville (168), Dallas -- Houston (243), Louisville – St. Louis (263), Louisville -- Pittsburgh (388), Pittsburgh -- Boston (561), Dallas – St. Louis (630).

25. A spanning tree for the 20 vertices will have exactly 19 edges and so the cost will be

$$19 \text{ edges} \times \frac{1 \text{ mile}}{2 \text{ edges}} \times \frac{\$40,000}{1 \text{ mile}} = \$380,000.$$

26. A spanning tree for the 30 vertices will have exactly 29 edges and so the cost will be

$$29 \text{ edges} \times \frac{1 \text{ mile}}{2 \text{ edges}} \times \frac{\$40,000}{1 \text{ mile}} = \$580,000.$$

D.   Steiner Points and Shortest Networks

27. (a) 580 miles.
The measure of angle *A* is $180° - 24° - 27° = 129°$. Since this is at least 120°, there is no Steiner point. Therefore, the shortest network is the minimum spanning tree, which consists of the edges *AB* and *AC*. The length is 270 miles + 310 miles = 580 miles.

(b) 385 miles.
The measure of angle *A* is $180° - 33° - 27° = 120°$. Since this is at least 120° (in fact, exactly that), there is no Steiner point. Therefore, the shortest

network is the minimum spanning tree, which consists of the edges *AB* and *AC*. The length is 212 miles + 173 miles = 385 miles.

28. (a) 642 miles.
The measure of angle *A* is 180° – 28° – 23° = 129°. Since this is at least 120°, there is no Steiner point. Therefore, the shortest network is the minimum spanning tree, which consists of the edges *AB* and *AC*. The length is 294 miles + 348 miles = 642 miles.

    (b) 375 miles.
The measure of angle *A* is 180° – 19° – 41° = 120°. Since this is at least 120°, there is no Steiner point. Therefore, the shortest network is the minimum spanning tree, which consists of the edges *AB* and *AC*. The length is 124 miles + 251 miles = 375 miles.

29. (a) 366 km
The measure of angle *A* is 180° – 20° – 20° = 140°. Since this is at least 120°, there is no Steiner point. Therefore, the shortest network is the minimum spanning tree. We can deduce that the length of side *AC* is 183 km because the measures of angles *B* and *C* are equal and so the lengths of the sides opposite those angles must be equal. Thus, the minimum spanning tree consists of the edges *AB* and *AC*, and the length is 183 km + 183 km = 366 km.

    (b) 334 km
Since side *AC* is shorter than side *AB*, we can deduce that the measure of angle *B* is less than the measure of angle *C*, or less than 28°. So the measure of angle *A* is at least 180° – 28° – 28° = 124°. Since this is at least 120°, there is no Steiner point. Therefore, the shortest network is the minimum spanning tree, which consists of the edges *AB* and *AC*. (Edge *BC* must be longer than either *AB* or *AC* since it is opposite the largest angle.) The length is 181 km + 153 km = 334 km.

30. (a) 430 km.
The measure of angle *A* is 130°. Since this is at least 120°, there is no Steiner point. Therefore, the shortest network is the minimum spanning tree. We can deduce that the length of side *AC* is 215 because the measures of angles *B* and *C*

are equal (both 25°) and so the lengths of the sides opposite those angles must be equal. Thus, the minimum spanning tree consists of the edges *AB* and *AC*, and the length is 215 km + 215 km = 430 km.

    (b) 450 km.
Since side *AB* is shorter than side *AC*, we can deduce that the measure of angle *C* is less than the measure of angle *B*, or less than 30°. So the measure of angle *A* is at least 180° – 30° – 30° = 120°. Since this is at least 120°, there is no Steiner point. Therefore, the shortest network is the minimum spanning tree, which consists of the edges *AB* and *AC*. (Edge *BC* must be longer than either *AB* or *AC* since it is opposite the largest angle.) The length is 180 km + 270 km = 450 km.

31. Since the measure of angle *CAB* is 120°, there is no Steiner point. Therefore, the shortest network is the minimum spanning tree, which consists of the edges *AB* and *AC*. In a 30-60-90 triangle, the hypotenuse is twice as long as the shortest leg (see Exercise 45(a)). Since the shortest leg of both of the 30-60-90 triangles in the figure is 85 miles, the hypotenuse for each 30-60-90 triangle is 170 miles. That is, *AB* = 170 miles and *AC* = 170 miles. The length of the shortest network is 170 miles + 170 miles = 340 miles.

32. 1500 km.
Since the measure of angle *CAB* is 134°, there is no Steiner point. Therefore, the shortest network is the minimum spanning tree, which consists of two edges *AB* and *AC* having the same length. By the Pythagorean theorem, the length of *AB* is $\sqrt{(293)^2 + (690.4)^2} \approx 750$ km. The length of the shortest network is 750 km + 750 km = 1500 km.

33. *Z* is the Steiner point.
The sum of the distances from *Z* to *A*, *B*, and *C* is 232 miles, the sum of the distances from *X* to *A*, *B*, and *C* is 240 miles, and the sum of the distances from *Y* to *A*, *B*, and *C* is 243 miles. Since one of the points is the Steiner point and the Steiner point is the point that makes the shortest network, *Z* is the Steiner point.

34. *Y* is the Steiner point.
The sum of the distances from *Y* to *A*, *B*, and *C* is 1260 miles, the sum of the distances from *X* to *A*, *B*, and *C* is 1300 miles, and the sum of the

distances from Z to A, B, and C is 1510 miles. Since one of the points is the Steiner point and the Steiner point is the point that makes the shortest network, Z is the Steiner point.

35. (a) $CE + ED + EB$ is larger since $CD + DB$ is the shortest network connecting the cities C, D, and B.

(b) $CD + DB$ is the shortest network connecting the cities C, D, and B since angle CDB is $120°$ and so the shortest network is the same as the minimum spanning tree.

(c) $CE + EB$ is the shortest network connecting the cities C, E, and B since angle CEB is more than $120°$ and so the shortest network is the same as the minimum spanning tree.

36. (a) $CA + AB$ is larger than $DC + DA + DB$ since D is a Steiner point for triangle ABC and therefore $DC + DA + DB$ is the length of the shortest network connecting A, B, and C.

(b) $EC + EA + EB$ is larger than $DC + DA + DB$. D is a Steiner point for triangle ABC and so $DC + DA + DB$ is the length of the shortest network connecting A, B, and C.

(c) DC, DA, and DB.

E.   Miscellaneous

37. (a) $k = 5, 2, 1, 0$ are all possible.
The network could have no circuits ($k=5$),

o - - - -o   o   o   o   o

or a circuit of length 3 ($k=2$),

o
∕ ⟍
o- - - -o   o- - - -o

or a circuit of length 4 ($k=1$),

or a circuit of length 5 ($k=0$).

(b) Using the same pattern as in (a), values of k = 123 and $0 \le k \le 120$ are all possible.

38. (a) $k = 7, 4, 3, 2, 1, 0$ are all possible.

(b) $k = 2481$ and $0 \le k \le 2478$ are all possible.

39. (a) Since $M = N - 1$, the network is a tree by Property 4. So, there are no circuits in the network.

(b) The redundancy of this network is $R = 1$ so one edge will need to be "discarded" in order to form a spanning tree. This means that there is one circuit in the network.

(c) 118. Each edge other than those in the circuit of length 5 is a bridge.

40. (a) There are no circuits in this network.

(b) There is one circuit in the network.

(c) 2,471. Each edge other than those in the circuit of length 10 is a bridge.

41. (a) Note that the graph is not connected.

(b) Other examples are possible.

(c) Other examples are possible.

42. (a) Note that the graph is not connected.

(b) Other examples are possible.

(c) Other examples are possible.

43. 15°.

Since S is a Steiner point, the measure of angle ASB is 120°. Since the triangle is isosceles, the measure of angle ASB is the same as the measure of angle BSC (half of 90°). That is, the measure of angle ASB is 45°. So, the measure of angle BAS is 180° − 120° − 45° = 15°.

44. 42°.

Since S is a Steiner point, the measure of angle ASB is 120°. Since the triangle is isosceles, the measure of angle ASB is the same as the measure of angle ASC (half of 36°). That is, the measure of angle ASB is 18°. So, the measure of angle ABS is 180° − 120° − 18° = 42°.

45. (a) $h = 2s$

Imagine that the figure is the top half of an equilateral triangle. Then, it becomes clear that h is twice the length of s. That is, $h = 2s$.

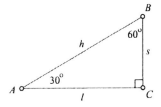

(b) $l = \sqrt{3}s$

By the Pythagorean theorem, $h^2 = s^2 + l^2$. Then, using the result of (a), we have $(2s)^2 = s^2 + l^2$ so that $4s^2 = s^2 + l^2$ and $3s^2 = l^2$. Since $l > 0$, it follows that $l = \sqrt{3}s$.

(c) $h = 2s = 2(21.0 \text{ cm}) = 42 \text{ cm}$

$l = \sqrt{3}s = \sqrt{3}(21.0 \text{ cm}) \approx 36.3 \text{ cm}$

(d) $s = \dfrac{1}{2}h = \dfrac{1}{2}(30.4 \text{ cm}) = 15.2 \text{ cm}$

$l = \sqrt{3}s = \sqrt{3}(15.2 \text{ cm}) \approx 26.3 \text{ cm}$

46. (a) $s = \dfrac{1}{2}h$; See Exercise 45(a).

(b) $l = \sqrt{3}s = \dfrac{\sqrt{3}}{2}h$; See Exercise 45(b).

(c) $h = \dfrac{2l}{\sqrt{3}}$

(d) $s = \dfrac{1}{\sqrt{3}}l = \dfrac{1}{\sqrt{3}}(173.0 \text{ cm}) \approx 100 \text{ cm}$

$h = \dfrac{2l}{\sqrt{3}} = \dfrac{2}{\sqrt{3}}(173.0 \text{ cm}) \approx 200 \text{ cm}$

47. In a 30°-60°-90° triangle, the side opposite the 30° angle is one half the length of the hypotenuse and the side opposite the 60° angle is $\dfrac{\sqrt{3}}{2}$ times the length of the hypotenuse (See Exercise 45). Therefore, the distance from C to J is $\dfrac{\sqrt{3}}{2} \times 500$ miles ≈ 433 miles and so the total length of the T-network (rounded to the nearest mile) is 433 miles + 500 miles = 933 miles.

48. In a 30°-60°-90° triangle, the side opposite the 30° angle is 1/2 the length of the hypotenuse and the side opposite the 60° angle is $\dfrac{\sqrt{3}}{2}$ times the length of the hypotenuse. Therefore, the distance from any one of the three cities to S (the Steiner point) is $\frac{2}{\sqrt{3}} \times 250 = \frac{500}{\sqrt{3}}$ miles and so the total length of the Y-network (rounded to the nearest mile) is $3 \times \left(\frac{500}{\sqrt{3}}\right) = 500\sqrt{3} \approx 866$ miles.

JOGGING

49. (a) 99.

Each spanning tree excludes one of the edges AB, BC, CA, and one of the edges HI, IJ, JH. Since the circuits C, D, E, C and D, E, I, F, D share a common edge there are two ways to exclude edges to form a spanning tree. If one of the excluded edges is the common edge DE, then any one of the other 5 edges CD, CE, EI, DF, or FI could be excluded to form a spanning tree. If, on the other hand, one of the excluded edges is not the common edge DE, then one excluded edge has to be either CE or CD

and the other excluded edge must be either
EI, *DF*, or *FI*. Thus, there are
$3 \times (5 + 2 \times 3) \times 3 = 99$ different spanning
trees.

(b) 171.

Each spanning tree excludes one of the
edges *AB*, *BL*, *LA*, and one of the edges *EJ*,
JK, *KE*. Since the circuits *C*, *D*, *I*, *H*, *C* and
B, *C*, D, *E*, *F*, *B* share a common edge there
are two ways to exclude edges to form a
spanning tree. If one of the excluded edges
is the common edge *CD*, then any one of the
other 7 edges *CH*, *HI*, *ID*, *BC*, *BF*, *EF*, or
DE could be excluded to form a spanning
tree. Or, if one of the excluded edges is not
the common edge *CD*, then one excluded
edge has to be either *CH*, *HI* or *ID* and the
other excluded edge must be either *BC*, *BF*,
EF, or *DE*. Thus, this network has
$3 \times (7 + 3 \times 4) \times 3 = 171$ different spanning
trees.

50. (a) $2N - 2$

A tree with *N* vertices has $N - 1$ edges, and,
in any graph, the sum of the degrees of all
the vertices is twice the number of edges.

(b) Exercise 52(a) shows that there are trees
with *N* vertices having just 2 vertices of
degree 1. To show that a tree cannot have
fewer than 2 vertices of degree 1, let *v* be
the number of vertices in the graph, *e* the
number of edges, and *k* the number of
vertices of degree 1. Recall that in a tree $v =
e + 1$ and in any graph the sum of the
degrees of all the vertices is $2e$. Now, since
we are assuming there are exactly *k* vertices
of degree 1, the remaining $v - k$ vertices
must have degree at least 2. Therefore, the
sum of the degrees of all the vertices must
be at least $k + 2(v - k)$. Putting all this
together we have
$2e = k + 2(v - k) = k + 2(e + 1 - k)$,
$\quad 2e = k + 2e + 2 - 2k$,
$\quad\quad k = 2.$

51. (a) A regular tree with $N = 2$ vertices:

(b) Suppose that a tree is regular. Since two
vertices of a tree must have degree 1 (see
Exercise 50(b)), every vertex must have
degree 1. So the sum of the degrees is *N*.
However, the sum of the degrees is also

twice the number of edges. So, there are
N/2 edges. In order to be a tree, it must be
that $N-1 = N/2$ (the number of edges must be
one fewer than the number of vertices).
Solving this equation gives $N = 2$ as the only
solution. So, if $N \geq 3$, the graph cannot be
regular.

52. (a)

(b)

(c)

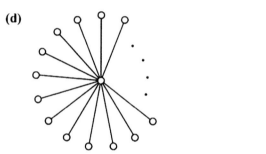

(d)

53. (a) If $R = 0$, then $M = N-1$ (the number of edges
is one less than the number of vertices). So,
the network is a tree.

(b) If $R = 1$, then $M = N$ (the number of edges is
the same as the number of vertices). So, the
network is not a tree. From the definition of
a tree, there must be at least one circuit.
Suppose that the graph had 2 (or more)
circuits. Then, there would be an edge of
one of the circuits that is not an edge of
another circuit. Removing such an edge
would leave us with a connected graph with
the number of vertices being one more than
the number of edges (i.e. a tree). But this
tree would have a circuit. This is
impossible, so there cannot be more than 1
circuit.

(c) The maximum redundancy occurs when the
degree of each vertex is *N*-1. In that case (a
complete graph), the number of edges is (*N*-
1) + (*N*-2) + ...+ 3 + 2 + 1. So, $R = (N-1) +
(N-2) + ... + 3 + 2 + 1 - (N-1) = (N-2) + ...
+ 3 + 2 + 1 = (N^2 - 3N + 2)/2$.

54. If $M \geq N$, then the redundancy of the network is at least 1 and the network has at least one circuit. The shortest length of that circuit is 3. None of the edges in the circuit are bridges, but the remaining $M - 3$ edges could all be bridges.

55. (a) According to Cayley's theorem, there are $3^{3-2} = 3$ spanning trees in a complete graph with 3 vertices, which is confirmed by the following figures.

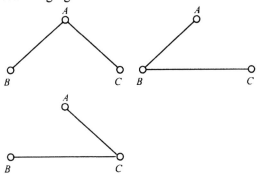

Likewise, for the completed graph with 4 vertices, Cayley's theorem predicts $4^{4-2} = 16$ spanning trees, which is confirmed by the following figures.

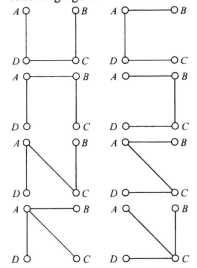

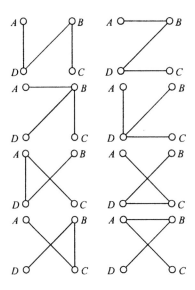

(b) The complete graph with N vertices has $(N-1)!$ Hamilton circuits and N^{N-2} spanning trees. Since $(N-1)! = 2 \times 3 \times 4 \times \ldots \times (N-1)$ and $N^{N-2} = N \times N \times N \times \ldots \times N$, and both expressions have the same number of factors, with each factor in $(N-1)!$ smaller than the corresponding factor in N^{N-2}, we know that for $N = 3$, $(N-1)! < N^{N-2}$. Thus, the number of spanning trees is larger than the number of Hamilton circuits.

56. The minimum spanning tree consists of the following edges (produced exactly in this order by Kruskal's algorithm): C_4C_7, C_3C_6, C_1C_8, C_1C_2, C_2C_5, C_2C_6, C_8C_9, and C_7C_9. (The total cost is 15 million dollars.)

57.

Edges in Spanning Tree	Junction Points	Total Cost
AB, AC, AD	A	85 + 50 + 45 + 25 = 205
AB, BC, BD	B	85 + 90 + 75 + 5 = 255
AC, BC, CD	C	50 + 90 + 70 + 15 = 225
AD, BD, CD	D	45 + 75 + 70 + 20 = 210
AD, AB, BC	A, B	45 + 85 + 90 + 25 + 5 = 250
AB, AC, BD	A, B	85 + 50 + 75 + 25 + 5 = 240
AB, BC, CD	B, C	85 + 90 + 70 + 5 + 15 = 265
BD, BC, AC	B, C	75 + 90 + 50 + 5 + 15 = 235
BC, CD, AD	C, D	90 + 70 + 45 + 15 + 20 = 240
AC, CD, BD	C, D	50 + 70 + 75 + 15 + 20 = 230
AB, AD, CD	A, D	85 + 45 + 70 + 25 + 20 = 245
AC, AD, BD	A, D	50 + 45 + 75 + 25 + 20 = 215
AD, AC, BC	A, C	45 + 50 + 90 + 25 + 15 = 225
AB, BD, CD	B, D	85 + 75 + 70 + 5 + 20 = 255
AD, BD, BC	B, D	45 + 75 + 90 + 20 + 5 = 235
AB, AC, CD	A, C	85 + 50 + 70 + 25 + 15 = 245

The minimum cost network connecting the 4 cities has a 3-way junction point at A and has a total cost of 205 million dollars.

58. 230 miles. Using the Pythagorean theorem, $AC = \sqrt{50^2 + 120^2} = \sqrt{16,900} = 130$ and so $AE = EC = DE = EB = 65$. Using Kruskal's algorithm, a minimum spanning tree has length $50 + 50 + 65 + 65 = 230$.

59. (a) The switching station should be located 1 mile north of the airport. [Most of the options can be eliminated by common sense. Since there are only a handful of viable options, trial and error will discover this solution.]

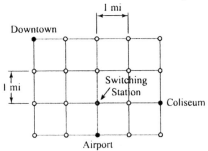

(b) Since the optimal network requires 7 miles of track and 1 switching station, the cost of the network is $7.5 million.

60. (a) The switching stations should be located 3 blocks north of the University and 1 block west of Slugger's Ballpark as shown below.

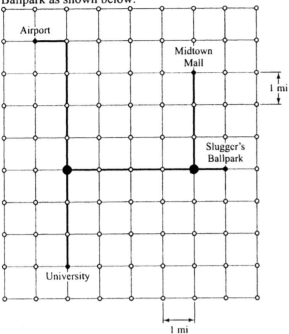

(b) Since the optimal network requires 16 miles of track and 2 switching stations, the cost of the network is $33 million.

61. (a) $m(\angle BFA) = 120°$ since $m(\angle EFG) = 60°$ (supplementary angles). Similarly, $m(\angle AEC) = 120°$ and $m(\angle CGB) = 120°$.

(b) In $\triangle ABF$, $m(\angle BFA) = 120°$ [from part (a)] and so $m(\angle BAF) + m(\angle ABF) = 60°$. It follows therefore that $m(\angle BAF) < 60°$ and $m(\angle ABF) < 60°$. Similarly, $m(\angle ACE) < 60°$, $m(\angle CAE) < 60°$, $m(\angle BCG) < 60°$, and $m(\angle CBG) < 60°$. Consequently, $m(\angle A) = m(BAF) + m(CAE) < 60° + 60° = 120°$. Likewise, $m(\angle B) < 120°$ and $m(\angle C) < 120°$. So, triangle ABC has a Steiner point S.

(c) Any point X inside or on $\triangle ABF$ (except vertex F) will have $m(\angle AXB) > 120°$. Any point X inside or on $\triangle ACE$ (except vertex E) will have $m(\angle AXC) > 120°$. Any point X inside or on $\triangle BCG$ (except vertex G) will have $m(\angle BXC) > 120°$. If S is the Steiner point, $m(\angle ASB) = m(\angle ASC) = m(BSC) = 120°$, and so S cannot be inside or on $\triangle ABF$ or $\triangle ACE$ or $\triangle BCG$. It follows that the Steiner point S must lie inside $\triangle EFG$.

62. The length of the network is $4x$ (see figure). Since the diagonals of a square are perpendicular, $\triangle AOB$ is a 45°-45°-90° triangle. So,

$$AO = x = \frac{AB}{\sqrt{2}} = \frac{500}{\sqrt{2}} = \frac{500\sqrt{2}}{2} = 250\sqrt{2}.$$ Thus, $4x = 1000\sqrt{2} \approx 1414$ miles.

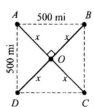

63.

The length of the network is $4x + (500 - x) = 3x + 500$, where $250^2 + \left(\dfrac{x}{2}\right)^2 = x^2$

(see figure). Rewriting the equation gives $250,000 + x^2 = 4x^2$ or $3x^2 = 250,000$.

Solving this gives $x = \sqrt{\dfrac{250,000}{3}} = \dfrac{500}{\sqrt{3}} = \dfrac{500\sqrt{3}}{3}$, and so the length of the network

is $3\dfrac{500\sqrt{3}}{3} + 500 = 500\sqrt{3} + 500 \approx 1366$ miles.

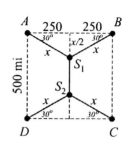

64. (a) The length of the network is $4x + (300 - x) = 3x + 300$ (see figure). The
triangle formed by A, S_1, and the midpoint of AB is a 30°-60°-90° triangle.

Therefore, $AS_1 = \dfrac{2}{\sqrt{3}} \times 200 = \dfrac{400}{\sqrt{3}} = \dfrac{400\sqrt{3}}{3} = x$, and so the length of the

network is $3\left(\dfrac{400\sqrt{3}}{3}\right) + 300 = 400\sqrt{3} + 300 \approx 993$ miles.

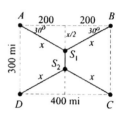

(b) The length of the network is $4x + (400 - x) = 3x + 400$, where

$150^2 + \left(\dfrac{x}{2}\right)^2 = x^2$ (see figure). Solving the equation gives $x = \dfrac{300\sqrt{3}}{3}$ and so

the length of the network is $3\left(\dfrac{300\sqrt{3}}{3}\right) + 400 = 300\sqrt{3} + 400 \approx 919.6$ miles.

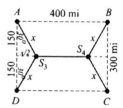

65. (a) There will be two subtrees formed as shown below.

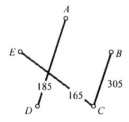

(b) The tree formed by Boruvka's algorithm is shown below.

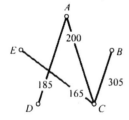

66. The city closest to the Steiner point on the map is Marion. Closer cities can be found on more detailed maps.

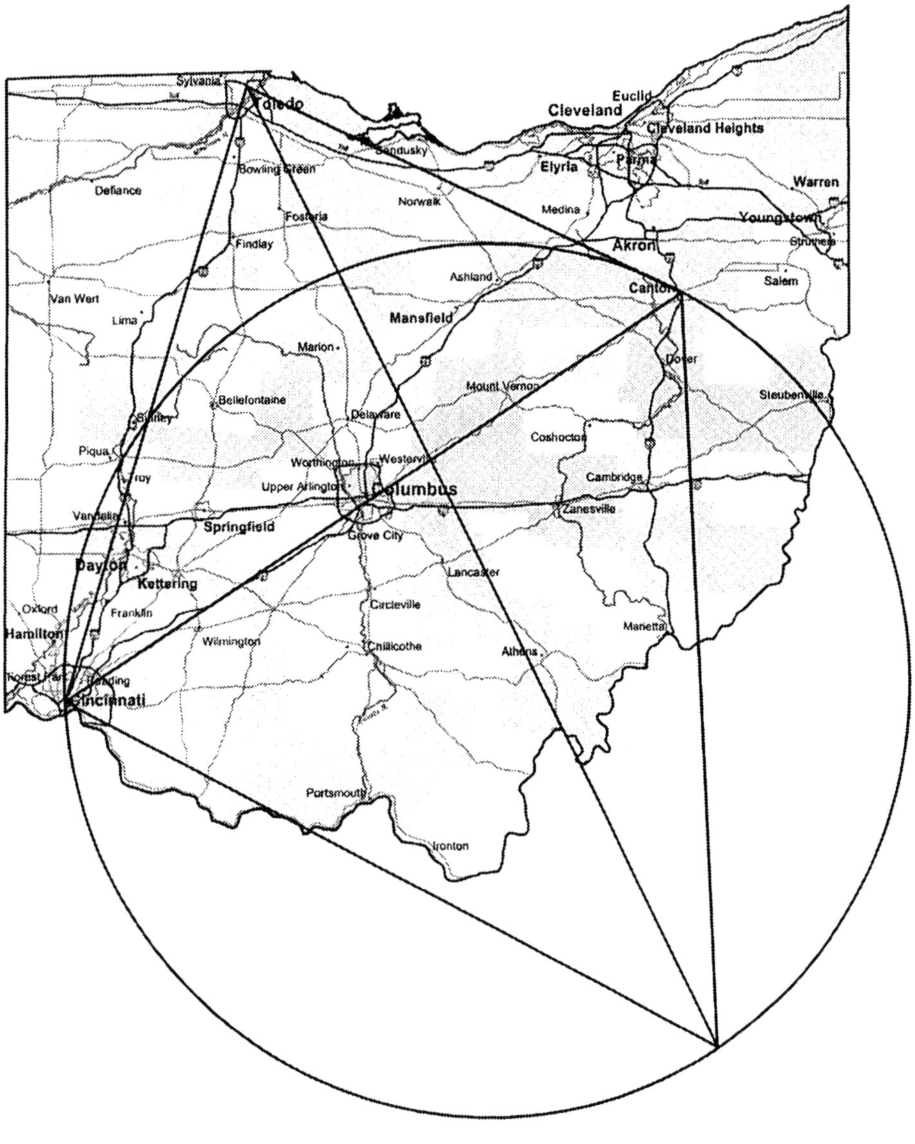

RUNNING

67. Let v be the number of vertices in the graph, e the number of edges, and t the number of vertices of degree 1. Recall that in a tree $v = e + 1$ and in any graph the sum of the degrees of all the vertices is $2e$. Now, since we are assuming there is a vertex of degree K and exactly t vertices of degree 1, the remaining $v - t - 1$ vertices must have degree at least 2. Therefore the sum of the degrees of all the vertices must be at least $t + K + 2(v - t - 1)$. Putting all this together we have $2e \geq t + K + 2(v - t - 1) = t + K + 2(e - t)$, or $2e \geq t + K + 2e - 2t$ which means $t \geq K$.

68. (a) $K = N - M$

   (b) 0 if $N = K$; 2 if $N > K$.

   (c) 0 if $N = K$; $2(N - K)$ if $K < N = 2K$; $N - 1$ if $N > 2K$.

69. (a) Start by marking the required edge in red. Proceed with Kruskal's algorithm as usual.

(b) The minimum spanning tree consists of the following edges (produced exactly in this order by the algorithm): C_3C_4, C_4C_7, C_3C_6, C_1C_8, C_1C_2, C_2C_5, C_2C_6, and C_8C_9. The total cost is 21 million dollars.

70. Without any loss of generality, we can assume that either X is located in the top half of the square or Y is located in the bottom half of the square. So assume that Y is located in the bottom half of the square. This means that the vertices A, B, and Y form a triangle in which each angle is less than 120°. But then the network AX, BX, and XY can be shortened by replacing X by a Steiner point S_1. But then the network S_1Y, YD, YC can be shortened by replacing Y by a second Steiner point S_2.

71. Note first that if we drop a perpendicular from vertex A to side DE, we see that $\triangle ADE$ is a 30°-60°-90° triangle since the shorter side is one-half the hypotenuse (see Fig. 1). Therefore $\angle ADE = 30°$.

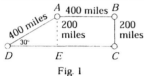
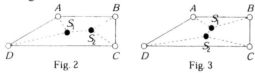

Fig. 1

If the figure had two interior Steiner points, they would have to be in one of two possible configurations as shown in Figs. 2 and 3.

Fig. 2   Fig. 3

It is easy to rule out Fig. 2 as a possibility, since $< S_1DC < 30°$, $< S_2DC < 90°$, and so the sum of the degrees of the angles of quadrilateral S_1DCS_2 would be **less than** 30° + 90° + 120° + 120° = 360°. This is impossible, since the sum of the degrees of the angles in any quadrilateral is 360°. It is harder to rule out Fig. 3 as a possibility. Figure 4 shows how Torricelli's method can be extended to quadrilateral $A'B'C'D'$ to find the two Steiner points S_1 and S_2. We leave the details of why this method works to the reader. Applying the method to the given quadrilateral $ABCD$, we see that the circles overlap and so no such Steiner points are possible (see Fig. 5).

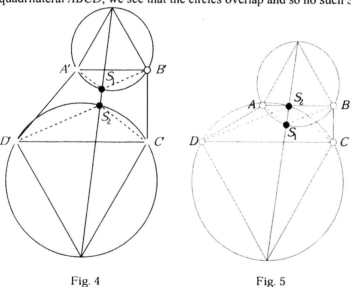

Fig. 4   Fig. 5

72. The length of the Steiner tree shown is $b\sqrt{3} + a$ [see Exercise 64(a)]. This Steiner tree is not necessarily the shortest network. The length of the MST is $b + 2a$. Consequently, the length of a MST is less than the length of the Steiner tree shown if and only if $b + 2a < b\sqrt{3} + a$, or equivalently, $a < b(\sqrt{3} - 1)$.

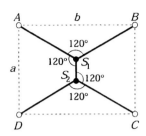

73. (a) $W = 120$ miles

(b) $Z = 30\left(\sqrt{2} + \sqrt{6}\right)$

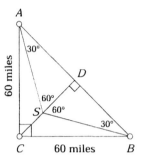

Draw CD perpendicular to AB and locate the Steiner point S on CD. Since $\triangle BCD$ is an isosceles right triangle (with sides in the ratio of $1{:}1{:}\sqrt{2}$), $CD = BD = 30\sqrt{2}$. Since $\triangle BDS$ is a 30°-60° right triangle (with sides in the ratio of $1{:}2{:}\sqrt{3}$), $DS = 10\sqrt{6}$ and $BS = 20\sqrt{6}$. This gives us $CS = CD - DS = 30\sqrt{2} - 10\sqrt{6}$. Putting this altogether, we get $CS + AS + BS = 30\left(\sqrt{2} + \sqrt{6}\right)$.

(c) $\dfrac{W - Z}{Z} = \dfrac{120 - 30\left(\sqrt{2} + \sqrt{6}\right)}{30\left(\sqrt{2} + \sqrt{6}\right)} \approx 3.528\%$

74. (a) The shortest network connecting the seven cities will contain four Steiner points (one of them being H itself).

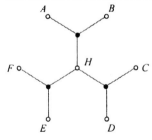

(b) $300\sqrt{3} \approx 519.6$ mi

75. (a)

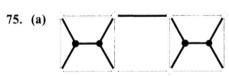

(b) $3 + 2\sqrt{3} \approx 6.464$

76. (a)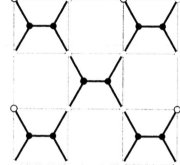

(b) $5 + 5\sqrt{3} \approx 13.66$

Chapter 8

WALKING

A. Directed Graphs

1. (a) Vertex set: V = {*A*, *B*, *C*, *D*, *E*}; Arc set: A = {*AB*, *AC*, *BD*, *CA*, *CD*, *CE*, *EA*, *ED*}

(b) indeg(*A*) = 2, indeg(*B*) = 1, indeg(*C*) = 1, indeg(*D*) = 3, indeg(*E*) = 1.

(c) outdeg(*A*) = 2, outdeg(*B*) = 1, outdeg(*C*) = 3, outdeg(*D*) = 0, outdeg(*E*) = 2.

2. (a) Vertex set: V = {*A*, *B*, *C*, *D*, *E*}; Arc set: A = {*AC*, *AD*, *AE*, *BA*, *BC*, *BE*, *EB*, *ED*}

(b) indeg(*A*) = 1, indeg(*B*) = 1, indeg(*C*) = 2, indeg(*D*) = 2, indeg(*E*) = 2.

(c) outdeg(*A*) = 3, outdeg(*B*) = 3, outdeg(*C*) = 0, outdeg(*D*) = 0, outdeg(*E*) = 2.

3. (a) *C* and *E*

(b) *B* and *C*

(c) *B*, *C*, and *E*

(d) No vertices are incident from *D*.

(e) *CD*, *CE* and *CA*

(f) No arcs are adjacent to *CD*.

4. (a) *B*

(b) *C*, *D* and *E*

(c) *A* and *E*

(d) No vertices are incident from *D*.

(e) *EB* and *ED*

(f) No arcs are adjacent to *BC*.

5.(a) 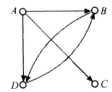   **(b)**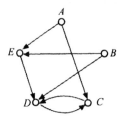

6. (a) 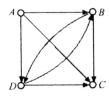   **(b)**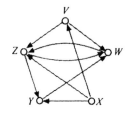

7. (a) 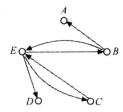   **(b)**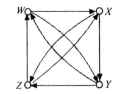

8. (a) 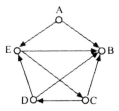   **(b)**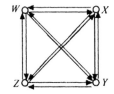

9. (a) 2 (these correspond to arcs *AB* and *AE*)

  (b) 1 (this corresponds to arc *EA*)

  (c) 1 (this corresponds to arc *DB*)

  (d) 0 (there are no arcs incident to *D*)

10. (a) 2 (these correspond to arcs *VW* and *VZ*)

  (b) 0 (there are no arcs incident to *V*)

  (c) 2 (this corresponds to arcs *ZY* and *ZW*)

  (d) 3 (this corresponds to arcs *VZ, WZ* and *XZ*)

11. (a) *A, B, D, E, F* is one possible path.

(b) *A, B, D, E, C, F*

(c) *B, D, E, B*

(d) The outdegree of vertex *F* is 0, so it cannot be part of a circuit.

(e) The indegree of vertex *A* is 0, so it cannot be part of a circuit.

12. **(a)** *A, E, C, D*

(b) The indegree of *D* is 1 and hence there is only one way to get to *D* and that is using the arc *CD*. Also, the indegree of *C* is 1 and so there is only one way to get to vertex *C* and that is using the arc *EC*. Finally, the outdegree of vertex *B* is 0 and so the only way to get to *D* from *A* is the given path.

(c) *E, C, D, E*

(d) The indegree of *A* is 0.

(e) The outdegree of *B* is 0.

(f) *E, C, D, E* is the only cycle.

13.

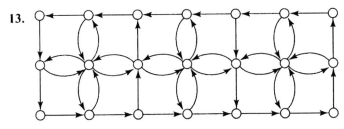

14.

15. **(a)** *B*, since *B* is the only person that everyone respects.

(b) *A*, since *A* is the only person that no one respects.

16. **(a)** *E*. The outdegree of *E* is 4, meaning *E* defeated every other team.

(b) *A*. The outdegree of *A* is 0, meaning *A* didn't win any games.

B.   Project Digraphs

17.

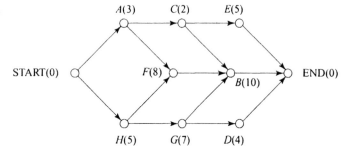

18.

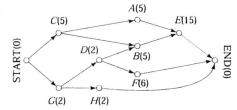

19.

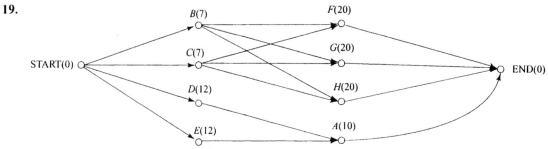

20.

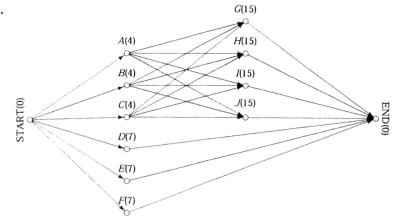

21.

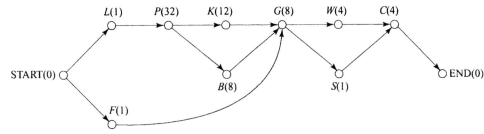

22.

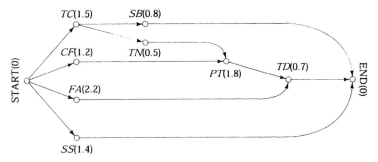

C.   Schedules, Priority Lists, and the Decreasing Time Algorithm

23. (a) There are $31 \times 3 = 93$ processor hours available. Of these,
$10 + 7 + 11 + 8 + 9 + 5 + 3 + 6 + 4 + 7 + 5 = 75$ hours are used. So there must be
$93 - 75 = 18$ hours idle time.

(b) There is a total of 75 hours of work to be done. Three processors working without any idle time
would take $\dfrac{75}{3} = 25$ hours to complete the project.

24. (a) There are $19 \times 5 = 95$ processor hours available. Of these,
$10 + 7 + 11 + 8 + 9 + 5 + 3 + 6 + 4 + 7 + 5 = 75$ hours are used. So there must be
$95 - 75 = 20$ hours idle time.

(b) There is a total of 75 hours of work to be done. Five processors working without any idle time
would take $\dfrac{75}{5} = 15$ hours to complete the project.

25. There is a total of 75 hours of work to be done. Dividing the work equally between the six processors
would require each processor to do $\dfrac{75}{6} = 12.5$ hours of work. Since there are no $\dfrac{1}{2}$-hour jobs, the
completion time could not be less than 13 hours.

26. (a) The completion time can never be less than 11 hours, since task C by itself takes 11 hours.

(b) There are 11 tasks, so clearly, having more than 11 processors makes no sense. To argue that 10
processors are enough, consider two cases: (i) if all tasks are independent then we can give two
"short" tasks [for example $F(5)$ and $G(3)$] to one processor and each of the remaining 9 tasks to a

different processor, and still meet the optimal completion time of 11 hours; (ii) if there is at least one precedence relation (call it $X \rightarrow Y$), then we can give tasks X and Y to one processor and each of the remaining 9 tasks to a different processor. In this case, the finishing time will be the critical time for the project, and thus the schedule will be an optimal schedule.

27.

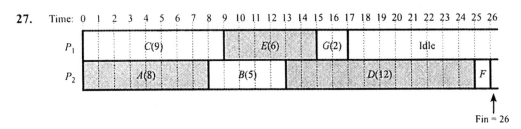

Fin = 26

28.

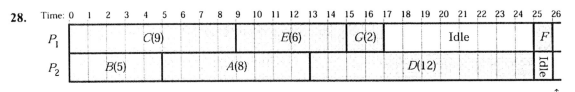

Finishing time = 26

29.

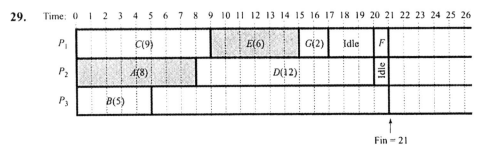

Fin = 21

30.

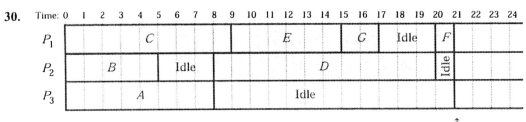

Finishing time = 21

31. There are many different priority lists that will produce the given schedule. Here are five: *B,C,A,E,D,G,F; B,C,A,E,D,F,G; B,C,A,E,G,F,D; B,C,A,E,G,D,F; B,C,A,D,E,G,F.*

32. There are many different priority lists that will produce the given schedule. Here are five: *C,A,B,E,D,G,F; C,A,B,D,E,G,F; C,A,B,E,F,D,G; C,A,B,F,D,E,G; C,A,B,F,E,D,G.*

33. According to the precedence relations, *G* cannot be started until *K* is completed.

34. According to the precedence relations, G cannot be started until K is completed.

35. Project Digraph:

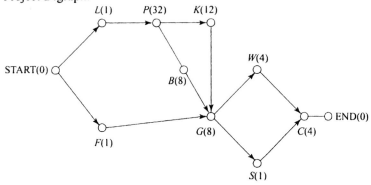

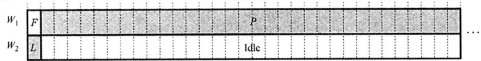

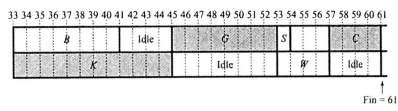

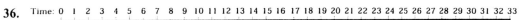

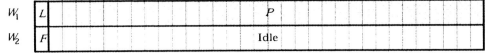

36.

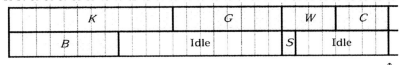

Finishing time = 61

D.   Decreasing Time Algorithm

37.   Decreasing-Time List: *D, C, A, E, B, G, F*; so schedule is:

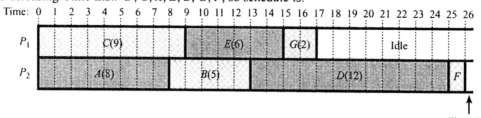

38.

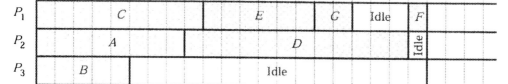

Finishing time = 21

39.   Refer to the project digraph from problem 35 to create the schedule. The Decreasing-Time List is *P, K, B, G, C, W, F, L, S.*

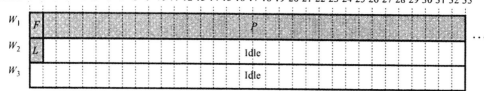

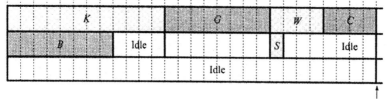

Fin = 61

40.

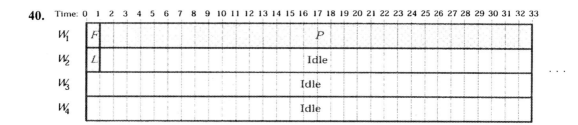

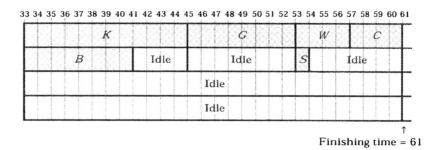

Finishing time = 61

41. (a) The 13 jobs *A–M* are already listed in decreasing order. So, the decreasing-time list is: *A, B, C, D, E, F, G, H, I, J, K, L, M* and (since the precedence relations play no role in this problem) the schedule is:

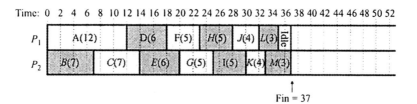

Fin = 37

(b)

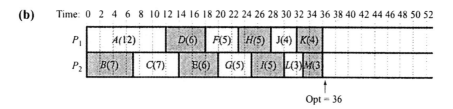

Opt = 36

42. (a) The 13 jobs *A–M* are already listed in decreasing order. So, the decreasing-time list is: *A, B, C, D, E, F, G, H, I, J, K, L, M* and (since the precedence relations play no role in this problem) the schedule is:

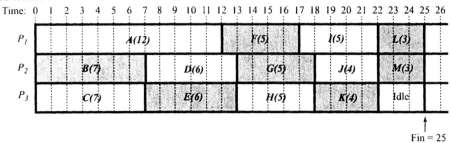

Fin = 25

(b)

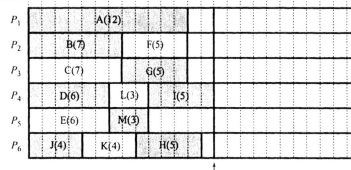

Fin = 24

43. (a) The 13 jobs *A–M* are already listed in decreasing order. So, the decreasing-time list is: *A, B, C, D, E, F, G, H, I, J, K, L, M* and since each task of length 5 cannot start until tasks *B* and *C* are completed the schedule is:

Time: 0 1 2 3 4 5 6 7 8 9 10 11 12 13 14 15 16 17 18 19 20 21 22 23 24

P_1	A(12)
P_2	B(7) F(5)
P_3	C(7) G(5)
P_4	D(6) L(3) I(5)
P_5	E(6) M(3)
P_6	J(4) K(4) H(5)

Fin = 14

(b)   Time: 0 1 2 3 4 5 6 7 8 9 10 11 12 13 14 15 16 17 18 19 20 21 22 23 24

P_1	M(3)		K(4)			I(5)																		
P_2	L(3)		J(4)			H(5)																		
P_3	C(7)					G(5)																		
P_4	B(7)					F(5)																		
P_5	E(6)				D(6)																			
P_6	A(12)																							

Opt = 12

(c) For six copiers, the completion time is 12 hours and one of the tasks takes 12 hours, thus the job cannot be completed in less than 12 hours.

44. (a)   Time: 0 1 2 3 4 5 6 7 8 9 10 11 12 13 14 15 16 17 18 19 20 21 22 23 24

P_1	A(12)											L(3)												
P_2	B(7)					F(5)				M(3)														
P_3	C(7)					G(5)				Idle														
P_4	D(6)				H(5)					J(4)														
P_5	E(6)				I(5)					K(4)														

Fin = 15

(b) There is a total of 72 hours of work to be done. Dividing the work equally between the five processors would require each processor to do 72/5 = 14.4 hours of work. But there are no partial-hour jobs, so the completion time could not be less than 15 hours.

(c) Any schedule with 15 hours completion time is optimal, so the schedule given in (a) is optimal.

E.   Critical Paths and Critical-Path Algorithm

45. (a)

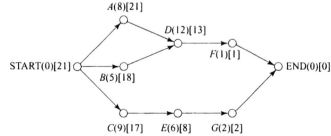

(b) START, *A*, *D*, *F*, END is the critical path, with a critical time of 21.

283

(c) The critical path list is: $A[21]$, $B[18]$, $C[17]$, $D[13]$, $E[8]$, $G[2]$, $F[1]$.
    The schedule is:

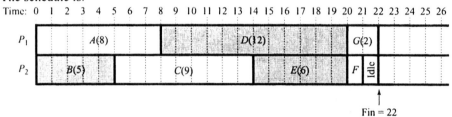

Fin = 22

(d) There are a total of 43 work units, so the shortest time the project can be completed by 2 workers is $\frac{43}{2} = 21.5$ time units. Since there are no tasks with less than 1 time unit, the shortest time the project can actually be completed is 22 hours.

46. (a)

Time: 0 1 2 3 4 5 6 7 8 9 10 11 12 13 14 15 16 17 18 19 20 21 22

P_1	A(8)	D(12)	F
P_2	B(5)	Idle	E(6)	G(2)	Idle
P_3	C(9)	Idle

Finishing time = 21

(b) The critical path of the project has length 21 hours, so the project cannot be completed in less than 21 hours.

47. The critical path list is: $B[46]$, $A[44]$, $E[42]$, $D[39]$, $F[38]$, $I[35]$, $C[34]$, $G[24]$, $K[20]$, $H[10]$, $J[5]$.
    The schedule is:

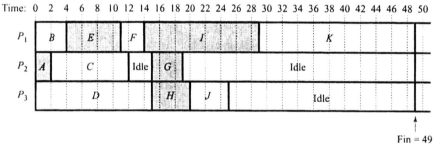

Fin = 49

48. (a)

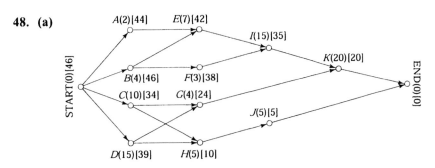

(b) Critical path: START, *B, E, I, K,* END.   Length of critical path: 46

(c)

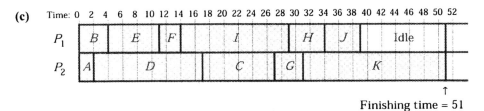

Finishing time = 51

49. The project digraph, with critical times is:

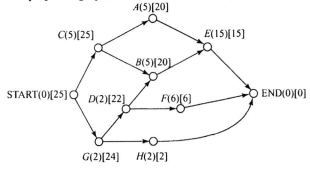

From this, we see the critical path list is: *C*[25], *G*[24], *D*[22], *A*[20], *B*[20], *E*[15], *F*[6], *H*[2].
The schedule is:

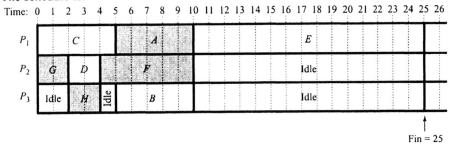

Fin = 25

50.

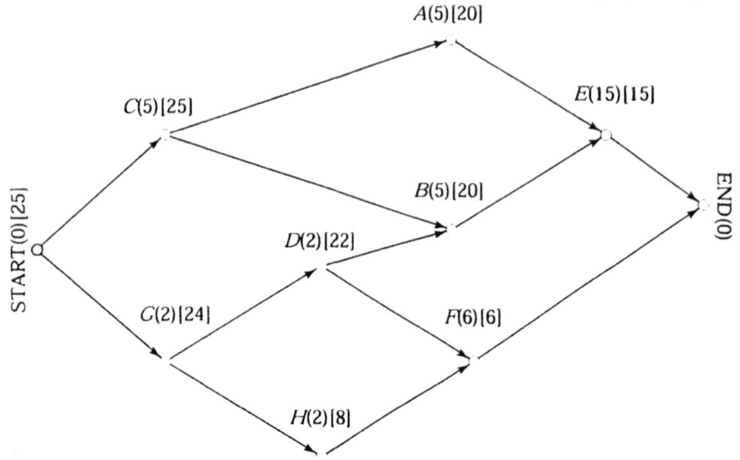
A(5)[20]
C(5)[25]
E(15)[15]
B(5)[20]
START(0)[25]
END(0)
D(2)[22]
C(2)[24]
F(6)[6]
H(2)[8]

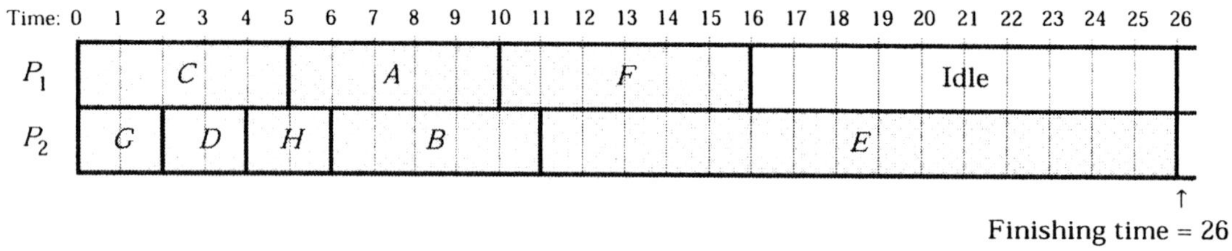
Time: 0 1 2 3 4 5 6 7 8 9 10 11 12 13 14 15 16 17 18 19 20 21 22 23 24 25 26
P_1
C
A
F
Idle
P_2
C
D
H
B
E
Finishing time = 26

F. Scheduling with Independent Tasks

51. (a)

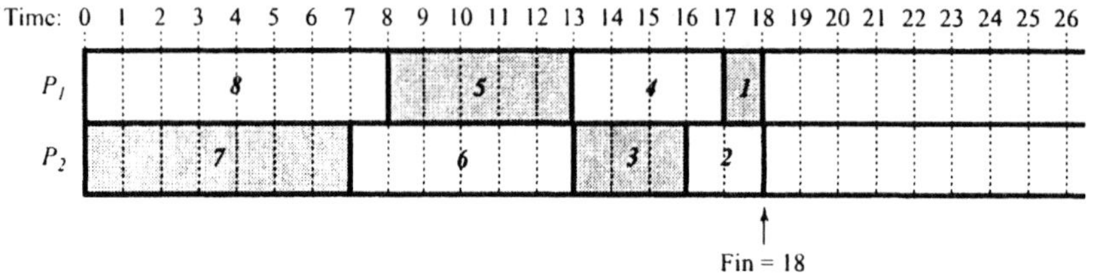
Time: 0 1 2 3 4 5 6 7 8 9 10 11 12 13 14 15 16 17 18 19 20 21 22 23 24 25 26
P_1
8
5
4
1
P_2
7
6
3
2
Fin = 18

(b) The optimal finishing time for $N = 2$ processors is $Opt = 18$ as shown in (a).

(c) The relative error expressed as a percent is $\varepsilon = \dfrac{Fin - Opt}{Opt} = \dfrac{18-18}{18} = 0\%$.

52. (a)

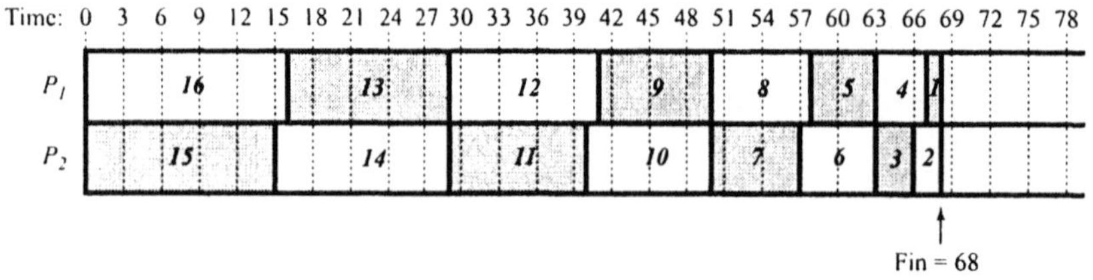
Time: 0 3 6 9 12 15 18 21 24 27 30 33 36 39 42 45 48 51 54 57 60 63 66 69 72 75 78
P_1
16
13
12
9
8
5
4
1
P_2
15
14
11
10
7
6
3
2
Fin = 68

(b) The optimal finishing time for $N = 2$ processors is $Opt = 68$ as shown in (a).

(c) The relative error expressed as a percent is $\varepsilon = \dfrac{Fin - Opt}{Opt} = \dfrac{68 - 68}{68} = 0\%$.

53. (a)   Time: 0 1 2 3 4 5 6 7 8 9 10

P_1	6	1
P_2	5	2
P_3	4	3

Fin = 7

(b) The optimal finishing time for $N = 3$ processors is $Opt = 7$ as shown in (a).

54. (a)   Time: 0 2 4 6 8 10 12 14 16 18 20 22 24 26 28 30 32 34 36 38 40 42 44 46 48 50 52 54 56 58

P_1	18	13 12 7 6 1
P_2	17	14 11 8 5 2
P_3	16	15 10 9 4 3

Fin = 57

(b) The optimal finishing time for $N = 3$ processors is $Opt = 57$ as shown in (a).

55. (a) Since all tasks are independent, the critical path list is identical to a decreasing-time list. The critical path list is: *E, I, D, H, C, G, A, B, F.*
The schedule using $N = 4$ processors is:

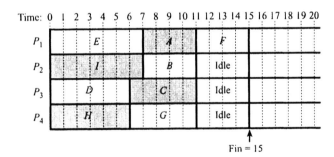

Time: 0 1 2 3 4 5 6 7 8 9 10 11 12 13 14 15 16 17 18 19 20

P_1	E	A	F
P_2	I	B	Idle
P_3	D	C	Idle
P_4	H	G	Idle

Fin = 15

(b)

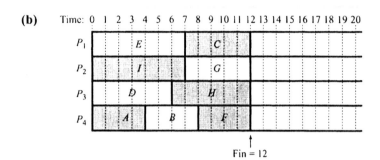

Fin = 12

(c) The relative error expressed as a percent is $\varepsilon = \dfrac{Fin - Opt}{Opt} = \dfrac{15 - 12}{12} = 25\%$.

56. (a)

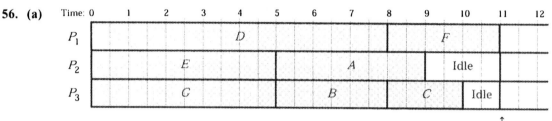

Finishing time = 11

(b)

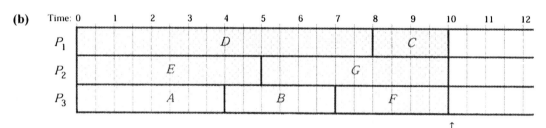

Finishing time = 10

The optimal finishing time is $Opt = 10$.

(c) The relative error expressed as a percent is $\varepsilon = \dfrac{Fin - Opt}{Opt} = \dfrac{11 - 10}{10} = 10\%$.

57. (a) Since all tasks are independent, the critical path list is identical to a decreasing-time list. The schedule using $N = 2$ processors is:

Time: 0 2 4 6 8 10 12 14 16 18 20 22 24 26 28 30 32 34 36 38 40 42 44 46 48 50 52

| P_1 | 34 | 8 | 2 |
| P_2 | 21 | 13 | 5 | 3 | 1 | 1 |

Fin = 44

(b)

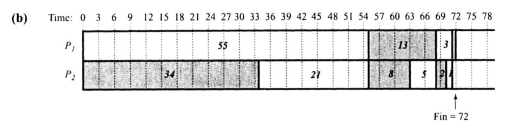

Fin = 72

58. (a) Since all tasks are independent, the critical path list is identical to a decreasing-time list. With a finishing time of *Fin* = 116, the schedule using N = 2 processors is:

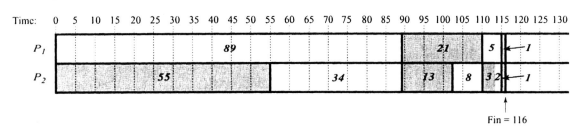

Fin = 116

(b)

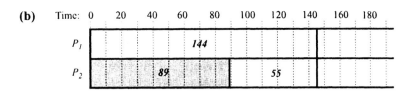

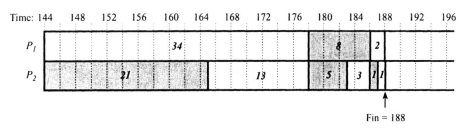

Fin = 188

G.   Miscellaneous

59. Each arc of the graph contributes 1 to the indegree sum and 1 to the outdegree sum.

60. (a) asymmetric

  (b) symmetric

  (c) neither

  (d) symmetric

  (e) asymmetric

61. (a) When $N = 7$, $\varepsilon = \dfrac{7-1}{3 \times 7} = \dfrac{6}{21} \approx 28.57\%$;

When $N = 8$, $\varepsilon = \dfrac{8-1}{3 \times 8} = \dfrac{7}{24} \approx 29.17\%$;

When $N = 9$, $\varepsilon = \dfrac{9-1}{3 \times 9} = \dfrac{8}{27} \approx 29.63\%$;

When $N = 10$, $\varepsilon = \dfrac{10-1}{3 \times 10} = \dfrac{9}{30} \approx 30\%$

(b) Since $M - 1 < M$, we have for every M that $\dfrac{M-1}{3M} \leq \dfrac{M}{3M} = \dfrac{1}{3}$.

62. (a)

Time: 0 1 2 3 4 5 6 7 8 9 10 11 12 13 14 15 16 17 18 19 20 21 22 23 24 25 26

| P_1 | C(6) | | | | | | G(3) | | | A | E | F | K(2) | | M | O | | | |
| P_2 | B(4) | | | D(4) | | | | H(3) | | | I | J | L | N | | | | |

Fin = 16

(b) No. The optimal finishing time for $N = 2$ processors is $Opt = 16$ as shown in (a).

63.

Time: 0 2 4 6 8 10 12 14 16 18 20 22 24 26 28 30 32 34 36 38 40 42 44 46 48 50 52 54 56

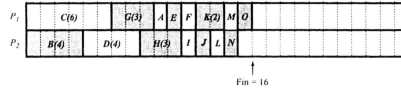

Fin = 44

64.

Time: 0 2 4 6 8 10 12 14 16 18 20 22 24 26 28 30 32 34 36 38 40 42

| P_1 | AD | AF | IF | IW | ID | PU | PD | FW | |
| P_2 | AP | AW | Idle | PL | Idle | IP | HU | EU/C | Idle |

Finishing time = 42

65. The schedule is:

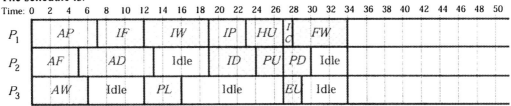

66. The schedule is:

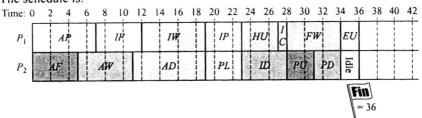

Finishing time = 34

JOGGING

67. (a)

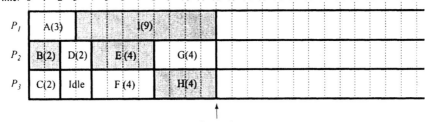

Fin = 12

(b)

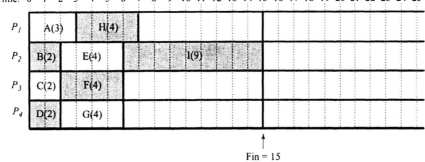

Fin = 15

(c) An extra processor was used and yet the finishing time of the project increased.

68. (a)

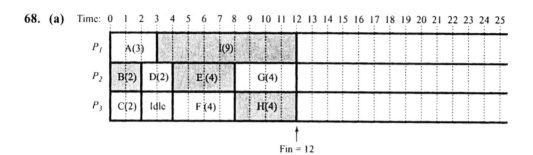

Fin = 12

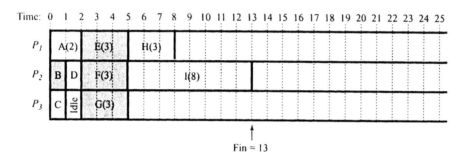

Fin = 13

(c) Each task was shorter and yet the finishing time of the project increased.

69. (a)

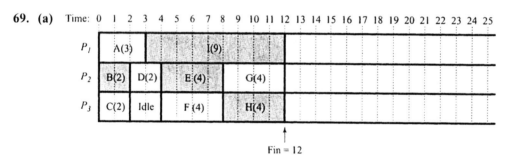

Fin = 12

(b)

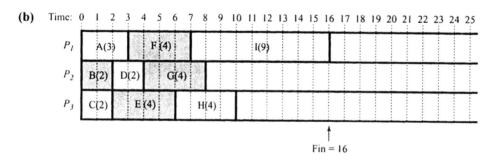

Fin = 16

(c) The project had fewer restrictions on the order of the assignments to the processors and yet the finishing time of the project increased.

70.

Time:	0	1	2	3	4	5	6	7	8	9	10	11	12	13	14	15	16	17	18	19	20	21	22	23	24
P_1		A			D			G			J			M			O			R					
P_2		B			E			H			K			N			Q			Idle					
P_3		C			F			I			L			P			Idle			Idle					

Finishing time = 21

71. (a) The finishing time of a project is always more than or equal to the number of hours of work to be done divided by the number of processors doing the work.

(b) The schedule is optimal with no idle time.

(c) The total idle time in the schedule.

72. (a) Answers will vary. One possible answer is *A, B, C, E, G, H, D, F, I.*

(b) Answers will vary. One possible answer is *A, B, G, I, C, D, H, E, F.*

RUNNING

73. Consider four cases: $N = 4M$, $4M+1$, $4M+2$, and $4M+3$ for some positive integer M. If $N = 4M$, then the optimal schedule is

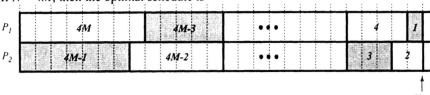

and the optimal completion time is $\dfrac{1+2+3+\ldots+4M}{2} = \dfrac{(4M+1)(4M)/2}{2} = \dfrac{(4M+1)(4M)}{4}$.

If $N = 4M+1$, then the optimal schedule is

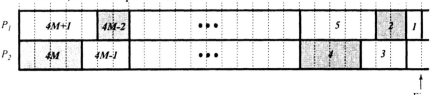

and the optimal completion time is $\dfrac{1+2+3+\ldots+(4M+1)}{2} = \dfrac{(4M+2)(4M+1)/2}{2} = \dfrac{(4M+2)(4M+1)}{4}$.

If $N = 4M+2$, then the optimal schedule is

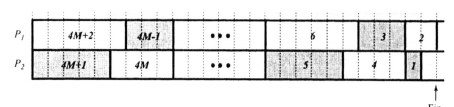

and the optimal completion time is $\dfrac{1+2+3+\ldots+(4M+2)}{2} = \dfrac{(4M+3)(4M+2)/2}{2} = \dfrac{(4M+3)(4M+2)}{4}$

If $N = 4M+3$, then the optimal schedule is

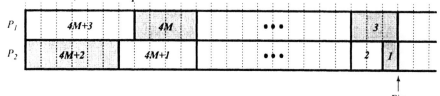

and the optimal completion time is $\dfrac{1+2+3+\ldots+(4M+3)}{2} = \dfrac{(4M+4)(4M+3)/2}{2} = \dfrac{(4M+4)(4M+3)}{4}$

74. Consider six cases: $N = 6M$, $6M+1$, $6M+2$, $6M+3$, $6M+4$, and $6M+5$ for some positive integer M. If $N = 6M$, then the optimal schedule is

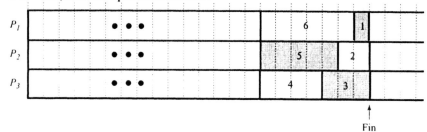

and the optimal completion time is $\dfrac{1+2+3+\ldots+6M}{2} = \dfrac{(6M+1)(6M)/2}{3} = \dfrac{(6M+1)(6M)}{6}$.

In a fashion, similar to Exercise 73, the optimal completion time for the other cases is given below:
If $N = 6M+1$, then the optimal completion time is

$\dfrac{1+2+3+\ldots+(6M+1)}{2} = \dfrac{(6M+2)(6M+1)/2}{3} = \dfrac{(6M+2)(6M+1)}{6}$.

If $N = 6M+2$, then the optimal completion time is

$\dfrac{1+2+3+\ldots+(6M+2)}{2} = \dfrac{(6M+3)(6M+2)/2}{3} = \dfrac{(6M+3)(6M+2)}{6}$.

In general, if $N = 6M+k$ ($k = 0,1,2,3,4$, or 5), then the optimal completion time is $\dfrac{(6M+k+1)(6M+k)}{6}$.

75. (a) Consider three cases: $M = 3k$, $M = 3k + 1$, and $M = 3k + 2$ where k is a positive integer.
       If $M = 3k$ for some k, then the optimal schedule is

294

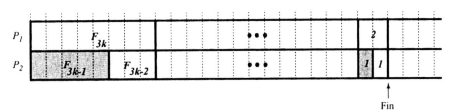

and the optimal completion time is $Opt = \dfrac{F_1 + F_2 + F_3 + \ldots + F_{3k}}{2} = \dfrac{F_{3k+2} - 1}{2}$.

If $M = 3k+1$ for some k, then the optimal schedule is

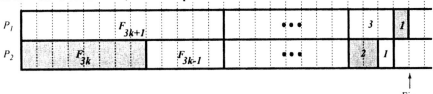

and the optimal completion time is $Opt = F_1 + \dfrac{F_2 + F_3 + \ldots + F_{3k+1}}{2} = 1 + \dfrac{(F_{3k+3} - 1) - 1}{2} = \dfrac{F_{3k+3}}{2}$.

If $M = 3k+2$ for some k, then the optimal schedule is

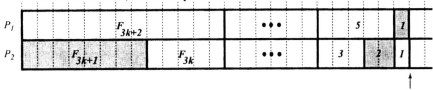

and the optimal completion time is $Opt = \dfrac{F_1 + F_2 + F_3 + \ldots + F_{3k+2}}{2} = \dfrac{F_{3k+2+2} - 1}{2} = \dfrac{F_{3k+4} - 1}{2}$.

(b) Part (a) shows that to schedule the tasks given by the first M-1 Fibonacci number using $N=2$ processors requires less than F_M . [Note: We have used the fact that $\dfrac{F_{3k+2} - 1}{2} \leq F_{3k+1}$, $\dfrac{F_{3k+3}}{2} \leq F_{3k+2}$, and $\dfrac{F_{3k+4} - 1}{2} \leq F_{3k+3}$]

So, if one uses the first processor to schedule task M (having length F_M) in the list, then the other two processors can process all of the remaining tasks in at most that much time. This makes $Opt = F_M$.

Chapter 9

A. Fibonacci Numbers

1. (a) $F_{10} = 55$

 (b) $F_{10} + 2 = 55 + 2 = 57$

 (c) $F_{10+2} = F_{12} = 144$

 (d) $F_{10} / 2 = 55 / 2 = 27.5$

 (e) $F_{10/2} = F_5 = 5$

2. (a) $F_{12} = 144$

 (b) $F_{12} - 1 = 144 - 1 = 143$

 (c) $F_{12-1} = F_{11} = 89$

 (d) $F_{12} / 4 = 144 / 4 = 36$

 (e) $F_{12/4} = F_3 = 2$

3. (a) $F_1 + F_2 + F_3 + F_4 + F_5 = 1 + 1 + 2 + 3 + 5$
$$= 12$$

 (b) $F_{1+2+3+4+5} = F_{15} = 610$

 (c) $F_3 \times F_4 = 2 \times 3 = 6$

 (d) $F_{3 \cdot 4} = F_{12} = 144$

 (e) $F_{F_4} = F_3 = 2$

4. (a) $F_1 + F_3 + F_5 + F_7 = 1 + 2 + 5 + 13 = 21$

 (b) $F_{1+3+5+7} = F_{16} = 987$

 (c) $F_{10} / F_5 = 55 / 5 = 11$

 (d) $F_{10/F_5} = F_{10/5} = F_2 = 1$

 (e) $F_{F_7} = F_{13} = 233$

5. (a) $3F_N + 1$ represents one more than three times the Nth Fibonacci number.

 (b) $3F_{N+1}$ represents three times the Fibonacci number in position $(N + 1)$.

 (c) $F_{3N} + 1$ represents one more than the Fibonacci number in the $3N$th position.

 (d) F_{3N+1} represents the Fibonacci number in position $(3N + 1)$.

6. (a) Subtract 3 from the Fibonacci number in position $2N$.

 (b) The Fibonacci number in position $(2N - 3)$

 (c) Subtract 3 from twice the Nth Fibonacci number.

 (d) Two times the Fibonacci number in position $(N - 3)$.

7. (a) $F_{38} = F_{37} + F_{36}$
$$= 24,157,817 + 14,930,352$$
$$= 39,088,169$$

 (b) $F_{35} = F_{37} - F_{36}$
$$= 24,157,817 - 14,930,352$$
$$= 9,227,465$$

8. (a) $F_{32} = F_{33} - F_{31}$
$$= 3,524,578 - 1,3469,269$$
$$= 2,178,309$$

 (b) $F_{34} = F_{33} + F_{32}$
$$= 3,524,578 + 2,178,309$$
$$= 5,702,887$$

9. (I) $F_{N+2} = F_{N+1} + F_N$, $N > 0$, is an equivalent way to express the fact that each term of the Fibonacci sequence is equal to the sum of the two preceding terms.

10. (II) $F_{N+1} - F_N = F_{N-1}$ is equivalent to $F_{N+1} = F_N + F_{N-1}$ which is another way to express the fact that each term of the Fibonacci sequence is equal to the sum of the two preceding terms.

11. (a) $47 = 34 + 13$

   (b) $48 = 34 + 13 + 1$

   (c) $207 = 144 + 55 + 8$

   (d) $210 = 144 + 55 + 8 + 3$

12. (a) $52 = 34 + 13 + 5$

   (b) $53 = 34 + 13 + 5 + 1$

   (c) $107 = 89 + 13 + 5$

   (d) $112 = 89 + 21 + 2$

13. (a) $1 + 2 + 5 + 13 + 34 + 89 = 144$

   (b) 22

   (c) $N+1$

14. (a) $2(13) - 21 = 5$

   (b) 14

   (c) N

15. (a) Choosing the Fibonacci numbers $F_4 = 3$, $F_5 = 5$, $F_6 = 8$, and $F_7 = 13$, the fact is verified by the equation $F_7 + F_4 = 13 + 3 = 16 = 2(8) = 2F_6$.

   (b) Denoting the first of these four Fibonacci numbers by F_N, a mathematical formula expressing this fact is $F_{N+3} + F_N = 2F_{N+2}$.

16. (a) $\dfrac{1+1+2+\ldots+55}{11} = \dfrac{143}{11}$
$$= 13$$

   (b) $\dfrac{(F_N + F_{N+1} + F_{N+2} + \ldots + F_{N+9})}{11} = F_{N+6}$

17. (a) $2F_6 - F_7 = 2 \times 8 - 13 = 3 = F_4$

   (b) $2F_{N+2} - F_{N+3} = F_N$

18. (a) $F_8 \cdot F_{11} = 21 \cdot 89 = 1869 = 3025 - 1156$
$$= 55^2 - 34^2 = F_{10}^2 - F_9^2$$

   (b) $F_N F_{N+3} = F_{N+2}^2 - F_{N+1}^2$

B.   **The Golden Ratio**

19. (a) $21\left(\dfrac{1+\sqrt{5}}{2}\right) + 13 \approx 46.97871$

   (b) $\left(\dfrac{1+\sqrt{5}}{2}\right)^8 \approx 46.97871$

   (c) $\dfrac{\left(\frac{1+\sqrt{5}}{2}\right)^8 - \left(\frac{1-\sqrt{5}}{2}\right)^8}{\sqrt{5}} = 21.00000$

20. (a) 122.99187

   (b) 122.99187

   (c) 55.00000

21. (a) $\dfrac{\phi^8}{\sqrt{5}} = \dfrac{\left[\frac{(1+\sqrt{5})}{2}\right]^8}{\sqrt{5}} \approx 21$

   (b) $\dfrac{\phi^9}{\sqrt{5}} = \dfrac{\left[\frac{(1+\sqrt{5})}{2}\right]^9}{\sqrt{5}} \approx 34$

   (c) Guess the 7th Fibonacci number, 13.

22. (a) $\dfrac{\phi^{10}}{\sqrt{5}} = \dfrac{\left[\frac{(1+\sqrt{5})}{2}\right]^{10}}{\sqrt{5}} \approx 55$

    (b) $\dfrac{\phi^{11}}{\sqrt{5}} = \dfrac{\left[\frac{(1+\sqrt{5})}{2}\right]^{11}}{\sqrt{5}} \approx 89$

    (c) Guess the 12th Fibonacci number, 144.

23. (a) $\phi^{9} = F_{9}\phi + F_{8}$
       $= 34\phi + 21$
       so $a = 34$ and $b = 21$.

    (b) $\phi^{9} = F_{9}\phi + F_{8}$
       $= 34\phi + 21$
       $= 34\left(\dfrac{1+\sqrt{5}}{2}\right) + 21$
       $= 17 + 17\sqrt{5} + 21$
       $= 38 + 17\sqrt{5}$
       So, $a = 17$ and $b = 38$.

24. (a) $\phi^{12} = F_{12}\phi + F_{11}$
       $= 144\phi + 89$
       so $a = 144$ and $b = 89$.

    (b) $161 + 72\sqrt{5}$
       $\phi^{12} = F_{12}\phi + F_{11}$
       $= 144\left(\dfrac{1+\sqrt{5}}{2}\right) + 89$
       $= 72\left(1 + \sqrt{5}\right) + 89$
       $= 161 + 72\sqrt{5}$
       So, $a = 72$ and $b = 161$.

25. $F_{500} \approx \phi \times F_{499}$
    $\approx 1.618 \times 8.617 \times 10^{103}$
    $\approx 1.394 \times 10^{104}$

26. $F_{1000} \approx F_{1002} / \phi^{2}$
    $\approx 1.138 \times 10^{209} / 2.61804$
    $\approx 4.347 \times 10^{208}$

27. (a) $A_{7} = 2A_{7-1} + A_{7-2}$
       $= 2A_{6} + A_{5}$
       $= 2(70) + 29$
       $= 169$

    (b) $\dfrac{A_{7}}{A_{6}} = \dfrac{169}{70}$
       ≈ 2.41429

    (c) $\dfrac{A_{11}}{A_{10}} = \dfrac{5,741}{2,378}$
       ≈ 2.41421

    (d) 2.41421 (Though not obvious, the ratio actually approaches $1 + \sqrt{2}$ as the value of N increases.)

28. (a) $A_{6} = 3A_{5} + A_{4}$
       $= 3 \cdot 109 + 33$
       $= 360$

    (b) $\dfrac{A_{6}}{A_{5}} = \dfrac{360}{109}$
       ≈ 3.30275

    (c) 3.30278

C. **Fibonacci Numbers and Quadratic Equations**

29. (a) $x = 1 + \sqrt{2}$ or $x = 1 - \sqrt{2}$
       ≈ 2.41421 ≈ -0.41421

    (b) $x = \dfrac{8}{3}$ or $x = -1$

30. (a) $x = \dfrac{3 + \sqrt{13}}{2}$ or $x = \dfrac{3 - \sqrt{13}}{2}$

≈ 3.30278 ≈ -0.30278

(b) $x = 1$, $x = -\dfrac{3}{8}$

31. (a) $x = 1$ is one solution.

(b) $x = \dfrac{34}{55} - 1 = -\dfrac{21}{55}$

32. (a) $x = -1$

(b) $x = 1 + \dfrac{34}{21} = \dfrac{55}{21}$

33. (a) Putting $x = 1$ in the equation gives $F_N = F_{N-1} + F_{N-2}$ which is a defining equation for the Fibonacci numbers.

(b) The sum of the roots of the equation is $-\dfrac{-F_{N-1}}{F_N} = \dfrac{F_{N-1}}{F_N}$ and so the other root is $\dfrac{F_{N-1}}{F_N} - 1$.

34. (a) Putting $x = -1$ in the equation gives $F_N = -F_{N+1} + F_{N+2}$, or $F_{N+2} = F_{N+1} + F_N$ which is a defining equation for the Fibonacci numbers.

(b) The sum of the roots of the equation is $-\dfrac{-F_{N+1}}{F_N} = \dfrac{F_{N+1}}{F_N}$ and so the other root is $\dfrac{F_{N+1}}{F_N} + 1$.

D.   Similarity

35. (a) Since R and R' are similar, each side length of R' is 3 times longer than the corresponding side in R. So, the perimeter of R' will be 3 times greater

than the perimeter of R. This means that the perimeter of R' is $3 \times 41.5 = 124.5$ inches.

(b) Since each side of R' is 3 times longer than the corresponding side in R, the area of R' will be $3^2 = 9$ times larger than the area of R. That is, the area of R' is $9 \times 105 = 945$ square inches.

36. (a) Since O and O' are similar, the outer radius of O' is 3 times longer than the outer radius of O. Since the outer radius of O is $\dfrac{14\pi}{2\pi} = 7$ feet, the outer radius of O' is 21 feet. Hence, the circumference of the outer circle of O' is $2 \cdot \pi \cdot 21 = 42\pi$.

(b) The area of an O-ring having inner radius r and outer radius R is $A = \pi R^2 - \pi r^2$. If the inner radius and outer radius are both tripled to form a new O-ring, the area will be $\pi (3R)^2 - \pi (3r)^2 = 3^2 [\pi R^2 - \pi r^2] = 9A$ Thus, the number of gallons to paint O' will be $9 \times 1.5 = 13.5$.

37. (a) 156 m.

The scaling factor is $\dfrac{60}{5} = 12$.

(b) 2880 sq. m.
In this problem we use the fact that the ratio of the areas of two similar triangles (or any two similar polygons) is the same as the ratio of their side lengths squared. Hence,

$\dfrac{A}{20 \text{ sq. in.}} = \left(\dfrac{60 \text{ m}}{5 \text{ in.}} \right)^2$

$A = \left(\dfrac{60 \text{ m}}{5 \text{ in.}} \right)^2 \times (20 \text{ sq. in.})$

$= 2880 \text{ sq. m}$

38. (a) 25

The scaling factor is $\dfrac{5}{2} = 2.5$.

(b) $\dfrac{375}{2}$

Since the scaling factor is $\dfrac{5}{2}$, the areas

change by a factor of $\left(\dfrac{5}{2}\right)^2 = \dfrac{25}{4}$.

39. There are two possible cases that need to be considered. First, we solve

$$\frac{3}{x} = \frac{5}{8-x}$$
$$24 - 3x = 5x$$
$$24 = 8x$$
$$3 = x$$

But, it could also be the case that the side of length 3 does not correspond to the side of length 5, but rather the side of length $8 - x$. In this case, we solve

$$\frac{3}{x} = \frac{8-x}{5}$$
$$15 = 8x - x^2$$
$$x^2 - 8x + 15 = 0$$
$$(x-5)(x-3) = 0$$
$$x = 3, 5$$

It follows that R and R' are similar if $x = 3$ or if $x = 5$ (as can easily be checked).

40. There are two possible cases that need to be considered. First, we solve

$$\frac{2}{x} = \frac{6}{x+1}$$
$$2x + 2 = 6x$$
$$2 = 4x$$
$$\frac{1}{2} = x$$

But, it could also be the case that the side of length 2 does not correspond to the side of length 6, but rather the side of length $x+1$.

In this case, we solve

$$\frac{2}{x} = \frac{x+1}{6}$$
$$12 = x^2 + x$$
$$x^2 + x - 12 = 0$$
$$(x-3)(x+4) = 0$$
$$x = 3, -4$$

It follows that R and R' are similar if $x = 3$ or if $x = 1/2$.

E.   Gnomons

41. $c = 24$

$$\frac{3}{9} = \frac{9}{c+3}$$

42. $x = 1.2$

$$\frac{6}{10} = \frac{6+x}{12}$$

43. $x = 4$

$$\frac{8}{12} = \frac{3+8+1}{2+12+x}$$
$$\frac{8}{12} = \frac{12}{14+x}$$

44. $x = 1.5$

$$\frac{2}{6} = \frac{3}{2x+6}$$

45.   20 by 30

$$\frac{10}{20} = \frac{20}{10+x}$$
$$x = 30$$

46. $x = 8$

$$\frac{8}{x} = \frac{1+8+1}{1+x+1}$$

$$\frac{8}{x} = \frac{10}{x+2}$$

47. (a) In the figure, the measure of angle CAD must be $180° - 108° = 72°$. Since triangle BDC must be similar to triangle BCA (in order for triangle ACD to be a gnomon), it must be that the measure of angle BDC must be $36°$. Using the fact that the sum of the measures of the angles in any triangle is $180°$, it follows that the measure of angle ACD is also $36°$.

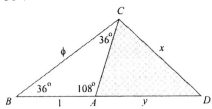

(b) Since triangle DBC is isosceles, $x = \phi$. Note that triangle ACD is also isosceles. Hence, $y = x = \phi$ as well.

48. We solve $\dfrac{4}{8} = \dfrac{6}{x} = \dfrac{8}{y+4}$. This gives $x = 12$ and $y = 12$.

49. $x = 12, y = 10$

$$\frac{3}{4} = \frac{9}{x} \text{ and } \frac{3}{5} = \frac{9}{5+y}$$

50. $x = 20, y = 16$

$$\frac{9}{12} = \frac{15}{x} \text{ and } \frac{9}{15} = \frac{15}{y+9}$$

JOGGING

51. $A_N = 5F_N$ (Each term in this sequence is 5 times more than the corresponding term in the Fibonacci sequence.)

52. (a) The expression $L_N = 2F_{N+1} - F_N$ satisfies the recursive rule:

$$\begin{aligned}
L_N &= 2F_{N+1} - F_N \\
&= 2(F_N + F_{N-1}) - (F_{N-1} + F_{N-2}) \\
&= 2F_N + F_{N-1} - F_{N-2} \\
&= 2F_N - F_{N-1} + (2F_{N-1} - F_{N-2}) \\
&= L_{N-1} + L_{N-2}
\end{aligned}$$

Also, this expression satisfies
$L_1 = 2F_2 - F_1 = 2 \cdot 1 - 1 = 1$ and
$L_2 = 2F_3 - F_2 = 2 \cdot 2 - 1 = 3$.

(b)

$$L_N = 2F_{N+1} - F_N$$

$$= 2 \left[\frac{\left(\frac{1+\sqrt{5}}{2}\right)^{N+1} - \left(\frac{1-\sqrt{5}}{2}\right)^{N+1}}{\sqrt{5}} \right] - \left[\frac{\left(\frac{1+\sqrt{5}}{2}\right)^{N} - \left(\frac{1-\sqrt{5}}{2}\right)^{N}}{\sqrt{5}} \right]$$

$$= \frac{2}{\sqrt{5}} \left(\frac{1+\sqrt{5}}{2}\right)\left(\frac{1+\sqrt{5}}{2}\right)^{N} - \frac{1}{\sqrt{5}}\left(\frac{1+\sqrt{5}}{2}\right)^{N}$$

$$\quad - \frac{2}{\sqrt{5}}\left(\frac{1-\sqrt{5}}{2}\right)\left(\frac{1-\sqrt{5}}{2}\right)^{N} + \frac{1}{\sqrt{5}}\left(\frac{1-\sqrt{5}}{2}\right)^{N}$$

$$= \left[\frac{2}{\sqrt{5}}\left(\frac{1+\sqrt{5}}{2}\right) - \frac{1}{\sqrt{5}}\right]\left(\frac{1+\sqrt{5}}{2}\right)^{N}$$

$$\quad + \left[-\frac{2}{\sqrt{5}}\left(\frac{1-\sqrt{5}}{2}\right) + \frac{1}{\sqrt{5}}\right]\left(\frac{1-\sqrt{5}}{2}\right)^{N}$$

$$= \left(\frac{1+\sqrt{5}}{2}\right)^{N} + \left(\frac{1-\sqrt{5}}{2}\right)^{N}$$

53. (a)
$$\begin{aligned}
T_1 &= 7F_2 + 4F_1 = 7 \cdot 1 + 4 \cdot 1 = 11 \\
T_2 &= 7F_3 + 4F_2 = 7 \cdot 2 + 4 \cdot 1 = 18 \\
T_3 &= 7F_4 + 4F_3 = 7 \cdot 3 + 4 \cdot 2 = 29 \\
T_4 &= 7F_5 + 4F_4 = 7 \cdot 5 + 4 \cdot 3 = 47 \\
T_5 &= 7F_6 + 4F_5 = 7 \cdot 8 + 4 \cdot 5 = 76 \\
T_6 &= 7F_7 + 4F_6 = 7 \cdot 13 + 4 \cdot 8 = 123 \\
T_7 &= 7F_8 + 4F_7 = 7 \cdot 21 + 4 \cdot 13 = 199 \\
T_8 &= 7F_9 + 4F_8 = 7 \cdot 34 + 4 \cdot 21 = 322
\end{aligned}$$

(b) $T_N = 7F_{N+1} + 4F_N$
$= 7(F_N + F_{N-1}) + 4(F_{N-1} + F_{N-2})$
$= (7F_N + 4F_{N-1}) + (7F_{N-1} + 4F_{N-2})$
$= T_{N-1} + T_{N-2}$

(c) $T_1 = 11$, $T_1 = 18$,
$T_N = T_{N-1} + T_{N-2}$

54. (a) $T_1 = aF_2 + bF_1 = a + b$
$T_2 = aF_3 = bF_2 = 2a + b$
$T_3 = aF_4 = bF_3 = 3a + 2b$
$T_4 = aF_5 = bF_4 = 5a + 3b$
$T_5 = aF_6 = bF_5 = 8a + 5b$

(b) $T_N = aF_{N+1} + bF_N$
$= a(F_N + F_{N-1}) + b(F_{N-1} + F_{N-2})$
$= (aF_N + bF_{N-1}) + (aF_{N-1} + bF_{N-2})$
$= T_{N-1} + T_{N-2}$

(c) To fit the description would require that
$T_1 = 5 = aF_2 + bF_1 = a + b$ and
$T_2 = 11 = aF_3 + bF_2 = 2a + b$. Subtracting
these equations gives $a = 11-5 = 6$ so that
$b = -1$.

55. $\dfrac{1+\sqrt{5}}{2} + \dfrac{1-\sqrt{5}}{2} = \dfrac{1+1}{2} = 1$

Since the first term is positive and the second
term is negative and the sum is a whole
number, it follows that the decimal parts are
the same.

56. (a) These values approach 0 as N gets
larger.

(b) Using Binet's formula,

$$F_N = \frac{\left(\dfrac{1+\sqrt{5}}{2}\right)^N - \left(\dfrac{1-\sqrt{5}}{2}\right)^N}{\sqrt{5}}$$

$$= \frac{\phi^N - \left(\dfrac{1-\sqrt{5}}{2}\right)^N}{\sqrt{5}}$$

It follows from (a), that $F_N \approx \dfrac{\phi^N}{\sqrt{5}}$.

(c) From (b), $\dfrac{F_N}{F_{N-1}} \approx \dfrac{\phi^N / \sqrt{5}}{\phi^{N-1} / \sqrt{5}} = \phi$.

57. We use the fact that $\phi^N = F_N\phi + F_{N-1}$ to
compute the ratio l/s. Since
$\dfrac{l}{s} = \dfrac{144\phi + 89}{89\phi + 55} = \dfrac{\phi^{12}}{\phi^{11}} = \phi$, it follows that R is a
golden rectangle.

58. Since $\phi^N = F_N\phi + F_{N-1}$, it follows that
$\phi^8 = F_8\phi + F_7 = 21\phi + 13$. That is, ϕ solves
$x^8 - 21x - 13 = 0$.

59. If the rectangle is a gnomon to itself, then the
rectangle in the figure below must be similar
to the original l by s rectangle.

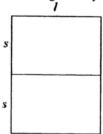

This means that $\dfrac{2s}{l} = \dfrac{l}{s}$. Letting $x = \dfrac{l}{s}$, we

solve $\dfrac{2}{x} = x$. The only positive solution to

this equation is $x = \dfrac{l}{s} = \sqrt{2}$. So, the only rectangles that are gnomons to themselves (homognomic) are those having this ratio.

60. The result of attaching a gnomon to the L-shaped figure must result in a new, larger L-shaped figure — it must be higher, wider, and thicker (all by the same proportions). The possible ways of attaching a square to the L-shaped figure and still maintaining a L-shaped figure are:

None of these figures can possibly be similar to the original L-shaped figure.

61. $x = 6, y = 12, z = 10$

Since the area of the white triangle is 6, the area of the shaded figure must be 48, which makes the area of the new larger similar triangle 54. Since the ratio of the areas of similar triangles is the square of the ratio of the sides, we have

$$\frac{3+x}{3} = \sqrt{\frac{54}{6}} = 3 \text{ and } \frac{y}{4} = \sqrt{\frac{54}{6}} = 3 \text{ and}$$

$$\frac{5+z}{5} = \sqrt{\frac{54}{6}} = 3 .$$

62. $x = 65, y = 25$

$$\frac{60}{156} = \frac{y}{x} \text{ and } \frac{60}{156} = \frac{x}{y + 144}$$

$$60x = 156y \text{ and}$$

$$60y + 8,640 = 156x$$

$$60\left(\frac{60}{156}x\right) + 8,640 = 156x$$

$$x = 65 \text{ so that}$$

$$y = \frac{60}{156}(65) = 25 .$$

63. $x = 3, y = 5$

Since the area of the white rectangle is 60 and the area of the shaded figure is 75, the area of the new larger similar rectangle is

135. Since the ratio of the area of similar rectangles is the square of the ratio of the sides, we have

$$\frac{6+x}{6} = \sqrt{\frac{135}{60}} = \sqrt{\frac{9}{4}} = \frac{3}{2} \text{ and } \frac{10+y}{10} = \frac{3}{2} .$$

64. From elementary geometry $\angle AEF \cong \angle DBA$. Consequently $\triangle AEF$ is similar to $\triangle DBA$ (since they are both right triangles and so have all their corresponding angles congruent). So $AF : FE = DA : AB$ which shows rectangle *ADEF* is similar to rectangle *ABCD*.

65. **(a)** Since we are given that $AB = BC = 1$, we know that $\angle BAC = 72°$ and so $\angle BAD = 180° - 72° = 108°$. This makes $\angle ABD = 180° - 108° - 36° = 36°$ and so triangle *ABD* is isosceles with $AD = AB = 1$. Therefore $AC = x - 1$. Using these facts and the similarity of triangle *ABC* and triangle *BCD* we have $\frac{x}{1} = \frac{1}{x-1}$ or, $x^2 = x + 1$ for which we know the solution is $x = \phi$.

  (b) 36°, 36°, 108°

  (c) $\frac{\text{longer side}}{\text{shorter side}} = \frac{x}{1} = x = \phi$

66. Follows from Exercise 65(a) and the following figure.

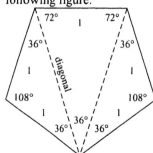

67. **(a)** The regular decagon can be split into ten 72° – 72° – 36° triangles as shown in the figure. In each of these triangles, the side opposite the $72°$ angle is the same length as the radius of the circle, namely r. In Exercise 65, it was shown that the length of the side opposite the $36°$ angle is $\dfrac{r}{\phi}$. Hence, the perimeter of the regular decagon is $10 \times \dfrac{1}{\phi} = \dfrac{10}{\phi}$.

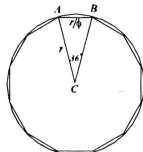

(b) Using part (a), the perimeter is found to be $\dfrac{10r}{\phi}$.

68. (a) Since $\phi + 1 = \phi^2$, we conclude that $\sqrt{\phi + 1} = \phi$. It then follows that

$$\sqrt{1 + \sqrt{1 + \sqrt{1 + \phi}}} = \sqrt{1 + \sqrt{1 + \phi}}$$
$$= \sqrt{1 + \phi}$$
$$= \phi$$

(b) Since $\phi + 1 = \phi^2$, we divide both sides by ϕ to conclude that $1 + \dfrac{1}{\phi} = \phi$. Hence,

$$1 + \cfrac{1}{1 + \cfrac{1}{1 + \cfrac{1}{\phi}}} = 1 + \cfrac{1}{1 + \cfrac{1}{\phi}}$$
$$= 1 + \frac{1}{\phi}$$
$$= \phi$$

RUNNING

69. (a) 3.

The possible paths are illustrated below.

(b) 21.

(c) F_N.

The path can end with either a vertical stone or two horizontal stones. There are F_{N-1} ways that a path of length N feet can end in a vertical stone (count all paths of length N-1). There are F_{N-2} ways that a path can of length N feet can end in two horizontal stones (count all paths of length N-2).

70.
$$\left(F_1\right)^2 + \left(F_2\right)^2 = 1 + 1 = 1 \cdot 2 = F_2 \cdot F_3$$
$$\left[\left(F_1\right)^2 + \left(F_2\right)^2\right] + \left(F_3\right)^2 = \left[F_2 \cdot F_3\right] + \left(F_3\right)^2$$
$$= F_3\left(F_2 + F_3\right)$$
$$= F_3 \cdot F_4$$
$$\left(F_1\right)^2 + \left(F_2\right)^2 + \left(F_3\right)^2 + \left(F_4\right)^2 = F_3 \cdot F_4 + \left(F_4\right)^2$$
$$= F_4\left(F_3 + F_4\right)$$
$$= F_4 \cdot F_5$$
$$\vdots$$
$$\left[\left(F_1\right)^2 + \left(F_2\right)^2 + \ldots \left(F_{N-1}\right)^2\right] + \left(F_N\right)^2 = \left[F_{N-1} \cdot F_N\right] + \left(F_N\right)^2$$
$$= F_N\left(F_{N-1} + F_N\right)$$
$$= F_N \cdot F_{N+1}$$

(A proper argument would involve induction.)

71.
$$F_1 = F_3 - F_2$$
$$F_2 = F_4 - F_3$$
$$\vdots$$
$$F_{N-1} = F_{N+1} - F_N$$
$$F_N = F_{N+2} - F_{N+1}$$

Adding the left and right hand sides respectively, yields
$$F_1 + F_2 + \cdots + F_N = F_{N+2} - F_2 = F_{N+2} - 1$$

72. $F_1 = F_2$

$F_3 = F_4 - F_2$

$F_5 = F_6 - F_4$

$\vdots$

$F_N = F_{N+1} - F_{N-1}$

Adding the left and right hand sides respectively, yields

$F_1 + F_3 + F_5 + \ldots + F_N = F_{N+1}$

73. Suppose M is a positive integer greater than 2. If M is a Fibonacci number ($M = F_N$), then it is certainly true that M can be written as the sum of distinct Fibonacci numbers ($M = F_N = F_{N-1} + F_{N-2}$). Otherwise, M falls somewhere between two Fibonacci numbers, say between F_N and F_{N+1}. Write

$M = F_N + (M - F_N)$. Now

$M - F_N < F_{N+1} - F_N = F_{N-1}$ is itself a

positive integer smaller than M and we can repeat the argument. Eventually the process must stop. (This is an argument by induction in disguise.)

Note: This argument gives an algorithm for finding a decomposition of M as a sum of Fibonacci numbers. Find the largest Fibonacci number that fits into M (call it F_N), then find the largest Fibonacci number that fits into the difference $M - F_N$, and so on.

74. We first express the ten consecutive Fibonacci numbers $F_K, F_{K+1}, F_{K+2}, F_{K+3}, F_{K+4}, F_{K+5}, F_{K+6}, F_{K+7}, F_{K+8}, F_{K+9}$ in terms of F_K and F_{K+1}.

$F_{K+2} = F_{K+1} + F_K$

$F_{K+3} = F_{K+2} + F_{K+1} = F_K + 2F_{K+1}$

$F_{K+4} = F_{K+3} + F_{K+2} = 2F_K + 3F_{K+1}$

$F_{K+5} = F_{K+4} + F_{K+3} = 3F_K + 5F_{K+1}$

$F_{K+6} = F_{K+5} + F_{K+4} = 5F_K + 8F_{K+1}$

$F_{K+7} = F_{K+6} + F_{K+5} = 8F_K + 13F_{K+1}$

$F_{K+8} = F_{K+7} + F_{K+6} = 13F_K + 21F_{K+1}$

$F_{K+9} = F_{K+8} + F_{K+7} = 21F_K + 34F_{K+1}$

So,

$F_K + F_{K+1} + F_{K+2} + F_{K+3} + F_{K+4} + F_{K+5} + F_{K+6} + F_{K+7} + F_{K+8} + F_{K+9} =$

$55F_K + 88F_{K+1} = 11(5F_K + 8F_{K+1})$.

75. (a) From Exercise 54, we see that if

$T_N = aF_{N+1} + bF_N$ then $T_1 = a + b$,

$T_2 = 2a + b$, and $T_N = T_{N-1} + T_{N-2}$.

Consequently we need only to choose a and b so that $a + b = c$ and $2a + b = d$.

Solving these equations, $a = d - c$ and $b = 2c - d$.

(b) $\dfrac{T_{N+1}}{T_N} = \dfrac{aF_{N+2} + bF_{N+1}}{aF_{N+1} + bF_N}$

$= \dfrac{F_{N+1}}{F_N} \left(\dfrac{a\left(\dfrac{F_{N+2}}{F_{N+1}}\right) + b}{a\left(\dfrac{F_{N+1}}{F_N}\right) + b} \right)$

$\approx \phi \left(\dfrac{a\phi + b}{a\phi + b} \right)$

$= \phi$

when N is large.

76. (a) $\dfrac{F_{N+2}}{F_N} = \dfrac{F_{N+2}}{F_{N+1}} \cdot \dfrac{F_{N+1}}{F_N}$ gets closer and

closer to $\phi \cdot \phi = \phi^2$ as N gets larger and larger.

(b) $\dfrac{F_{N+3}}{F_N} = \dfrac{F_{N+3}}{F_{N+2}} \cdot \dfrac{F_{N+2}}{F_{N+1}} \cdot \dfrac{F_{N+1}}{F_N}$ gets closer

and closer to $\phi \cdot \phi \cdot \phi = \phi^3$ as N gets larger and larger.

77. The area of triangle II is $\dfrac{1}{2}x^2$. The area of triangle III is $\dfrac{1}{2}y(x + y)$. Setting the areas equal gives $\dfrac{1}{2}x^2 = \dfrac{1}{2}y(x + y)$ or $x^2 = y(x + y)$ or, equivalently,

$\dfrac{x}{y} = \dfrac{x+y}{x} = 1 + \dfrac{y}{x}$. Letting $r = \dfrac{x}{y}$ the

equation becomes $r = 1 + \dfrac{1}{r}$ or

$r^2 = r + 1$ which has the solution

$\dfrac{x}{y} = r = \dfrac{1 + \sqrt{5}}{2} = \phi$.

78. (a) From Exercise 65, $x = \phi y$ and so

$\dfrac{x}{y} = \phi$. (See figure.) Since $z = x$,

$\dfrac{x+y}{z} = \dfrac{x+y}{x} = 1 + \dfrac{y}{x} = 1 + \dfrac{1}{\phi} = \phi$.

Therefore, $\dfrac{x+y+z}{x+y} = 1 + \dfrac{z}{x+y} =$

$1 + \dfrac{1}{\phi} = \phi$.

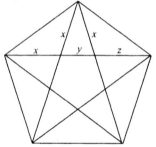

(b) From part (a), $x = \phi y = \phi$;

$x + y = z\phi = x\phi = \phi^2$;

$x + y + z = (x+y)\phi$

$\qquad = \phi^2 \cdot \phi$

$\qquad = \phi^3$

Chapter 10

WALKING

A. Linear Growth and Arithmetic Sequences

1. (a) $P_1 = 205$, $P_2 = 330$, $P_3 = 455$

   $P_1 = P_0 + 125 = 80 + 125 = 205$

   $P_2 = P_1 + 125 = 205 + 125 = 330$

   $P_3 = P_2 + 125 = 330 + 125 = 455$

   (b) $P_{100} = 12,580$

   $P_{100} = 80 + 125 \times 100 = 12,580$

   (c) $P_N = 80 + 125N$

2. (a) $P_1 = 80$, $P_2 = 103$, $P_3 = 126$

   $P_1 = P_0 + 23 = 57 + 23 = 80$;

   $P_2 = P_1 + 23 = 80 + 23 = 103$;

   $P_3 = P_2 + 23 = 103 + 23 = 126$.

   (b) $P_{200} = 4657$

   $P_{200} = 57 + 200 \times 23 = 4657$

   (c) $P_N = 57 + 23N$

3. (a) 225

   $P_{30} = P_0 + 30 \times 5 = 74 + 5 \times 30 = 225$

   (b) 185

   $1000 = 75 + 5N$

   $925 = 5N$

   $N = 185$

   (c) 186

   Solving $P_N = 75 + 5N = 1002$ for N gives $N = 185.4$. Since N must be an integer, $N = 186$.

4. (a) $P_{24} = 40$

   $P_{24} = P_0 + 24 \times (-20) = 520 - 480 = 40$

   (b) 26

   Solving $P_N = 520 + (-20)N = 10$ for N gives $N = 25.5$. Since N must be an integer, $N = 26$.

   (c) 26

   Solving $P_N = 520 + (-20)N = 0$ for N gives $N = 26$.

5. (a) $d = 3$

   $38 = 8 + d \times 10$

   $30 = 10d$

   (b) $P_{50} = 8 + 3 \times 50 = 158$

   (c) $P_N = 8 + 3N$

6. (a) $d = 5$

   $47 = P_7 = P_0 + 7d$

   $37 = P_5 = P_0 + 5d$

   $47 - 37 = 7d - 5d$

   $10 = 2d$

   (b) $P_0 = 12$

   $37 = P_5 = P_0 + 5d = P_0 + 5 \times 5$

   Hence, $P_0 = 37 - 25 = 12$.

   (c) $P_N = 12 + 5N$

7. (a) $A_3 = -19$

   $d = A_2 - A_1 = -4 - 11 = -15$

   $A_3 = A_2 + (-15) = -4 - 15 = -19$

   (b) $A_0 = 26$

   $A_1 = A_0 + (-15)$

   $11 = A_0 - 15$

   (c) None, the sequence is decreasing and starts at 26.

8. (a) $A_7 = -30$

$d = -5 - 20 = -25$

$A_7 = A_6 + (-25) = -5 - 25 = -30$

(b) $A_4 = 45$

$A_4 = A_5 - (-25) = 20 + 25 = 45$

(c) 4

The sequence starts at 145 and the common difference is -25. Thus, the first terms are 145, 120, 95, 70, 45, 20, -5,...

9. (a) $P_N = P_{N-1} + 5; P_0 = 3$

(b) $P_N = 3 + 5N$

(c) $P_{300} = 1503$

$P_{300} = 3 + 5 \times 300 = 1503$

10. (a) $P_N = P_{N-1} + 12; P_0 = 25$

(b) $P_N = 25 + 12N$

(c) Between the ends of the 39th and 40th months (i.e. during the 40th month).

$P_N = 25 + 12N = 500$ implies

$N = \dfrac{475}{12} \approx 39.6$

11. (a) $2 + 5 \times 99 = 497$

(b) $A_0 = 2, d = 5$

The 100th term is

$A_{99} = 2 + 5 \times 99 = 497$.

$2 + 7 + 12 + \ldots + 497 = \dfrac{(2 + 497) \times 100}{2}$

$= 24,950$

12. (a) $21 + 56 \times 7 = 413$

(b) 12,369

$A_0 = 21, d = 7$

The last term is $A_{56} = 21 + 56 \times 7 = 413$.

$21 + 28 + 35 + \ldots + 413 = \dfrac{(21 + 413) \times 57}{2}$

$= 12,369$

13. (a) $d = 3$

If 309 is the Nth term of the sequence,

$309 = 12 + 3(N - 1)$

$309 = 12 + 3N - 3$

$300 = 3N$

$N = 100$

So, 309 is the 100th term of the sequence.

(b) $12 + 15 + 18 + \ldots + 309 = \dfrac{(12 + 309) \times 100}{2}$

$= 16,050$

14. (a) $A_0 = 1, d = 9$

The last (Nth) term is

$A_{N-1} = 1 + 9(N - 1) = 2701$. Thus, $N = 301$

(b) The sum is

$1 + 10 + 19 + \ldots + 2701 = \dfrac{(1 + 2701) \times 301}{2}$

$= 406,651$

15. (a) 3,519,500

$P_{999} = 23 + 7 \times 999 = 7016$

$P_0 + P_1 + P_2 + \ldots + P_{999}$

$= \dfrac{(23 + 7016) \times 1000}{2}$

$= 3,519,500$

(b) 3,482,550

$P_{99} = 23 + 7 \times 99 = 716$

$P_0 + P_1 + P_2 + \ldots + P_{99}$

$= \dfrac{(23 + 716) \times 100}{2}$

$= 36,950$

$$P_{100} + P_{101} + \ldots + P_{999}$$
$$= (P_0 + P_1 + P_2 + \ldots + P_{999})$$
$$\quad - (P_0 + P_1 + P_2 + \ldots + P_{99})$$
$$= 3,519,500 - 36,950$$
$$= 3,482,550$$

16. (a) 504,507

$$P_{500} = 7 + 500 \times 4 = 2007$$
$$P_0 + P_1 + P_2 + \ldots + P_{500}$$
$$= \frac{(7 + 2007) \times 1000}{2}$$
$$= 504,507$$

(b) 484,007

$$P_{99} = 7 + 99 \times 4 = 403$$
$$P_0 + P_1 + P_2 + \ldots + P_{99}$$
$$= \frac{(7 + 403) \times 100}{2}$$
$$= 20,500$$
$$P_{100} + P_{101} + \ldots + P_{500}$$
$$= (P_0 + P_1 + P_2 + \ldots + P_{500})$$
$$\quad - (P_0 + P_1 + P_2 + \ldots + P_{99})$$
$$= 504,507 - 20,500$$
$$= 484,007$$

17. (a) 213

$$P_{38} = 137 + 2 \times 38 = 213$$

(b) $P_N = 137 + 2N$

(c) \$7124

$$137 \times \$1 \times 52 = \$7124$$

(c) \$2652
When just counting the newly installed lights, $P_0 = 0$ and $P_{51} = 2 \times 51 = 102$.
(The lights installed in the 52nd week aren't in operation during the 52-week period.)

$$0 + 2 + 4 + \ldots + 102 = \frac{(0 + 102) \times 52}{2}$$
$$= 2652$$
The cost is \$2652.

18. (a) 1164

$$387 + 37 \times 21 = 1164$$

(b) $387 + 37N$

(c) \$4024.80

$$137 \times \$0.10 \times 104 = \$4024.80$$

(d) \$19,817.20

$$3.70 + 7.40 + 11.10 + \ldots + 381.10$$
$$= \frac{(3.70 + 381.10) \times 103}{2}$$
$$= 19,817.20$$

B.   Exponential Growth and Geometric Sequences

19. (a) $P_1 = 11 \times 1.25 = 13.75$

(b) $P_9 = 11 \times (1.25)^9 \approx 81.956$

(c) $P_N = 11 \times (1.25)^N$

20. (a) $r = \dfrac{P_1}{P_0} = \dfrac{12}{8} = 1.5$

(b) $P_9 = 8 \times (1.5)^9 \approx 307.547$

(c) $P_N = 8 \times (1.5)^N$

21. (a) $P_1 = 4 \times P_0 = 4 \times 5 = 20$
$P_2 = 4 \times P_1 = 4 \times 20 = 80$
$P_3 = 4 \times P_2 = 4 \times 80 = 320$

(b) $P_N = 5 \times 4^N$

(b) 9 generations
We solve $P_N = 5 \times 4^N \geq 1,000,000$ for N. By trial and error, we find that

$5 \times 4^8 = 327,680$ and

$5 \times 4^9 = 1,310,720$.

22. (a) $P_5 = r^5 \times P_0 = (0.75)^5 \times 3072 = 729$

(b) $P_N = 3072 \times (0.75)^N$

(c) 10 generations

We solve $P_N = 3072 \times (0.75)^N < 200$

for N. By trial and error, we find that

$3072 \times (0.75)^9 \approx 230.66$ and

$3072 \times (0.75)^{10} \approx 173$.

23. (a) $P_N = 1.50 P_{N-1}$ where $P_0 = 200$

We multiply by 1.50 each year to account for an *increase* by 50%.

(b) $P_N = 200 \times 1.5^N$

(c) $P_{10} = 200 \times 1.5^{10} \approx 11,533$

A good estimate would be to say that about 11,500 crimes will be committed in 2010.

24. (a) $P_N = 0.8 P_{N-1}$ where $P_0 = 100,000$

We multiply by 0.8 each year to account for a *decrease* by 20%.

(b) $P_N = 100,000 \times 0.8^N$

(c) $P_{15} = 100,000 \times 0.8^{15} \approx 3518$

A good estimate would be to say that about 3,500 cases will be reported in 2015.

25. (a) $P_{100} = 3 \times 2^{100}$

(b) $P_N = 3 \times 2^N$

(c) $a = 3, r = 2, N = 101$.

$P_0 + P_1 + \ldots + P_{100}$

$= 1 + 1 \times 2 + 1 \times 2^2 + \ldots + 1 \times 2^{100}$

$= \dfrac{3 \times (2^{101} - 1)}{2 - 1}$

$= 3 \times (2^{101} - 1)$

(d) $P_0 + P_1 + \ldots + P_{49} = \dfrac{3 \times (2^{50} - 1)}{2 - 1}$

$= 3 \times (2^{50} - 1)$

$P_{50} + P_{51} + \ldots + P_{100}$

$= (P_0 + P_1 + \ldots + P_{100}) - (P_{50} + P_{51} + \ldots + P_{100})$

$= 3 \times (2^{101} - 1) - 3 \times (2^{50} - 1)$

$= 3 \times 2^{101} - 3 \times 2^{50}$

$= 3 \times 2^{50} \times (2^{51} - 1)$

26. (a) $P_{100} = 3^{100}$

(b) $P_N = 3^N$

(c) $\dfrac{(3^{101} - 1)}{2}$

$P_0 + P_1 + \ldots + P_{100}$

$= 1 + 3 + 3^2 + \ldots + 3^{100}$

$= \dfrac{(3^{101} - 1)}{3 - 1}$

(d) $\dfrac{(3^{101} - 3^{50})}{2}$

$P_{50} + P_{51} + \ldots + P_{100}$

$= 3^{50} + 3^{51} + \cdots + 3^{100}$

$= \dfrac{3^{101} - 1}{2} - \dfrac{3^{50} - 1}{2}$

$= \dfrac{3^{101} - 3^{50}}{2}$

C.   **Financial Applications**

27. **(a)** Case 1: Coupon before 30% discount
Price after coupon:
$100 - 0.15 3 ($100) = 85
Final price:
$\$85 - 0.30 3 (\$85) = \$59.50$
Amount of discount:
$\$100 - \$59.50 = \$40.50$
Case 2: Coupon after 30% discount
Price after discount:
$\$100 - 0.30 3 (\$100) = \$70$
Final price:
$\$70 - 0.15 3 \$70 = \$59.50$
Amount of discount:
$\$100 - \$59.50 = \$40.50$

    (b) $\dfrac{\$40.50}{\$100} \times 100\% = 40.5\%$

    (c) Case 1: Coupon before 30% discount
Price after coupon:
$P - 0.15P = 0.85P$
Final price:
$0.85P - 0.30(0.85P) = 0.85P - 0.255P$
$\qquad\qquad\qquad\qquad = 0.595P$
Amount of discount:
$P - 0.595P = 0.405P$
Percent of discount is 40.5%.
Case 2: Coupon after 30% discount
Price after discount:
$P - 0.30P = 0.70P$
Final price:
$0.70P - 0.15(0.70P) = 0.70P - 0.105P$
$\qquad\qquad\qquad\qquad = 0.595P$
Amount of discount:
$P - 0.595P = 0.405P$
Percent of discount is 40.5%.
The percentage discount does not
depend on the original price.

28. 35%
Letting C denote the store cost of an item, a
member pays $0.90(1.50C) = 1.35C$. The
store realizes a 35% markup when an item is
sold to a member.

29. $P_4 = \$3250 \times (1.09)^4 = \$4587.64$

30. $\approx \$1569.74$
$P_3 = \$1237.80 \times (1.0825)^3 = \$1569.74$

31. The initial deposit of \$3420 grows at a
$6\dfrac{5}{8}\%$ annual interest rate for 3 years. At
the end of three years (on Jan. 1, 2009), the
amount in the account is
$\$3420 \times (1.06625)^3 = \$4145.75$. This
amount then grows at a $5\dfrac{3}{4}\%$ annual
interest rate for 4 years. At the end of that
time (on Jan. 1, 2013), the amount in the
account is $\$4145.75 \times (1.0575)^4 = \$5184.71$.

32. The initial deposit of \$2500 grows at a
$5\dfrac{3}{8}\%$ annual interest rate for 3 years. At the
end of three years (on Jan. 1, 2008), the
amount in the account is
$\$2500 \times (1.05375)^4 = \$3082.41$. This
amount then grows at a $4\dfrac{3}{4}\%$ annual
interest rate for 3 years. At the end of that
time (on Jan. 1, 2011), the amount in the
account is $\$3082.41 \times (1.0475)^3 = \$3542.85$.

33. The balance on December 31, 2004 is
$P_2 = \$3420 \times (1.06625)^2 = \$3888.16$.
The balance on January 1, 2005 is
$\$3888.16 - \$1500 = \$2388.16$.
The balance on December 31, 2005 is
$\$2388.16 \times (1.06625)^1 = \$2546.38$.
The balance on January 1, 2006 is
$\$2546.38 - \$1000 = \$1546.38$.
The balance on January 1, 2009 is
$\$1546.38 \times (1.06625)^3 = \$1874.53$.

34. $\approx \$2696.15$
$\left[(2500)(1.05375)^3 - 850 \right] (1.05375)^5$
≈ 2696.15

35. (a) The periodic interest rate is given by

$$p = \frac{0.12}{12} = 0.01.$$

(b) The amount in the account after 5 years (60 months) is

$$P_{60} = \$5000 \times (1.01)^{60} = \$9083.48$$

(c) Each \$1 invested grows to

$$\$\left(1 + \frac{0.12}{12}\right)^{12} \approx \$1.126825$$

So, the annual yield is 12.6825%.

36. (a) $p = \dfrac{0.0775}{365}$

(b) The amount in the account after 2 years (730 days) is

$$P_{730} = \$874.83 \times \left(1 + \frac{0.0775}{365}\right)^{365 \times 2}$$

$$= \$1021.49$$

(c) 8.0573%
Each \$1 invested grows to

$$\$\left(1 + \frac{0.0775}{365}\right)^{365} \approx \$1.080573$$

37. Great Bulldog Bank: 6%;
First Northern Bank:
Each \$1 invested grows to

$$\$\left(1 + \frac{0.0575}{12}\right)^{12} \approx \$1.05904$$

The annual yield is thus 5.904%;
Bank of Wonderland:
Each \$1 invested grows to

$$\$\left(1 + \frac{0.055}{365}\right)^{365} \approx \$1.0564$$

The annual yield is thus 5.654%.

38. At an annual interest rate of 12%, the annual yields are as follows:

Compounded	Annual Yield
Yearly	12%
Semiannually	12.36%
Quarterly	12.551%
Monthly	12.683%
Daily	12.747%
Hourly	12.750%

39. (a) $\approx \$10,834.71$

$$\$1000 \times (1.1)^{25} = \$10,834.71$$

(b) $\approx \$11,338.09$

$$\$1000 \times (1.102)^{25} = \$11,338.09$$

(c) $\approx \$10,736.64$

$$\$1000 \times (1.0996)^{25} = \$10,736.64$$

40. 11%
$500(1 + r) = 555$ gives $1 + r = 1.11$ so that
$r = 0.11$

41. $\approx \$1133.56$
The periodic interest rate is

$$p = \frac{0.06}{12} = 0.005.$$

The Jan. 1 deposit will grow to $100(1.005)^{11}$. The Feb. 1 deposit will grow to $100(1.005)^{10}$. The Mar. 1 deposit will grow to $100(1.005)^{9}$, and so on. The total amount in the account will be
$100(1.005) + 100(1.005)^{2} + \ldots + 100(1.005)^{11}$.
So, $a = 100(1.005)$, $r = 1.005$, and $N = 11$.
The sum is

$$\frac{100(1.005)[(1.005)^{11} - 1]}{1.005 - 1} \approx \$1133.56.$$

42. $\approx \$12,241.75$

The periodic interest rate is

$p = \dfrac{0.08}{12} \approx 0.0066667$.

The total amount in the account will be

$300(1.0066667) + 300(1.0066667)^2$

$+300(1.0066667)^3 + \ldots + 300(1.0066667)^{36}$

$= \dfrac{300(1.0066667)[(1.0066667)^{36} - 1]}{1.0066667 - 1}$

$\approx \$12,241.75$.

43. (a) $6209.21

The amount after 5 years is

$P_5 = \$10,000$.

The periodic interest rate is $p = 0.10$.
The number of years is $N = 5$. Thus, we
solve for the initial investment P_0.

$10,000 = P_0 \times (1.10)^5$

$\quad P_0 \approx 6209.21$

(b) $6102.71

$P_5 = \$10,000, \quad p = \dfrac{0.10}{4} = 0.025,$

$N = 20$

$10,000 = P_0 \times (1.025)^{20}$

$\quad P_0 \approx \$6102.71$

(c) $6077.89

$P_5 = \$10,000, p = \dfrac{0.10}{12}, \ N = 60$

$10,000 = P_0 \times \left(1 + \dfrac{0.10}{12}\right)^{60}$

$\quad P_0 \approx \$6077.89$

44. 9 years

$1000 \times (1.085)^N \geq 2000$ is equivalent to

$1.085^N \geq 2$. Then, note that $1.085^8 \approx 1.92$
and $1.085^9 \approx 2.08$.

D.   Logistic Growth Model

45. (a) $p_1 = 0.8 \times (1 - 0.3) \times 0.3 = 0.1680$

(b) $p_2 = 0.8 \times (1 - 0.168) \times 0.168 \approx 0.1118$

(b) 7.945% of the habitat's carrying
capacity is taken up by the third
generation.

$P_3 = 0.8 \times (1 - 0.11182) \times 0.11182$

$\quad \approx 0.07945$

46. (a) $p_1 = 0.6 \times (1 - 0.7) \times 0.7 = 0.1260$

(b) $p_2 = 0.6 \times (1 - 0.126) \times 0.126 \approx 0.06607$

(c) 3.702% of the habitat's carrying
capacity is taken up by the third
generation.

$P_3 = 0.6 \times (1 - 0.06607) \times 0.06607$

$\quad \approx 0.03702$

47. (a) $p_1 = 0.1680, p_2 \approx 0.1118, p_3 \approx 0.0795,$
$p_4 \approx 0.0585, p_5 \approx 0.0441, p_6 \approx 0.0337,$
$p_7 \approx 0.0261, p_8 \approx 0.0203, p_9 \approx 0.0159,$
$p_{10} \approx 0.0125$.

(c) This logistic growth model predicts
extinction for this population.

48. (a) $p_1 \approx 0.1260, p_2 \approx 0.0661, p_3 \approx 0.0370,$
$p_4 \approx 0.0214, p_5 \approx 0.0126, p_6 \approx 0.0074,$
$p_7 \approx 0.0044, p_8 \approx 0.0026, p_9 \approx 0.0016,$
$p_{10} \approx 0.0009$.

(b) This logistic growth model predicts
extinction for this population.

49. (a) $p_1 = 0.4320, p_2 \approx 0.4417, p_3 \approx 0.4439,$
$p_4 \approx 0.4443, p_5 \approx 0.4444, p_6 \approx 0.4444,$
$p_7 \approx 0.4444, p_8 \approx 0.4444, p_9 \approx 0.4444,$
$p_{10} \approx 0.4444$.

(b) The population becomes stable at
44.44% of the habitat's carrying
capacity.

50. (a) $p_1 = 0.2400$, $p_2 \approx 0.2736$, $p_3 \approx 0.2981$,

$p_4 \approx 0.3139$, $p_5 \approx 0.3230$, $p_6 \approx 0.3280$,

$p_7 \approx 0.3306$, $p_8 \approx 0.3320$, $p_9 \approx 0.3327$,

$p_{10} \approx 0.3330$.

(b) The population becomes stable at 33.33% of the habitat's carrying capacity.

51. (a) $p_1 = 0.3570$, $p_2 \approx 0.6427$, $p_3 \approx 0.6429$,

$p_4 \approx 0.6428$, $p_5 \approx 0.6429$, $p_6 \approx 0.6428$,

$p_7 \approx 0.6429$, $p_8 \approx 0.6428$, $p_9 \approx 0.6429$,

$p_{10} \approx 0.6428$

(b) The population becomes stable at

$\dfrac{9}{14} \approx 64.29\%$ of the habitat's carrying capacity.

52. (a) $p_1 = 0.4$, $p_2 \approx 0.6$, $p_3 \approx 0.6$,

$p_4 \approx 0.6$, $p_5 \approx 0.6$, $p_6 \approx 0.6$,

$p_7 \approx 0.6$, $p_8 \approx 0.6$, $p_9 \approx 0.6$,

$p_{10} \approx 0.6$

(b) The population becomes stable at 60% of the habitat's carrying capacity.

53. (a) $p_1 = 0.5200$, $p_2 = 0.8112$, $p_3 \approx 0.4978$,

$p_4 \approx 0.8125$, $p_5 \approx 0.4952$, $p_6 \approx 0.8124$,

$p_7 \approx 0.4953$, $p_8 \approx 0.8124$, $p_9 \approx 0.4953$,

$p_{10} \approx 0.8124$

(c) The population settles into a two-period cycle alternating between a high-population period at 81.24% and a low-population period at 49.53% of the habitat's carrying capacity.

54. (a) $p_1 = 0.8424$, $p_2 = 0.4660$, $p_3 \approx 0.8734$,

$p_4 \approx 0.3880$, $p_5 \approx 0.8335$, $p_6 \approx 0.4872$,

$p_7 \approx 0.8769$, $p_8 \approx 0.3788$, $p_9 \approx 0.8260$,

$p_{10} \approx 0.5045$

(b) The population settles into a four-period cycle with the following approximate percentages of the habitat's carrying capacity: 38%, 83%, 51%, 88%.

E.   Miscellaneous

55. (a) Exponential ($r = 2$)

(b) Linear ($d = 2$)

(c) Logistic

(d) Exponential ($r = \dfrac{1}{3}$)

(e) Logistic

(f) Linear ($d = -0.15$)

(g) Linear ($d = 0$), Exponential ($r = 1$), and Logistic

56. (a) Linear

(b) Logistic

(d) Exponential

(e) Logistic

(f) Linear

(g) Exponential

57. (a) $P_2 = 10 + 2 \times 6 = 22$

$P_3 = 22 + 2 \times 10 = 42$

(b) The first two numbers in this sequence are even. Thereafter, the sum and product of two even numbers is also even.

58. (a) $P_2 = 2P_1 + P_0 = 2 \times 5 - 3 = 7$

$P_3 = 2P_2 + P_1 = 2 \times 7 - 5 = 9$

(b) An even number minus an odd number is an odd number.

(c) $P_N = 3 + 2N$

JOGGING

59. 6%

Given the initial deposit of $P_0 = \$500$, we solve $P_2 = P_0(1+r)^2$ for the annual yield r. But,

$$561.80 = 500(1+r)^2$$
$$561.80 = 500r^2 + 1000r + 500$$
$$0 = 500r^2 + 1000r - 61.80$$

and the quadratic equation gives

$$r = \frac{-1000 \pm \sqrt{1000^2 - 4(500)(-61.8)}}{2(500)}$$
$$= \frac{-1000 \pm \sqrt{1,123,600}}{1000}$$
$$= \frac{-1000 \pm 1060}{1000}$$
$$= \frac{60}{1000}, \frac{-2060}{1000}$$
$$= 0.06, -2.06$$

Taking the positive value of r gives an annual yield of 6%.

60. 20%

$$\left(1 + \frac{r}{2}\right)^2 = 1.21$$
$$1 + \frac{r}{2} = 1.1$$
$$r = 0.2 = 20\%$$

61. (a) Let a be the length of the shortest side of such a triangle. Then the other sides are of length $a + 2$ and $a + 4$. By the Pythagorean theorem,

$$a^2 + (a+2)^2 = (a+4)^2$$
$$a^2 + a^2 + 4a + 4 = a^2 + 8a + 16$$
$$a^2 - 4a - 12 = 0$$
$$(a - 6)(a + 2) = 0$$

So, $a = 6$ or $a = -2$. Since $a > 0$, the only right triangles for which the sides are in an arithmetic sequence having $d = 2$ are 6-8-10 triangles.

(b) A $1 - \sqrt{\Phi} - \Phi$ triangle.

Suppose the shortest side of such a triangle is 1. By the Pythagorean theorem, when the sides are in a geometric sequence with common ratio r, we must have $1^2 + r^2 = r^4$. Let $x = r^2$. Then $1 + x = x^2$. So,

$x = \frac{1 \pm \sqrt{5}}{2}$. Since $x > 0$, we have

$x = r^2 = \frac{1 + \sqrt{5}}{2}$ (the golden ratio Φ).

So $r = \sqrt{\Phi}$ and $r^2 = \Phi$. So, one right triangle for which the sides are in a geometric sequence is a $1 - \sqrt{\Phi} - \Phi$ triangle.

62. 100%

Let m be the markup and c be the retailer's cost.

$$0.75(1 + m)p = 1.5p$$
$$0.75 + 0.75m = 1.5$$
$$0.75m = 0.75$$
$$m = 1$$

The markup should be 100%.

63. 39.15%

If T was the starting tuition, then the tuition at the end of one year is 110% of T. That is, $(1.10)T$. The tuition at the end of two years is 115% of what it was after one year. That is, after two years, the tuition was $(1.15)(1.10)T$. Likewise, the tuition at the end of the three years was $(1.10)(1.15)(1.10)T = 1.3915T$. The total percentage increase was 39.15%.

64. (a) $1,335.90

The Nth newspaper of the year must be stored online for $(365 - N) + 1$ days (assuming the newspaper must be stored for the day it comes out). Thus,

we add
$$0.02 + 0.04 + 0.06 + \ldots + 365(0.02)$$
$$= (0.02)\left[1 + 2 + 3 + \ldots + 365\right]$$
$$= 0.02\left[\frac{365 \times 366}{2}\right]$$
$$= \$1,335.90$$

(b) $40,236.27
$$3000 + 3000(1.02) + 3000(1.02)^2$$
$$+ \ldots + 3000(1.02)^{11}$$
$$= \frac{3000 - 3000(1.02)^{12}}{-0.02}$$
$$= \$40,236.27$$

65. $10,737,418.23
We sum $\underbrace{0.01 + 0.02 + 0.04 + 0.08 + \ldots}_{30 \text{ terms}}$

This is a sum of terms in a geometric sequence having $a = 0.01$, $r = 2$, and $N = 30$. We compute
$$0.01 + 0.01 \times 2 + 0.01 \times 2^2 + \ldots + 0.01 \times 2^{29}$$
$$= \frac{0.01 \times (2^{30} - 1)}{2 - 1}$$
$$= \$10,737,418.24$$

66. $2^{13} + 1 - \left(\frac{1}{2}\right)^{12}$

Combining alternate terms of the sum gives two separate sums of geometric sequences – the first with common ratio 2 and the second with common ratio 1/2:
$$(1 + 2 + 4 + 8 + \ldots + 4096) +$$
$$\left(1 + \frac{1}{2} + \frac{1}{4} + \frac{1}{8} + \ldots + \frac{1}{4096}\right)$$
$$= \left(\frac{2^{13} - 1}{2 - 1}\right) + \left(\frac{\left(\frac{1}{2}\right)^{13} - 1}{\frac{1}{2} - 1}\right) .$$
$$= 2^{13} + 1 - \left(\frac{1}{2}\right)^{12}$$

67. $r = \dfrac{1 \pm \sqrt{5}}{2}$

If a is a term of the geometric sequence with common ratio r, then ar and ar^2 are the following two terms. From the recursive rule we get $ar^2 = ar + a$. Assuming $a \neq 0$, this is equivalent to $r^2 = r + 1$, which gives us $r = \dfrac{1 \pm \sqrt{5}}{2}$.

68. **(a)** Reading the sum from right to left, $a = 100(1.005)$, $r = 1.005$, and $N = 216$.

   (b) $b(1.005)^{216} + b(1.005)^{215} + \cdots + b(1.005)$
$$= \frac{b}{a} \cdot S$$

   (c) We compute
$$400\left(1 + \frac{0.06}{12}\right)^{108} + 400\left(1 + \frac{0.06}{12}\right)^{107}$$
$$+ 400\left(1 + \frac{0.06}{12}\right)^{106} + \ldots + 400\left(1 + \frac{0.06}{12}\right)^{1}$$
where each term is the amount to which a $400 deposit grows. By the geometric sum formula, this sum is
$$\frac{400\left(1 + \frac{0.06}{12}\right)\left[\left(1 + \frac{0.06}{12}\right)^{108} - 1\right]}{1 + \frac{0.06}{12} - 1} .$$

69. $\left(a + ar + ar^2 + \ldots + ar^{N-1}\right)(r - 1)$
$$= \quad ar + ar^2 + ar^3 + \ldots + ar^{N-1} + ar^N$$
$$- a - ar - ar^2 - ar^3 - \ldots - ar^{N-1}$$
$$= -a + ar^N$$
$$= a(r^N - 1)$$

So, after dividing both sides by $(r - 1)$, we arrive at
$$a + ar + ar^2 + \ldots + ar^{N-1} = \frac{a(r^N - 1)}{r - 1} .$$

70. The first N terms of the arithmetic sequence are $c, c+d, c+2d, \ldots c+(N-1)d$. Their sum is

$$\frac{(c+[c+(N-1)d]) \times N}{2} = \frac{N}{2}\left[2c+(N-1)d\right].$$

71. One example is $P_0 = 8, r = \dfrac{1}{2}$.

$$P_1 = 4, P_2 = 2, P_3 = 1, P_4 = \frac{1}{2}, P_5 = \frac{1}{4} \ldots$$

72. $r = 10/3$

If the population is constant, $p_0 = p_1 = 0.7$.
Thus $r \times 0.7 \times (1-0.7) = 0.7$, i.e., $0.3r = 1$.
Solving for r gives $r = 10/3$.

73. No. A constant population would require
$p_0 = p_1 = 0.8(1-p_0)p_0$ and so
$1 = 0.8(1-p_0)$ or $p_0 = -0.25$.

74. $p_0 = \dfrac{r-1}{r}$

If the population is constant, $p_1 = p_0$. Thus,

$rp_0(1-p_0) = p_0$, i.e., $r(1-p_0) = 1$. Solving

for p_0 gives $p_0 = \dfrac{r-1}{r}$.

75. $\approx 14{,}619$ snails

$p_0 = \dfrac{5000}{20{,}000} = 0.25$

$p_1 = 3.0 \times (1-0.25) \times 0.25 = 0.5625$

$p_2 \approx 0.7383$

$p_3 \approx 0.5797$

$p_4 \approx 0.7310$

$p_4 \times 20{,}000 \approx 14{,}619$ snails

RUNNING

76. The loan from Bank A would be \$90,000 with a monthly interest rate of $\dfrac{.10}{12}$. Thus, the monthly compounding rate would be $\left(1 + \dfrac{.10}{12}\right)$, which for convenience we will abbreviate as r. Letting p denote the monthly payment, the following table shows how much would be owed after making each payment.

Payment	Balance Owed After Payment
1	$90{,}000r - p$
2	$[90{,}000r - p]r - p = 90{,}000r^2 - p[1+r]$
3	$90{,}000r^3 - p\left[1 + r + r^2\right]$
4	$90{,}000r^4 - p\left[1 + r + r^2 + r^3\right]$
$\vdots$	$\vdots$
360	$90{,}000r^{360} - p\left[1 + r + r^2 + \ldots + r^{358} + r^{359}\right]$

Since there must be a 0 balance after the 360th payment, we get the equation

$90000r^{360} = p\left[1 + r + r^2 + \ldots + r^{358} + r^{359}\right]$. The equation above simplifies to $90000r^{360} = p\left(\dfrac{r^{360} - 1}{r - 1}\right)$.

Solving this equation for p and remembering that $r = 1 + \dfrac{.10}{12}$ gives $p \approx \$789.81$.

The loan from Bank B would be \$92,783.51 (leaving \$90,000 after paying the 3% loan fee). Using the same ideas as above, the monthly payment turns out to be \$780.17 for 360 months. Consequently, the loan from Bank B is \$9.64 a month less than the loan from Bank A, saving \$3470.40 over the 360 months.

77. \$1125.51

Let B denote the amount you should pay for the note. The following table shows how much would be owed you after each payment had been made.

Payment	Balance Owed After Payment
1	$B(1.01) - 100$
2	$\left[B(1.01) - 100\right](1.01) - 100 = B(1.01)^2 - 100\left[1 + (1.01)\right]$
3	$B(1.01)^3 - 100\left[1 + (1.01) + (1.01)^2\right]$
$\vdots$	$\vdots$
12	$B(1.01)^{12} - 100\left[1 + (1.01) + (1.01)^2 + \ldots + (1.01)^{11}\right]$

Since there must be a zero balance after the 12th payment we get the equation

$$B(1.01)^{12} = 100\left[1 + (1.01) + (1.01)^2 + \ldots + (1.01)^{11}\right] = 100\left[\frac{(1.01)^{12} - 1}{.01}\right].$$

Solving this equation for B gives $B = 100\left[\dfrac{(1.01)^{12} - 1}{.01(1.01)^{12}}\right] \approx \$1125.51$.

78. (a) If $r > 4$, and $p_N = 0.5$, $p_{N+1} = r(1 - p_N)p_N = 4(1 - 0.5)(0.5) = 0.25r > 1$.
     This is impossible since the population cannot be more than 100% of the carrying capacity.

   (b) If $r > 4$, and $p_N = 0.5$, $p_{N+1} = r(1 - p_N)p_N = 4(1 - 0.5)(0.5) = 1$ and hence $p_K = 0$ for all $K > N + 1$
        (i.e. the population becomes extinct.)

   (c) ¼
        The graph of $(1 - p)p = -p^2 + p$ is an inverted parabola which crosses the x-axis at 0 and 1. Thus,

        its maximum value occurs when $p = \dfrac{1}{2}$.

   (d) From part (c), if $0 < p < 1$, $0 < (1 - p)p < \dfrac{1}{4}$ and so if we also have $0 < r < 4$, then $0 < r(1 - p)p < 1$.

        Consequently, if we start with $0 < p_0 < 1$ and $0 < r < 4$, then $0 < p_N < 1$ for every positive integer N.

79. We have $p_1 = rp_0(1 - p_0)$ and $p_0 = p_2 = rp_1(1 - p_1)$. Eliminating p_1 and p_2 from these equations gives $r^3 p_0^4 - 2r^3 p_0^3 + (r^3 + r^2)p_0^2 + (1 - r^2)p_0 = 0$. Since both $p_0 = 0$ and $p_0 = \dfrac{r-1}{r}$ are solutions that we don't want, we may divide both sides of the equation by $p_0 \left(p_0 - \dfrac{r-1}{r} \right)$ or alternatively by $p_0 \left[rp_0 - (r-1) \right]$. This results in the equation $r^2 p_0^2 - (r^2 + r)p_0 + (r+1) = 0$. Solving this equation for p_0 gives the two solutions $p_0 = \dfrac{(r+1) \pm \sqrt{(r+1)(r-3)}}{2r}$, both of which work.

80. If $P_0, P_1, P_2, \ldots$ is arithmetic, then $P_N = P_0 + N \cdot d$. So, the sequence $2^{P_0}, 2^{P_1}, 2^{P_2}, \ldots$ is given by $2^{P_0}, 2^{P_0 + d}, 2^{P_0 + 2d}, 2^{P_0 + 3d}, \ldots$ which is the same as $2^{P_0} \cdot 1, 2^{P_0} \cdot \left(2^d\right), 2^{P_0} \cdot \left(2^d\right)^2, 2^{P_0} \cdot \left(2^d\right)^3, \ldots$. But this is a geometric sequence with common ratio 2^d.

Mini-Excursion 3

WALKING

A.   The Geometric Sum Formula

1. In this sum, we have $a = 10$, $r = 1.05$, and $N = 36$. Thus,

$$\$10 + \$10(1.05) + \$10(1.05)^2 + \ldots + \$10(1.05)^{35} = \$10\frac{1.05^{36} - 1}{1.05 - 1}$$
$$= \$958.36$$

2. $\$500 + \$500(1.01) + \$500(1.01)^2 + \ldots + \$500(1.01)^{59} = \$500\dfrac{1.01^{60} - 1}{1.01 - 1} = \$40,834.83$

3. In this sum, we have $a = 10(1.05)^{-35}$, $r = 1.05$, and $N = 36$. Thus,

$$\$10 + \$10(1.05)^{-1} + \$10(1.05)^{-2} + \ldots + \$10(1.05)^{-35} = \$10(1.05)^{-35}\frac{1.05^{36} - 1}{1.05 - 1}$$
$$= \$10\frac{1.05 - (1.05)^{-35}}{0.05}$$
$$= \$173.74$$

We could also take $a = 10$, $r = (1.05)^{-1}$, and $N = 36$ giving

$$\$10 + \$10(1.05)^{-1} + \$10(1.05)^{-2} + \ldots + \$10(1.05)^{-35} = \$10\frac{(1.05)^{-36} - 1}{(1.05)^{-1} - 1}$$
$$= \$173.74$$

4. $\$500 + \$500(1.01)^{-1} + \$500(1.01)^{-2} + \ldots + \$500(1.01)^{-59} = \$500(1.01)^{-59}\dfrac{1.01^{60} - 1}{1.01 - 1} = \$22,702.29$

5. In this sum, we can take $a = 10(1.05)^{-36}$, $r = 1.05$, and $N = 36$. Thus,

$$\$10(1.05)^{-1} + \$10(1.05)^{-2} + \ldots + \$10(1.05)^{-35} + \$10(1.05)^{-36} = \$10(1.05)^{-36}\frac{1.05^{36} - 1}{1.05 - 1}$$
$$= \$10\frac{1 - (1.05)^{-36}}{0.05}$$
$$= \$165.47$$

6. $\$500(1.01)^{-1} + \$500(1.01)^{-2} + \$500(1.01)^{-3} + \ldots + \$500(1.01)^{-60} = \$500(1.01)^{-60}\dfrac{1.01^{60} - 1}{1.01 - 1} = \$22,477.52$

7. **(a)** In this sum, we take $a = 399(1.0075)^{-72}$, $r = 1.0075$, and $N = 72$. Then, by the geometric sum

formula, $\$399(1.0075)^{-1} + \$399(1.0075)^{-2} + \ldots + \$399(1.0075)^{-72} = \$399(1.0075)^{-72}\dfrac{(1.0075)^{72} - 1}{1.0075 - 1}$.

    (b) To obtain the right hand side of this equation from the left hand side, distribute $(1.0075)^{-72}$ and note

that $(1.0075)^{-72}(1.0075)^{72} = 1$.

8. **(a)** In this sum, if we take $a = PMT(1 + p)^{-N}$ and $r = 1 + p$ we have, by the geometric sum formula,

$$\$PMT(1 + p)^{-1} + \$PMT(1 + p)^{-2} + \ldots + \$PMT(1 + p)^{-N} = \$PMT(1 + p)^{-N}\dfrac{(1 + p)^{N} - 1}{(1 + p) - 1}.$$

    (b) To obtain the right hand side of this equation from the left hand side, distribute $(1 + p)^{-N}$ and note

that $(1 + p)^{-N}(1 + p)^{N} = 1$.

B.   **Annuities, Investments and Loans**

9. Markus' first \$2,000 deposit grows for 39 years to a future value of $\$2000(1.075)^{39}$. His second \$2,000

deposit grows for 38 years to a future value of $\$2000(1.075)^{38}$. His third \$2,000 deposit grows for 37

years to a future value of $\$2000(1.075)^{37}$. And so on. His second to last deposit of \$2,000 grows for

one year to a future value of $\$2000(1.075)^{1}$. Markus' last deposit is \$2,000 and does not grow.

The future value of this deferred annuity is the sum of the future values of all the deposits. In this case,
that is $\$2000(1.075)^{39} + \$2000(1.075)^{38} + \ldots + \$2000(1.075)^{1} + \$2000$. Writing this sum in the reverse
order allows us to recognize that $a = PMT = \$2000$, $r = 1.075$, and $N = 40$. So,

$FV = a\dfrac{r^{N} - 1}{r - 1} = \$2000\dfrac{(1.075)^{40} - 1}{1.075 - 1} \approx \$454{,}513.04$.

10. Using $a = PMT = \$400$, $r = 1 + 0.045/12$, and $N = 36$, Celine will have a future value of

$FV = a\dfrac{r^{N} - 1}{r - 1} = \$400\dfrac{\left(1 + \dfrac{0.045}{12}\right)^{36} - 1}{1 + \dfrac{0.045}{12} - 1} \approx \$15{,}386.44$. If this is a 20% down payment, then the

maximum price of a house she can buy is five times as much or \$76,932.20.

11. The periodic interest rate in this problem is $p = 0.06/12 = 0.005$ so that $r = 1 + p = 1.005$. The number of
periods N that Donald will make a payment is $N = 12 \times 35 = 420$. We solve the formula for the future

value of a fixed deferred annuity $FV = a\dfrac{r^{N} - 1}{r - 1}$ where $FV = \$1{,}000{,}000$, $r = 1.005$, and $N = 420$ for $a =$

PMT. This gives $a = PMT = FV\dfrac{r-1}{r^N-1} = \$1,000,000\dfrac{1.005-1}{(1.005)^{420}-1} \approx \$701.90$. Donald should sock away a little more than \$700 each month.

12. The periodic interest rate in this problem is $p = 0.0468/52$ and $r = 1 + p$. The number of periods N that Layla will make a payment is $N = 52 \times 12 = 624$. We solve the formula for the future value of a fixed deferred annuity $FV = a\dfrac{r^N-1}{r-1}$ where $FV = \$150,000$, $r = 1+0.0468/52$, and $N = 624$ for $a = PMT \cdot r$.

This gives $a = FV\dfrac{r-1}{r^N-1} = \$150,000\dfrac{1+\dfrac{0.0468}{52}-1}{\left(1+\dfrac{0.0468}{52}\right)^{624}-1} \approx \$179.28$. Layla should place $PMT = a/r \approx$

\$179.11 each week into the trust fund.

13. Since Freddy only made a single deposit, we can use the compound interest formula to give us the future value of the account. Using $i = 0.07$ and $N = 15$, we solve $\$1172.59 = P_0(1.07)^{15}$ for Freddy's initial deposit P_0. But then $P_0 = \dfrac{\$1172.59}{(1.07)^{15}} = \$425.00$.

14. The purchase price of the bond is given by $P_0 = \dfrac{\$10,000}{(1.035)^7} = \$7,859.91$.

15. We find the present value of a fixed immediate annuity. In this case, the payment is $PMT = \$100,000,000$, $N = 10$ years, and $p = 0.15$. Hence

$$PV = \$PMT\dfrac{1-(1+p)^{-N}}{p} = \$100,000,000\dfrac{1-(1.15)^{-10}}{0.15} = \$501,876,863.$$

16. (a) $PV = \$PMT\dfrac{1-(1+p)^{-N}}{p} = \$30,000\dfrac{1-(1.06)^{-25}}{0.06} = \$383,500.68$

(b) $PV = \$PMT\dfrac{1-(1+p)^{-N}}{p} = \$30,000\dfrac{1-(1.07)^{-25}}{0.07} = \$349,607.50$

(c) The interest rate is proportional to the amount of risk present in the investment. If the amount of risk goes up, the amount that a person would be willing to pay for such an annuity will go down.

17. We find the present value of a fixed immediate annuity. Here the payment is $PMT = \$50$, $N = 52 \times 60 = 3120$ weeks, and $p = 0.055/52$. Hence

$$PV = \$PMT \frac{1-(1+p)^{-N}}{p} = \$50 \frac{1-\left(1+\frac{0.055}{52}\right)^{-3120}}{\frac{0.055}{52}} = \$45,526.11 \, .$$

18. The amortization formula can be used the find the payment for this fixed immediate annuity. Here the present value is $PV = \$16,000,000,000$, $N = 40$ years, and $p = 0.03$. Hence

$$PMT = \$PV \frac{p}{1-(1+p)^{-N}} = \$16,000,000,000 \frac{0.03}{1-(1+0.03)^{-40}} \approx \$692,198,046 \, .$$ That is, Michael Dell

can expect a yearly payment of almost $700 million.

19. (a) The amortization formula can be used the find the payment for this fixed immediate annuity. The present value of the loan is $160,000, $N = 12 \times 30 = 360$ months, and the periodic rate is $p = 0.0575/12$. Hence

$$PMT = \$PV \frac{p}{1-(1+p)^{-N}} = \$160,000 \frac{\frac{0.0575}{12}}{1-\left(1+\frac{0.0575}{12}\right)^{-360}} = \$933.72 \, .$$

(b) The Simpsons will make 360 payments of $933.72 for a total of $336,139.20. This means they will pay $336,139.20 - $160,000 = $176,139.20 in interest.

20. (a) The amortization formula can be used the find the payment for the new mortgage. The present value of the loan is $95,000, $N = 12 \times 15 = 180$ months, and the periodic rate is $p = 0.0525/12$. So the monthly payments on the new mortgage are given by

$$PMT = \$PV \frac{p}{1-(1+p)^{-N}} = \$95,000 \frac{\frac{0.0525}{12}}{1-\left(1+\frac{0.0525}{12}\right)^{-180}} = \$763.68 \, .$$ To the nearest dollar, the

Smiths will be saving $\$1104 - \$764 = \$340$ each month by refinancing.

(b) The Smiths will pay $180 \times \$764 - \$95,000 = \$42,520$ in interest over the life of the new loan.

21. We find the present value of a fixed immediate annuity and then add $25,000. In this case, the payment is $PMT = \$950$, $N = 12 \times 20 = 240$ months, and $p = 0.055/12$. So,

$$PV = \$PMT \frac{1-(1+p)^{-N}}{p} = \$950 \frac{1-\left(1+\frac{0.055}{12}\right)^{-240}}{\frac{0.055}{12}} = \$138,104.01 \, .$$ Adding the $25,000 down

payment, we find the selling price of the house that Ken just bought to be approximately $163,104.

RUNNING

22. Option 1: Suppose you were to choose the $4000 rebate. Then you would need to finance $20,035 from the bank at the 6% rate. Using the amortization formula, the monthly payment would be

$$PMT = \$PV \frac{p}{1-(1+p)^{-N}} = \$20,035 \frac{\dfrac{0.06}{12}}{1-\left(1+\dfrac{0.06}{12}\right)^{-72}} = \$332.04 \; .$$

Option 2: Suppose you were to choose the 0% financing. The monthly payment would be

$$PMT = \frac{\$24,035}{72} = \$333.82 \; .$$

Though a close call, it is slightly better to choose the $4000 rebate.

23. (a) In this sum, we apply the geometric sum formula with $a = C(1+p)^{-N}$ and $r = 1+p$. Then,

$$\$C(1+p)^{-1} + \$C(1+p)^{-2} + \ldots + \$C(1+p)^{-N} = \$C(1+p)^{-N}\frac{(1+p)^N - 1}{(1+p)-1}$$

$$= \$C\frac{1-(1+p)^{-N}}{p}$$

(b) As N gets larger, $(1+p)^{-N}$ gets closer to 0 since $p > 0$. So, $\$C\dfrac{1-(1+p)^{-N}}{p}$ gets closer and closer to $\$C/p$.

24. (a) First, we show that the increase in monthly payment $\$x$ that will pay the mortgage off in 21 years is indeed close to $100 using the amortization formula. The monthly payment on a 30-year mortgage

would be $PMT = \$PV \dfrac{p}{1-(1+p)^{-N}} = \$100,000 \dfrac{\dfrac{0.06}{12}}{1-\left(1+\dfrac{0.06}{12}\right)^{-360}} \approx \$600$. To pay off a $100,000 in

21 years would require a payment of $PMT = \$100,000 \dfrac{\dfrac{0.06}{12}}{1-\left(1+\dfrac{0.06}{12}\right)^{-252}} \approx \$700$. The amount of

interest paid over 30 years would be approximately $360 \times \$600 - \$100,000 = \$116,000$. The amount of interest paid if the mortgage were paid off in 21 years would be $252 \times \$700 - \$100,000 = \$76,400$ which equates to a savings of $40,000.

(b) To pay off a $100,000 in 15 years would require a payment of

$$PMT = \$100,000\frac{\dfrac{0.06}{12}}{1-\left(1+\dfrac{0.06}{12}\right)^{-180}} \approx \$843.86 \text{ . This is an increase of approximately}$$

$844 - $600 = 244 each month. The amount of interest saved in paying the loan off 15 years early would be $360 \times \$600 - 180 \times \$844 = \$64,080$.

(c) To pay off a $100,000 in t $(t < 30)$ years would require a payment of

$$PMT = \$100,000\frac{\dfrac{0.06}{12}}{1-\left(1+\dfrac{0.06}{12}\right)^{-12t}} \text{ . This is an increase of}$$

$$\$100,000\left(\frac{\dfrac{0.06}{12}}{1-\left(1+\dfrac{0.06}{12}\right)^{-12t}} - \frac{\dfrac{0.06}{12}}{1-\left(1+\dfrac{0.06}{12}\right)^{-360}}\right) \text{ each month.}$$

25. The first deposit (July 1, 2006) of $1000 grows for 29 years at 6% interest to $\$1000(1.06)^{29}$.

The second deposit (in 2007) of $\$(1.06)1000$ grows for 28 years at 6% interest to $\$(1.06)1000(1.06)^{28}$.

The third deposit (in 2008) of $\$(1.06)^2 1000$ grows for 27 years at 6% interest to $\$(1.06)^2 1000(1.06)^{27}$.

The fourth deposit (in 2009) of $\$(1.06)^3 1000$ grows for 26 years at 6% interest to $\$(1.06)^3 1000(1.06)^{26}$.

...

The 30th deposit (in 2035) of $\$(1.06)^{29}1000$ grows for 0 years to $\$(1.06)^{29}1000$.

Each of these 30 terms has a value of $\$(1.06)^{29}1000$ so that the future value of Sam's retirement account is $30 \times \$(1.06)^{29}1000 = \$162,551.64$.

26. (a) $PMT_1 = \$150,000\dfrac{\dfrac{0.075}{12}}{1-\left(1+\dfrac{0.075}{12}\right)^{-360}} \approx \$1,048.82$

(b) With this monthly payment, the amount of the loan outstanding after three years of payments is

$$PV = \$PMT_1\frac{1-(1+p)^{-N}}{p} = \$1,048.82\frac{1-\left(1+\dfrac{0.075}{12}\right)^{-324}}{\dfrac{0.075}{12}} = \$145,521.13 \text{ .}$$

(c) So, the monthly payment on the new 27-year loan (at 6%) will

$$be \; PMT_2 = \$145,521.13 \frac{\dfrac{0.06}{12}}{1-\left(1+\dfrac{0.06}{12}\right)^{-324}} \approx \$872.47 \; .$$

(d) $MS = \$1,048.82 - \$872.47 = \$176.35$. The present value of these monthly savings is

$$PV = \$176.35 \frac{1-\left(1+\dfrac{0.03}{12}\right)^{-324}}{\dfrac{0.03}{12}} = \$28,261.88 \; .$$

(e) The cost of refinancing, C, is given by $\$1,500 + (0.02)(\$145,521.13) = \$4,410.42$. The present value of refinancing the loan is $PV = \$28,261.88 - \$4,410.42 = \$23,851.46$.

Chapter 11

WALKING

A.   Reflections

1. (a) *C*   **(b)** *F*   **(c)** *E*   **(d)** *B*

2. (a) *E*   **(b)** *A*   **(c)** *C*   **(d)** *G*

3. (a)
(b)
(c)

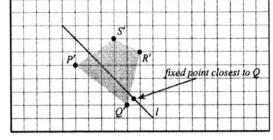

4. (a)
(b)
(c)

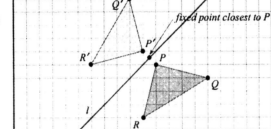

5. (a)
(b)
(c)
(d)

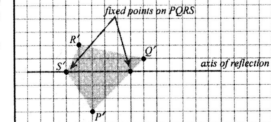

6. (a)
(b)
(c)
(d)

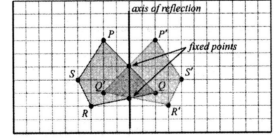

7.

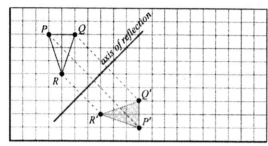

8.

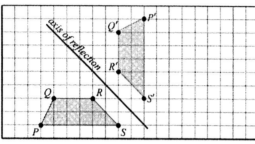

9.

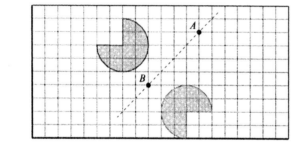

Since points *A* and *B* are fixed points, the axis of reflection must pass through these points.

10.

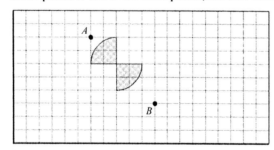

B.   Rotations

11. **(a)** *I*   **(b)** *E*   **(c)** *G*   **(d)** *A*

     (e) *F*   **(f)** *C*   **(g)** *E*   **(h)** *D*

12. **(a)** *H*   **(b)** *G*   **(c)** *A*   **(d)** *B*

     (e) *D*   **(f)** *B*   **(g)** *C*   **(h)** *H*

13. (a) 110°   **(b)** 350°   **(c)** 10°   **(d)** 81°

14. (a) 140°   **(b)** 220°   **(c)** 320°   **(d)** 40°

15. (a)
(b)

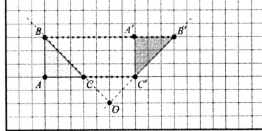

Since *BB'* and *CC'* are parallel, the intersection of *BC* and *B'C'* locates the rotocenter *O*. This is a 90° clockwise rotation.

16. (a)
(b)

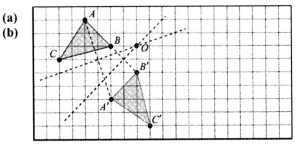

17. (a)
(b)
(c)

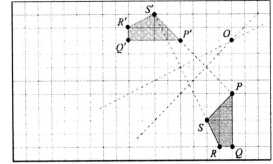

The rotocenter *O* is located at the intersection of the perpendicular bisectors to *PP'* and *SS'*. This is a 90° counterclockwise rotation.

18. **(a)**
    (b)
    (c)

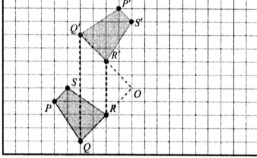

This is a 90° clockwise rotation about rotocenter *O*.

19. **(a)**
    (b)

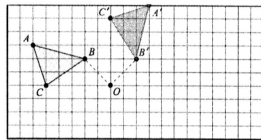

The rotocenter *O* is located somewhere on the perpendicular bisector of *BB'*. Since the 90° rotation is clockwise, *O* is located below *BB'* rather than above *BB'*.

20. **(a)**
    (b)

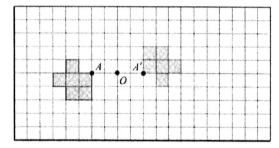

C.   **Translations**

21. **(a)** *C*   **(b)** *C*   **(c)** *A*   **(d)** *D*

22. **(a)** *D*   **(b)** *A*   **(c)** *B*   **(d)** *C*

23. **(a)**
    (b)

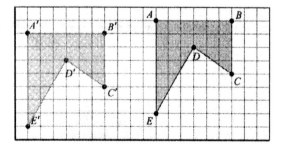

24. (a)
   (b)

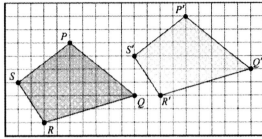

25. One possible answer: One translation is right (East) 4 miles. A second translation is up (North) 3 miles (see figure).

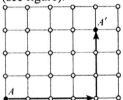

26. One translation is left 4 miles and up 3 miles (Northwest) as shown in the figure. The distance of the translation is 5 miles.

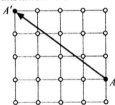

D. Glide Reflections

27.

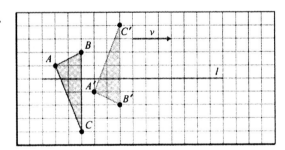

28.

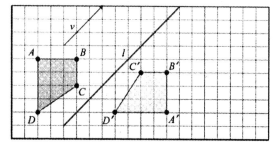

29. (a)
(b)
(c)

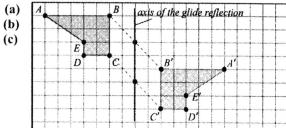

30. (a)
(b)
(c)

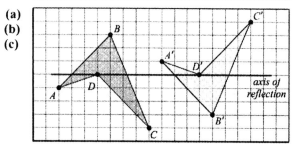

31. (a)
(b)

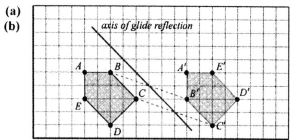

32. (a)
(b)

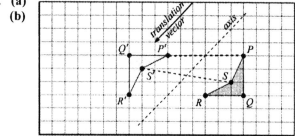

33. (a)
(b)

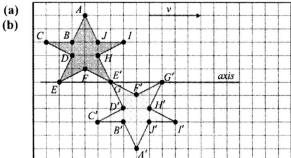

The axis of reflection cannot be determined by the midpoints of *PP'* and *QQ'* (since they are the same point). So, the axis of reflection is the line perpendicular to *PQ*.

34. (a)
(b)

E.   Symmetries of Finite Shapes

35. (a) Reflection with axis going through the midpoints of *AB* and *DC*; reflection with axis going through the midpoints of *AD* and *BC*; rotations of 180° and 360° with rotocenter the center of the rectangle.

(b) No Reflections. Rotations of 180° and 360° with rotocenter the center of the parallelogram.

(c) Reflection with axis going through the midpoints of *AB* and *DC*; rotation of 360° with rotocenter the center of the trapezoid.

36. (a) Reflection with axis going through *C* and the midpoint of *AB*; rotation of 360° with rotocenter the center of the triangle.

(b) Reflections (three of them) with axis going through a vertex and the midpoint of the opposite side; rotations of 120°, 240°, and 360° with rotocenter the center of the triangle.

(c) Rotation of 360° with rotocenter the center of the triangle.

37. (a) Reflections (three of them) with axis going through pairs of opposite vertices; reflections (three of them) with axis going through the midpoints of opposite sides of the hexagon; rotations of 60°, 120°, 180°, 240°, 300°, 360° with rotocenter the center of the hexagon.

(b) Reflections with axis *AD, GJ, BE, HK, CF, IL*; rotations of 60°, 120°, 180°, 240°, 300°, 360° with rotocenter the center of the star.

38. (a) Reflections (five of them) with axis going through a vertex and midpoint of the opposite side; rotations of $72°, 144°, 216°, 288°, 360°$ with rotocenter the center of the pentagon.

(b) Reflections (five of them) with axis AH, FD, BI, GE, CJ; rotations of $72°, 144°, 216°, 288°, 360°$ with rotocenter the center of the star.

39. (a) D_2 **(b)** Z_2 **(c)** D_1

40. (a) D_1 **(b)** D_3 **(c)** Z_1

41. (a) D_6 **(b)** D_6

42. (a) D_5 **(b)** D_5

43. (a) D_1 **(b)** D_1 **(c)** Z_1 **(d)** Z_2 **(e)** D_1 **(f)** D_2

44. (a) D_1 **(b)** D_1 **(c)** Z_2 **(d)** D_2 **(e)** D_2 **(f)** Z_1

45. (a) J   **(b)** T   **(c)** Z   **(d)** I

46. (a) 5   **(b)** 3   **(c)** 96   **(d)** 8

47. Answers will vary.

(a) Symmetry type D_5 is common among many types of flowers (daisies, geraniums, etc.). The only requirements are that the flower have 5 equal, evenly spaced petals and that the petals have a reflection symmetry along their long axis. In the animal world, symmetry type D_5 is less common, but it can be found among certain types of starfish, sand dollars, and in some single celled organisms called diatoms.

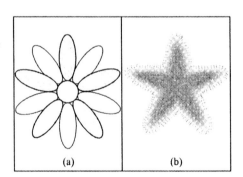

(a)   (b)

(b) The Chrysler Corporation logo is a classic example of a shape with symmetry D_5. Symmetry type D_5 is also common in automobile wheels and hubcaps. One of the largest and most unusual buildings in Washington, DC has symmetry of type D_5.

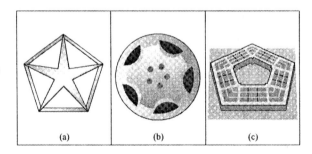

(a)   (b)   (c)

(c) Objects with symmetry type Z_1 are those whose only symmetry is the identity. Thus, any "irregular" shape fits the bill. Tree leaves, seashells, plants, and rocks more often than not have symmetry type Z_1.

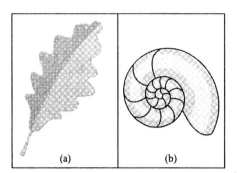

(d) Examples of manmade objects with symmetry of type Z_1 abound.

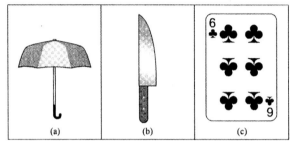

48. **(a)** Snowflakes, some types of jelly fish, a beehive cell, are all examples of natural objects with symmetry type D_6, often called hexagonal symmetry.

   (b) A hex nut, some hubcaps, some bathroom tiles, etc., are all examples of man-made objects with hexagonal symmetry.

   (c) Answers will vary.

   (d) Answers will vary.

F.   Symmetries of Border Patterns

49. **(a)** $m1$ **(b)** $1m$ **(c)** 12 **(d)** 11

50. **(a)** 11 **(b)** $m1$ **(c)** $1m$ **(d)** 12

51. **(a)** $m1$ **(b)** 12 **(c)** $1g$ **(d)** mg

52. **(a)** 12 **(b)** $1g$ **(c)** $m1$ **(d)** mg

53. 12

54. 11

G.   Miscellaneous

55. Since every proper rigid motion is equivalent to either a rotation or a translation, and a translation has no fixed points, the specified rigid motion must be equivalent to a rotation.

56. Since every rigid motion is equivalent to either a reflection, rotation, translation, or a glide reflection, and a rotation has only one fixed point while translations and glide reflections have no fixed points, the specified rigid motion must be equivalent to a reflection.

57. (a) D (b) D (c) B (d) E (e) G

58. (a) C (b) P (c) D (d) D

59. (a) improper   (b) proper   (c) improper   (d) proper

60. (a) exactly one fixed point. The rigid motion is a rotation (see Exercise 57).

    (b) no fixed points. The rigid motion is a translation (see Exercise 58).

61. The combination of two improper rigid motions is a proper rigid motion. Since C is a fixed point, the rigid motion must be a rotation with rotocenter C.

62. M is a proper rigid motion (an improper rigid motion combined with an improper rigid motion is a proper rigid motion). Moreover M has no fixed points. (See Exercise 58 for details.) It follows that M must be a translation.

JOGGING

63. (a) The result of applying the reflection with axis l_1, followed by the reflection with axis l_2, is a clockwise rotation with center C and angle of rotation $\lambda + \lambda + \beta + \beta = 2(\lambda + \beta) = 2\alpha$. One example is shown below.

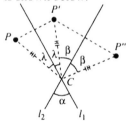

    (b) The result of applying the reflection with axis l_2, followed by the reflection with axis l_1, is a counter-clockwise rotation with center C and angle of rotation 2α.

64. (a)

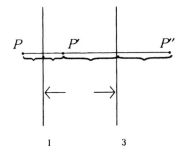

The distance from P to P'' is $x + x + y + y = 2x + 2y = 2(x + y) = 2d$. This is a translation by a vector perpendicular to l_1 and l_2 of length $2d$ and going from left to right.

(b)

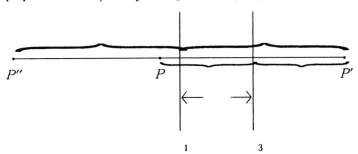

The distance from P to P'' is $y - (x + x - y) = 2y - 2x = 2(y - x) = 2d$. This is a translation by a vector perpendicular to l_1 and l_2 of length $2d$ and going from right to left.

65. (a)

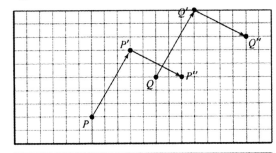

(b)

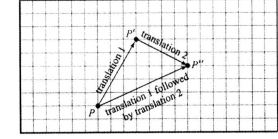

66. (a)

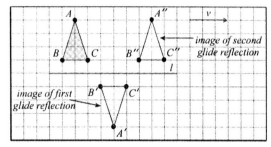

(b) The result of applying the same glide reflection twice is equivalent to a translation in the direction of the glide of twice the amount of the original glide. [See figure in part (a).]

67. (a) By definition, a border has translation symmetries in exactly one direction (let's assume the horizontal direction). If the pattern had a reflection symmetry along an axis forming 45° with the horizontal direction, there would have to be a second direction of translation symmetry (vertical).

(b) If a pattern had a reflection symmetry along an axis forming an angle of $\alpha°$ with the horizontal direction, it would have to have translation symmetry in a direction that forms an angle of $2\alpha°$ with the horizontal. This could only happen for $\alpha = 90°$ or $\alpha = 180°$ (since the only allowable direction for translation symmetries is the horizontal).

68. (a)

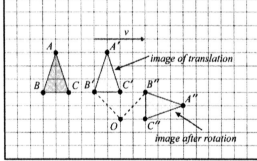

(b) Rotations and translations are proper rigid motions, and hence preserve clockwise-counterclockwise orientations. The given motion is a proper rigid motion. However, the given motion cannot be a translation since points A, B, and C are each moved different distances. The resulting rigid motion is a 90° clockwise rotation about rotocenter O as shown in the figure.

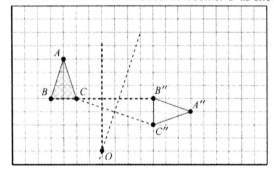

69. (a)

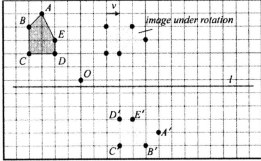

(b) Rotations and translations are proper rigid motions, and hence preserve clockwise-counterclockwise orientations. The given motion is an improper rigid motion (it reverses the clockwise-counterclockwise orientation). Since performing the same rotation and glide reflection again results in the original figure, this is a reflection (rather than a glide reflection) whose axis is shown in the figure below.

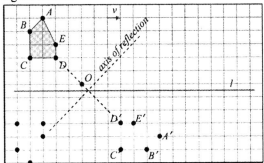

[The figure in the bottom left is the result of rotation $A'B'C'D'E'$ 90° about O. Performing the glide reflection on that figure results in $ABCDE$.]

70. (a)

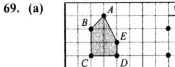

(b)

(c)

(d)

(e)

(f)

(g)

71. Rotations and translations are proper rigid motions, and hence preserve clockwise-counterclockwise orientations. The given motion is an improper rigid motion (it reverses the clockwise-counterclockwise orientation). If the rigid motion was a reflection, then PP', RR', and QQ' would all be perpendicular to the axis of reflection and hence would all be parallel. It must be a glide reflection (the only rigid motion left).

72. (a) If a word has vertical reflection symmetry then the word remains unchanged when the word is reflected about a vertical line through the center of the word. Consequently, the word must be a palindrome.

    (b) DAD

    (c) Each letter must have vertical reflection symmetry.

    (d) SOS

RUNNING

73.

	r_1	r_2	r_3	R_1	R_2	I
r_1	I	R_1	R_2	r_2	r_3	r_1
r_2	R_2	I	R_1	r_3	r_1	r_2
r_3	R_1	R_2	I	r_1	r_2	r_3
R_1	r_3	r_1	r_2	R_2	I	R_1
R_2	r_2	r_3	r_1	I	R_1	R_2
I	r_1	r_2	r_3	R_1	R_2	I

74.

	r_1	r_2	r_3	r_4	R_1	R_2	R_3	I
r_1	I	R_1	R_2	R_3	r_2	r_3	r_4	r_1
r_2	R_3	I	R_1	R_2	r_3	r_4	r_1	r_2
r_3	R_2	R_3	I	R_1	r_4	r_1	r_2	r_3
r_4	R_1	R_2	R_3	I	r_1	r_2	r_3	r_4
R_1	r_4	r_1	r_2	r_3	R_2	R_3	I	R_1
R_2	r_3	r_4	r_1	r_2	R_3	I	R_1	R_2
R_3	r_2	r_3	r_4	r_1	I	R_1	R_2	R_3
I	r_1	r_2	r_3	r_4	R_1	R_2	R_3	I

75. *pm*
    The identity is the only rotation symmetry. There is a reflection (vertical). However, there is not a glide reflection with an axis that is not a reflection axis.

76. *p2*

The pattern has 2-fold rotational symmetry. There are no reflections. There are also no glide reflections.

77. *cm*

The identity is the only rotation symmetry. There is a reflection (vertical). There are also glide reflections that do not have the same axis as the vertical reflection axes. These vertical axes are ¼ and ¾ of the distance between two horizontal clubs.

78. *pm*

The identity is the only rotation symmetry. There is a reflection (vertical). However, there is not a glide reflection with an axis that is not a reflection axis.

79. *p4m*

The pattern has 4-fold rotational symmetry. There are reflections. In fact, there are reflections that intersect at 45° angles.

80. *p6m*

The pattern has 6-fold rotational symmetry. Furthermore, there are reflections.

Chapter 12

WALKING

A. **The Koch Snowflake and Variations**

1.

	Start	Step 1	Step 2	Step 3	Step 4	...	Step 30	Step N
Number of sides	3	12	48	192	768		3×4^{30}	3×4^{N}
Length of each side	1 in	1/3 in	1/9 in	1/27 in	1/81 in		$\dfrac{1}{3^{30}}$ in	$\dfrac{1}{3^{N}}$ in
Length of the boundary	3 in	4 in	48/9 in	192/27 in	768/81 in		≈ 0.265 mi	$3 \times \left(\dfrac{4}{3}\right)^{N}$ in

The number of sides increases by a factor of 4 at each step since each side is replaced by 4 sides of 1/3 the length. The length of the boundary can be found by multiplying the number of sides at step N by the length of each side at step N.

2.

	Start	Step 1	Step 2	Step 3	Step 4	...	Step 30	Step N
Number of sides	3	12	48	192	768		3×4^{30}	3×4^{N}
Length of each side	6 cm	2 cm	2/3 cm	2/9 cm	2/27 cm		$6 \times \dfrac{1}{3^{30}}$ cm	$6 \times \dfrac{1}{3^{N}}$ cm
Length of the boundary	18 cm	24 cm	32 cm	$\dfrac{128}{3}$ cm	$\dfrac{512}{9}$ cm		≈ 1.008 km	$18 \times \left(\dfrac{4}{3}\right)^{N}$ cm

3.

	Start	Step 1	Step 2	Step 3	Step 4
Area	24 in^2	32 in^2	$\dfrac{320}{9}$ in^2	$\dfrac{3,008}{81}$ in^2	$\dfrac{27,584}{729}$ in^2

At step 1, three triangles are added each having 1/9 the area of the original triangle. That is, the area at step 1 is $24 \text{ in}^2 + \dfrac{3 \times 24}{9} \text{ in}^2 = 32 \text{ in}^2$.

At step 2, $3 \times 4 = 12$ triangles are added each having $\dfrac{1}{9^2}$ the area of the original triangle. That is, the area at step 2 is $24 \text{ in}^2 + \dfrac{3 \times 24}{9} \text{ in}^2 + \dfrac{12 \times 24}{9^2} \text{ in}^2 = \dfrac{2,880}{81} \text{ in}^2 = \dfrac{320}{9} \text{ in}^2.$

At step 3, $3 \times 4^2 = 48$ triangles are added each having $\dfrac{1}{9^3}$ the area of the original triangle. That is, the

area at step 3 is $24 \text{ in}^2 + \dfrac{3 \times 24}{9} \text{ in}^2 + \dfrac{3 \times 4 \times 24}{9^2} \text{ in}^2 + \dfrac{3 \times 4^2 \times 24}{9^3} \text{ in}^2 = \dfrac{27,072}{729} \text{ in}^2 = \dfrac{3,008}{81} \text{ in}^2.$

At step 4, $3 \times 4^3 = 192$ triangles are added each having $\dfrac{1}{9^4}$ the area of the original triangle. That is, the

area at step 4 is $24 \text{ in}^2 + \dfrac{3 \times 24}{9} \text{ in}^2 + \dfrac{3 \times 4 \times 24}{9^2} \text{ in}^2 + \dfrac{3 \times 4^2 \times 24}{9^3} \text{ in}^2 + \dfrac{3 \times 4^3 \times 24}{9^4} \text{ in}^2 = \dfrac{27,584}{729} \text{ in}^2.$

4.

	Start	Step 1	Step 2	Step 3	Step 4
Area	$\dfrac{\sqrt{3}}{4} \text{ in}^2$	$\dfrac{3\sqrt{3}}{9} \text{ in}^2$	$\dfrac{30\sqrt{3}}{81} \text{ in}^2$	$\dfrac{282\sqrt{3}}{729} \text{ in}^2$	$\dfrac{2586\sqrt{3}}{6561} \text{ in}^2$

At step 1, three triangles are added each having 1/9 the area of the original triangle. That is, the area at

step 1 is $\dfrac{\sqrt{3}}{4} \text{ in}^2 + \dfrac{3 \times \sqrt{3}/4}{9} \text{ in}^2 = \dfrac{3\sqrt{3}}{9} \text{ in}^2.$

At step 2, $3 \times 4 = 12$ triangles are added each having $\dfrac{1}{9^2}$ the area of the original triangle. That is, the

area at step 2 is $\dfrac{\sqrt{3}}{4} \text{ in}^2 + \dfrac{3 \times \sqrt{3}/4}{9} \text{ in}^2 + \dfrac{3 \times 4 \times \sqrt{3}/4}{9^2} \text{ in}^2 = \dfrac{30\sqrt{3}}{81} \text{ in}^2.$

At step 3, $3 \times 4^2 = 48$ triangles are added each having $\dfrac{1}{9^3}$ the area of the original triangle. That is, the

area at step 3 is $\dfrac{\sqrt{3}}{4} \text{ in}^2 + \dfrac{3 \times \sqrt{3}/4}{9} \text{ in}^2 + \dfrac{3 \times 4 \times \sqrt{3}/4}{9^2} \text{ in}^2 + \dfrac{3 \times 4^2 \times \sqrt{3}/4}{9^3} \text{ in}^2 = \dfrac{282\sqrt{3}}{729} \text{ in}^2.$

At step 4, $3 \times 4^3 = 192$ triangles are added each having $\dfrac{1}{9^4}$ the area of the original triangle. That is, the

area at step 4 is

$\dfrac{\sqrt{3}}{4} \text{ in}^2 + \dfrac{3 \times \sqrt{3}/4}{9} \text{ in}^2 + \dfrac{3 \times 4 \times \sqrt{3}/4}{9^2} \text{ in}^2 + \dfrac{3 \times 4^2 \times \sqrt{3}/4}{9^3} \text{ in}^2 + \dfrac{3 \times 4^3 \times \sqrt{3}/4}{9^4} \text{ in}^2 = \dfrac{2586\sqrt{3}}{6561} \text{ in}^2.$

5. $1.6 \times 24 = 38.4 \text{ in}^2$

6. $1.6 \times \dfrac{\sqrt{3}}{4} = \dfrac{2\sqrt{3}}{5} \text{ in}^2$

7.

	Start	Step 1	Step 2	Step 3	Step 4	...	Step 50	Step N
Number of sides	4	20	100	500	2500		4×5^{50}	4×5^{N}
Length of each side	1 in	1/3 in	1/9 in	1/27 in	1/81 in		$\dfrac{1}{3^{50}}$ in	$\dfrac{1}{3^{N}}$ in
Length of the boundary	4 in	20/3 in	100/9 in	500/27 in	2500/81 in		$\approx 7{,}810{,}562$ mi	$4 \times \left(\dfrac{5}{3}\right)^{N}$

The number of sides increases by a factor of 5 at each step since each side is replaced by 5 sides of 1/3 the length. The length of the boundary can be found by multiplying the number of sides at step N by the length of each side at step N.

8.

	Start	Step 1	Step 2	Step 3	Step 4	...	Step N
Number of sides	4	20	100	500	2500		4×5^{N}
Length of each side	a	$a/3$	$a/9$	$a/27$	$a/81$		$\dfrac{a}{3^{N}}$
Length of the boundary	$4a$	$(20/3)a$	$(100/9)a$	$(500/27)a$	$(2500/81)a$		$4a \times \left(\dfrac{5}{3}\right)^{N}$

9.

	Start	Step 1	Step 2	Step 3	Step 4
Area	$1\ \text{in}^2$	$\dfrac{13}{9}\ \text{in}^2$	$\dfrac{137}{81}\ \text{in}^2$	$\dfrac{1333}{729}\ \text{in}^2$	$\dfrac{12{,}497}{6561}\ \text{in}^2$

At step 1, four squares are added each having 1/9 the area of the original square. That is, the area at step 1 is $1\ \text{in}^2 + \dfrac{4 \times 1}{9}\ \text{in}^2 = \dfrac{13}{9}\ \text{in}^2$.

At step 2, $4 \times 5 = 20$ squares are added each having $\dfrac{1}{9^2}$ the area of the original square. That is, the area at step 2 is $1\ \text{in}^2 + \dfrac{4 \times 1}{9}\ \text{in}^2 + \dfrac{20 \times 1}{9^2}\ \text{in}^2 = \dfrac{137}{81}\ \text{in}^2$.

At step 3, $4 \times 5^2 = 100$ squares are added each having $\dfrac{1}{9^3}$ the area of the original square. That is, the

area at step 3 is $1 \text{ in}^2 + \dfrac{4 \times 1}{9} \text{ in}^2 + \dfrac{4 \times 5 \times 1}{9^2} \text{ in}^2 + \dfrac{4 \times 5^2 \times 1}{9^3} \text{ in}^2 = \dfrac{1333}{729} \text{ in}^2$.

At step 4, $4 \times 5^3 = 500$ squares are added each having $\dfrac{1}{9^4}$ the area of the original square. That is, the

area at step 4 is $1 \text{ in}^2 + \dfrac{4 \times 1}{9} \text{ in}^2 + \dfrac{4 \times 5 \times 1}{9^2} \text{ in}^2 + \dfrac{4 \times 5^2 \times 1}{9^3} \text{ in}^2 + \dfrac{4 \times 5^3 \times 1}{9^4} \text{ in}^2 = \dfrac{12{,}497}{6561} \text{ in}^2$.

10.

	Start	**Step 1**	**Step 2**	**Step 3**	**Step 4**
Area	A	$\dfrac{13}{9}A$	$\dfrac{137}{81}A$	$\dfrac{1333}{729}A$	$\dfrac{12{,}497}{6561}A$

11.

	Start	**Step 1**	**Step 2**	**Step 3**	**Step 4**	**...**	**Step 40**	**Step N**
Number of sides	3	12	48	192	768		3×4^{40}	3×4^N
Length of each side	a	$a/3$	$a/9$	$a/27$	$a/81$		$\dfrac{a}{3^{40}}$	$\dfrac{a}{3^N}$
Length of the boundary	$3a$	$4a$	$\dfrac{48}{9}a$	$\dfrac{192}{27}a$	$\dfrac{768}{81}a$		$\dfrac{3 \times 4^{40}}{3^{40}}a$	$3a \times \left(\dfrac{4}{3}\right)^N$

The number of sides increases by a factor of 4 at each step since each side is replaced by 4 sides of 1/3 the length. The length of the boundary can be found by multiplying the number of sides at step N by the length of each side at step N.

12.

	Start	**Step 1**	**Step 2**	**Step 3**	**Step 4**	**...**	**Step 30**	**Step N**
Number of sides	3	12	48	192	768		3×4^{30}	3×4^N
Length of each side	1 in	1/3 in	1/9 in	1/27 in	1/81 in		$\dfrac{1}{3^{30}}$	$\dfrac{1}{3^N}$ in
Length of the boundary	3 in	4 in	$\dfrac{48}{9}$ in	$\dfrac{192}{27}$ in	$\dfrac{768}{81}$ in		$\approx 0.2651 \text{ mi}$	$3 \times \left(\dfrac{4}{3}\right)^N$ in

13.

	Start	Step 1	Step 2	Step 3	Step 4	Step 5
Area	81 in^2	54 in^2	42 in^2	$\dfrac{110}{3} \text{ in}^2$	$\dfrac{926}{27} \text{ in}^2$	$\dfrac{8{,}078}{243} \text{ in}^2$

At step 1, three triangles are subtracted each having 1/9 the area of the original triangle. That is, the area at step 1 is $81 \text{ in}^2 - \dfrac{3 \times 81}{9} \text{ in}^2 = 54 \text{ in}^2$.

At step 2, $3 \times 4 = 12$ triangles are subtracted each having $\dfrac{1}{9^2}$ the area of the original triangle. That is, the area at step 2 is $81 \text{ in}^2 - \dfrac{3 \times 81}{9} \text{ in}^2 - \dfrac{12 \times 81}{9^2} \text{ in}^2 = 42 \text{ in}^2$.

At step 3, $3 \times 4^2 = 48$ triangles are subtracted each having $\dfrac{1}{9^3}$ the area of the original triangle. That is, the area at step 3 is $81 \text{ in}^2 - \dfrac{3 \times 81}{9} \text{ in}^2 - \dfrac{3 \times 4 \times 81}{9^2} \text{ in}^2 - \dfrac{3 \times 4^2 \times 81}{9^3} \text{ in}^2 = \dfrac{26{,}730}{729} \text{ in}^2 = \dfrac{110}{3} \text{ in}^2$.

At step 4, $3 \times 4^3 = 192$ triangles are subtracted each having $\dfrac{1}{9^4}$ the area of the original triangle. That is, the area at step 4 is $81 \text{ in}^2 - \dfrac{3 \times 81}{9} \text{ in}^2 - \dfrac{3 \times 4 \times 81}{9^2} \text{ in}^2 - \dfrac{3 \times 4^2 \times 81}{9^3} \text{ in}^2 - \dfrac{3 \times 4^3 \times 81}{9^4} \text{ in}^2$

$= \dfrac{225{,}018}{6{,}561} \text{ in}^2 = \dfrac{2{,}778}{81} \text{ in}^2 = \dfrac{926}{27} \text{ in}^2$.

At step 5, $3 \times 4^4 = 768$ triangles are subtracted each having $\dfrac{1}{9^5}$ the area of the original triangle. That is, the area at step 5 is $81 \text{ in}^2 - \dfrac{3 \times 81}{9} \text{ in}^2 - \dfrac{3 \times 4 \times 81}{9^2} \text{ in}^2 - \dfrac{3 \times 4^2 \times 81}{9^3} \text{ in}^2 - \dfrac{3 \times 4^3 \times 81}{9^4} \text{ in}^2 - \dfrac{3 \times 4^4 \times 81}{9^5} \text{ in}^2$

$= \dfrac{1{,}962{,}954}{59{,}049} \text{ in}^2 = \dfrac{24{,}234}{729} \text{ in}^2 = \dfrac{8{,}078}{243} \text{ in}^2$.

14.

	Start	Step 1	Step 2	Step 3	Step 4	Step 5
Area	A	$\dfrac{2}{3} A$	$\dfrac{42}{81} A$	$\dfrac{330}{729} A$	$\dfrac{2778}{6561} A$	$\dfrac{24{,}234}{59{,}049} A$

15.

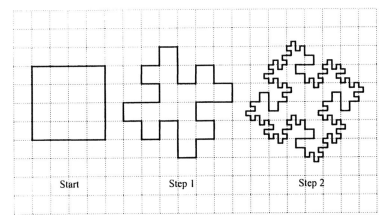

	Start	Step 1	Step 2	Step 3	Step 4	... Step N
16.						
Number of sides	4	28	196	1372	9604	4×7^N
Length of the boundary	4	8	16	32	64	4×2^N

17. (a)

	Start	Step 1	Step 2	Step 3	Step 4
Area	A	A	A	A	A

At each step, the area added is the same as the area subtracted.

(b) If the area of the starting square is A, then the area of the resulting quadratic Koch island is also A (what the rule giveth, the rule taketh away).

18. Since the perimeter doubles at each step, the perimeter of the quadratic Koch island becomes infinitely large.

B. The Sierpinski Gasket and Variations

	Start	Step 1	Step 2	Step 3	Step 4	...	Step N
19.							
Area	1	$\dfrac{3}{4}$	$\left(\dfrac{3}{4}\right)^2$	$\left(\dfrac{3}{4}\right)^3$	$\left(\dfrac{3}{4}\right)^4$		$\left(\dfrac{3}{4}\right)^N$

At each step of construction, ¾ of each triangle remains.

20.

	Start	Step 1	Step 2	Step 3	Step 4	...	Step N
Number of triangles	1	3	9	27	81		3^N
Perimeter of each triangle	P	$(1/2)P$	$(1/4)P$	$(1/8)P$	$(1/16)P$		$\dfrac{1}{2^N}P$
Length of the boundary	P	$(3/2)P$	$\dfrac{9}{4}P$	$\dfrac{27}{8}P$	$\dfrac{81}{16}P$		$\left(\dfrac{3}{2}\right)^N P$

21. The area of the Sierpinski gasket is smaller than the area of the gasket formed during any step of construction. That is, if the area of the original triangle is 1, then the area of the Sierpinski gasket is less than $\left(\dfrac{3}{4}\right)^N$ for every positive value of N. Since $0 < 3/4 < 1$, the value of $\left(\dfrac{3}{4}\right)^N$ can be made smaller than any positive quantity for a large enough choice of N. It follows that the Sierpinski gasket can also be made smaller than any positive quantity.

22. Since the perimeter grows by a factor of 1.5 at each step, the perimeter of the Sierpinski gasket becomes infinitely large.

23.

	Start	Step 1	Step 2	Step 3	Step 4	...	Step N
Number of triangles	1	3	9	27	81		3^N
Perimeter of each triangle	24 in	12 in	6 in	3 in	1.5 in		$24 \times \left(\dfrac{1}{2}\right)^N$ in
Length of the boundary	24 in	36 in	54 in	81 in	121.5 in		$24 \times \left(\dfrac{3}{2}\right)^N$ in

24.

	Start	Step 1	Step 2	Step 3	Step 4	...	Step N
Area	24	$24 \times \dfrac{3}{4} = 18$	$24 \times \left(\dfrac{3}{4}\right)^2 = \dfrac{27}{2}$	$24 \times \left(\dfrac{3}{4}\right)^3 = \dfrac{81}{8}$	$24 \times \left(\dfrac{3}{4}\right)^4 = \dfrac{243}{32}$		$24 \times \left(\dfrac{3}{4}\right)^N$

25.

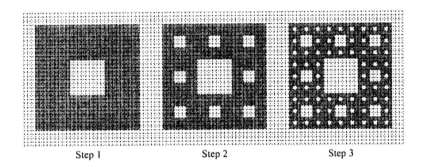

Step 1   Step 2   Step 3

26.

	Start	Step 1	Step 2	Step 3	...	Step N
Area	1 sq. in.	$\dfrac{8}{9}$ sq. in.	$\left(\dfrac{8}{9}\right)^2$ sq. in.	$\left(\dfrac{8}{9}\right)^3$ sq. in.		$\left(\dfrac{8}{9}\right)^N$ sq. in.

27. (a)

	Start	Step 1	Step 2	Step 3	Step 4
Perimeter	4	16/3	80/9	496/27	3536/81

Note that the boundary will include the outside perimeter and the perimeters of all removed squares. We also note that each removed square will have sides of length $\dfrac{1}{3}$ that of the square it was removed from. Since each side of the original square has length 1, we have:

Start: $4 \cdot 1 = 4$;

Step 1: $4 + 4 \cdot \dfrac{1}{3} = 4 + \dfrac{4}{3} = \dfrac{12}{3} + \dfrac{4}{3} = \dfrac{16}{3}$

(Previous boundary plus boundary of new hole with sides of length $\dfrac{1}{3}$)

Step 2: $\dfrac{16}{3} + 8 \cdot \dfrac{4}{9} = \dfrac{80}{9}$

(Previous boundary plus boundary of 8 new holes, each with sides of length $\dfrac{1}{3} \cdot \dfrac{1}{3} = \dfrac{1}{9}$)

Step 3: $\dfrac{80}{9} + 8^2 \cdot \dfrac{4}{27} = \dfrac{496}{27}$

(Previous boundary plus boundary of 8^2 new holes, each with sides of length $\dfrac{1}{3} \cdot \dfrac{1}{3} \cdot \dfrac{1}{3} = \dfrac{1}{27}$)

Step 4: $\dfrac{496}{27} + 8^3 \cdot \dfrac{4}{81} = \dfrac{3536}{81}$

(Previous boundary plus boundary of 8^3 new holes, each with sides of length $\left(\dfrac{1}{3}\right)^4 = \dfrac{1}{81}$)

(b) At step $N+1$, there are 8^N new holes, each with sides of length $\left(\dfrac{1}{3}\right)^{N+1} = \dfrac{1}{3^{N+1}}$ so, perimeter of the

"carpet" at step $N + 1$ is $L + 8^N \cdot \dfrac{4}{3^{N+1}}$.

28.

Step	Number of square holes	Explanation
1	1	
2	$1 + 8 = 9$	The hole at step 1 + 8 new smaller holes.
3	$1 + 8 + 8^2 = 73$	All the holes at step 2 + 8^2 new smaller holes.
4	$1 + 8 + 8^2 + 8^3 = 585$	All the holes at step 3 + 8^3 new smaller holes.
5	$1 + 8 + 8^2 + 8^3 + 8^4 = 4681$	All the holes at step 4 + 8^4 new smaller holes.

29.

	Start	Step 1	Step 2	Step 3	Step 4	...	Step N
Number of triangles	1	6	$6^2 = 36$	$6^3 = 216$	$6^4 = 1296$		6^N
Area of each triangle	A	$\dfrac{1}{9}A$	$\dfrac{1}{9^2}A$	$\dfrac{1}{9^3}A$	$\dfrac{1}{9^4}A$		$\dfrac{1}{9^N}A$
Area of gasket	A	$\dfrac{2}{3}A$	$\left(\dfrac{2}{3}\right)^2 A$	$\left(\dfrac{2}{3}\right)^3 A$	$\left(\dfrac{2}{3}\right)^4 A$		$\left(\dfrac{2}{3}\right)^N A$

The area of the gasket at step N of the construction will be the product of the number of triangles at that step and the area of each such triangle. The length of each side of each triangle in step N is 1/3 of the length of a side in step N-1. So, the area at step N is 1/9 that of the area of a triangle in step N-1.

30.

	Start	Step 1	Step 2	Step 3	Step 4	...	Step N
Number of triangles	1	6	$6^2 = 36$	$6^3 = 216$	$6^4 = 1296$		6^N
Perimeter of each triangle	P	$(1/3)P$	$(1/9)P$	$(1/27)P$	$(1/81)P$		$\left(\dfrac{1}{3}\right)^N P$
Length of the boundary	P	$2P$	$4P$	$8P$	$16P$		$2^N P$

At any step, a black triangle produces 6 smaller black triangles with sides 1/3 the length of the previous sides.

31. The area of the Sierpinski ternary gasket is smaller than the area of the gasket formed during any step of construction. That is, if the area of the original triangle is A, then the area of the Sierpinski ternary gasket is less than $\left(\dfrac{2}{3}\right)^N A$ for every positive value of N. Since $0 < 2/3 < 1$, the value of $\left(\dfrac{2}{3}\right)^N A$ can be made smaller than any positive quantity for a large enough choice of N. It follows that the Sierpinski ternary gasket can also be made smaller than any positive quantity.

32. Since the length of the boundary doubles at each step, the perimeter of the Sierpinski ternary gasket becomes infinitely large.

C. The Chaos game and Variations

33. The coordinates of each point are:
P_1 : $(32, 0)$; P_2 : $(16, 0)$, the midpoint of A and P_1; P_3 : $(8, 16)$, the midpoint of C and P_2; P_4 : $(20, 8)$, the midpoint of B and P_3; P_5 :$(10, 20)$, the midpoint of C and P_4; P_6 : $(5, 26)$, the midpoint of C and P_5.

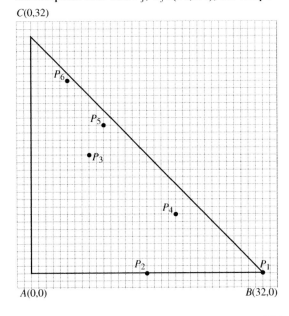

34. The coordinates of each point are:

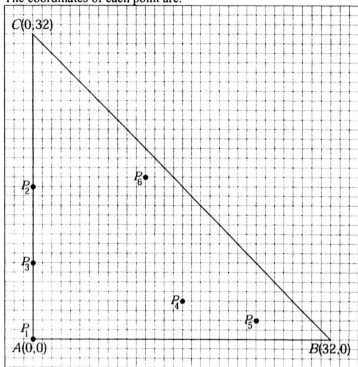

35. P_3 : (8, 0), the midpoint of A and P_2;

   P_4 : (20, 0), the midpoint of B and P_3;

   P_5 : (10, 16), the midpoint of C and P_4;

   P_6 : (5, 24), the midpoint of C and P_5.

Number rolled	3	1	2	3	5	5
Point	P_1	P_2	P_3	P_4	P_5	P_6
Coordinates	(32,0)	(16,0)	(8,0)	(20,0)	(10,16)	(5,24)

36. The results are found in the table below.

Number rolled	2	6	5	1	3	6
Point	P_1	P_2	P_3	P_4	P_5	P_6
Coordinates	(0,0)	(0,16)	(0,24)	(0,12)	(16,6)	(8,19)

37. General note: Find new coordinate by picking new *x*-value to be $\frac{2}{3}$ of way from *x*-coordinate of first

point to *x*-coordinate of second point and picking new *y*-value to be $\frac{2}{3}$ of way from *y*-coordinate of first

point to *y*-coordinate of second point.

(a) The coordinates of each point are:

P_1 : (0, 27);

P_2 : (18, 9), $\frac{2}{3}$ of way from P_1 to B;

P_3 : (6, 3), $\frac{2}{3}$ of way from P_2 to A;

P_4 : (20, 1), $\frac{2}{3}$ of way from P_3 to B.

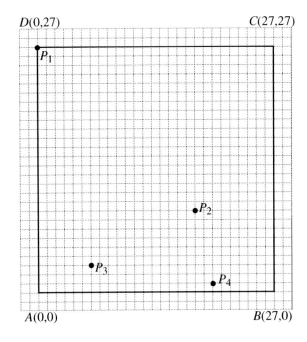

(b) The coordinates of each point are:

P_1 : $(27, 27)$;

P_2 : $(27, 9)$, $\dfrac{2}{3}$ of way from P_1 to B;

P_3 : $(9, 3)$, $\dfrac{2}{3}$ of way from P_2 to A;

P_4 : $(21, 1)$, $\dfrac{2}{3}$ of way from P_3 to B.

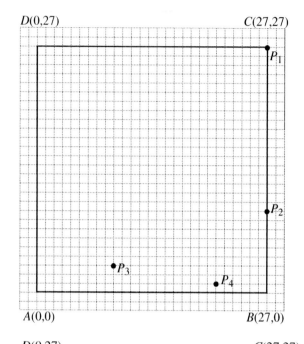

(c) The coordinates of each point are:

P_1 : $(27, 27)$;

P_2 : $(27, 27)$;

P_3 : $(9, 9)$, $\dfrac{2}{3}$ of way from P_2 to A;

P_4 : $(3, 3)$, $\dfrac{2}{3}$ of way from P_3 to A.

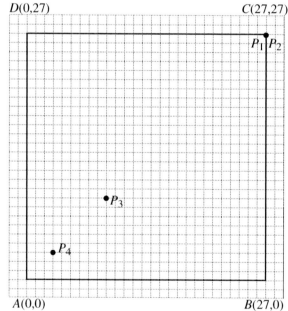

38. (a)

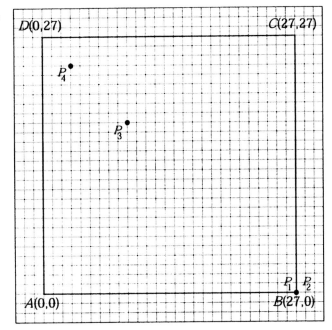

(b)

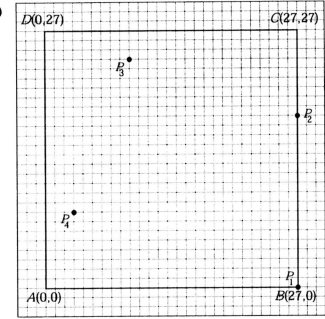

(c)

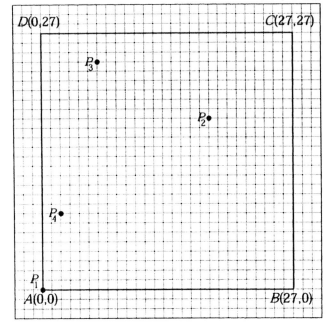

39. **(a)** P_1 : (0, 27);

P_2 : (18, 9), $\dfrac{2}{3}$ of way from P_1 to B;

P_3 : (6, 3), $\dfrac{2}{3}$ of way from P_2 to A;

P_4 : (20, 1), $\dfrac{2}{3}$ of way from P_3 to B.

(b) P_1 : (27, 27);

P_2 : (9, 9), $\dfrac{2}{3}$ of way from P_1 to A;

P_3 : (3, 3), $\dfrac{2}{3}$ of way from P_2 to A;

P_4 : (19, 19), $\dfrac{2}{3}$ of way from P_3 to C.

(c) P_1 : (0, 0);

P_2 : (18, 18), $\dfrac{2}{3}$ of way from P_1 to C;

$P_3 : (6, 24),\ \dfrac{2}{3}$ of way from P_2 to D;

$P_4 : (20, 8),\ \dfrac{2}{3}$ of way from P_3 to B.

40. (a) $P_1 : (27, 0);\ P_2 : (27, 18),\ P_3 : (9, 24),\ P_4 : (3, 8).$

   (b) $P_1 : (0, 27);\ P_2 : (18, 9),\ P_3 : (24, 3),$
$P_4 : (8, 19).$

   (c) $P_1 : (27, 27);\ P_2 : (9, 9),\ P_3 : (21, 3),$
$P_4 : (7, 19).$

D.   Operations with Complex Numbers

41. (a) $(1+i)^2 + (1+i) = 1 + 2i - 1 + (1+i) = 1 + 3i$

   (b) $(1-i)^2 + (1-i) = 1 - 2i - 1 + (1-i) = 1 - 3i$

   (c) $(-1+i)^2 + (-1+i) = 1 - 2i - 1 + (-1+i) = -1 - i$

42. (a) $(2+3i)^2 + (2+3i) = 4 + 12i - 9 + (2+3i) = -3 + 15i$

   (b) $(2-3i)^2 + (2-3i) = 4 - 12i - 9 + (2-3i) = -3 - 15i$

   (c) $(-2+3i)^2 + (3-2i) = 4 - 12i - 9 + (3-2i) = -2 - 14i$

43. (a) $(-0.25+0.25i)^2 + (-0.25+0.25i) = 0.0625 - 0.125i - 0.0625 + (-0.25+0.25i) = -0.25 + 0.125i$

   (b) $(-0.25-0.25i)^2 + (-0.25-0.25i) = 0.0625 + 0.125i - 0.0625 + (-0.25-0.25i) = -0.25 - 0.125i$

44. (a) $(-0.25+0.125i)^2 + (-0.25+0.125i) = 0.0625 - 0.625i - 0.015625 + (-0.25+0.125i) = -0.203125 - 0.5i$

   (b) $(-0.2+0.8i)^2 + (-0.2+0.8i) = 0.04 + 0.16i - 0.64 + (-0.2+0.8i) = -0.8 + 0.96i$

45. (a) Since the value of $i(1+i) = -1+i$, $i^2(1+i) = -1-i$, and $i^3(1+i) = 1-i$ we plot $1+i$, $-1+i$, $-1-i$, and $1-i$.

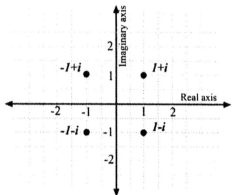

(b) Since the value of $i(3-2i) = 2+3i$, $i^2(3-2i) = -3+2i$, and $i^3(3-2i) = -2-3i$ we plot $3-2i$, $2+3i$, $-3+2i$, and $-2-3i$.

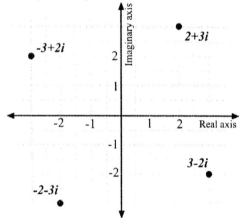

(c) The effect of multiplying each point in (a) and (b) by i is a 90-degree counterclockwise rotation.

46. **(a)** **Note: Exercise 46(a) is intended to read: Plot the points corresponding to the complex**
   numbers $(1+i)$, $-i(1+i)$, $(-i)^2(1+i)$, **and** $(-i)^3(1+i)$.

   Since the value of $-i(1+i) = 1-i$, $(-i)^2(1+i) = -1-i$, and $(-i)^3(1+i) = -1+i$ we plot $1+i$, $1-i$,
   $-1-i$ and $-1+i$.

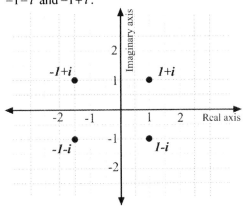

(b) Since the value of $-i(0.8+1.2i) = 1.2-0.8i$, $(-i)^2(0.8+1.2i) = -0.8-1.2i$, and

   $(-i)^3(0.8+1.2i) = -1.2+0.8i$ we plot $0.8+1.2i$, $1.2-0.8i$, $-0.8-1.2i$ and $-1.2+0.8i$.

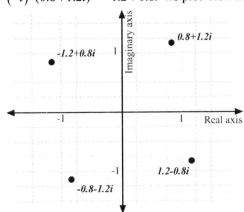

(c) The effect of multiplying each point in (a) and (b) by *-i* is a 90-degree *clockwise* rotation.

E. **Mandelbrot Sequences**

47. **(a)** $s_1 = (-2)^2 + (-2) = 4 - 2 = 2$; $s_2 = (2)^2 + (-2) = 4 - 2 = 2$; $s_3 = (2)^2 + (-2) = 4 - 2 = 2$;
   $s_4 = (2)^2 + (-2) = 4 - 2 = 2$.

(b) The sequence is attracted to 2, so $s_{100} = 2$.

(c) Each number in the sequence is 2. In this case, the sequence could be considered periodic (with period 1) or attracted to 2 (in the sense that a sequence of 2's could be considered getting closer and closer to the attractor 2).

48. (a) $s_1 = 2^2 + 2 = 6$; $s_2 = 6^2 + 2 = 38$; $s_3 = 38^2 + 2 = 1446$; $s_4 = 1446^2 + 2 = 2,090,918$.

(b) Escaping

49. (a) $s_1 = (-0.5)^2 + (-0.5) = -0.25$; $s_2 = (-0.25)^2 + (-0.5) = -0.4375$; $s_3 = (-0.4375)^2 + (-0.5) \approx -0.3086$;
$s_4 = (-0.3086)^2 + (-0.5) \approx -0.4048$; $s_5 = (-0.4048)^2 + (-0.5) \approx -0.3361$.

(b) $s_{N+1} = (-0.366)^2 + (-0.5) \approx -0.3660$

(c) From part (b), we see that $s_N = s_{N+1}$, so the sequence must be attracted to -0.3660 (rounded to 4 decimal places).

50. (a) $s_1 = -0.1875$, $s_2 = -0.214844$, $s_3 = -0.203842$, $s_4 = -0.208448$, $s_5 = -0.206549$,
$s_6 = -0.207337$, $s_7 = -0.207011$, $s_8 = -0.207146$, $s_9 = -0.207090$, $s_{10} = -0.207114$.

(b) -0.207107

(c) Attracted to the number -0.207107 (rounded to six decimal places).

51. (a) $s_1 = \left(\dfrac{1}{2}\right)^2 + \dfrac{1}{2} = \dfrac{1}{4} + \dfrac{1}{2} = \dfrac{3}{4}$; $s_2 = \left(\dfrac{3}{4}\right)^2 + \dfrac{1}{2} = \dfrac{9}{16} + \dfrac{1}{2} = \dfrac{17}{16}$; $s_3 = \left(\dfrac{17}{16}\right)^2 + \dfrac{1}{2} = \dfrac{289}{256} + \dfrac{1}{2} = \dfrac{417}{256}$.

(b) If $s_N > 1$, we have $(s_N)^2 > s_N$, and so $(s_N)^2 + \dfrac{1}{2} > s_N + \dfrac{1}{2}$. But $(s_N)^2 + \dfrac{1}{2} = s_{N+1}$, so we have

$$s_{N+1} > s_N + \dfrac{1}{2} > s_N.$$

(c) Notice from part (a) that $s_2 > 1$. From part (b) this implies that the sequence is escaping.

52. (a) $s_1 = 1.3125$, $s_2 = -0.02734$, $s_3 = -1.74925$, $s_4 = 1.30988$, $s_5 = -0.03423$, $s_6 = -1.74883$,
$s_7 = 1.30840$, $s_8 = -0.03807$, $s_9 = -1.74855$, $s_{10} = 1.30742$, $s_{11} = -0.04064$, $s_{12} = -1.74835$.

(b) The Mandelbrot sequence is periodic ($s_7 \approx s_{10}$, $s_8 \approx s_{11}$, $s_9 \approx s_{12}, \dots$).

53. (a) $s = 2$
$$s_{N+1} = (s_N)^2 + s$$
$$38 = (6)^2 + s$$
$$38 = 36 + s$$
$$s = 2$$

(b) $N = 1$
$$s_1 = (2)^2 + 2$$
$$= 4 + 2$$
$$= 6;$$

54. (a) $s = -3/2$

     (b) $N = 2$

JOGGING

55. At each step, one new hole is introduced for each solid triangle and the number of solid triangles is tripled (multiplied by three).

Step	Holes	Solid Triangles
1	1	3
2	$1 + 3$	3^2
3	$1 + 3 + 3^2$	3^3
4	$1 + 3 + 3^2 + 3^3$	3^4

Using the formula for the sum of the terms in a geometric sequence in which $r = 3$ (found in chapter 10), we see that at the Nth step there will be $1 + 3 + 3^2 + 3^3 + \cdots + 3^{N-1} = \dfrac{1 - 3^N}{1 - 3} = \dfrac{3^N - 1}{2}$ holes.

56. At each step, one new hole is introduced for each solid square and the number of solid squares is multiplied by eight.

Step	Holes	Solid Squares
1	1	8
2	$1 + 8$	8^2
3	$1 + 8 + 8^2$	8^3
4	$1 + 8 + 8^2 + 8^3$	8^4

Using the formula for the sum of the terms in a geometric sequence in which $r = 8$ (found in chapter 10), we see that at the Nth step there will be $1 + 8 + 8^2 + 8^3 + \cdots + 8^{N-1} = \dfrac{1 - 8^N}{1 - 8} = \dfrac{8^N - 1}{7}$ holes.

57. At the first step, a cube is removed from each of the six faces and from the center for a total of 7 cubes removed. At the next step, each of the 20 remaining cubes has 7 cubes removed (i.e, 20×7 cubes are removed). In the second step, there are 20^2 remaining cubes each of which has 7 cubes removed (i.e. $20^2 \times 7$ cubes are removed). Continuing in this fashion, we see that $20^{N-1} \times 7$ are removed from the 20^{N-1} remaining cubes in step N.

	Number of cubes removed
Start	0
Step 1	7
Step 2	20×7
Step 3	$20^2 \times 7$
...	
Step N	$20^{N-1} \times 7$

58. (a) At each step, the volume of the figure is found by multiplying by 20/27.

	Volume of the figure
Start	1
Step 1	20/27
Step 2	$(20/27)^2$
Step 3	$(20/27)^3$
...	
Step N	$(20/27)^N$

(b) Since $20/27 < 1$, the volume of the Menger Sponge is 0.

(c) The surface area of the Menger Sponge at the start of the construction is 6. The surface area after Step 1 is 8.

(d) For each square hole cut out of a side of a sub-cube, four such squares are added to the surface area.

59. (a) Reflection with axis a vertical line passing through the center of the snowflake; reflections with axes lines making 30°, 60°, 90°, 120°, 150° angles with the vertical axis of the snowflake and passing through the center of the snowflake.

(b) Rotations of 60°, 120°, 180°, 240°, 300°, 360° with rotocenter the center of the snowflake.

(c) D_6

60. (a) Reflections with vertical and horizontal lines passing through the center of the carpet; reflections with 45° (clockwise and counterclockwise from horizontal) diagonal axes passing through the center of the carpet.

(b) Rotations of 90°, 180°, 270°, 360° with rotocenter the center of the carpet.

(c) D_4

61. (a) Using the formula for the sum of the terms in a geometric sequence in which $r = 4/9$ (found in chapter 10), we have $1 + \left(\frac{4}{9}\right) + \left(\frac{4}{9}\right)^2 + \cdots + \left(\frac{4}{9}\right)^{N-1} = \dfrac{1-\left(\frac{4}{9}\right)^N}{\left(\frac{5}{9}\right)} = \frac{9}{5}\left[1-\left(\frac{4}{9}\right)^N\right]$.

(b) Using the result in (a) we have $\left(\frac{A}{3}\right) + \left(\frac{A}{3}\right)\left(\frac{4}{9}\right) + \left(\frac{A}{3}\right)\left(\frac{4}{9}\right)^2 + \ldots + \left(\frac{A}{3}\right)\left(\frac{4}{9}\right)^{N-1} =$

$\left(\frac{A}{3}\right)\left[1 + \left(\frac{4}{9}\right) + \left(\frac{4}{9}\right)^2 + \ldots + \left(\frac{4}{9}\right)^{N-1}\right] = \left(\frac{A}{3}\right)\left(\frac{9}{5}\right)\left[1-\left(\frac{4}{9}\right)^N\right] = \left(\frac{3}{5}\right)A\left[1-\left(\frac{4}{9}\right)^N\right]$.

62. If it is attracted to a number, then we have $s_{N+1} = (s_N)^2 + (-0.75)$ and $s_{N+1} = s_N$. Substituting, we have

$s_N = (s_N)^2 - 0.75$ so $s_N{}^2 - s_N - 0.75 = 0$. Solve via the Quadratic Equation: $s_N = \dfrac{1 \pm \sqrt{1 - 4\left(-\frac{3}{4}\right)}}{2}$.

Solving yields $s_N = -\dfrac{1}{2}$ or $s_N = \dfrac{3}{2}$. Examining the first few terms of the sequence indicates that the

sequence is attracted to $-\dfrac{1}{2}$.

63. If it is attracted to a number, then we have $s_{N+1} = (s_N)^2 + (0.2)$ and we set $s_{N+1} = s_N$. Substituting, we

have $s_N = (s_N)^2 + 0.2$ so $s_N{}^2 - s_N + 0.2 = 0$. Solve via the Quadratic Equation:

$s_N = \dfrac{1 \pm \sqrt{1 - 4(0.2)}}{2} = \dfrac{1 \pm \sqrt{0.2}}{2}$.

Solving yields $s_N = \dfrac{1 + \sqrt{0.2}}{2}$ or $s_N = \dfrac{1 - \sqrt{0.2}}{2}$. We proceed to examine a few terms of the sequence:

Step 10: 0.276241069;
Step 20: 0.2763927972;
Step 30: 0.2763932012.

This sequence is attracted to $\dfrac{1 - \sqrt{0.2}}{2} \approx 0.276393....$

64. If it is attracted, there will be a solution to $s_{N+1} = (s_N)^2 + 0.25$ with $s_{N+1} = s_N$. Substituting, we have

$s_N = s_N{}^2 + 0.25$ or $s_N{}^2 - s_N + 0.25 = 0$. Solving via the Quadratic Equation:

$s_N = \dfrac{1 \pm \sqrt{1 - 4\left(\frac{1}{4}\right)}}{2} = \dfrac{1 \pm 0}{2} = \dfrac{1}{2}.$ Examining several terms of the sequence indicates that the sequence is

attracted to $\dfrac{1}{2}$.

65. The first twenty steps: 0.3125, -1.15234375, 0.0778961182, -1.24393219, 0.297367305, -1.16157269, 0.0992511044, -1.24014922, 0.287970084, -1.16707323, 0.112059926, -1.23744257, 0.281264121, -1.17089049, 0.120984549, -1.23536274, 0.276121097, -1.17375714, 0.127705824, -1.23369122. The numbers oscillate, alternating between positive and negative values, but always staying within the interval $-1.25 \le x \le 0.3125$. The sequence is periodic.

66. Consider the first term of the sequence: $s_1 = \left(\sqrt{2}\right)^2 + \sqrt{2} = 2 + \sqrt{2}$

    Since $s_1 > 1$ and $\sqrt{2} \ge 0$, we are guaranteed that $s_{N+1} > s_N$ and so the sequence is escaping.

RUNNING

67. $0.4A$

    This follows from the fact that the area of the Koch snowflake is $1.6A$ and the fact that the construction of the anti-snowflake reverses the construction of the snowflake: what's added to the starting triangle to get the snowflake is removed from the starting triangle to get the anti-snowflake.

68. $2A$

    The area of the figure at step N of the construction of the square snowflake (see Exercise 10) is

    $$\text{Area} = A + \tfrac{4}{9}A + \tfrac{4}{9}\left(\tfrac{5}{9}\right)A + \tfrac{4}{9}\left(\tfrac{5}{9}\right)^2 A + \tfrac{4}{9}\left(\tfrac{5}{9}\right)^3 A + \cdots + \tfrac{4}{9}\left(\tfrac{5}{9}\right)^{N-1} A = A + \tfrac{4}{9}A\left(\dfrac{1 - \left(\frac{5}{9}\right)^N}{1 - \frac{5}{9}}\right) = A + A\left(1 - \left(\tfrac{5}{9}\right)^N\right)$$

    Note that all but the first term form the sum of the first N terms of a geometric sequence with $r = \dfrac{5}{9}$.

    As N gets larger, $\left(\dfrac{5}{9}\right)^N$ approaches 0 and the above expression approaches $A+A$.

69. The critical observation is the following: Suppose that P is an arbitrary point inside (or on the boundary) of triangle AM_1M_2. Then the midpoint Q of the segment PB is inside (or on the boundary) of triangle BM_1M_3. (Why? Because segment M_1M_3 is parallel to AC and therefore Y is the midpoint of segment BX, which forces Q to be between Y and B.) The argument above implies that the chaos game will force us to keep hopping among the insides (or boundaries) of the triangles AM_1M_2, BM_1M_3, and CM_2M_3, but never into a point inside triangle $M_1M_2M_3$.

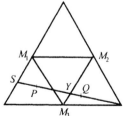

70. The first twenty steps: $-0.25 + 0.125i$, $-0.203125 + 0.1875i$, $-0.243896484 + 0.173828125i$,
$-0.220730722 + 0.165207863i$, $-0.228571586 + 0.177067098i$, $-0.229107787 + 0.169054985i$,
$-0.22608921 + 0.172536373i$, $-0.228652469 + 0.171982776i$, $-0.227296123 + 0.171351427i$,
$-0.227697784 + 0.17210497i$, $-0.22777384 + 0.17162416i$, $-0.22757393 + 0.171817012i$,
$-0.227731192 + 0.171797854i$, $-0.227653007 + 0.17175254i$, $-0.227673043 + 0.171800036i$,
$-0.227680238 + 0.171771526i$, $-0.227667167 + 0.171782036i$, $-0.227676729 + 0.171781741i$,
$-0.227672274 + 0.17177859i$, $-0.22767322 + 0.171781556i$.
The sequence is attracted to $-0.22767 + 0.17178i$ (rounded to 5 decimal places).

71. The first twenty steps: $-0.25 - 0.125i$, $-0.203125 - 0.1875i$, $-0.243896484 - 0.173828125i$,
$-0.220730722 - 0.165207863i$, $-0.228571586 - 0.177067098i$, $-0.229107787 - 0.169054985i$,
$-0.22608921 - 0.172536373i$, $-0.228652469 - 0.171982776i$, $-0.227296123 - 0.171351427i$,
$-0.227697784 - 0.17210497i$, $-0.22777384 - 0.17162416i$, $-0.22757393 - 0.171817012i$,
$-0.227731192 - 0.171797854i$, $-0.227653007 - 0.17175254i$, $-0.227673043 - 0.171800036i$,
$-0.227680238 - 0.171771526i$, $-0.227667167 - 0.171782036i$, $-0.227676729 - 0.171781741i$,
$-0.227672274 - 0.17177859i$, $-0.22767322 - 0.171781556i$.
The sequence is attracted to $-0.22767 - 0.17178i$ (rounded to 5 decimal places).

72. Suppose that $s = a + bi$ and $\bar{s} = a - bi$. The Mandelbrot replacement process with seed s produces the
sequence of complex numbers $s, s^2 + s, (s^2 + s)^2 + s, \ldots$. The Mandelbrot replacement process with seed
$\bar{s}$ produces the sequence of complex numbers $\bar{s}, \overline{s^2 + s} = \overline{s^2} + \bar{s}, \overline{(s^2 + s)^2 + s} = \overline{(s^2 + s)^2} + \bar{s}, \ldots$. (In
other words, each term in the second sequence is the complex conjugate of the corresponding term in the
first sequence. This follows because $\overline{z^2} = \overline{z}^2$ and $\overline{u + v} = \overline{u} + \overline{v}$ for all complex numbers z, u, and v.) It
follows that the two sequences either both stay bounded or both are escaping and therefore if the point z
is black (white) then its reflection across the x-axis, $\bar{z}$, is also black (white).

73. The Koch curve consists of $N = 4$ self-similar copies of itself with each copy having been reduced by a
scaling factor of $S = 3$. So, the dimension of the Koch curve is $D = \dfrac{\log 4}{\log 3} \approx 1.26$.

74. The Sierpinski carpet consists of $N = 8$ self-similar copies of itself with each copy having been reduced
by a scaling factor of $S = 3$. So, the dimension of the Sierpinski carpet is $D = \dfrac{\log 8}{\log 3} \approx 1.89$.

75. The Menger sponge consists of $N = 20$ self-similar copies of itself with each copy having been reduced
by a scaling factor of $S = 3$. So, the dimension of the Menger sponge is $D = \dfrac{\log 20}{\log 3} \approx 2.73$.

Chapter 13

WALKING

A. Surveys and Public Opinion Polls

1. (a) The population for this survey is the gumballs in the jar.

(b) The sample for this survey is the 25 gumballs draw out of the jar.

(c) 32%
The proportion of red gumballs in the sample is $\frac{8}{25} = 0.32$.

(d) The sampling method used for this survey was simple random sampling. Each set of n gumballs had the same probability of being selected as any other set of n gumballs.

2. (a) 12.5% (25/200)

(b) 64
The proportion of red gumballs in the sample is $\frac{8}{25} = 0.32$. Assuming that the sample is representative of the population, we estimate that there are $0.32 \times 200 = 64$ red gumballs in the candy jar.

3. (a) 25%
The parameter for the proportion of red gumballs in the jar is $\frac{50}{200} = 0.25$.

(b) 7%
The sampling error is 32% - 25% = 7%.

(c) Sampling variability.
Simple random sampling was used. This survey method does not suffer from selection bias.

4. (a) The target population and the sampling frame are identical for this survey. Both consist of the jar full of gumballs.

(b) A census.

5. (a) The sampling rate for this survey is $\frac{680}{8325} \approx 0.082$; that is, approximately 8.2%.

(b) 306/680 = 45%

6. (a) The registered voters in Cleansburg.

(b) The 680 registered voters that are polled by telephone.

(c) Simple random sampling.

7. Of the people surveyed, 45% indicated they would vote for Smith $\left(\frac{306}{680} = 0.45 \right)$. The actual percentage was 42%. Since 45% - 42% = 3%, the sampling error for Smith was 3%.
Similarly, the sampling error for Jones was 43% - 40% = 3% and the sampling error for Brown was 15% - 15% = 0%.

8. The sampling error should be attributed primarily to chance, since the sample was chosen randomly (this eliminates selection bias) and there was a 100% response rate (this eliminates nonresponse bias).

9. (a) The sample for this survey is the 350 students attending the Eureka High football game before the election.

(b) $\frac{350}{1250} = 28\%$

10. The sampling method used in this survey is convenience sampling.

11. **(a)** The population consists of all 1250 students at Eureka High School while the sampling frame consists only of those students that attended the football game a week prior to the election.

    (b) The sampling error is mainly a result of sampling bias. The sampling frame (and hence any sample taken from it) is not representative of the population. Students that choose to attend a football game are not representative of all Eureka High students.

12. **(a)** Based on the sample, we expect the following results: Tomlinson – 58%, Garcia – 12%, and Marsalis – 30%.

    (b) The sampling error for Tomlinson was 58% - 19% = 39%.
    The sampling error for Garcia was 51% - 12% = 39%.
    The sampling error for Marsalis was 30% - 30% = 0%.

13. **(a)** The sampling frame is all married people who read Dear Abby's column.

    (b) Abby's target population appears to be all married people. However, she is sampling from a subset of the population – a sampling frame that consists of those married couples that read her column. The sampling frame is quite different than the target population.

    (c) The sample chose itself. That is, the sample was chosen via self-selection.

    (d) 85% is a statistic, since it is based on data taken from a sample.

14. **(a)** If we assume that the target population consisted of all married people then Dear Abby's readers are far from a representative sample. Second (and this applies even if we assume the target population consisted only of Dear Abby's married readers), the sample

was self-selected — only those who took the trouble to write back were in the sample.

    (b) A very small percentage (probably less than 10%) of Dear Abby's readers (in the millions) took the trouble to respond.

15. **(a)** $\dfrac{44,807}{60,550} = 74.0\%$

    (b) $\dfrac{127,318 + 44,807}{210,336} \approx 81.8\%$

    (c) These estimates are probably not very accurate. The sample was far from being representative of the entire target population. One reason is that the sampling frame is so different from the target population. Another reason is that even if the sampling frame was similar to the target population, the survey is subject to nonresponse bias.

16. **Problem 1:** Defining the target population. The target population of this survey consists of (presumably) all married Americans. A reasonably accurate list of this population could be compiled from state records (almost all marriages within a state are certified and recorded by the state).
    Problem 2: Choosing a representative sample. We know that the best way to do this is by simple random sampling. Usually, a sample of about 1500-2000 individuals provides sufficient accuracy for a survey like this.
    Problem 3: Getting truthful responses. It is obvious that how the question is asked is a critical issue in this survey. Many respondents will be reluctant to answer or will not answer truthfully unless complete confidentiality can be guaranteed. Mail questionnaires are likely to produce a high nonresponse rate, and telephone interviews are almost guaranteed to produce a lot of untruthful responses. So this pretty much leaves personal interviews as the only

reasonable alternative. A few more things can be done to improve the chances of getting people to respond truthfully. For example, the interview should be held somewhere other than the home (office, a restaurant, etc.) and males should be interviewed by males, females by females.

17. **(a)** The target population of this survey is the citizens of Cleansburg.

    (b) The sampling frame is limited to that part of the target population that passes by a city street corner between 4:00 p.m. and 6:00 p.m.. It excludes citizens of Cleansburg having other responsibilities during that time of day.

18. **(a)** 475

    (b) Yes, this survey is subject to nonresponse bias. The total number of respondents was 475 (add the numbers in the first two columns). The total number of nonrespondents was 1313. The response rate was
    $$\frac{475}{1313+475} \approx 0.266 .$$ That is, only 26.6% of the people asked to participate in this survey actually did.

19. **(a)** The choice of street corner could make a great deal of difference in the responses collected.

    (b) *D.* (We are making the assumption that people who live or work downtown are much more likely to answer yes than people in other parts of town.)

    (c) Yes, the survey was subject to selection bias for two main reasons. (i) People out on the street between 4 p.m. and 6 p.m. are not representative of the population at large. For example, office and white collar workers are much more likely to be in the sample than homemakers and school teachers. (ii) The five street corners were chosen by

the interviewers and the passersby are unlikely to represent a cross section of the city.

    (d) No, no attempt was made to use quotas to get a representative cross section of the population.

20. Sending people out to interview passersby in a fixed location is not a good idea. Fixing a particular time of the day made it even worse. A telephone poll, based on a random sample of 500 registered voters in the city of Cleansburg would probably produce much more accurate data. Before asking the actual question ("Are you in favor, blah, blah, blah,...") the interviewer should introduce himself as representing the City Planning Department and, indicate that the survey consists of only one question and the survey will be used by the city to make important planning decisions. In this case, a better response rate can be expected.

21. **(a)** Assuming that the registrar has a complete list of the 15,000 undergraduates at Tasmania State University, the target population and the sampling frame both consist of all undergraduates at TSU.

    (b) $N = 15,000$

22. **(a)** $n = 135$ (90% of 1% of 15,000)

    (b) 0.9%

23. **(a)** In simple random sampling, any two members of the population have as much chance of both being in the sample as any other two. But in this sample, two people with the same last name—say Len Euler and Linda Euler—have no chance of both being in the sample.

    (b) Sampling variability. The students sampled appear to be a fair cross section of all TSU undergraduates that would attempt to enroll in Math 101.

24. (a) The proportion of students in the sample who responded by saying that they were unable to enroll in Math 101 is $\dfrac{8}{0.90 \times 150} = \dfrac{8}{135} \approx 0.059$. Assuming that those who responded are representative of the population, we estimate that there are $0.059 \times 15,000 \approx 889$ TSU undergraduates that tried but were unable to enroll in Math 101 this semester.

(b) The only possible flaw with this survey is the size of the sample (too small). A larger sample, of course, would result in a more accurate (but also more expensive) survey. The decision on how big is big enough depends on how important is accuracy and how much money one is willing to spend. In any case, a sample of 150 students is probably too small.

25. (a) Stratified sampling. The trees are broken into three different strata (by variety) and then a random sample is taken from each stratum.

(b) Quota sampling. The grower is using a systematic method to force the sample to fit a particular profile. However, because the grower is human, sampling bias could then be introduced. When selecting 300 trees of variety A, the grower does not select them at random. Selecting 300 trees in one particular part of the orchard could bias the yield.

26. (a) 80 oranges per tree
$0.50 \times 100 + 0.25 \times 50 + 0.25 \times 70 = 80$

(b) A statistic. (This is information about a sample, not about a population.)

27. (a) Convenience sampling.
George is selecting those units in the population that are easily accessible.

(b) Census.
The evaluation is a survey of all the students in the population.

(c) Stratified sampling.
The student newspaper is dividing the population into strata and then selecting a proportionately sized random sample from each stratum.

(d) Simple random sampling.
Every subset of 3 players has the same chance of being selected as any other subset of 3 players.

(e) Quota sampling.
The coach is attempting to force the sample to fit a particular profile (he wants only seniors to be a captain).

28. (a) Census.

(b) Convenience sampling.

(c) Stratified sampling.

B.   The Capture-Recapture Method

29. $N = \dfrac{n_2}{k} \cdot n_1 = \dfrac{120}{30} \cdot 500 = 2000$

30. 20,500
$$N = \dfrac{n_2}{k} \cdot n_1 = \dfrac{900}{218} \cdot 4965$$
$$= 20,497.7$$
$$\approx 20,500$$

31. 84 quarters
$N = \dfrac{n_2}{k} \cdot n_1 = \dfrac{28}{4} \cdot 12 = 84$ quarters. (Note:
To estimate the number of quarters, we disregard the nickels and dimes—they are irrelevant.)

32. 87 nickels
$$N = \dfrac{n_2}{k} \cdot n_1 = \dfrac{29}{5} \cdot 15 = 87$$

33. 124 dimes

$$N = \frac{n_2}{k} \cdot n_1 = \frac{43}{8} \cdot 23 = 123.625; \text{ Rounding to}$$

the nearest integer gives us 124 dimes.

34. The capture-recapture method could be a reasonable way to estimate the number of coins in the jar. Unlike animals, the coins are easy to "capture", they are equally accessible (one coin doesn't have more "smarts" than another coin), and they are not disturbed by tagging. The main issue in using the capture-recapture method with coins is that it is hard to get a good random sample for both the capture and the recapture. Unlike animals, the coins do not disperse on their own. Thus, the jar needs to be shaken well and the coins thoroughly mixed before drawing the capture and the recapture. One should also be careful not to draw all the coins from the top (or bottom) of the jar.

35. $N = \dfrac{n_2}{k} \cdot n_1 = \dfrac{660}{7} \cdot 1700 \approx 160,285$

Rounding to the nearest thousand gives an estimate of 160,000 lake sturgeon in the Lake of the Woods.

36. $N = \dfrac{n_2}{k} \cdot n_1 = \dfrac{10,300}{208} \cdot 24,000 \approx 1,188,462$

Rounding to the nearest hundred thousand gives an estimate of 1.2 million carp in Utah Lake in 2004.

37. **(a)** $N = \dfrac{n_2}{k} \cdot n_1 = \dfrac{1540}{171} \cdot 4064 \approx 36,600$

(b) $\dfrac{1}{3}(0.89 \times 36,600) \approx 10,860$

38. The capture and recapture of this study may sample two very different segments of the population. The capture may capture drug users wealthy enough to receive treatment; the recapture may capture a poorer segment of the population. Further, one would not

expect the proportion of tagged individuals that are recaptured to be as high as the proportion of the population that are tagged simply because going through treatment should, in theory at least, decrease the potential of being recaptured. Simply put, a drug user does not have the same likelihood of being in both captures.

C.　Clinical Studies

39. **(a)** The target population for this study is anyone who could have a cold and would consider buying vitamin X (i.e., pretty much all adults).

(b) The sampling frame is only a small portion of the target population. It only consists of college students in the San Diego area that are suffering from colds.

(c) Yes. This sample would likely under represent older adults and those living in colder climates.

40. **(a)** No, there was no control group.

(b) 1. San Diego residents are not typical of the population at large in several critical aspects (age, health, exposure to inclement weather, etc.).
2. The volunteers were paid to participate.
3. The subjects themselves determined the length of their cold.
4. There was no control group.

41. Four different problems with this study that indicate poor design include
(i) using college students (College students are not a representative cross section of the population in terms of age and therefore in terms of how they would respond to the treatment.),
(ii) using subjects only from the San Diego area,
(iii) offering money as an incentive to participate, and

(iv) allowing self-reporting (the subjects themselves determine when their colds are over).

42. (i) Choose the subjects randomly from the population at large.
(ii) Divide the subjects randomly into a treatment group (gets vitamin X) and a control group (gets a fake pill).
(iii) Have trained professionals (nurses) measure the length of each subject's cold.
(iv) Neither the subjects nor the nurses should know who is getting the real vitamin X and who is getting a placebo.

43. The target population for this study is all potential knee surgery patients.

44. **(a)** The sample consists of 180 potential knee surgery patients at the Houston VA Medical Center who volunteered to be in the study.

(b) $n = 180$

(c) No, the subjects volunteered. 144 of the 324 declined to participate.

45. **(a)** Yes, this was a controlled placebo experiment. There was one control group receiving the sham-surgery (placebo) and two treatment groups.

(b) The first treatment group consisted of those patients receiving arthroscopic debridement. The second treatment group consisted of those patients receiving arthroscopic lavage.

(c) Yes, this study could be considered a randomized controlled experiment since the 180 patients in the study were assigned to a treatment group at random.

(d) This was a blind experiment. The doctors certainly knew which surgery they were performing on each patient.

46. **(a)** Some patients that really do need surgery do not receive treatment.

(b) It is, at best, unclear whether arthroscopic debridement or arthroscopic lavage have any positive effect in treating knee surgery patients.

47. The professor was conducting a clinical study because he was, after all, trying to establish the connection between a cause (10 milligrams of caffeine a day) and an effect (improved performance in college courses). Other than that, the experiment had little going for it: it was not controlled (no control group); not randomized (the subjects were chosen because of their poor grades); no placebo was used and consequently the study was not double blind.

48. **(a)** The target population for this study can be assumed to be all college students. The sample for the study was the set of students that were invited to come to the professor's office for "individual tutoring."

(b) $n = 13$

(c) The sampling rate is much, much less than 0.01%. [With $n = 13$, a sampling rate of 0.01% (0.0001) would correspond to a population of 130,000 (13/130,000 = 0.0001). The population of college students is obviously much, much larger than 130,000.]

49. **(a)** It is likely that the study was blind but not double-blind since the professor knew who was in the study.

(b) Three possible causes that could have confounded the results of this study include the following.
(i) A regular visit to the professor's office could in itself be a boost to a student's self-confidence and help improve his or her grades.
(ii) The "individualized tutoring" that took place during the office meetings

could also be the reason for improved performance.
(iii) The students selected for the study all got F's on their first midterm, making them likely candidates to show some improvement.

50. (i) Use a much larger sample.
(ii) Use a random sample.
(iii) Use students in courses other than his own.
(iv) Use more than a couple of midterms to measure improvements in a student's performance.

51. The target population consists of all people having a history of colorectal adenomas. The point of the study is to determine the effect that Vioxx had on this population. That is, whether recurrence of colorectal polyps could be prevented in this population.

52. (a) The sample consisted of 2,586 participants all of whom had a history of colorectal adenomas.

(b) $n = 2,586$

53. (a) The treatment group consisted of the 1287 patients that were given 25 daily milligrams of Vioxx. The control group consisted of the 1299 patients that were given a placebo.

(b) This is an experiment since members of the population received a treatment. It is a controlled placebo experiment since there was a control group that did not receive the treatment, but instead received a placebo. It is a randomized controlled experiment since the 2586 participants were randomly divided into the treatment and control groups. The study was double blind since neither the participants nor the doctors involved in the clinical trial knew who was in each group.

54. The clinical study described is a double-blind randomized controlled placebo experiment. As such, a person suffering from arthritis and having a history of colorectal adenomas should avoid taking Vioxx as it this study suggests the potential for an increase in the occurrence of cardiovascular events.

D.   Miscellaneous

55. (a) Spurlock's study was a clinical trial since a treatment was imposed (eating three meals at McDonald's every day for 30 days) on a sample of the population.

(b) The target population is the "average American."

(c) The sample consisted of one person (that being Mr. Spurlock himself).

(d) Three problems with this study that indicate poor design include the following (there are countless others).
(i) The use of a sample that is not representative of the population.
(ii) A small sample size (1 person).
(iii) The lack of a control group in which a sample of "average Americans" curtailed their physical activity and ate the same number of calories as the treatment group.

56. (a) Morgan's treatment group consisted of Merab Morgan.

(b) Merab may have exercised more than usual during the study. Meal plans of less than 1,400 calories a day may cause an average person to lose weight no matter what they eat. The choice of foods that Merab ate at McDonald's may also not be those of the average American.

(c) Since the experiment is far from legitimate, not many legitimate conclusions can be drawn. However, one might be able to say that combined with wise dietary behavior, it is possible to lose weight while eating only at McDonald's.

57. **(a)** This study was a clinical trial since a treatment was imposed (the heavy reliance on supplemental materials, online practice exercises and interactive tutorials) on a sample of the population.

    (b) Some possible confounding variables in this study include the following.
(i) The instructors used in the treatment group may be more excited about this new curricular approach or they may be better teachers.
(ii) If students in this particular intermediate algebra class were self-selected, they may not be representative of the target population.
(iii) Students in the treatment group may have benefited simply by being forced to put more time studying into the course. To eliminate this possible confounding variable, the control groups should be asked to spend the same amount of time studying out of class.

58. Yes. Each student has a 20% chance of being selected.

59. **(a)** parameter
This statement refers to the entire population of students taking the SAT math test.

    (b) statistic
A sample of the population of new automobiles are crash tested.

    (c) statistic
A sample of the population of Mr. Johnson's blood tested positive.

    (d) statistic
The poll did not sample all Americans; the statement refers to a sample of the population.

60. **(a)** Association is not causation.

    (b) placebo effect

    (c) sampling variability

    (d) selection bias

JOGGING

61. **(a)** The populations are (i) the entire sky; (ii) all the coffee in the cup; (iii) the entire Math 101 class.

    (b) In none of the three examples is the sample random.

    (c) (i) In some situations one can have a good idea as to whether it will rain or not by seeing only a small section of the sky, but in many other situations rain clouds can be patchy and one might draw the wrong conclusions by just peeking out the window. (ii) If the coffee is burning hot on top, it is likely to be pretty hot throughout, so Betty's conclusion is likely to be valid. (iii) Since Carla used convenience sampling and those students sitting next to her are not likely to be a representative sample, her conclusion is likely to be invalid.

62. Answers will vary.

63. **(a)** The results of this survey might be invalid because the question was worded in a way that made it almost impossible to answer yes.

    (b) "Will you support some form of tax increase if it can be proven to you that such a tax increase is justified?" is better, but still not neutral. "Do you support or oppose some form of tax increase?" is bland but probably as neutral as one can get.

    (c) Many such examples exist. A very real example is a question such as "Would you describe yourself as pro-life or not?" or "Would you describe yourself as pro-choice or not?"

64. **(a)** People are very unlikely to tell IRS representatives that they cheated on their taxes even when they are promised confidentiality.

(b) The critical issue in this survey is to get the respondents to given an honest answer to the question. In this regard two points are critical: (i) the survey is much more likely to get honest responses when sponsored by a "neutral" organization (a newspaper poll, for example); (ii) a mailed questionaire is the safest way to guarantee anonimity for the respondent and in this case it is much better than a telephone or (heaven forbid) personal interview. This is a situation where a tradeoff must be made — some nonresponse bias is still preferable to dishonest answers. The nonresponse bias can be reduced by the use of an appropriate inducement or reward (book, magazine, or newspaper subscription, etc.) to those who can show proof of having mailed back the questionnaire (for example by showing a post office receipt, etc.). Note: In 1984 the public opinion firm of Yankelovitch, Skelley, and White conducted a poll in which approximately 2200 taxpayers were asked if they had ever cheated on their federal income taxes. Approximately 20% responded yes. (Hah!)

65. **(a)** Under method 1, people whose phone numbers are unlisted are automatically ruled out from the sample. At the same time, method 1 is cheaper and easier to implement than method 2. Method 2 will typically produce more reliable data since the sample selected would better represent the population.

(b) For this particular situation, method 2 is likely to produce much more reliable data than method 1. The two main reasons are (i) people with unlisted phone numbers are very likely to be the same kind of people that would seriously consider buying a burglar alarm, and (ii) the listing bias is more likely to be significant in a place like New York City. (People with unlisted phone numbers make up a much higher percentage of the population in a large city such as New York than in a small town or rural area. Interestingly enough, the largest percentage of unlisted phone numbers for any American city is in Las Vegas, Nevada.)

66. **(a)** As discussed in the chapter, an Area Code 900 telephone poll represents an extreme case of selection bias. People that respond to these polls usually represent the extreme view points (strongly for or strongly against), leaving out much of the middle of the road point of view. Economics also plays some role in the selection bias. (While 50 cents is not a lot of money anymore, poor people are much more likely to think twice before spending the money to express their opinion.)

(b) This survey was based on fairly standard modern-day polling techniques (random sample telephone interviews, etc.) but it had one subtle flaw. How reliable can a survey about the conduct of the newsmedia be when the survey itself is conducted by a newsmedia organization? ("The fox guarding the chicken-coop" syndrome.)

(c) Both surveys seem to have produced unreliable data — survey 1 overestimating the public's dissapproval of the role played by the newsmedia and survey 2 overestimating the public's support for the press coverage of the war.

(d) Any reasoned out answer should be acceptable. (Since Area Code 900 telephone polls are particularly unreliable, survey 2 gets our vote.)

67. (a) Fridays, Saturdays, and Sundays make up 3/7 or about 43% of the week. It follows that proportionally, there are fewer fatalities due to automobile accidents on Friday, Saturday, and Sunday (42%) than there are on Monday through Thursday.

(b) On Saturday and Sunday there are fewer people commuting to work. The number of cars on the road and miles driven is significantly less on weekends. The number of accidents due to fatalities should be proportionally much less. The fact that it is 42% indicates that there are other factors involved and increased drinking is one possible explanation.

68. (a) Both samples should be a representative cross section of the same population. In particular, it is essential that the first sample, after being released, be allowed to disperse evenly throughout the population, and that the population should not change between the time of the capture and the time of the recapture.

(b) It is possible (especially when dealing with elusive types of animals) that the very fact that the animals in the first sample allowed themselves to be captured makes such a sample biased (they could represent a slower, less cunning group). This type of bias is compounded with the animals that get captured the second time around. A second problem is the effect that the first capture can have on the captured animals. Sometimes the animal may be hurt (physically or emotionally) making it more (or less) likely to be captured the second time around. A third source of bias is the possibility that some of the tags will come off.

Chapter 14

WALKING

A.   Frequency Tables, Bar Graphs, and Pie Charts

1.

Score	10	50	60	70	80	100
Frequency	1	3	7	6	5	2

2.

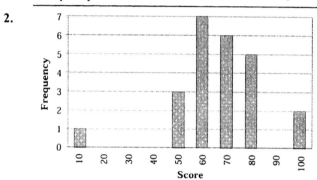

3. (a)

Grade	A	B	C	D	F
Frequency	7	6	7	3	1

(b)

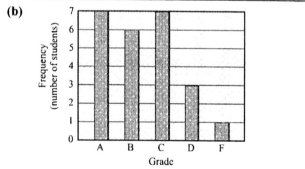

4. (a) $3 / 24 = 12.5\%$

(b) $0.125 \times 360° = 45°$

(c)

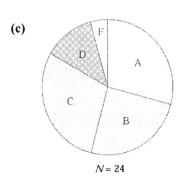

$N = 24$

5. (a) 80

$24 + 16 + 20 + 12 + 5 + 3 = 80$

(b) 30% $\left(\dfrac{24}{80} = 0.30 \right)$

(c)

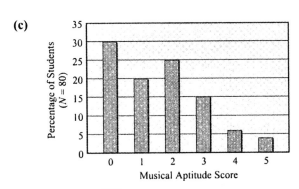

6.

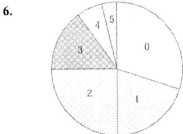

$N = 80$

7.	Distance (miles) to school	0.0	0.5	1.0	1.5	2.0	2.5	3.0	5.0	8.5
	Frequency	4	3	4	6	3	2	1	1	1

8.

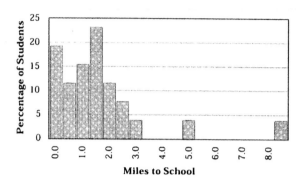

9. (a)

Class Interval	Very close	Close	Nearby	Not too far	Far
Frequency	7	10	5	1	2

(b)

$N = 25$

Slice "Very close": $\dfrac{7}{25} \times 360° = 100.8°$; Slice "Close": $\dfrac{10}{25} \times 360° = 144°$;

Slice "Nearby": $\dfrac{5}{25} \times 360° = 72°$; Slice "Not too far": $\dfrac{1}{25} \times 360° = 14.4°$;

Slice "Far": $\dfrac{2}{25} \times 360° = 28.8°$.

10.

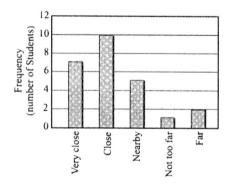

11. (a) 30

$N = 2 + 5 + 6 + 4 + 4 + 5 + 3 + 1 = 30$

(b) 0%

(c) approximately 56.67%

$$\frac{4 + 4 + 5 + 3 + 1}{30} \approx 0.5667$$

12.

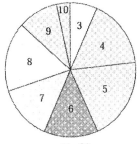

$N = 30$

13. Accidents: $0.43023 \times 360° \approx 155°$
Homicide: $0.17297 \times 360° \approx 62°$
Suicide: $0.12982 \times 360° \approx 47°$
Cancer: $0.05236 \times 360° \approx 19°$
Heart Disease: $0.03208 \times 360° \approx 12°$
Other: $0.18254 \times 360° \approx 66°$

14. (a)

Category	Accidents	Homicide	Suicide	Cancer	Heart Disease	Other
Frequency	8,275	3,327	2,497	1,007	617	3,511

Accidents: $0.43023 \times 19,234 \approx 8,275$
Homicide: $0.17297 \times 19,234 = 3,327$
Suicide: $0.12982 \times 19,234 = 2,497$
Cancer: $0.05236 \times 19,234 = 1,007$
Heart Disease: $0.03208 \times 19,234 = 617$
Other: $0.18254 \times 19,234 = 3,511$

(b)

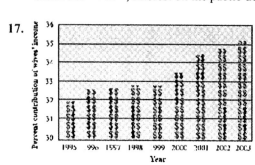

15. **(a)** $0.09 \times \$2,100,000,000,000 = \$189,000,000,000$ (\$189 billion)

   (b) $0.44 \times \$2,100,000,000,000 = \$924,000,000,000$ (\$924 billion)

16. Defense: $0.18 \times 360° \approx 65°$; Social Security: $0.26 \times 360° \approx 94°$; Medicare and Medicaid: $0.18 \times 360° \approx 65°$; Interest on the public debt: $0.09 \times 360° \approx 32°$; Other expenses: $0.29 \times 360° \approx 104°$.

17.

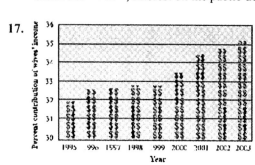
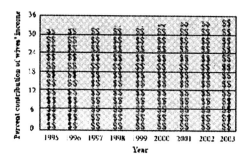

18.

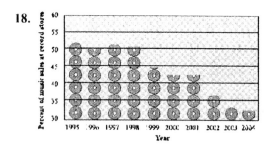
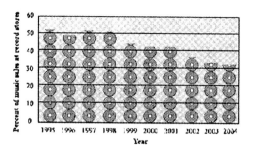

B.   Histograms

19. **(a)** $60 - 48 = 12$ ounces

   (b) The third class interval: "more than 72 ounces and less than or equal to 84 ounces." Values that fall exactly on the boundary between two class intervals belong to the class interval to the left.

(c) $N = 15 + 24 + 41 + 67 + 119 + 184 + 142 + 26 + 5 + 2 = 625$

Frequency	15	24	41	67	119	184	142	26	5	2
Percent	2.4	3.8	6.6	10.7	19.0	29.4	22.7	4.2	0.8	0.3

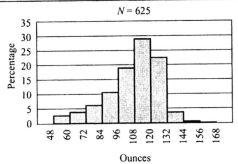

20. (a) The following is a frequency table for birth weights in Cleansburg using class intervals of length equal to 24 ounces.

Weight in Ounces		
More than	Less than or Equal	Frequencies
48	72	39
72	96	108
96	120	303
120	144	168
144	168	7

(b)

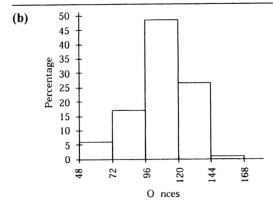

21. (a) $8 + 3 = 11$

    (b) \$20,000,000 (\$20 million)

    (c) Payrolls of \$20 million, \$40 million, \$60 million, \$80 million, or \$100 million would belong to the class interval on the right.

22.	Payroll	$20-$40 million	$40-$60 million	$60-$80 million	$80-$100 million	>$100 million
	Frequency	4	7	8	8	3

C. Means and Medians

23. **(a)** 2

$$\text{average} = \frac{3-5+7+4+8+2+8-3-6}{9} = 2$$

(b) 3

The ordered data set is {-6, -5, -3, 2, 3, 4, 7, 8, 8}. The locator of the 50th percentile is L = (0.50)(9) = 4.5. Since L is not a whole number, the 50th percentile is located in the 5th position in the list. Hence, the median is 3.

(c) Average: 2; Median: 2.5

The average of the new data set is found by computing $\frac{(9 \times 2) + 2}{10} = 2$ The new ordered data set is {-6, -5, -3, 2, 2, 3, 4, 7, 8, 8}. The locator of the 50th percentile is L = (0.50)(10) = 5. Since L is a whole number, the 50th percentile is the average of the 5th and 6th numbers (2 and 3) in the ordered list. Hence, the median of this new data set is 2.5.

24. **(a)** 0.1625

(b) -3.8

(c) Average: -1.7; Median: -3.8

25. **(a)** Average: 4.5; Median: 4.5

$$\text{average} = \frac{0+1+2+3+4+5+6+7+8+9}{10} = \frac{45}{10} = 4.5$$

Since the data set is already ordered, the locator of the median is L = (0.50)(10) = 5. Since L is a whole number, the median is the average of the 5th and 6th numbers (4 and 5) in the data set. Hence the median is 4.5.

(b) Average: 5; Median: 5

$$\text{average} = \frac{1+2+3+4+5+6+7+8+9}{9} = \frac{45}{9} = 5$$

The locator of the median is L = (0.50)(9) = 4.5. Since L is not a whole number, the median is the 5th number in the data set. Hence the median is 5.

(c) Average: 5.5; Median: 5.5

$$\text{average} = \frac{1+2+3+4+5+6+7+8+9+10}{10} = \frac{55}{10} = 5.5$$

The locator of the median is L = (0.50)(10) = 5. Since L is a whole number, the median is the average of the 5th and 6th numbers (5 and 6) in the data set. Hence the median is 5.5.

26. **(a)** Average: 1.5; Median: 1.5

(b) Average: 2.5; Median: 2.5

(c) Average: 3; Median: 3

27. **(a)** 50

(b) 50

28. **(a)** 500.5

$$\text{average} = \frac{1+2+3+4+5+\ldots+999+1000}{1000} = \frac{\frac{1000 \times 1001}{2}}{1000} = 500.5$$

(b) 500.5
The locator for the median is L = (0.50)(1000) = 500. Since L is a whole number, the median is the average of the 500th and 501st numbers (500 and 501) in the data set. Hence the median is 500.5.

29. **(a)** 1.5875

$$\text{average} = \frac{24 \times 0 + 16 \times 1 + 20 \times 2 + 12 \times 3 + 5 \times 4 + 3 \times 5}{24 + 16 + 20 + 12 + 5 + 3} = \frac{127}{80} = 1.5875$$

(b) 1.5
The locator for the median is L = (0.50)(80) = 40. So, the median is the average of the 40th and 41st scores. The 40th score is 1, and the 41st score is 2. Thus, the median is 1.5.

30. **(a)** 31.05

$$\text{average} = \frac{25 \times 2 + 27 \times 7 + 28 \times 6 + 29 \times 9 + 30 \times 15 + 31 \times 12 + 32 \times 9 + 33 \times 9 + 37 \times 6 + 39 \times 4}{2 + 7 + 6 + 9 + 15 + 12 + 9 + 9 + 6 + 4} = 31.05$$

(b) 31
The locator for the median is L = (0.50)(79) = 39.5. So, the median is the 40th age which is 31.

31. **(a)** 6.77
Since the number of quiz scores N is not given, we can compute the average as
$$\frac{(0.07N) \times 4 + (0.11N) \times 5 + (0.19N) \times 6 + (0.24N) \times 7 + (0.39N) \times 8}{N}$$
$$= 0.07 \times 4 + 0.11 \times 5 + 0.19 \times 6 + 0.24 \times 7 + 0.39 \times 8$$
$$= 6.77$$

(As the calculation shows, the number of scores is not important. If one likes, they can assume that there were 100 scores.)

(b) 7

Since 50% of the scores were at 7 or below, the median is 7.

32. (a) 6.2

$$\frac{2\times3+5\times4+6\times5+4\times6+4\times7+5\times8+3\times9+1\times10}{2+5+6+4+4+5+3+1} \approx 6.2$$

(b) 6

The locator for the median is L = (0.50)(30) = 15. So, the median is the average of the 15th and 16th scores which are both 6.

D.   Percentiles and Quartiles

33. The ordered data set is {-6, -5, -3, 2, 3, 4, 7, 8, 8}.

(a) $Q_1 = -3$

The locator of the 25th percentile is L = (0.25)(9) = 2.25. By rounding up, we find that the first quartile is the 3rd number in the ordered list. That is, $Q_1 = -3$.

(b) $Q_3 = 7$

The locator of the 75th percentile is L = (0.75)(9) = 6.75. By rounding up, we find that the third quartile is the 7th number in the ordered list. That is, $Q_3 = 7$.

(c) $Q_1 = -3$; $Q_3 = 7$

The new ordered data set is {-6, -5, -3, 2, 2, 3, 4, 7, 8, 8}. The locator of the 25th percentile is L = (0.25)(10) = 2.5. Rounding up, we find that the first quartile is the 3rd number in the ordered list. That is, $Q_1 = -3$. The locator of the 75th percentile is L = (0.75)(10) = 7.5. Rounding up, we find that the third quartile is the 8th number in the ordered list. That is, $Q_3 = 7$.

34. (a) $Q_1 = -5.9$

(b) $Q_3 = 8.3$

(c) $Q_1 = -7.3$; $Q_3 = 8.3$

35. (a) 75th percentile : 75.5; 90th percentile : 90.5

Since the data set is already ordered, the locator of the 75th percentile is given by L = (0.75)(100) = 75. Since this is a whole number, the 75th percentile is the average of the 75th and 76th numbers in the list. That is, the 75th percentile is 75.5.
The locator of the 90th percentile is given by L = (0.90)(100) = 90. Since this is a whole number, the 90th percentile is the average of the 90th and 91st numbers in the list. That is, the 90th percentile is 90.5.

(b) 75th percentile : 75; 90th percentile : 90

The locator of the 75th percentile is given by L = (0.75)(101) = 75.75. Since this not is a whole number, the 75th percentile is the 76th number in the list. That is, the 75th percentile is 75.

The locator of the 90th percentile is given by $L = (0.90)(101) = 90.9$. Since this is not a whole number, the 90th percentile is the 91st number in the list. That is, the 90th percentile is 90.

(c) 75th percentile : 75; 90th percentile : 90
The locator of the 75th percentile is given by $L = (0.75)(99) = 74.25$. Since this not is a whole number, the 75th percentile is the 75th number in the list. That is, the 75th percentile is 75.
The locator of the 90th percentile is given by $L = (0.90)(99) = 89.1$. Since this is not a whole number, the 90th percentile is the 90th number in the list. That is, the 90th percentile is 90.

(d) 75th percentile : 74; 90th percentile : 89
The locator of the 75th percentile is given by $L = (0.75)(98) = 73.5$. Since this not is a whole number, the 75th percentile is the 74th number in the list. That is, the 75th percentile is 74.
The locator of the 90th percentile is given by $L = (0.90)(98) = 88.2$. Since this is not a whole number, the 90th percentile is the 89th number in the list. That is, the 90th percentile is 89.

36. (a) 10th percentile : 5.5; 25th percentile : 13

   (b) 10th percentile : 5; 25th percentile : 13

   (c) 10th percentile : 5; 25th percentile : 13

37. (a) $Q_1 = 29$
The Cleansburg Fire Department consists of $2 + 7 + 6 + 9 + 15 + 12 + 9 + 9 + 6 + 4 = 79$ firemen. The locator of the first quartile is thus given by $L = (0.25)(79) = 19.75$. So, the first quartile is the 20th number in the ordered data set. That is, $Q_1 = 29$.

   (b) $Q_3 = 32$
The locator of the third quartile is given by $L = (0.75)(79) = 59.25$. So, the third quartile is the 60th number in the ordered data set. That is, $Q_3 = 32$.

   (c) The 90th percentile is 37.
The locator of the 90th percentile is given by $L = (0.90)(79) = 71.1$. So, the 90th percentile is the 72nd number in the ordered data set or 37.

38. (a) $Q_1 = 5$
There were 30 scores on the math quiz. The locator of the first quartile is given by $L = (0.25)(30) = 7.5$. So, the first quartile is the 8th number in the ordered data set or 5.

   (b) $Q_3 = 8$
The locator of the third quartile is given by $L = (0.75)(30) = 22.5$. So, the first quartile is the 23rd number in the ordered data set or 8.

   (c) The 70th percentile is 7.5.

39. (a) The $709,504^{th}$ score, $d_{709,504}$.
The locator is given by $L = 709,503.5$.

(b) The 354,752[th] score, $d_{354,752}$.
The locator is given by L = 354,751.75.

(c) The 1,064,256[th] score, $d_{1,064,256}$.
The locator is given by L = 1,064,255.25.

40. (a) Since the locator is given by L = 638,160, the median is located halfway between the 638,160[th] and 638,161[st] scores.

(b) Since the locator is given by L = 319,080, the first quartile is located halfway between the 319,080[th] and 319,081[st] scores.

(c) Since the locator is given by L = 957,240, the third quartile is located halfway between the 957,240[th] and 957,241[st] scores.

E.   Box Plots and Five-Number Summaries

41. (a) *Min* = –6, Q_1 = –3, *M* = 3, Q_3 = 7, *Max* = 8

(b)

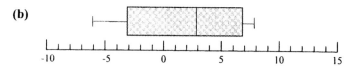

42. (a) *Min* = –9.1, Q_1 = –5.9, *M* = –3.8, Q_3 = 8.3, *Max* = 13.2

(b)

43. (a) *Min* = 25, Q_1 = 29, *M* = 31, Q_3 = 32, *Max* = 39

(b)

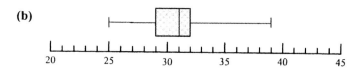

44. (a) *Min* = 3, Q_1 = 5, *M* = 6, Q_3 = 8, *Max* = 8

(b)

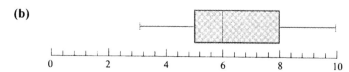

45. (a) Between $33,000 and $34,000

(b) $40,000

(c) The vertical line indicating the median salary in the engineering box plot is to the right of the box in the agriculture box plot.

46. (a) 459
$35,000 is the first quartile of engineering salaries, so $0.75 \times 612 = 459$ engineering majors made $35,000 or more.

(b) 960
$25,000 is the first quartile of the N agriculture salaries, so $0.25 \times N = 240$ agriculture majors made $25,000 or less. Thus, $N = 240 \times 4 = 960$.

F.   Ranges and Interquartile Ranges

47. (a) $8 - (-6) = 14$

(b) 10
From Exercise 33, $Q_1 = -3, Q_3 = 7$.
$IQR = 7 - (-3) = 10$

48. (a) 22.3

(b) 14.2

49. (a) $156,000 - $115,000 = $41,000

(b) At least 171 homes.

50. (a) Approximately $53,500 - $22,500 = $31,000.

(b) Approximately $8,500.

(c) At least 306 students.

51. (a) Note that $1.5 \times IQR = 1.5 \times 3 = 4.5$. So any number bigger than $12 + 4.5 = 16.5$ is an outlier.

(b) Any number smaller than $9 - 4.5 = 4.5$ is also an outlier.

(c) Since 1 is the only number smaller than 4.5 and 24 is the only number bigger than 16.5, the numbers 1 and 24 are the only outliers in this data set.

52. There are 10 outliers: 6 ages of 37 and 4 ages of 39.
Note that $1.5 \times IQR = 1.5 \times 3 = 4.5$. Hence, outliers are ages above $32 + 4.5 = 36.5$ or below $29 - 4.5 = 24.5$.

53. The *IQR* for the 2001 SAT math scores is $590 - 440 = 150$. Since $1.5 \times IQR = 1.5 \times 150 = 225$, an outlier is any score bigger than $590 + 225 = 815$ or any score smaller than $440 - 225 = 215$. Since the maximum score on the SAT is 800 and the minimum SAT score is 200, the only outliers are scores less than 215. That is, only SAT math scores of 200 or 210 would be considered outliers.

54. The *IQR* for the 2004 SAT math scores is $600 - 440 = 160$. Since $1.5 \times IQR = 1.5 \times 160 = 240$, an outlier is any score bigger than $600 + 240 = 840$ or any score smaller than $440 - 240 = 200$. Since the maximum score on the SAT is 800 and the minimum SAT score is 200, there are no possible scores that are outliers.

G. Standard Deviations

55. (a) 0

$A = 5$, so $x - A = 0$ for every number x in the data set. The standard deviation is 0.

(b) Approximately 3.5

$$A = \frac{0+5+5+10}{4} = 5$$

x	$x - 5$	$(x-5)^2$
0	-5	25
5	0	0
5	0	0
10	5	25
		50

Standard deviation $= \sqrt{\dfrac{50}{4}} = \dfrac{5\sqrt{2}}{2} \approx 3.5$

(c) Approximately 11.7

$$A = \frac{-5+0+0+25}{4} = 5$$

x	$x - 5$	$(x-5)^2$
-5	-10	100
0	-5	25
0	-5	25
25	20	400
		550

Standard deviation $= \sqrt{\dfrac{550}{4}} \approx 11.7$

56. (a) 0

$A = 10$, so $x - A = 0$ for every number x in the data set. The standard deviation is 0.

(b) Approximately 7.2; $A = \dfrac{1 + 6 + 13 + 20}{4} = 10$

x	$x - 10$	$(x-10)^2$
1	−9	81
6	-4	16
13	3	9
20	10	100
		206

Standard deviation $= \sqrt{\dfrac{206}{4}} \approx 7.2$

(b) Approximately 9; $A = \dfrac{1 + 1 + 18 + 20}{4} = 10$

x	$x - 10$	$(x-10)^2$
1	−9	81
1	−9	81
18	8	64
20	10	100
		326

Standard deviation $= \sqrt{\dfrac{326}{4}} \approx 9$

57. (a) $A = \dfrac{0 + 1 + 2 + 3 + 4 + 5 + 6 + 7 + 8 + 9}{10} = 4.5$

x	$x - 4.5$	$(x-4.5)^2$
0	−4.5	20.25
1	−3.5	12.25
2	−2.5	6.25
3	−1.5	2.25
4	−0.5	0.25
5	0.5	0.25

6	1.5	2.25
7	2.5	6.25
8	3.5	12.25
9	4.5	20.25
		82.5

Standard deviation $= \sqrt{\dfrac{82.5}{10}} \approx 2.87$

(b) $A = \dfrac{1+2+3+4+5+6+7+8+9+10}{10} = 5.5$

x	$x - 5.5$	$(x-5.5)^2$
1	−4.5	20.25
2	−3.5	12.25
3	−2.5	6.25
4	−1.5	2.25
5	−0.5	0.25
6	0.5	0.25
7	1.5	2.25
8	2.5	6.25
9	3.5	12.25
10	4.5	20.25
		82.5

Standard deviation $= \sqrt{\dfrac{82.5}{10}} \approx 2.87$

Note that each data point is simply located 1 unit to the right of that data set given in (a). So, the spread of the data set has not changed.

(c) $A = \dfrac{6+7+8+9+10+11+12+13+14+15}{10} = 10.5$

x	$x - 10.5$	$(x-10.5)^2$
6	−4.5	20.25
7	−3.5	12.25
8	−2.5	6.25

9	−1.5	2.25
10	−0.5	0.25
11	0.5	0.25
12	1.5	2.25
13	2.5	6.25
14	3.5	12.25
15	4.5	20.25
		82.5

Standard deviation = $\sqrt{\dfrac{82.5}{10}} \approx 2.87$

Note again that each data point is 6 units to the right of where it appeared in (a). So, the mean has changed (it is 6 units bigger), but the spread of the data has not. So, the standard deviation is the same as in (a).

(d) $A = \dfrac{5 + 15 + 25 + 35 + 45 + 55 + 65 + 75 + 85 + 95}{10} = 50$

x	$x - 50$	$(x-50)^2$
5	−45	2025
15	−35	1225
25	−25	625
35	−15	225
45	−5	25
55	5	25
65	15	225
75	25	625
85	35	1225
95	45	2025
		8250

Standard deviation = $\sqrt{\dfrac{8250}{10}} \approx 28.7$

Note that each data point is 10 times farther away from the mean as in (a). So the spread (standard deviation) is 10 times larger.

58. **(a)** $A = \dfrac{-4 - 3 - 2 - 1 + 1 + 2 + 3 + 4}{8} = 0$

x	$x - 0$	$(x-0)^2$
-4	-4	16
-3	-3	9
-2	-2	4
-1	-1	1
1	1	1
2	2	4
3	3	9
4	4	16
		60

Standard deviation = $\sqrt{\dfrac{60}{8}} \approx 2.74$

(b) Note that each data point is simply located 1 unit to the right of that data set given in (a). So, the spread of the data set has not changed. Thus, standard deviation = $\sqrt{\dfrac{60}{8}} \approx 2.74$.

(c) Note again that each data point is 5 units to the right of where it appeared in (a). So, the mean has changed (it is 5 units bigger), but the spread of the data has not. Thus, the standard deviation is the same as in (a). That is, standard deviation = $\sqrt{\dfrac{60}{8}} \approx 2.74$.

H.   Miscellaneous

59. 10 (Frequency 16)

60. 55%, 70%, and 74%

61. 4, 5, and 8 (Frequency 5)

62. C

63. Caucasian (Has largest percent.)

64. There is no mode.

JOGGING

65. 100

Let x = Mike's score on the next exam.

$$\frac{5 \times 88 + x}{6} = 90$$

$$5 \times 88 + x = 540$$

$$x = 100$$

66. 58 points

The lowest possible score on the first exam is when all the rest of the scores are as high as possible:

$$\frac{x + 100 + 100 + 100 + 200}{6} = 93 \, ; x = 558 - 500 = 58.$$

67. Ramon gets 85 out of 100 on each of the first four exams and 60 out of 100 on the fifth exam. Josh gets 80 out of 100 on all 5 of the exams.

68. Kelly gets 75 out of 100 on all six exams while Karen gets 100 on three of the exams and 50 on the other three. Kelly's scores have a standard deviation of 0, but Karen's scores have a standard deviation of 25.

69. **(a)** $\{1, 1, 1, 1, 6, 6, 6, 6, 6, 6\}$ Average = 4; Median = 6.

(b) $\{1, 1, 1, 1, 1, 1, 6, 6, 6, 6\}$ Average = 3; Median =1.

(c) $\{1, 1, 6, 6, 6, 6, 6, 6, 6, 6\}$ Average = 5; $Q_1 = 6$.

(d) $\{1, 1, 1, 1, 1, 1, 1, 1, 6, 6\}$ Average = 2; $Q_3 = 1$.

70. **(a)** The ten numbers add up to 75. Since *Min* = 3, the remaining nine largest numbers add up to 72. The smallest possible value of Max is *Max* = 8. (It occurs when the ten numbers are 3, 8, 8, 8, 8, 8, 8, 8, 8, 8.)

(b) The largest possible value of *Max* is *Max* = 48. (It occurs when the ten numbers are 3, 3, 3, 3, 3, 3, 3, 3, 3, 48.)

71. **(a)** The five-number summary for the original scores was $Min = 1$, $Q_1 = 9$, $M = 11$, $Q_3 = 12$, and $Max = 24$. When 2 points are added to each test score, the five-number summary will also have 2 points added to each of its numbers (i.e., $Min = 3$, $Q_1 = 11$, $M = 13$, $Q_3 = 14$, and $Max = 26$).

(b) When 10% is added to each score (i.e., each score is multiplied by 1.1) then each number in the five-number summary will also be multiplied by 1.1 (i.e., $Min = 1.1$, $Q_1 = 9.9$, $M = 12.1$, $Q_3 = 13.2$, and $Max = 26.4$).

72. **(a)** The average of $\{a, a, a, ..., a\}$ is a. This implies that all the deviations from the average are 0. It follows that the average of the squared deviations is 0, and thus the standard deviation is 0.

(b) If the standard deviation is 0, then the average of the squared deviations is 0. The squared deviations cannot be negative, so if their average is 0, they must all be 0. It follows that all deviations from the average must be 0. This means that each data value is equal to the average a, i.e., the data set is constant.

73. (a) 4

$$\frac{\text{Column area over interval } 30-35}{\text{Column area over interval } 20-30} = \frac{5 \times h}{10 \times 1} = \frac{50\%}{25\%} \text{ and so } 5h = 20, \ h = 4.$$

(b) 0.4

$$\frac{\text{Column area over interval } 35-45}{\text{Column area over interval } 20-30} = \frac{10 \times h}{10 \times 1} = \frac{10\%}{25\%} \text{ and so } h = 0.4.$$

(c) 0.4

$$\frac{\text{Column area over interval } 45-60}{\text{Column area over interval } 20-30} = \frac{15 \times h}{10 \times 1} = \frac{15\%}{25\%} \text{ and so } h = 0.4.$$

74.

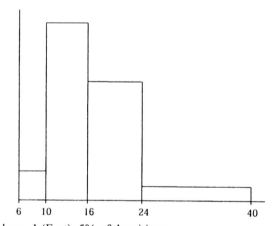

Column 1 (Fast): 5% of the citizens.
Column 2 (Fit): 45% of the citizens.
Column 3 (Average): 40% of the citizens.
Column 4 (Slow): 10% of the citizens.
Let the height of the first column be 1.

$$\frac{\text{Col. 2 area}}{\text{Col. 1 area}} = \frac{6 \times h}{4 \times 1} = \frac{45\%}{5\%} \text{ so the height of the second column is } h = 6.$$

$$\frac{\text{Col. 3 area}}{\text{Col. 1 area}} = \frac{8 \times h}{4 \times 1} = \frac{40\%}{5\%} \text{ so the height of the third column is } h = 4.$$

$$\frac{\text{Col. 4 area}}{\text{Col. 1 area}} = \frac{16 \times h}{4 \times 1} = \frac{10\%}{5\%} \text{ so the height of the fourth column is } h = 0.5.$$

75. (a) Male: 10%, Female: 20%

(b) Male: 80%, Female: 90%

(c) The figures for both schools were combined. A total of 820 males were admitted out of a total of 1200 that applied–an admission rate for males of approximately 68.3%. Similarly, a total of 460 females were admitted out of a total of 900 that applied–an admission rate for females of approximately 51.1%.

(d) In this example, females have a higher percentage $\left(\dfrac{100}{500} = 20\%\right)$ than males $\left(\dfrac{20}{200} = 10\%\right)$ for admissions to the School of Architecture and also a higher percentage $\left(\dfrac{360}{400} = 90\%\right)$ than males $\left(\dfrac{800}{1000} = 80\%\right)$ for the School of Engineering. When the numbers are combined, however, females have a lower percentage $\left(\dfrac{100+360}{500+400} \approx 51.1\%\right)$ than males $\left(\dfrac{20+800}{200+1000} \approx 68.3\%\right)$ in total admissions. The reason that this apparent paradox can occur is purely a matter of arithmetic: Just because $\dfrac{a_1}{a_2} > \dfrac{b_1}{b_2}$ and $\dfrac{c_1}{c_2} > \dfrac{d_1}{d_2}$ it does not necessarily follow that $\dfrac{a_1+c_2}{a_2+c_2} > \dfrac{b_1+d_1}{b_2+d_2}$. The majority of males applied to the engineering school, which has a much higher acceptance rate than the School of Architecture. This, combined with the fact that more females applied to the School of Architecture than the School of Engineering, is why, overall, the percentage of males admitted is higher than the percentage of females admitted.

76. (a)
$$\frac{(x_1+c)+(x_2+c)+(x_3+c)+\ldots+(x_N+c)}{N} = \frac{(x_1+x_2+x_3+\ldots+x_N)+cN}{N}$$
$$= \frac{(x_1+x_2+x_3+\ldots+x_N)}{N} + \frac{cN}{N}$$
$$= A + c$$

(b) Adding c to each value of a data set adds c to the average as well. Hence, subtracting the average A from each value of a data set (adding $-A$ to each value) subtracts A from the average creating a new average of 0.

77. The relative sizes of the numbers are not changed by adding a constant c to every number. Thus (assuming the original data set is sorted) if the median of the data set is $M = x_k$, then the median of the new data set will be $x_k + c = M + c$. If the median of the original set is $M = \dfrac{x_k + x_{k+1}}{2}$, then the median of the new data set will be $\dfrac{(x_k+c)+(x_{k+1}+c)}{2} = \dfrac{x_k+x_{k+1}}{2} + \dfrac{2c}{2} = M + c$. In either case, we see that the median of the new data set is $M + c$.

78. (a) Let M be the maximum value of $\{x_1, x_2, x_3, \ldots, x_N\}$. The maximum value of $\{x_1+c, x_2+c, x_3+c, \ldots, x_N+c\}$ is $M + c$. Similarly, if the minimum value of $\{x_1, x_2, x_3, \ldots, x_N\}$ is m, then the minimum value of $\{x_1+c, x_2+c, x_3+c, \ldots, x_N+c\}$ is $m - c$. So, the range of

$\{x_1 + c, x_2 + c, x_3 + c, \ldots, x_N + c\}$ is $M + c - (m + c) = M - m$. That is, the same as the range of $\{x_1, x_2, x_3, \ldots, x_N\}$.

(b) Adding c to each value of a data set does not change how spread out the data set is. Since the standard deviation is a measure of spread, the standard deviation does not change. Specifically, the average of the data set will increase by c, but the deviations from the mean (and hence the standard deviation) will remain the same.

79. (a)

Chapter	1	2	3	4	5	6	7	8	9	10	11	12	13	14	15	16
Exercises	80	78	84	67	73	75	76	75	78	80	80	75	68	89	86	81

average $= \dfrac{1245}{16} = 77.8125$ exercises

(b) 78

The sorted data set: {67, 68, 73, 75, 75, 75, 76, 78, 78, 80, 80, 80, 81, 84, 86, 89}
The median is the average of the 8th and 9th elements of this sorted data set. That is, the average of 78 and 78.

(c) $Min = 67$, $Q_1 = 75$, $M = 78$, $Q_3 = 80.5$, $Max = 89$

(d)

x	$x - 77.8125$	$(x - 77.8125)^2$
80	2.1875	4.78515625
78	0.1875	0.03515625
84	6.1875	38.28515625
67	-10.8125	116.9101563
73	-4.8125	23.16015625
75	-2.8125	7.91015625
76	-1.8125	3.28515625
75	-2.8125	7.91015625
78	0.1875	0.03515625
80	2.1875	4.78515625
80	2.1875	4.78515625
75	-2.8125	7.91015625
68	-9.8125	96.28515625
89	11.1875	125.1601563
86	8.1875	67.03515625
81	3.1875	10.16015625
		518.4375

$$\text{standard deviation} = \sqrt{\frac{518.4375}{16}} \approx 5.69 \text{ exercises}$$

RUNNING

80. (a) The smallest possible standard deviation for such a data set occurs when as many values in the data set as possible lie close to (or at) the mean. In this particular case, it occurs when 8 of the numbers take on the value of the average ($A=7$), one value takes on the minimum (Min = 2), and one value takes on the maximum (Max = 12).

The average of the data set $\{2, 7, 7, 7, 7, 7, 7, 7, 7, 12\}$ is $A = 7$.

x	*Freq. f*	$x - 7$	$f \cdot (x-7)^2$
2	1	−5	25
7	8	0	0
12	1	5	25
			50

So, the smallest value of $\sigma = \sqrt{\dfrac{50}{10}} = \sqrt{5}$.

(b) The largest possible standard deviation for such a data set occurs when as many values in the data set as possible lie as far away as possible from the mean. In this particular case, in order to have a mean of 7, this occurs when 5 of the numbers take on the value of the minimum (Min = 2), and 5 values take on the maximum (Max = 12).

The average of the data set $\{2, 2, 2, 2, 2, 12, 12, 12, 12, 12\}$ is $A = 7$.

x	*Freq. f*	$x - 7$	$f \cdot (x-7)^2$
2	5	−5	125
12	5	5	125
			250

So, the largest value of $\sigma = \sqrt{\dfrac{250}{10}} = 5$.

81. Consider a data set $\{x_1, x_2, x_3, \ldots, x_N\}$ and assume $\text{Min} = x_1 \le x_2 \le x_3 \le \ldots \le x_N = \text{Max}$. Then since the average A satisfies the inequality $\text{Min} \le A \le \text{Max}$, we see that $(x_k - A)^2 \le (\text{Max} - \text{Min})^2 = \text{Range}^2$ for each $k = 1, 2, 3, \ldots, N$. Therefore, $\sigma = \sqrt{\dfrac{(x_1 - A)^2 + (x_2 - A)^2 + \ldots + (x_N - A)^2}{N}} \le \sqrt{\dfrac{N \times \text{Range}^2}{N}} = \text{Range}$.

82. (a) Since $\sigma = \sqrt{\dfrac{(x_1 - A)^2 + (x_2 - A)^2 + \ldots + (x_N - A)^2}{N}} \geq \sqrt{\dfrac{(x_i - A)^2}{N}} = \dfrac{|x_i - A|}{\sqrt{N}}$ for every data value

$x_1 + x_2 + \cdots + x_N - NA = 0$, we have $x_1 + x_2 + \cdots + x_N - NA = 0$ for every data value

$x_1 + x_2 + \cdots + x_N - NA = 0$.

(b) From (a), $-\sigma\sqrt{N} \leq x_i - A \leq \sigma\sqrt{N}$ or equivalently, $A - \sigma\sqrt{N} \leq x_i \leq A + \sigma\sqrt{N}$.

83. (a) The two numbers are $A + \sigma$ and $A - \sigma$.

It is easy to verify that their average is A and their standard deviation is σ. An algebraic derivation of the solution can be obtained by setting up the system of equations

(1) $\dfrac{x+y}{2} = A$ and   (2) $\sqrt{\dfrac{(x-A)^2 + (y-A)^2}{2}} = \sigma$

and solving for x and y.

(b) Since the three numbers are equally spaced, the average is the middle one. We can write the three numbers as $A - c, A, A + c$ ($c > 0$). The standard deviation of these three numbers is

$\sigma = \sqrt{\dfrac{c^2 + 0 + c^2}{3}} = c\sqrt{\dfrac{2}{3}}$. It follows that $c = \sigma\sqrt{\dfrac{3}{2}}$ and the three numbers are

$A - \sigma\sqrt{\dfrac{3}{2}}, A$, and $A + \sigma\sqrt{\dfrac{3}{2}}$.

(c) Case 1: N is odd. Say $N = 2k + 1$. The "middle" number is the average A. If we write the N numbers as

$\{A - kc, \ldots, A - c, A, A + c, \ldots, A + kc\}$ (*)

then

$\sigma = \sqrt{\dfrac{2[c^2 + (2c)^2 + \ldots + (kc)^2]}{N}} = c\sqrt{\dfrac{2(1^2 + 2^2 + \ldots + k^2)}{N}}$ and we have

$c = \sigma\sqrt{\dfrac{N}{2(1^2 + \ldots + k^2)}}$.

Replacing this value of c in (*) completely describes the N numbers.

Case 2: N is even. Here the N numbers can be written in the form

$\left\{A - (N-1)\cdot\dfrac{c}{2}, \ldots, A - 3\cdot\dfrac{c}{2}, A - \dfrac{c}{2}, A + \dfrac{c}{2}, A + 3\cdot\dfrac{c}{2}, \ldots, A + (N-1)\cdot\dfrac{c}{2}\right\}$ (**)

and therefore

$\sigma = \sqrt{\dfrac{2\left[\left(\frac{c}{2}\right)^2 + \left(\frac{3c}{2}\right)^2 + \left(\frac{5c}{2}\right)^2 + \ldots + \left(\frac{(N-1)c}{2}\right)^2\right]}{N}} = \dfrac{c}{2}\sqrt{\dfrac{2\left[1^2 + 3^2 + 5^2 + \ldots + (N-1)^2\right]}{N}}$.

It follows that

$$c = 2\sigma \sqrt{\frac{N}{2\left[1^2 + 3^2 + \ldots + (N-1)^2\right]}}$$

and replacing this value of c in (**) completely describes the N numbers.

84. $1 + 2 + \ldots + N = \dfrac{N(N+1)}{2}$ implies the average $A = \dfrac{1+2+\ldots+N}{N} = \dfrac{N+1}{2}$. If N is odd, the median

M is the "middle" number $M = \dfrac{N+1}{2}$. If N is even the median M is the average of $\dfrac{N}{2}$ and $\dfrac{N}{2}+1$,

which is $M = \dfrac{N+1}{2}$.

85. $V = \dfrac{(x_1 - A)^2 + \ldots + (x_N - A)^2}{N} = \dfrac{(x_1^2 - 2Ax_1 + A^2) + \ldots + (x_N^2 - 2Ax_N + A^2)}{N} =$

$\dfrac{(x_1^2 + \ldots + x_N^2)}{N} - 2A\dfrac{(x_1 + \ldots + x_N)}{N} + \dfrac{NA^2}{N} = B - 2A^2 + A^2 = B - A^2$

86. If A is the average of $x_1, x_2, \ldots, x_N$, then the average of $ax_1, ax_2, \ldots, ax_N$ is aA. Thus,

$$\sqrt{\frac{(ax_1 - aA)^2 + \ldots + (ax_N - aA)^2}{N}} = \sqrt{\frac{a^2(x_1 - A)^2 + \ldots + a^2(x_N - A)^2}{N}} = a\sqrt{\frac{(x_1 - A)^2 + \ldots + (x_N - A)^2}{N}} = a\sigma.$$

87. (a) Approximately 28.58. The average of the data set $\{1, 2, 3, \ldots, 99\}$ is $A = 50$.

$\dfrac{1+2+\cdots+99}{99} = \dfrac{99 \times 100}{2 \times 99} = 50$

The average of the data set $\{1^2, 2^2, \ldots, 99^2\}$ is B $= \dfrac{100 \times 199}{6}$.

$\dfrac{1^2 + 2^2 + \cdots + 99^2}{99} = \dfrac{99 \times 100 \times 199}{6 \times 99} = \dfrac{100 \times 199}{6}$

By Exercise 85, $V = \dfrac{100 \times 199}{6} - 50^2 = \dfrac{4900}{6} \approx 816.67$ and so $\sigma \approx \sqrt{816.67} \approx 28.58$.

(b) The average of the data set $\{1, 2, 3, \ldots, N\}$ is $A = (N + 1)/2$.

$\dfrac{1+2+\ldots+N}{N} = \dfrac{N(N+1)}{2N} = \dfrac{N+1}{2}$

The average of the data set $\{1^2, 2^2, \ldots, N^2\}$ is B $= \dfrac{(N+1)(2N+1)}{6}$

$\dfrac{1^2 + 2^2 + \ldots + N^2}{N} = \dfrac{N(N+1)(2N+1)}{6N} = \dfrac{(N+1)(2N+1)}{6}$

By Exercise 85, $V = \dfrac{(N+1)(2N+1)}{6} - \left(\dfrac{N+1}{2}\right)^2 = \dfrac{N^2-1}{12}$ and so $\sigma = \sqrt{\dfrac{N^2-1}{12}}$.

88. (a) The data set $\{315, 316, ..., 412, 413\}$ can be written as $\{1+c, 2+c, ..., 99+c\}$ where $c = 314$. By Exercise 76(a), the average is $50 + 314 = 364$. From Exercise 78(b), the standard deviation is the same as the standard deviation of the data set $\{1, 2,..., 99\}$ which is $\sigma \approx 28.58$.

(b) From Exercise 76(a), the average is $A = (N+1)/2$. Using Exercise 78(b), the standard deviation is the same as the standard deviation of the set $\{1, 2, ..., N\}$ which is $\sigma = \sqrt{\dfrac{N^2 - 1}{12}}$.

89. (a) 8/9 or approximately 89%

(b) 10

(c) Since $k > 0$, $1 - \dfrac{1}{k^2} < 1$ will always be the case.

Chapter 15

WALKING

A. Random Experiments and Sample Spaces

1. (a) {*HHH, HHT, HTH, THH, TTH, THT, HTT, TTT*}

   (b) {0, 1, 2, 3}

   (c) {0, 1, 2, 3}

2. (a) {*HHHH, HHHT, HHTH, HHTT, HTHH, HTHT, HTTH, HTTT, THHH, THHT, THTH, THTT, TTHH, TTHT, TTTH, TTTT*}

   (b) {*FFFF, FFFT, FFTF, FFTT, FTFF, FTFT, FTTF, FTTT, TFFF, TFFT, TFTF, TFTT, TTFF, TTFT, TTTF, TTTT*}

3. (a) {*ABCD, ABDC, ACBD, ACDB, ADBC, ADCB, BACD, BADC, BCAD, BCDA, BDAC, BDCA, CABD, CADB, CBAD, CBDA, CDAB, CDBA, DABC, DACB, DBAC, DBCA, DCAB, DCBA*}

   (b) $N = 4 \times 3 \times 2 \times 1 = 24$ (4 choices for first name chosen, 3 choices for second name chosen, etc.)

4. {*AA, AB, AC, AD, BB, BC, BD, CC, CD, DD*}

5. Answers will vary. A typical outcome is a string of 10 letters each of which can be either an *H* or a *T*. An answer like {*HHHHHHHHHH*, …,*TTTTTTTTTT*} is not sufficiently descriptive. An answer like{… *HTTHHHTHTH*, …, *TTHTHHTTHT*, …, *HHHTHTTHHT*, …} is better. An answer like $\{(X_1 X_2 X_3 X_4 X_5 X_6 X_7 X_8 X_9 X_{10})$: each X_i is either *H* or *T*} is best. Note: This sample space consists of $N = 2^{10} = 1024$ outcomes (2 possible outcomes at each of 10 stages of the experiment).

6. A typical outcome is a string of 10 letters each of which can be either an *T* or a *F*. An answer like {… *FFFFFFFFFF*, …,*TTTTTTTTTT*} is not sufficiently descriptive. An answer like{… *FTTFFFFTFTF*, …, *TTFTFFTTFT*, …, *FFFTFTTFFT*, …} is better. An answer like $\{(X_1 X_2 X_3 X_4 X_5 X_6 X_7 X_8 X_9 X_{10})$: each X_i is either *T* or *F* for positive integers $1 = i = 10$} is best.

7. Answers will vary. An outcome is an ordered sequence of four numbers, each of which is an integer between 1 and 6 inclusive. The best answer would be something like $\{(n_1, n_2, n_3, n_4)$: each n_i is 1, 2, 3, 4, 5, or 6}. An answer such as {(1,1,1,1), …, (1,1,1,6), …,(1,2,3,4),…, (3,2,6,2), …, (6,6,6,6)} showing a few typical outcomes is possible, but not as good. An answer like {(1,1,1,1),…, (2,2,2,2), …, (6,6,6,6)} is not descriptive enough. Note: This sample space consists of $N = 6^4 = 1296$ outcomes (6 possible outcomes at each of 4 stages of the experiment).

8. An outcome consists of ten letters. The letters can be *A*, *B*, *C*, *D* or *E* only. Because the order in which the letters are listed is relevant, the best answer would then be of the form $\{X_1 X_2 X_3 X_4 X_5 X_6 X_7 X_8 X_9 X_{10}$: each X_i is one of the letters *A*, *B*, *C*, *D* or *E*}. Other acceptable answers involve listing a few typical outcomes separated by …'s.

B.   The Multiplication Rule.

9. (a) $9 \times 26^3 \times 10^3 = 158,184,000$

   (b) $1 \times 26^3 \times 10^2 \times 1 = 1,757,600$

   (c) $9 \times 26 \times 25 \times 24 \times 9 \times 8 \times 7 = 70,761,600$

10. (a) $26^4 \times 10 = 4,569,760$

   (b) $26^4 = 456,976$

   (c) $25 \times 26^3 \times 10 = 4,394,000$

   (d) $25^4 \times 10 = 3,906,250$

11. (a) $52^4 \times 10 = 73,116,160$

   (b) $52^3 \times 10 = 1,406,080$

   (c) $50 \times 52^3 \times 10 = 70,304,000$

   (d) $50^4 \times 10 = 62,500,000$

12. (a) $3 \times 4 \times 9 = 108$

   (b) $3 \times 6 \times 9 \times 5 = 810$

   (c) $(2 + 4 + 2 \times 4) \times 9 = 126$

13. (a) $8! = 40,320$

   (b) $40,320 - 1 = 40,319$ (there is only one way in which all of the books are in order)

14. (a) $8! = 40,320$

   (b) $4 \times 7! = 20,160$

   (c) $4 \times 4 \times 3 \times 3 \times 2 \times 2 \times 1 \times 1 = 576$

15. (a) $35 \times 34 \times 33 = 39,270$

   (b) $15 \times 34 \times 33 = 16,830$

   (c) 29,700
        The total number of all-girl committees is $15 \times 14 \times 13 = 2730$.

The total number of all-boy committees is $20 \times 19 \times 18 = 6840$.

The remaining $35 \times 34 \times 33 - (15 \times 14 \times 13 + 20 \times 19 \times 18) = 39,270 - (2730 + 6840) = 29,700$ committees are mixed.

16. **(a)** $35 \times 34 \times 33 \times 32 = 1,256,640$

    (b) $15 \times 14 \times 33 \times 32 = 221,760$
    Note that we picked the girl president first and the girl treasurer second, the vice-president (girl or boy) third and the secretary (girl or boy) last.

    (c) $15 \times 14 \times 20 \times 19 = 79,800$

    (d) $6 \times 15 \times 14 \times 20 \times 19 = 478,800$
    Note that the answer in (c) is one of 6 different ways to pick 2 offices for the girls and two offices for the boys.

17. **(a)** $9 \times 10^5 \times 5 = 4,500,000$
    There are 9 choices for the first digit (1-9), 10 choices for the next 5 digits (0-9), and 5 digits for the last digit (0, 2, 4, 6, 8).

    (b) $9 \times 10^5 \times 2 = 1,800,000$

    (c) $9 \times 10^4 \times 4 = 360,000$
    The last 2 digits must be 00, 25, 50 or 75.

18. **(a)** $9 \times 9! = 3,265,920$
    The first digit cannot be 0.

    (b) $9 \times 9 \times 8 \times 7 \times 6 = 27,216$
    A 10 digit palindrome is completely determined by its first 5 digits.

C.   Permutations and Combinations

19. **(a)** $_{10}P_2 = 10 \times 9 = 90$

    (b) $_{10}C_2 = \dfrac{10 \times 9}{2 \times 1} = \dfrac{90}{2} = 45$

    (c) $_{10}P_3 = 10 \times 9 \times 8 = 720$

    (d) $_{10}C_3 = \dfrac{720}{3!} = \dfrac{720}{6} = 120$

20. **(a)** $_{11}P_2 = 11 \times 10 = 110$

(b) $_{11}C_2 = \dfrac{11 \times 10}{2 \times 1} = \dfrac{110}{2} = 55$

(c) $_{20}P_2 = 20 \times 19 = 380$

(d) $_{20}C_2 = \dfrac{20 \times 19}{2!} = \dfrac{380}{2} = 190$

21. (a) $_{10}C_9 = \dfrac{10!}{(10-9)!9!} = \dfrac{10!}{1!9!} = 10$

(b) $_{10}C_8 = \dfrac{10!}{(10-8)!8!} = \dfrac{10!}{2!8!} = \dfrac{10 \times 9}{2 \times 1} = 45$

(c) $_{100}C_{99} = \dfrac{100!}{(100-99)!99!} = \dfrac{100!}{1!99!} = 100$

(d) $_{100}C_{98} = \dfrac{100!}{(100-98)!98!} = \dfrac{100!}{2!98!} = \dfrac{100 \times 99}{2 \times 1} = 4950$

22. (a) $_{12}P_2 = \dfrac{12!}{(12-2)!} = \dfrac{12!}{10!} = 12 \times 11 = 132$

(b) $_{12}P_3 = \dfrac{12!}{(12-3)!} = \dfrac{12!}{9!} = 12 \times 11 \times 10 = 1320$

(c) $_{12}P_4 = \dfrac{12!}{(12-4)!} = \dfrac{12!}{8!} = 12 \times 11 \times 10 \times 9 = 11,880$

(d) $_{12}P_5 = \dfrac{12!}{(12-5)!} = \dfrac{12!}{7!} = 12 \times 11 \times 10 \times 9 \times 8 = 95,040$

23. (a) $_{20}C_2 = \dfrac{20!}{(20-2)!2!} = \dfrac{20!}{18!2!} = \dfrac{20 \times 19}{2 \times 1} = 190$

(b) $_{20}C_{18} = \dfrac{20!}{(20-18)!18!} = \dfrac{20!}{2!18!} = \dfrac{20 \times 19}{2 \times 1} = 190$

(c) $_{20}C_3 = \dfrac{20!}{(20-3)!3!} = \dfrac{20!}{17!3!} = \dfrac{20 \times 19 \times 18}{3 \times 2 \times 1} = 1140$

(d) $\ _{20}C_{17} = \dfrac{20!}{(20-17)!17!} = \dfrac{20!}{3!17!} = \dfrac{20 \times 19 \times 18}{3 \times 2 \times 1} = 1140$

24. (a) Calculating this by hand is very illustrative.

$$\begin{aligned}
_{10}C_3 + _{10}C_4 &= \dfrac{10!}{(10-3)!3!} + \dfrac{10!}{(10-4)!4!} \\
&= \dfrac{10!}{7!3!} + \dfrac{10!}{6!4!} \\
&= \dfrac{10 \times 9 \times 8}{3 \times 2 \times 1} + \dfrac{10 \times 9 \times 8 \times 7}{4 \times 3 \times 2 \times 1} \\
&= \dfrac{4 \times 10 \times 9 \times 8}{4 \times 3 \times 2 \times 1} + \dfrac{10 \times 9 \times 8 \times 7}{4 \times 3 \times 2 \times 1} \\
&= \dfrac{(4+7) \times 10 \times 9 \times 8}{4 \times 3 \times 2 \times 1} \\
&= 330
\end{aligned}$$

(b) $\ _{11}C_4 = \dfrac{11!}{(11-4)!4!} = \dfrac{11!}{7!4!} = \dfrac{11 \times 10 \times 9 \times 8}{4 \times 3 \times 2 \times 1} = 330$

(c) 120

(d) 120

25. (a) $\begin{aligned}[t]
_3C_0 + _3C_1 + _3C_2 + _3C_3 &= \dfrac{3!}{(3-0)!0!} + \dfrac{3!}{(3-1)!1!} + \dfrac{3!}{(3-2)!2!} + \dfrac{3!}{(3-3)!3!} \\
&= 1+3+3+1 \\
&= 8
\end{aligned}$

(b) $\begin{aligned}[t]
&_4C_0 + _4C_1 + _4C_2 + _4C_3 + _4C_4 \\
&= \dfrac{4!}{(4-0)!0!} + \dfrac{4!}{(4-1)!1!} + \dfrac{4!}{(4-2)!2!} + \dfrac{4!}{(4-3)!3!} + \dfrac{4!}{(4-4)!4!} \\
&= 1+4+6+4+1 \\
&= 16
\end{aligned}$

(c) $1 + 5 + 10 + 10 + 5 + 1 = 32$

(d) The pattern in (a)-(c) is that each of these sums is a power of two. In (a), the sum was $2^3 = 8$. In (b), the sum was $2^4 = 16$. In (c), the sum was $2^5 = 32$. It should then be that the last sum is $2^{10} = 1,024$. (One should also note that values found in the rows of Pascal's triangle are being added.)

26. (a) 0

(b) 0

(c) 0

(d) 0 [Note: Exercise 26(d) in the text should read $_{1000}C_{498} - _{1000}C_{502}$.]

27. First, note that $_{150}P_{50} = \dfrac{150!}{100!} = \dfrac{150 \times 149 \times 148 \times \cdots \times 3 \times 2 \times 1}{100 \times 99 \times 98 \times \cdots \times 3 \times 2 \times 1}$ and

$_{150}P_{51} = \dfrac{150!}{99!} = \dfrac{150 \times 149 \times 148 \times \cdots \times 3 \times 2 \times 1}{99 \times 98 \times 97 \times \cdots \times 3 \times 2 \times 1}$. It follows that $_{150}P_{51} = 100 \times _{150}P_{50}$. That is, $_{150}P_{51}$ is 100

times bigger than $_{150}P_{50}$. Thus, $_{150}P_{51} = 6.12 \times 10^{104} \times 100 = 6.12 \times 10^{106}$.

28. First, note that $_{150}C_{50} = \dfrac{150!}{100!50!} = \dfrac{150 \times 149 \times 148 \times \cdots \times 3 \times 2 \times 1}{\left(100 \times 99 \times 98 \times \cdots \times 3 \times 2 \times 1\right) \times \left(50 \times 49 \times 48 \times \cdots \times 3 \times 2 \times 1\right)}$ and

$_{150}C_{51} = \dfrac{150!}{99!51!} = \dfrac{150 \times 149 \times 148 \times \cdots \times 3 \times 2 \times 1}{\left(99 \times 98 \times 97 \times \cdots \times 3 \times 2 \times 1\right) \times \left(51 \times 50 \times 49 \times \cdots \times 3 \times 2 \times 1\right)}$. It follows that

$51 \times _{150}C_{51} = 100 \times _{150}C_{50}$. That is, $_{150}C_{51}$ is $\dfrac{100}{51}$ times bigger than $_{150}C_{50}$. Thus,

$_{150}C_{51} = 2.01 \times 10^{40} \times \dfrac{100}{51} \approx 3.94 \times 10^{40}$.

29. (a) $_{20}P_{10} \approx 6.7 \times 10^{11}$

    (b) $_{52}C_{20} \approx 1.26 \times 10^{14}$

    (c) $_{52}C_{32} \approx 1.26 \times 10^{14}$

    (d) $_{53}P_{20} \approx 2.02 \times 10^{14}$

30. (a) $_{18}P_{10} \approx 1.6 \times 10^{11}$

    (b) $_{51}C_{21} \approx 1.14 \times 10^{14}$

    (c) $_{51}C_{30} \approx 1.14 \times 10^{14}$

    (d) $_{51}P_{30} \approx 3.0 \times 10^{46}$

31. (a) $_{15}P_{4}$

    (b) $_{15}C_{4}$

32. (a) $_{10}C_{3}$

    (b) $_{10}P_3$

33. **(a)** $_{20}C_2$

    (b) $_{20}P_2$

    (c) $_{20}C_5$

34. **(a)** $_{119}P_{25}$

    (b) $_{119}C_8$

D.   **General Probability Spaces**

35. **(a)** $\Pr(o_3) = 0.18$

$$\Pr(o_1) + \Pr(o_2) + \Pr(o_3) + \Pr(o_4) + \Pr(o_5) = 1$$
$$0.22 + 0.24 + 3\Pr(o_3) = 1$$
$$\Pr(o_3) = 0.18$$

    (b) $\Pr(o_3) = 0.27$

$$\Pr(o_1) + \Pr(o_2) + \Pr(o_3) + \Pr(o_4) + \Pr(o_5) = 1$$
$$0.22 + 0.24 + 2\Pr(o_3) = 1$$
$$\Pr(o_3) = 0.27$$

    (c) The probability assignment is $\Pr(o_1) = 0.22$, $\Pr(o_2) = 0.24$, $\Pr(o_3) = 0.27$, $\Pr(o_4) = 0.17$, $\Pr(o_5) = 0.1$.

$$\Pr(o_1) + \Pr(o_2) + \Pr(o_3) + \Pr(o_4) + \Pr(o_5) = 1$$
$$0.22 + 0.24 + 0.27 + \Pr(o_4) + 0.1 = 1$$
$$\Pr(o_4) = 0.17$$

36. **(a)** $\Pr(o_2) = 0.35$

$$\Pr(o_1) + \Pr(o_2) = \Pr(o_3) + \Pr(o_4) = \frac{1}{2}$$

    (b) $\Pr(o_1) = 0.15$, $\Pr(o_2) = 0.35$, $\Pr(o_3) = 0.22$, $\Pr(o_4) = 0.28$

37. $S = \{P_1, P_2, P_3, P_4, P_5, P_6, P_7\}$

The probability assignment is $\Pr(P_1) = \dfrac{2}{8}, \Pr(P_2) = \Pr(P_3) = \Pr(P_4) = \Pr(P_5) = \Pr(P_6) = \Pr(P_7) = \dfrac{1}{8}.$

$$\Pr(P_1) + \Pr(P_2) + \Pr(P_3) + \Pr(P_4) + \Pr(P_5) + \Pr(P_6) + \Pr(P_7) = 1$$
$$8\Pr(P_2) = 1$$
$$\Pr(P_2) = \dfrac{1}{8}$$
$$\Pr(P_1) = 2\Pr(P_2) = 2\left(\dfrac{1}{8}\right) = \dfrac{2}{8}$$

38. $S = \{P_1, P_2, P_3, P_4, P_5, P_6\}$; The probability assignment is
$\Pr(P_1) = 0.25, \Pr(P_2) = 0.15, \Pr(P_3) = 0.09, \Pr(P_4) = \Pr(P_5) = \Pr(P_6) = 0.17.$

39. **(a)** $S = \{\text{red, blue, white, green, yellow}\}$

(b) $\Pr(\text{blue}) = \Pr(\text{white}) = \dfrac{72°}{360°} = 0.2$

$\Pr(\text{green}) = \Pr(\text{yellow}) = \dfrac{54°}{360°} = 0.15$

The probability assignment is $\Pr(\text{red}) = 0.3$, $\Pr(\text{blue}) = \Pr(\text{white}) = 0.2$, $\Pr(\text{green}) = \Pr(\text{yellow}) = 0.15.$

40. **(a)** $S = \{\text{white, yellow, blue, red}\}$

(b) The probability assignment is:

$\Pr(\text{blue}) = \dfrac{144°}{360°} = 0.4$; $\Pr(\text{red}) = \dfrac{126°}{360°} = 0.35$

$\Pr(\text{yellow}) = \dfrac{54°}{360°} = 0.15$; $\Pr(\text{white}) = \dfrac{36°}{360°} = 0.1$

E.   Events

41. **(a)** $E_1 = \{HHT, HTH, THH\}$

(b) $E_2 = \{HHH, TTT\}$

(c) $E_3 = \{\}$

(d) $E_4 = \{TTH, TTT\}$

42. **(a)** $E_1 = \{TTFF, TFTF, TFFT, FTTF, FTFT, FFTT\}$

(b) $E_2 = \{TTFF, TFTF, TFFT, FTTF, FTFT, FFTT, TTTF, TTFT, TFTT, FTTT, TTTT\}$

(c) $E_3 = \{FFTT, FTFT, FTTF, TFFT, TFTF, TTFF, FFFT, FFTF, FTFF, TFFF, FFFF\}$

(d) $E_4 = \{TTFF, TTFT, TTTF, TTTT\}$

43.   **(a)** $E_1 = \{(1,1),(2,2),(3,3),(4,4),(5,5),(6,6)\}$

(b) $E_2 = \{(1,1),(1,2),(2,1)\}$

(c) $E_3 = \{(1,6),(2,5),(3,4),(4,3),(5,2),(6,1),(5,6),(6,5)\}$

44.   *Note:* A convenient notation for describing the cards in a standard deck is useful here. The quickest might be to use one of the symbols *A*, 2, 3, 4, 5, 6, 7, 8, 9, 10, *J*, *Q*, K for the face value followed by *H*, *S*, *D*, *C* for the suit. Fortunately, all symbols are different so there is no chance of ambiguity. Thus, the Queen of Hearts is written *QH*, *AD* is the Ace of Diamonds, and so on.

(a) $E_1 = \{QH\}$

(b) $E_2 = \{QH, QD, QS, QC\}$

(c) $E_3 = \{AH, 2H, 3H, 4H, 5H, 6H, 7H, 8H, 9H, 10H, JH, QH, KH\}$

(d) $E_4 = \{JH, JD, JS, JC, QH, QD, QS, QC, KH, KD, KS, KC\}$

45.   **(a)** $E_1 = \{HHHHHHHHHH\}$

(b) $E_2 = \{HHHHHHHHHT, HHHHHHHHTH, HHHHHHHTHH, HHHHHHTHHH, HHHHHTHHHH,$
$HHHHTHHHHH, HHHTHHHHHH, HHTHHHHHHH, HTHHHHHHHH, THHHHHHHHH\}$

(c) $E_3 = \{\ \}$

46. $\{\ \}, \{A\}, \{B\}, \{C\}, \{D\}, \{A, B\}, \{A, C\}, \{A, D\}, \{B, C\}, \{B, D\}, \{C, D\}, \{A, B, C\}, \{A, B, D\},$
$\{A, C, D\}, \{B, C, D\}, \{A, B, C, D\}$

F.   **Equiprobable Spaces**

47.   **(a)** $\Pr(E_1) = \dfrac{3}{8} = 0.375$

(b) $\Pr(E_2) = \dfrac{2}{8} = 0.25$

(c) $\Pr(E_3) = 0$

(d) $\Pr(E_4) = \dfrac{2}{8} = 0.25$

48. (a) $\Pr(E_1) = \dfrac{6}{16} = 0.375$

(b) $\Pr(E_2) = \dfrac{11}{16} = 0.6875$

(c) $\Pr(E_3) = \dfrac{11}{16} = 0.6875$

(d) $\Pr(E_4) = \dfrac{4}{16} = 0.25$

49. (a) $T_6 = \{(1,5),(2,4),(3,3),(4,2),(5,1)\}$ and $T_8 = \{(2,6),(3,5),(4,4),(5,3),(6,2)\}$

So, $\Pr(T_6) = \dfrac{5}{36}$ and $\Pr(T_8) = \dfrac{5}{36}$.

(b) $T_5 = \{(1,4),(2,3),(3,2),(4,1)\}$ and $T_9 = \{(3,6),(4,5),(5,4),(6,3)\}$

So, $\Pr(T_5) = \dfrac{4}{36} = \dfrac{1}{9}$ and $\Pr(T_9) = \dfrac{4}{36} = \dfrac{1}{9}$.

(c) $\Pr(E_1) = \dfrac{6}{36} = \dfrac{1}{6} \approx 0.167$ (see Exercise 43(a))

(d) $\Pr(E_2) = \dfrac{3}{36} \approx 0.083$ (see Exercise 43(b))

(e) $\Pr(E_3) = \dfrac{8}{36} = \dfrac{2}{9} \approx 0.222$ (see Exercise 43(c))

50. (a) $\Pr(E_1) = \dfrac{1}{52}$

(b) $\Pr(E_2) = \dfrac{4}{52} = \dfrac{1}{13}$

(c) $\Pr(E_3) = \dfrac{13}{52} = \dfrac{1}{4}$

(d) $\Pr(E_4) = \dfrac{12}{52} = \dfrac{3}{13}$

51. (a) $\Pr(E_1) = \dfrac{1}{1024} \approx 0.001$

(b) $\Pr(E_2) = \dfrac{10}{1024} \approx 0.01$

(c) $\Pr(E_3) = 0$

52. (a) $\Pr(E_1) = \dfrac{_4C_2}{_{52}C_2} = \dfrac{6}{1326} \approx 0.0045$

(b) $\Pr(E_2) = 13 \cdot \dfrac{6}{1326} \approx 0.059$

53. (a) $\Pr(\text{"roll 8"}) = \dfrac{5}{36} \approx 0.139$

(b) $\Pr(\text{"not roll 8"}) = 1 - \dfrac{5}{36} = \dfrac{31}{36} \approx 0.861$

(c) $\Pr(\text{"roll 8 or 9"}) = \dfrac{9}{36} = 0.25$

(d) $\Pr(\text{"roll 8 or more"}) = \dfrac{15}{36} \approx 0.417$

54. (a) 0

(b) 1

55. The total number of outcomes in this random experiment is $2^{10} = 1024$.

(a) There is only one way to get all ten correct. So, $\Pr(\text{getting 10 points}) = \dfrac{1}{1024}$.

(b) There is only one way to get all ten incorrect (and hence a score of –5). So,
$\Pr(\text{getting -5 points}) = \dfrac{1}{1024}$.

(c) In order to get 8.5 points, the student must get exactly 9 correct answers and 1 incorrect answer. There are $_{10}C_1 = 10$ ways to select which answer would be answered incorrectly. So,
$\Pr(\text{getting 8.5 points}) = \dfrac{10}{1024}$.

(d) In order to get 8 or more points, the student must get at least 9 correct answers (if they only get 8 correct answers, they lose a point for guessing two incorrect answers and score 7 points). So,

Pr(getting 8 or more points) = Pr(getting 8.5 points) + Pr(10 points) = $\dfrac{10}{1024} + \dfrac{1}{1024} = \dfrac{11}{1024}$.

(e) If the student gets 6 answers correct, they score $6 - 4 \times 0.5 = 4$ points. If the student gets 7 answers correct, they score $7 - 3 \times 0.5 = 5.5$ points. So, there is no chance of getting exactly 5 points. Hence, Pr(getting 5 points) = 0.

(f) If the student gets 8 answers correct, they score $8 - 2 \times 0.5 = 7$ points. There are $_{10}C_2 = 45$ ways to select which 8 answers would be answered correctly. So, Pr(getting 7 points) = $\dfrac{45}{1024}$.

In order to get 7 or more points, the student needs to answer at least 8 answers correctly.
Pr(getting 7 or more points) = Pr(getting 7 points) + Pr(getting 8.5 points) + Pr(10 points)

$$= \frac{45}{1024} + \frac{10}{1024} + \frac{1}{1024}$$

$$= \frac{56}{1024}$$

56. The total number of ways to choose four names when order matters is

(a) If A is the first name chosen then there are $_9P_3 = 504$ ways to choose the other three names.

Pr(A first) = $\dfrac{504}{5040} = 0.1$

(b) There are $_9P_4 = 3024$ ways to have A not chosen, so there are 5040 – 3024 = 2016 ways to choose A as one of the names.

Pr(A chosen) = $\dfrac{2016}{5040} = 0.4$

(c) Pr(A not chosen) = $\dfrac{3024}{5040} = 0.6$

(d) Pr(A,B,C,D) = $\dfrac{1}{5040} = 0.0002$

57. (a) There are $_{15}C_4 = 1365$ ways to choose four delegates. If Alice is selected, there are $_{14}C_3 = 364$ ways to choose the other three delegates.

Pr(Alice selected) = $\dfrac{364}{1365} \approx 0.267$

(b) $\Pr(\text{Alice not selected}) = 1 - \dfrac{364}{1365} = \dfrac{1001}{1365} \approx 0.733$

(c) There are $_{15}C_4 = 1,365$ ways to select four members, but only one way to select Alice, Bert, Cathy, and Dale.

$\Pr(\text{Alice, Bert, Cathy, and Dale selected}) = \dfrac{1}{_{15}C_4} = \dfrac{1}{1,365} \approx 0.0007326$

58. (a) $\Pr(\text{all 4 girls}) = \dfrac{1}{2^4} = \dfrac{1}{16} = 0.0625$

(b) $\Pr(\text{2 girls and 2 boys}) = \dfrac{_4C_2}{2^4} = \dfrac{6}{16} = 0.375$

(c) $\Pr(\text{youngest child is a girl}) = \dfrac{1}{2}$

G.   Odds

59. (a) The odds in favor of E are 4 to 3.
$a = 4, b = 7, b - a = 7 - 4 = 3$

(b) The odds in favor of E are 6 to 4, or 3 to 2.
$a = 6, b = 10, b - a = 10 - 6 = 4$

60. (a) The odds in favor of E are 3 to 8.
$a = 3, b = 11, b - a = 8$

(b) The odds in favor of E are 3 to 5.
$a = 3, b = 8, b - a = 5$

61. (a) $\Pr(E) = \dfrac{3}{3+5} = \dfrac{3}{8}$

(b) $\Pr(E) = 1 - \dfrac{8}{8+15} = 1 - \dfrac{8}{23} = \dfrac{15}{23}$

(c) $\Pr(E) = \dfrac{1}{1+1} = \dfrac{1}{2}$

62. (a) $\Pr(E) = \dfrac{4}{4+3} = \dfrac{4}{7}$

(b) $\Pr(E) = \dfrac{5}{12+5} = \dfrac{5}{17}$

(c) $\Pr(E) = \dfrac{1}{2}$

JOGGING

63. There are 35 ways to select a chair and 34 ways to select a secretary. From the remaining 33 members of the ski club, there are $_{33}C_3 = 5456$ ways to select three at-large members. This makes a total of $35 \times 34 \times 5456 = 6,492,640$ ways to select a planning committee.

64. **(a)** The event that R wins the match in game 5 can be described by {*AARRR, ARARR, ARRAR, RAARR, RARAR, RRAAR*}.

    (b) The event that R wins the match can be described by {*RRR, ARRR, RARR, RRAR, AARRR, ARARR, ARRAR, RAARR, RARAR, RRAAR*}.

    (c) The event that the match goes five games can be described by { *AARRR, ARARR, ARRAR, RAARR, RARAR, RRAAR, RRAAA, RARAA, RAARA, ARRAA, ARARA, AARRA*}.

65. **(a)** The event that X wins in 5 games can be described by {*YXXXX, XYXXX, XXYXX, XXXYX*}.

    (b) The event that the series is over in 5 games can be described by {*YXXXX, XYXXX, XXYXX, XXXYX, XYYYY, YXYYY, YYXYY, YYYXY*}.

    (c)

	X wins	Y wins
6 game series	YYXXXX, YXYXXX, YXXYXX, YXXXYX, XYYXXX, XYXYXX, XYXXYX, XXYYXX, XXYXYX, XXXYYX	XXYYYY, XYXYYY, XYYXYY, XYYYXY, YXXYYY, YXYXYY, YXYYXY, YYXXYY, YYXYXY, YYYXXY

    The event "the series is over in game 6" can be described by { *YYXXXX, YXYXXX, YXXYXX, YXXXYX, XYYXXX, XYXYXX, XYXXYX, XXYYXX, XXYXYX, XXXYYX, XXYYYY, XYXYYY, XYYXYY, XYYYXY, YXXYYY, YXYXYY, YXYYXY, YYXXYY, YYXYXY, YYYXXY*}

66. 64
    There are 2 choices for each topping—put it on or leave it off. Thus there are $2^6 = 64$ possible pizzas.

67. **(a)** $10! = 3,628,800$

    (b) 362,880
    A circle of 10 people can be broken to form a line in 10 different ways.
    So there are $\dfrac{3,628,800}{10} = 362,880$ ways to form a circle.

    (c) 28,800
    There are 2 choices as to which sex will start the line. Then, there are 5! ways to order the boys in

the line and 5! ways to order the girls in the line.   So, there are $2 \times 5! \times 5! = 28,800$ ways to form such a line.

(d) $\dfrac{2 \times 5! \times 5!}{10} = 2,880$ ways

68. (a) $_8C_2 = 28$

A chord is determined by choosing 2 of the 8 points in either order.

(b) $_8C_3 = 56$

A triangle is determined by choosing 3 of the 8 points in either order.

69. 126,126. Suppose, for the moment, that the order the teams (but not their members) were selected mattered. There are $\left(_{15}C_5\right) \cdot \left(_{10}C_5\right) \cdot \left(_5C_5\right) = 756,756$ ways to select the teams. Since the order that the teams are selected does not matter, and there are 3! = 6 ways to rearrange the teams, there are actually $\dfrac{756,756}{6} = 126,126$ ways to select the teams.

As an alternative method of solution, think in the following way: Start with an ordered list of the study group. The first person on the list must be in *some* group. Then, select 4 of the remaining 14 members to be in that group ($_{14}C_4 = 1001$ ways to do this). The first person on the list of the remaining members must be in some group (one of the two groups left to be formed). Then, select 4 of the remaining 9 members to be in that group ($_9C_4 = 126$ ways to do this). Finally, the remaining 5 people on the list must belong to the study group not yet formed. So, there are $1001 \times 126 = 126,126$ ways to form the three groups.

70. (a) A sample space S for this random experiment might be taken to consist of all ways that 3 balls could be selected from the 10 in the urn (*without* regard to order). That is $N = {_{10}C_3} = 120$. The number of outcomes in the event that two balls drawn are blue and one is red is $_3C_2 \times {_7C_1} = 21$. So, Pr(two are blue and one is red) = 21/120 = 7/40.

(b) In this random experiment, each draw is an independent event. So, we can multiply the probabilities of each event. Pr(only first and third balls are blue) = $\dfrac{3}{10} \times \dfrac{7}{10} \times \dfrac{3}{10} = \dfrac{63}{1000}$.

(c) A sample space S for this random experiment might be taken to consist of all ways that 3 balls could be selected from the 10 in the urn (*with* regard to order). That is $N = {_{10}P_3} = 720$. The number of outcomes in the event that only the first and third balls drawn are blue (making the second ball drawn red) is $_3P_2 \times {_7P_1} = 42$. So, Pr(first and third balls are blue) = 42/720 = 7/120.

71. The total number of possible outcomes is $_7P_7 = 7! = 5040$

(a) Choose the positions of the H's: $_{20}C_{10} = 184{,}756$.

$$\Pr(10 \ H\text{'s and } 10 \ T\text{'s}) = \frac{184{,}756}{1{,}048{,}576} \approx 0.176$$

(b) Choose the positions of the H's: $_{20}C_3 = 1140$.

$$\Pr(3 \ H\text{'s and } 17 \ T\text{'s}) = \frac{1140}{1{,}048{,}576} \approx 0.001$$

(c) $\Pr(3 \text{ or more } H\text{'s}) = 1 - \Pr(0 \ H\text{'s}) - \Pr(1 \ H\text{'s}) - \Pr(2 \ H\text{'s})$

$$= 1 - \frac{_{20}C_0}{2^{20}} - \frac{_{20}C_1}{2^{20}} - \frac{_{20}C_2}{2^{20}}$$

$$= 1 - \frac{1}{2^{20}} - \frac{20}{2^{20}} - \frac{190}{2^{20}}$$

$$= 1 - \frac{211}{1{,}048{,}576}$$

$$= \frac{1{,}048{,}365}{1{,}048{,}576} \approx 0.9998$$

72. $\Pr(4 \text{ of a kind}) = \dfrac{13 \times 48}{2{,}598{,}960} = \dfrac{1}{4165} \approx 0.0002$

The denominator is $_{52}C_5 = 2{,}598{,}960$, the total number of unordered draw poker hands [see Example 15.16(b)]. The numerator represents the 13 ways to choose the value of the 4 of a kind times the 48 ways to choose the 5th card.

73. $\Pr(\text{all 5 same color}) = \dfrac{131{,}560}{2{,}598{,}960} \approx 0.05$

The total number of 5-card draw poker hands is $_{52}C_5 = 2{,}598{,}960$. The number of hands with all 5 cards

the same color is $2 \times {}_{26}C_5 = \dfrac{52 \times 25 \times 24 \times 23 \times 22}{5!} = 131{,}560$.

74. $\Pr(\text{all 5 same suit}) = \dfrac{4 \times {}_{13}C_5}{2{,}598{,}960} = \dfrac{33}{16{,}660} \approx 0.00198$

The total number of 5-card draw poker hands is $_{52}C_5 = 2{,}598{,}960$. The number of hands with all 5 cards

the same color is $4 \times {}_{13}C_5 = \dfrac{52 \times 25 \times 24 \times 23 \times 22}{5!} = 131{,}560$. The numerator represents the 4 ways to

choose the suit times the number of (unordered) ways to choose 5 cards from the 13 cards of the chosen suit.

75. $\Pr(\text{ace-high straight}) = \dfrac{1020}{2{,}598{,}960} = \dfrac{1}{2548} \approx 0.00039$

The total number of 5-card draw poker hands is $_{52}C_5 = 2{,}598{,}960$. The number of ways to get 10, J, Q,

K, A of any suit (including all the same suit) is $\dfrac{20 \times 16 \times 12 \times 8 \times 4}{5!} = 1024.$ There are 4 ways for these cards to all be the same suit. So there are $1024 - 4 = 1020$ ways to get an ace-high straight.

76. $\Pr(\text{full house}) = \dfrac{3744}{2,598,960} = \dfrac{6}{4165} \approx 0.00144$

The total number of 5-card draw poker hands is $_{52}C_5 = 2,598,960.$ There are 13 ways to choose the value of the 3 cards and then $_4C_3 = 4$ ways to choose the 3 cards from the chosen value. Once that has been done, there are 12 ways to choose the value of the 2 other cards and then $_4C_2 = 6$ ways to choose the 2 cards from the chosen value. Thus, there are $13 \times 4 \times 12 \times 6 = 3744$ ways to choose a full house.

77. $\Pr(\text{win}) = 1 - \Pr(\text{never roll a 7})$

$$= 1 - \left(\frac{30}{36}\right)^5$$

$$= 1 - \left(\frac{5}{6}\right)^5 \approx 0.6$$

78. Bet 1 (that of rolling at least one 6 in four rolls of a die) is better.
  $\Pr(\text{winning Bet 1}) = 1 - \Pr(\text{never roll a 6})$

$$= 1 - \left(\frac{5}{6}\right)^4 \approx 0.5178$$

$\Pr(\text{winning Bet 2}) = 1 - \Pr(\text{never roll boxcars})$

$$= 1 - \left(\frac{35}{36}\right)^{24} \approx 0.4914$$

79. (a) $(1 - 0.02)^{12} = (0.98)^{12} \approx 0.78.$ We are assuming that the events are independent.

  (b) $\Pr(\text{at most 1 defective}) = \Pr(\text{none defective}) + \Pr(1 \text{ defective})$
$$= (0.98)^{12} + 12(0.98)^{11}(0.02)$$
$$\approx 0.98$$

80. The key word in this exercise is "at least." The sample space consists of all possible outcomes. There are $_{500}C_5$ ways in which 5 tickets can be selected from the 500 to be "winning" tickets. For the event that you win at least one prize to occur, it could happen that you win one prize, two prizes, or three prizes. So,

$\Pr(\text{winning at least one prize}) = \Pr(\text{win 1 prize}) + \Pr(\text{win 2 prizes}) = \Pr(\text{win 3 prizes})$

$$= \frac{_5C_1 \cdot {}_{495}C_2}{_{500}C_5} + \frac{_5C_2 \cdot {}_{495}C_1}{_{500}C_5} + \frac{_5C_3 \cdot {}_{495}C_0}{_{500}C_5}$$

RUNNING

81. If N is odd, the probability is 0 (there can't be the same number of H's as T's). If N is even, say $N = 2K$,
then the probability is $_NC_K \left(\frac{1}{2} \right)^N = \frac{N!}{2^N K! K!} = \frac{(2K)!}{2^N K! K!}$.

82. (a) $_7P_7 = 7! = 5040$

(b) 60

There are 6 slots to fill. There are 6 ways to choose which slot the R will occupy. From the
remaining 5 slots, we much choose 3 for the P's—this can be done in $_5C_3 = \frac{5!}{3! 2!} = 10$ ways. The
remaining slots will be occupied by the E's. Thus there are $6 \times 10 = 60$ possible "words."

83. $\Pr(\text{win}) = \frac{8}{36} + 2 \times \frac{1}{36} + 2 \times \frac{2}{45} + 2 \times \frac{25}{396} \approx 0.4929$.

The player can win if any one of the following mutually exclusive events occurs:

W_f : first roll is 7 or 11,

W_4 : first roll is 4 and player rolls another 4 before rolling a 7,

W_5 : first roll is 5 and player rolls another 5 before rolling a 7,

W_6 : first roll is 6 and player rolls another 6 before rolling a 7,

W_8 : first roll is 8 and player rolls another 8 before rolling a 7,

W_9 : first roll is 9 and player rolls another 9 before rolling a 7,

W_{10} : first roll is 10 and player rolls another 10 before rolling a 7.

Thus,

$\Pr(\text{win}) = \Pr(W_f) + \Pr(W_4) + \Pr(W_5) + \Pr(W_6) + \Pr(W_8) + \Pr(W_9) + \Pr(W_{10})$

$\Pr(W_f) = \frac{6}{36} + \frac{2}{36} = \frac{8}{36}$.

To compute $\Pr(W_4)$ we use the following reasoning: The first roll must be a 4. This has probability 3/36.
After the first roll the only rolls that matter are 4's (good) or 7's (bad). All other possible numbers are
inconsequential. The 7 (with probability 6/36) is twice as likely to come up as the 4 (with probability
3/36), and we can interpret this by saying that there are 3 chances in favor and 6 chances against rolling a
4 before a 7, so the probability of this happening is $\frac{3}{3+6} = \frac{3}{9}$. From this we get $\Pr(W_4) = \frac{3}{36} \times \frac{3}{9} = \frac{1}{36}$. By a
similar argument, we can get $\Pr(W_5) = \frac{4}{36} \times \frac{4}{10} = \frac{2}{45}$ and $\Pr(W_6) = \frac{5}{36} \times \frac{5}{11} = \frac{25}{396}$. Also, $\Pr(W_8) = \Pr(W_6)$,
$\Pr(W_9) = \Pr(W_5)$, and $\Pr(W_{10}) = \Pr(W_4)$.

Putting it altogether we have, $\Pr(\text{win}) = \frac{8}{36} + 2 \times \frac{1}{36} + 2 \times \frac{2}{45} + 2 \times \frac{25}{396} \approx 0.4929$.

84. 0.706

We compute the probability that all 30 individuals have different birthdays. Needless to say, we assume
that each of the 365 days of the year are equally likely to be an individual's birthday. Imagine that we
line up the 30 individuals and call them P_1, P_2, ..., P_{30}. We start by recording P_1's birthday.

The probability that P_2's birthday is different from P_1's is $\frac{364}{365}$.

The probability that P_3's birthday is different from P_1's and P_2's is $\frac{363}{365}$.

$\vdots$

The probability that P_{30}'s birthday is different from P_1's, P_2's, ..., P_{29}'s is $\frac{336}{365}$.

Since every birthday is independent from every other birthday, the probability that P_1, P_2, ..., P_{30} all have different birthdays is $\frac{364}{365} \times \frac{363}{365} \times ... \times \frac{336}{365} \approx 0.294$. It follows that the probability that there are two people in the room with the same birthday is $1 - 0.294 = 0.706$, a fact that most people find nothing short of amazing.

85. **(a)** $\Pr(\text{YAHTZEE}) = \dfrac{6}{6^5} = \dfrac{6}{7776} \approx 0.00077$

The denominator, 7776, is the number of ordered outcomes possible. The numerator consists of the only 6 outcomes that give YAHTZEE (six 1's, six 2's, etc...).

(b) $\Pr(\text{four of a kind}) = \dfrac{5 \times 6 \times 5}{6^5} = \dfrac{150}{7776} \approx 0.019$

There are 5 choices as to which die will not match the other 4. There are 6 choices for what will constitute the four of kind (four sixes, four fives, etc...) and there are 5 choices for what will constitute the other die.

(c) $\Pr(\text{large straight}) = \dfrac{2 \times 5!}{6^5} = \dfrac{240}{7776} \approx 0.031$

There are 2 choices as to what the large straight will be – it will either be 1-5 or 2-6. For each there are 5! ways to rearrange the the order that the dice are rolled.

(d) $\Pr(\text{trips}) = \dfrac{_5C_3 \times 6 \times 5 \times 4}{6^5} = \dfrac{1200}{7776} \approx 0.154$

There are $_5C_3 = \frac{5!}{3!2!} = 10$ choices as to which 3 dice will match each other. There are then 6 choices as to what the three of a kind will consist of (three 1's, three 2's, etc...). There are 5 choices for one of the remaining dice and 4 choices for the value of the other.

86.

Hand	Probability
Four of a kind	0
Flush (five cards of same suit)	$\dfrac{3 \times {}_{13}C_5}{{}_{39}C_5} = \dfrac{3861}{575,757} \approx 0.0067$
Full house (3 cards of equal value and two others of equal value)	$\dfrac{13 \times 1 \times 12 \times {}_3C_2}{{}_{39}C_5} = \dfrac{468}{575,757} \approx 0.00081$
Three of a kind	$\dfrac{13 \times {}_3C_3 \times 12 \times {}_3C_1 \times 11 \times {}_3C_1}{{}_{39}C_5} = \dfrac{15,444}{575,757} \approx 0.0268$
Two pair	$\dfrac{13 \times {}_3C_2 \times 12 \times {}_3C_2 \times 11 \times {}_3C_1}{{}_{39}C_5} = \dfrac{46,332}{575,757} \approx 0.0805$

Mini-Excursion 4

WALKING

A.   Weighted Averages

1. Using the fact that 90/120 = 75% and 144/180 = 80%, Paul's score is
    $0.15 \times 77\% + 0.15 \times 83\% + 0.15 \times 91\% + 0.1 \times 75\% + 0.25 \times 87\% + 0.2 \times 80\% = 82.9\%$

2. $0.014 \times 2 + 0.361 \times 3 + 0.5 \times 4 + 0.111 \times 5 + 0.014 \times 6 = 3.75$

3. 100% - 7% - 22% - 24% - 23% - 19% = 5% are 19 years old. So, the average age at Thomas Jefferson
    HS is $0.07 \times 14 + 0.22 \times 15 + 0.24 \times 16 + 0.23 \times 17 + 0.19 \times 18 + 0.05 \times 19 = 16.4$.

4. $0.47 \times 4,000 + 0.27 \times 3,000 + 0.19 \times 1,500 + 0.07 \times 100 = 2,982$

B.   Expected Values

5. The expected value of this random variable is $E = \frac{1}{5} \times 5 + \frac{2}{5} \times 10 + \frac{2}{5} \times 15 = 11$.

6. $E = 0.2 \times 10 + 0.3 \times 20 + 0.4 \times 30 + 0.1 \times 40 = 24$

7. **(a)**

Outcome	$1	$5	$10	$20	$100
Probability	1/2	1/4	1/8	1/10	1/40

   (b) $E = \frac{1}{2} \times \$1 + \frac{1}{4} \times \$5 + \frac{1}{8} \times \$10 + \frac{1}{10} \times \$20 + \frac{1}{40} \times \$100 = \$7.50$

   (c) $7.50

8. **(a)**

Outcome	0 points	1 point	2 points
Probability	0.0625	0.375	0.5625

   (b) $E = 0.0625 \times 0 + 0.375 \times 1 + 0.5625 \times 2 = 1.5$ points

9. **(a)**

Outcome	0	1	2	3
Probability	1/8	3/8	3/8	1/8

   (b) $E = \frac{1}{8} \times 0 + \frac{3}{8} \times 1 + \frac{3}{8} \times 2 + \frac{1}{8} \times 3 = 1.5$ heads

10. (a)

Outcome	$18	$54	$(-9)
Probability	1/6	1/18	14/18

$$E = \frac{1}{6} \times \$18 + \frac{1}{18} \times \$54 + \frac{14}{18} \times \$(-9) = \$(-1)$$

(b) You should pay $(-1) for the right to play this game. That is, in order to play the game, you must be offered $1.

11. (a)

Outcome (Profit)	$1 (red)	$(-1) (black)	$(-1) (green)
Probability	18/38	18/38	2/38

$$E = \frac{18}{38} \times \$1 + \frac{18}{38} \times \$(-1) + \frac{2}{38} \times \$(-1) = \$ - \frac{1}{19} \approx \$ - 0.05$$

(b) $E = \frac{18}{38} \times \$N + \frac{18}{38} \times \$(-N) + \frac{2}{38} \times \$(-N) = \$ - \frac{1}{19}N \approx \$ - 0.05N$. So, for every $100 bet on red, you should expect to lose about $5 ($5.26 to be more precise). For every $1,000,000 bet on red, you should expect to lose about $52,631.

12. (a)

Outcome (Profit)	$36	$(-1)
Probability	1/38	37/38

$$E = \frac{1}{38} \times \$36 + \frac{37}{38} \times \$(-1) = \$ - \frac{1}{38} \approx \$ - 0.0263$$

(b) $E = \frac{1}{38} \times \$36N + \frac{37}{38} \times \$(-N) = \$ - \frac{1}{38}N \approx \$ - 0.0263N$. So, for every $100 bet on 10, you should expect to lose $2.63. For every $1,000,000 bet on 10, you should expect to lose about $26,316.

13. (a) $E = \frac{1}{6} \times \$1 + \frac{1}{6} \times \$(-2) + \frac{1}{6} \times \$3 + \frac{1}{6} \times \$(-4) + \frac{1}{6} \times \$5 + \frac{1}{6} \times \$(-6) = \$ - 0.50$

(b) Pay $0.50 to play a game in which you roll a single die. If an odd number comes up, you have to pay the amount of your roll ($1, $3, or $5). If an even number (2, 4, or 6) comes up, you win the amount of your roll.

14. (a) We solve $0.002 \times \$(P - 100,000) + 0.998 \times \$P = \$0$ for P which gives $P - 200 = 0$ and $P = 200$.

(b) For a fair premium on a $100,000 one-year term life insurance policy,
$E = 0.003 \times \$(P - 100,000) + 0.997 \times \$P = \$0$ when $P = \$300$.

C. Miscellaneous

15.

Outcome (Benefit to Joe)	$320	$(-80)
Probability	24%	76%

$E = 0.24 \times \$320 + 0.76 \times \$(-80) = \$16$

Joe should take this risk since his expected payoff is greater than 0 ($16). That is, if he made this transaction on thousands of plasma TVs, in the long run he could expect to save $16 for each warranty he purchases.

16.

Outcome (Benefit to Jackie)	$31	$(-19)
Probability	5%	95%

$E = 0.05 \times \$31 + 0.95 \times \$(-19) = \$-16.50$

Jackie should not buy this extended warranty since her expected payoff is less than 0.

17.

Payoff (to insurer)	$P	$(P-500)	$(P-1,500)	$(P-4,000)
Probability	50%	35%	12%	3%

In order to make an average profit of $50 per policy, we solve
$E = 0.5 \times \$P + 0.35 \times \$(P - 500) + 0.12 \times \$(P - 1,500) + 0.03 \times \$(P - 4,000) = \$50$ for P. Doing this gives
$P = \$525$. That is, the insurance company should charge $525 per policy.

18.

Payoff (to insurer)	$P	$(P-250,000)
Probability	$\dfrac{2,492,500}{2,500,000}$	$\dfrac{7,500}{2,500,000}$

In order to make an average profit of $50 per policy, we solve

$E = \dfrac{2,492,500}{2,500,000} \times \$P + \dfrac{7,500}{2,500,000} \times \$(P - 250,000) = \$50$ for P. Doing this we find that the insurance

company should charge $P = \$800$ per policy.

19. **(a)** There are three ways to select which of the three dice will not land as a 4. There are five numbers that this die can land on (1, 2, 3, 5, or 6). The multiplication rule tells us that there are
$3 \times 5 = 15$ ways to select an outcome in which exactly two 4's are rolled. Since there are $6^3 = 216$

(again by the multiplication rule) possible outcomes in this random experiment, the probability of such an outcome is 15/216.

(b) There are three ways to select which of the three dice will land as a 4. There are five numbers that each other die can land on (1, 2, 3, 5, or 6). The multiplication rule tells us that there are $3 \times 5 \times 5 = 75$ ways to select an outcome in which exactly one 4 is rolled. Hence, the probability of such an outcome is 75/216.

(c) There are five numbers that each die can land on (1, 2, 3, 5, or 6). So, there are $5 \times 5 \times 5 = 125$ ways to select an outcome in which no 4 is rolled. So, the probability of not rolling any 4's is 125/216.

20. We solve $P_4 = P_0 (1+r)^4$ for r where $P_0 = \$10$ and $P_4 = \$15.25$. That is, we solve $\dfrac{15.25}{10} = (1+r)^4$ for r to give $r = \sqrt[4]{1.525} - 1 \approx 0.11$. That is, the expected annual yield is about 11%.

21.

Outcome (Winnings)	\$29,999,999	\$(-1)
Probability	$\dfrac{1}{_{47}C_5 \times\, _{27}C_1}$	$1 - \dfrac{1}{_{47}C_5 \times\, _{27}C_1}$

$$E = \frac{1}{_{47}C_5 \times\, _{27}C_1} \times \$29,999,999 + \left(1 - \frac{1}{_{47}C_5 \times\, _{27}C_1}\right) \times \$(-1) =$$

$$\frac{1}{41,416,353} \times \$29,999,999 + \frac{41,415,352}{41,416,353} \times \$(-1) \approx \$-0.28$$

That is, on each \$1 lottery ticket purchased, you should expect to lose about \$0.28. [In general, the question is slightly more complicated than this since it is not reasonable to expect never to need to split the jackpot. Also, in most lotteries of this sort there are other (lesser) prizes that can be won.]

22.

Outcome (Winnings)	\$63,999,999	\$(-1)
Probability	$\dfrac{1}{_{56}C_5 \times\, _{46}C_1}$	$1 - \dfrac{1}{_{56}C_5 \times\, _{46}C_1}$

$$E = \frac{1}{_{56}C_5 \times\, _{46}C_1} \times \$63,999,999 + \left(1 - \frac{1}{_{56}C_5 \times\, _{46}C_1}\right) \times \$(-1) =$$

$$\frac{1}{175,711,536} \times \$63,999,999 + \frac{175,711,535}{175,711,536} \times \$(-1) \approx \$-0.64$$

That is, on each \$1 lottery ticket purchased, you should expect to lose about \$0.64. [In general, the question is slightly more complicated than this since it is not reasonable to expect never to need to split the jackpot. Also, in most lotteries of this sort there are other (lesser) prizes that can be won.]

Chapter 16

A. Normal Curves

1. (a) 83 lb

   (b) 83 lb

   (c) 90 lb. − 83 lb. = 7 lb

2. (a) 253 m.

   (b) 253 m.

   (c) 61 m.

3. (a) $Q_1 = 81.2$ lb. $- 0.675 \times 12.4$ lb. ≈ 72.8 lb

   (b) $Q_3 = 81.2$ lb. $+ 0.675 \times 12.4$ lb. ≈ 89.5 lb

4. (a) $Q_1 \approx 2038$ points

   (b) $Q_3 \approx 2670$ points

5. Since $Q_1 = \mu - 0.675 \times \sigma$,
   $72.8 = \mu - 0.675 \times 12.4$ so that
   $\mu = 81.17$ lb.
   Thus,
   $Q_3 = 81.17$ lb. $+ 0.675 \times 12.4$ lb. ≈ 89.6 lb.

6. $2670 = \mu + 0.675 \times 468$ so that $\mu = 2354.1$ points. Thus,
   $Q_1 = 2354.1 - 0.675 \times 468 \approx 2038$ points.

7. $94.7 = 81.2 + 0.675 \times \sigma$
   $\sigma = 20$ in.

8. $4,520

9. (a) $\dfrac{72 \text{ in.} + 78 \text{ in.}}{2} = 75$ in.

   (b) $\sigma = 78$ in. $- 75$ in. $= 3$ in.

(c) $Q_1 = 75$ in. $- 0.675 \times 3$ in. ≈ 73 in.
$Q_3 = 75$ in. $+ 0.675 \times 3$ in. ≈ 77 in.

10. (a) 530 points

    (b) 120 points

    (c) $Q_1 = 449$ points, $Q_3 = 611$ points (since $\sigma = 120$, $0.675 \times \sigma = 81$.)

11. $\mu \neq M$

12. $\mu \neq M$

13. In a normal distribution the first and third quartiles are the same distance from the mean. In this distribution,
    $\mu - Q_1 = 453 - 343 = 110$ and
    $Q_3 - \mu = 553 - 453 = 100$.

14. In a normal distribution the first quartile 0.675 standard deviations below the mean. Rather than having a value of 35, the first quartile in this distribution should be
    $\mu - 0.675 \times \sigma = 47 - 0.675 \times 10 = 40.25$.

B. Standardizing Data

15. (a) $\dfrac{45 \text{ kg} - 30 \text{ kg}}{15 \text{ kg}} = \dfrac{15 \text{ kg}}{15 \text{ kg}} = 1$

    (b) $\dfrac{54 \text{ kg} - 30 \text{ kg}}{15 \text{ kg}} = \dfrac{24 \text{ kg}}{15 \text{ kg}} = 1.6$

    (c) $\dfrac{0 \text{ kg} - 30 \text{ kg}}{15 \text{ kg}} = \dfrac{-30 \text{ kg}}{15 \text{ kg}} = -2$

    (d) $\dfrac{3 \text{ kg} - 30 \text{ kg}}{15 \text{ kg}} = \dfrac{-27 \text{ kg}}{15 \text{ kg}} = -1.8$

16. (a) $\dfrac{128 \text{ points} - 110 \text{ points}}{12 \text{ points}} = 1.5$

(b) $\dfrac{100 \text{ points} - 110 \text{ points}}{12 \text{ points}} = -\dfrac{5}{6}$

(c) $\dfrac{110 \text{ points} - 110 \text{ points}}{12 \text{ points}} = 0$

(d) $\dfrac{71 \text{ points} - 110 \text{ points}}{12 \text{ points}} = \dfrac{-39}{12} = -3.25$

17. (a) ≈ 0.22

In a normal distribution, the third quartile is about 0.675 standard deviations above the mean. That is, $Q_3 \approx \mu + (0.675)\sigma$. In this case, it means $278.58 \approx 253.45 + (0.675)\sigma$ so that the standard deviation is $\sigma \approx 37.23$. Hence, the standardized value of 261.71 is $\dfrac{261.71 - 253.45}{37.23} \approx 0.22$.

(b) $\dfrac{185.79 - 253.45}{37.23} \approx -1.82$

(c) $\dfrac{253.45 - 253.45}{37.23} = 0$

18. (a) -1

In a normal distribution, the first quartile is about 0.675 standard deviations below the mean. That is, $Q_1 \approx \mu - (0.675)\sigma$. In this case, it means $44.1 \approx 49.5 - (0.675)\sigma$ so that the standard deviation is $\sigma = 8$. Hence, the standardized value of 41.5 lb. is $\dfrac{41.5 \text{ lb.} - 49.5 \text{ lb.}}{8 \text{ lb.}} = -1$.

(b) $\dfrac{61.5 \text{ lb.} - 49.5 \text{ lb.}}{8 \text{ lb.}} = 1.5$

(c) $\dfrac{35.1 \text{ lb.} - 49.5 \text{ lb.}}{8 \text{ lb.}} = -1.8$

19. -0.675

20. 0.675

21. (a) 152.3 ft
$$\dfrac{x - 183.5}{31.2} = -1$$
$$x - 183.5 = -31.2$$
$$x = 152.3 \text{ ft}$$

(b) 199.1 ft
$$\dfrac{x - 183.5}{31.2} = 0.5$$
$$x - 183.5 = 15.6$$
$$x = 199.1 \text{ ft}$$

(c) 111.74 ft
$$\dfrac{x - 183.5}{31.2} = -2.3$$
$$x - 183.5 = -71.76$$
$$x = 111.74 \text{ ft}$$

(d) 183.5 ft
$$\dfrac{x - 183.5}{31.2} = 0$$
$$x - 183.5 = 0$$
$$x = 183.5 \text{ ft}$$

22. (a) 92.4 gal.
$$\dfrac{x - 83.2}{4.6} = 2$$
$$x - 83.2 = 9.2$$
$$x = 92.4 \text{ gal}$$

(b) 76.3 gal.
$$\dfrac{x - 83.2}{4.6} = -1.5$$
$$x - 83.2 = 6.9$$
$$x = 76.3 \text{ gal}$$

(c) 81.222 gal.

$$\frac{x - 83.2}{4.6} = -0.43$$

$$x - 83.2 = -1.978$$

$$x = 81.222 \text{ gal}$$

(d) 83.2 gal.

$$\frac{x - 83.2}{4.6} = 0$$

$$x = 83.2 \text{ gal}$$

23. $\dfrac{84 - 50}{\sigma} = 2$

$$34 = 2\sigma$$

$$\sigma = 17 \text{ lb.}$$

24. 30

$$\frac{-60 - 30}{\sigma} = -3$$

$$-90 = -3\sigma$$

$$\sigma = 30$$

25. $\mu = 5$

$$\frac{50 - \mu}{15} = 3$$

$$50 - \mu = 45$$

$$\mu = 5$$

26. $\mu = 50$

$$\frac{10 - \mu}{20} = -2$$

$$10 - \mu = -40$$

$$\mu = 50$$

27. $\mu = 52; \ \sigma = 16$

$$\frac{20 - \mu}{\sigma} = -2; \frac{100 - \mu}{\sigma} = 3$$

$$20 - \mu = -2\sigma; 100 - \mu = 3\sigma$$

$$\mu = 20 + 2\sigma, \text{ so } 100 - (20 + 2\sigma) = 3\sigma$$

$$100 - 20 - 2\sigma = 3\sigma$$

$$80 = 5\sigma$$

$$\sigma = 16$$

$$\mu = 20 + 2 \times 16 = 52$$

28. $\mu = -10; \ \sigma = 30$

$$\frac{-10 - \mu}{\sigma} = 0; \frac{50 - \mu}{\sigma} = 2$$

$$-10 - \mu = 0; 50 - \mu = 2\sigma$$

$$\mu = -10, \text{ so } 50 - (-10) = 2\sigma$$

$$60 = 2\sigma$$

$$\sigma = 30$$

C.   The 68 – 95 – 99.7 Rule

29. $\mu = 55; \ \sigma = 5$

P is one standard deviation above the mean, and P' is one standard deviation below the mean.

$$\mu = \frac{50 + 60}{2} = 55$$

$$\sigma = 60 - 55 = 5$$

30. $\mu = 51, \ \sigma = 16$

P is one standard deviation above the mean, and P' is one standard deviation below the mean.

$$\mu = \frac{35 + 67}{2} = 51$$

$$\sigma = 67 - 51 = 16$$

31. $\mu = 92, \ \sigma = 3.4$

98.8 is 2 standard deviations above the mean and 85.2 is 2 standard deviations below the mean.

$$\mu = \frac{85.2 + 98.8}{2} = 92$$

$$\sigma = \frac{1}{2}(98.8 - 92) = 3.4$$

32. $\mu = 112, \ \sigma = 9.5$

131 is 2 standard deviations above the mean

and 93 is 2 standard deviations below the mean.

$$\mu = \frac{93 + 131}{2} = 112$$

$$\sigma = \frac{1}{2}(131 - 112) = 9.5$$

33. $\mu = 80, \sigma \approx 10$

73.25 is the first quartile and 86.75 is the third quartile.

$$\mu = \frac{73.25 + 86.75}{2} = 80$$

$$Q_3 - \mu \approx 86.75 - 80 = 6.75$$

$$0.675\sigma \approx 6.75$$

$$\sigma \approx 10$$

34. $\mu = 150, \sigma \approx 20$

136.5 is the first quartile and 163.5 is the third quartile.

$$\mu = \frac{136.5 + 163.5}{2} = 150$$

$$Q_3 - \mu = 163.5 - 150 = 13.5$$

$$0.675\sigma \approx 13.5$$

$$\sigma \approx 20$$

35. (a) 97.5%

95% of the data lies within two standard deviations of the mean. Hence, 2.5% of the data are not within two standard deviations on each side of the mean. So, 97.5% of the data fall below the point two standard deviations above the mean.

(b) $\dfrac{95\% - 68\%}{2} = 13\%$

36. (a) 99.85%

99.7% of the data lies within three standard deviations of the mean. Hence, 0.3% of the data are not within three standard deviations on each side of the mean. So, 99.85% of the data fall above the point three standard deviations below the mean.

(b) $\dfrac{99.7\% - 95\%}{2} = 2.35\%$

37. Since 84% of the data lies above one standard deviation of the mean, $\mu - \sigma = 50.2$ cm.
Thus, $\mu = 6.1$ cm. $+ 50.2$ cm. $= 56.3$ cm.

38. 6.1 cm
$\sigma = 56.3 - 50.2 = 6.1$ cm.

39. 9.9 has a standardized value of
$\dfrac{9.9 - 12.6}{4} = -0.675$. Also, 16.6 has a standardized value of $\dfrac{16.6 - 12.6}{4} = 1$. So, 25% of the data is below the first quartile of 9.9. Also, 84% of the data is below 16.6. So, 84% - 25% = 59% of the data is between 9.9 and 16.6.

40. 465 has a standardized value of
$\dfrac{465 - 500}{35} = -1$. Also, 605 has a standardized value of $\dfrac{605 - 500}{35} = 3$
So, 16% of the data is below 465. Also, about 100% of the data is below 605. So, 100% - 16% = 84% of the data is between 465 and 605.

D. **Approximately Normal Data Sets**

41. (a) 52 points

(b) 50%

(c) 68%

$$\frac{41 - 52}{11} = -1, \frac{63 - 52}{11} = 1$$

(d) $\dfrac{1}{2}(100\% - 68\%) = 16\%$

42. (a) 2375 students
30 is two standard deviations below the

mean and 74 is two standard deviations above the mean. Hence, 95% of 2500 students (or 2375) scored between 30 and 74.

(b) ≈ 63 students
$0.025 \times 2500 = 62.5$

(c) ≈ 4 students
$0.0015 \times 2500 = 3.75$

43. **(a)** $Q_1 \approx 52 - 0.675 \times 11 \approx 44.6$ points

(b) $Q_3 \approx 52 + 0.675 \times 11 \approx 59.4$ points

(c) interquartile range $= Q_3 - Q_1$
$$\approx 59.4 - 44.6$$
$$= 14.8 \text{ points}$$

44. **(a)** The correct answer is 46.5, but a reasonable estimate is anywhere between 45 and 49.
Since the 50th percentile is 52, a score of 51 should be somewhat below the 50th percentile and any number between 45 and 49 should be considered a reasonable guess (and therefore an acceptable answer). Most students guess the 49th percentile and are surprised to find out that the true answer is approximately 46.5. There is a useful lesson for the student here: a one point difference can produce different effects on the corresponding percentiles depending on where the scores are, and the closer the scores are to the center of the normal distribution, the bigger the change in the percentile.

(b) Any answer above the 84th percentile (but reasonably close to it) is an acceptable estimate. (The actual value is approximately 86.2.)

(c) Any answer above the 75th percentile (but reasonably close to it) is an acceptable estimate. (The actual value is 76.4.)

(d) 99.85th percentile

45. **(a)** 1900 patients
$$\frac{99 - 125}{13} = -2, \frac{151 - 125}{13} = 2$$
95% have blood pressure between 99 and 151 mm.
$0.95(2000) = 1900$ patients

(b) 1630 patients
112 is one standard deviation below the mean. 151 is two standard deviations above the mean. The percentage of patients falling between one standard deviation below the mean and two standard deviations above the mean is 68% + 13.5% = 81.5%. 81.5% of the 2000 patients is 1630 patients.

46. **(a)** 1950 patients
$$\frac{99 - 125}{13} = -2$$
97.5% have blood pressure above 99 mm.
$0.975(2000) = 1950$ patients

(b) 1630 patients
99 is two standard deviations below the mean. 138 is one standard deviation above the mean. The percentage of patients falling between two standard deviations below the mean and one standard deviation above the mean is 68% + 13.5% = 81.5%. 81.5% of the 2000 patients is 1630 patients.

47. **(a)** $\dfrac{100 - 125}{13} = -1.92$

approximately the 3rd percentile

(b) $\dfrac{112 - 125}{13} = -1$

the 16th percentile

(c) $\dfrac{138 - 125}{13} = 1$

the 84th percentile

(d) $\dfrac{164-125}{13}=3$

the 99.85th percentile

48. (a) *Min* $\approx$ 86 mm, *Max* $\approx$ 164 mm.

(b) *Min* $\approx$ 86 mm, Q_1 $\approx$ 116 mm, Q_2 = 125 mm, Q_3 $\approx$ 134 mm, *Max* $\approx$ 164 mm.

49. (a) 95%

$\dfrac{11-12}{0.5}=-2, \dfrac{13-12}{0.5}=2$

(b) 47.5%

$\dfrac{12-12}{0.5}=0, \dfrac{13-12}{0.5}=2$

$\dfrac{1}{2}(95\%)=47.5\%$

(c) 97.5%

Because the chance of the bag weighing between 11 and 12 ounces is the same as the chance that it weighs between 12 and 13 ounces, we can use our answer to part (b) and symmetry to obtain an answer of 47.5% + 50% = 97.5%.

50. (a) 68%

(b) 34%

(c) 16%

51. (a) 13 bags

$\dfrac{11-12}{0.5}=-2$

$\dfrac{1}{2}(100\%-95\%)=2.5\%$

$0.025 \times 500 = 12.5 \approx 13$ bags

(b) 80 bags

$\dfrac{11.5-12}{0.5}=-1$

$\dfrac{1}{2}(100\%-68\%)=16\%$

$0.16 \times 500 = 80$ bags

(c) 250 bags

$0.50 \times 500 = 250$ bags

(d) 420 bags

$\dfrac{12.5-12}{0.5}=1$

$\dfrac{1}{2}(68\%)+50\%=84\%$

$0.84 \times 500 = 420$ bags

(e) 488 bags

$\dfrac{13-12}{0.5}=2$

$\dfrac{1}{2}(95\%)+50\%=97.5\%$

$0.975 \times 500 = 487.5 \approx 488$ bags

(f) 499 bags

$\dfrac{13.5-12}{0.5}=3$

$\dfrac{1}{2}(99.7\%)+50\%=99.85\%$

$0.9985 \times 500 = 499.25 \approx 499$ bags

52. (a) 202 or 203
13.5% of 1500

(b) 510
34% of 1500

(c) 510

(d) 202 or 203

(e) 35

53. (a) 16th percentile

$$\frac{15.25 - 17.25}{2} = -1$$

(b) 97.5th percentile

$$\frac{21.25 - 17.25}{2} = 2$$

(c) 18.6 lb.
weight = $17.25 + 0.675 \times 2 = 18.6$ lb

54. (a) 2.5th percentile

$$\frac{16.6 - 21}{2.2} = -2$$

(b) 16th percentile

$$\frac{18.8 - 21}{2.2} = -1$$

(c) 22.5 lb.
weight = $21 + 0.675 \times 2.2 = 22.485$ lb

55. (a) 97.5th percentile

$$\frac{11 - 8.75}{1.1} \approx 2$$

(b) 99.85th percentile

$$\frac{12 - 8.75}{1.1} \approx 3$$

(c) 8 lb.
weight = $8.75 - 0.675 \times 1.1 \approx 8$ lb

56. (a) 75th percentile

$$\frac{24 - 22.5}{2.2} \approx 0.682 \approx 0.675$$

(b) 25th percentile

$$\frac{21 - 22.5}{2.2} \approx -0.682$$

(c) 24.7 lb.
weight = $22.5 + 2.2 \approx 24.7$ lb

E.   **The Honest- and Dishonest-Coin Principles**

57. (a) $\mu = \dfrac{3600}{2} = 1800, \sigma = \dfrac{\sqrt{3600}}{2} = 30$

(b) 68%

$$\frac{1770 - 1800}{30} = -1, \frac{1830 - 1800}{30} = 1$$

(c) $\dfrac{1}{2}(68\%) = 34\%$

(d) 13.5%

$$\frac{1860 - 1800}{30} = 2$$

$$\frac{1}{2}(95\%) = 47.5\%$$

$$47.5\% - 34\% = 13.5\%$$

58. (a) $\mu = 3200, \sigma = 40$

(b) $\approx 95\%$

(c) $\approx 50\%$

(d) $\approx 13.5\%$

59. (a) $\approx 68\%$

(b) $\approx \dfrac{1}{2}(100\% - 68\%) = 16\%$

(c) $\approx \dfrac{1}{2}(68\%) + 50\% = 84\%$

60. (a) 0.5
According to the honest coin principle
$\mu = 2500/2 = 1250$ and
$\sigma = \sqrt{2500}/2 = 25.$

Not losing any money means winning
1250 times or more—a 50% chance.

(b) 0.475

$1300 = \mu + 2\sigma$ so that there is a 95% chance that the number of rolls will fall between 1200 and 1300.

(c) 0.025

Winning $100 or more means winning 1300 times or more—a 2.5% chance since $1300 = \mu + 2\sigma$.

(d) 0

Winning 1300 times (and hence losing 1200 times) results in a net gain of $100; winning 1301 times (and hence losing 1199 times) results in a net gain of $102. Thus, it is impossible to win exactly $101.

61. (a) $\mu = 600 \times 0.4 = 240$,

$\sigma = \sqrt{600 \times 0.4 \times (1 - 0.4)} = 12$

(b) $Q_1 \approx 240 - 0.675 \times 12 \approx 232$

$Q_3 \approx 240 + 0.675 \times 12 \approx 248$

(c) 0.95

$\dfrac{216 - 240}{12} = -2, \dfrac{264 - 240}{12} = 2$

62. (a) $\mu = 1200 \times 0.75 = 900$,

$\sigma = \sqrt{1200 \times 0.75 \times (1 - 0.75)} = 15$

(b) $Q_1 \approx 900 - 0.675 \times 15 \approx 890$

$Q_3 \approx 900 + 0.675 \times 15 \approx 910$

(c) ≈ 0.50

900 to 945 consists of 3 standard deviations.

63. (a) $\mu = 180 \times \dfrac{1}{6} = 30$,

$\sigma = \sqrt{180 \times \dfrac{1}{6} \times \left(1 - \dfrac{1}{6}\right)} = 5$

(b) 0.025

$\dfrac{40 - 30}{5} = 2$

$\dfrac{1}{2}(1 - 0.95) = 0.025$

(c) ≈ 0.34

$\dfrac{35 - 30}{5} = 1$

$\dfrac{1}{2}(0.68) = 0.34$

64. (a) ≈ 0.34

(b) ≈ 0.475

(c) ≈ 0.0015

65. We assume that the defects are distributed normally so that the mean number of defects on a given day is $\mu = 90,000 \times 0.10 = 9,000$ by the Dishonest-Coin principle. The standard deviation is given by $\sigma = \sqrt{90,000 \times 0.10 \times (1 - 0.10)} = 90$. So, 9,180 is 2 standard deviations above the mean. It follows that the machine needs to be recalibrated 2.5% of the time.

66. 97.5%

$\mu = 2000 \times 0.89 = 1780$,

$\sigma = \sqrt{2000 \times 0.89 \times (1 - 0.89)} \approx 14$

Thus, 1750 is 2 standard deviations below the mean.

JOGGING

67. (a) weight = 17.25 + 1.65 × 2 = 20.55 lb

(b) weight = 17.25 - 0.25 × 2 = 16.75 lb

68. (a) 55 + 12 × 2.33 = 82.96 ≈ 83 points

(b) 55 - 12 × 0.52 = 48.76 ≈ 49 points

69. (a) 60th percentile

$17.25 + 2 \times w = 17.75$

$w = 0.25$

(b) 30th percentile

$17.25 - 2 \times w = 16.2$

$w = 0.525$

70. (a) 99th percentile

$55 + 12 \times w = 83$

$w = 2.33$

(b) 20th percentile

$55 - 12 \times w = 45$

$w = 0.84$

(c) 5000

$55 - 12 \times w = 35$

$w = 1.666$

So a score of 35 is at the 5th percentile.

5% of $N = 250$ gives $N = 5000$ students.

71. (a) score $= 520 + (0.675)(115) = 597.625 \approx$ 600 points

(b) $\dfrac{750 - 520}{115} = 2$. Thus, a score of 750 is

2 standard deviations above the mean. This means a score of 750 is at the 97.5th percentile.

72. (a) 1.28

(b) -1.28

(c) 0.84

(d) -0.84

(e) -1.04

73. (a) The 90th percentile of the data is located at $\mu + 1.28 \times \sigma = 65.2 + 1.28 \times 10 = 78$ points.

(b) The 70th percentile of the data is located at $\mu + 0.52 \times \sigma = 65.2 + 0.52 \times 10 = 70.4$ points.

(c) The 30th percentile of the data is located at $\mu - 0.52 \times \sigma = 65.2 - 0.52 \times 10 = 60$ points.

(d) The 5th percentile of the data is located at $\mu - 1.65 \times \sigma = 65.2 - 1.65 \times 10 = 48.7$ points.

74. Since $Q_1 = \mu - 0.675 \times \sigma$ and

$Q_3 = \mu + 0.675 \times \sigma$, $Q_3 - Q_3 = 1.35 \times \sigma$.

That is, 1.35 standard deviations describe the IQR of an approximately normal distribution.

75. $\mu = \dfrac{n}{2}$

There is a 95% chance when X is within 2 standard deviations of the mean.

$15 = 2\sigma$

$\sigma = 7.5$

$7.5 = \dfrac{\sqrt{n}}{2}$ $\left(\text{using } \sigma = \dfrac{\sqrt{n}}{2}\right)$

$15 = \sqrt{n}$

$n = 225$

76. $n = 400$

$\mu = \dfrac{n}{2}$

There is a 16% chance when Y is more than one standard deviation above the mean.

$\sigma = 10$

$10 = \dfrac{\sqrt{n}}{2}$ $\left(\text{using } \sigma = \dfrac{\sqrt{n}}{2}\right)$

$20 = \sqrt{n}$

$n = 400$

77. For $p = \dfrac{1}{2}$, $\mu = n \times p = \dfrac{n}{2}$, and

$$\sigma = \sqrt{n \times p \times (1-p)} = \sqrt{n \times \dfrac{1}{2} \times \dfrac{1}{2}} = \sqrt{\dfrac{n}{4}} = \dfrac{\sqrt{n}}{2}.$$

RUNNING

78. $n = 2500$

X has an approximately normal distribution

with mean $\mu = \dfrac{n}{10}$ and standard deviation

$\sigma = \sqrt{n \cdot \dfrac{1}{10} \cdot \dfrac{9}{10}} = \dfrac{3}{10}\sqrt{n}$. If there is a 95%

chance that X will be between $\dfrac{n}{10} - 30$ and

$\dfrac{n}{10} + 30$, then $30 = 2\sigma$ and $\sigma = 15$. Solving

$\dfrac{3}{10}\sqrt{n} = 15$ gives $n = 2500$.

79. $n = 720$

The probability of rolling a total of 7 is

$p = \dfrac{6}{36} = \dfrac{1}{6}$. Thus, . Thus, Y has an

approximately normal distribution with

mean $\mu = \dfrac{n}{6}$ and standard deviation

$\sigma = \sqrt{n \cdot \dfrac{1}{6} \cdot \dfrac{5}{6}} = \dfrac{1}{6}\sqrt{5n}$. If there is a 95%

chance that Y will be between $\dfrac{n}{6} - 20$ and

$\dfrac{n}{6} + 20$, then $20 = 2\sigma$ and $\sigma = 10$. Solving

$\dfrac{1}{6}\sqrt{5n} = 10$ gives $n = 720$.

80. (a) The probability of losing a bet on red is
$20/38 \approx 0.53$. By the dishonest coin
principle, Y has an approximately
normal distribution with center
$\mu \approx 10,000 \times 0.53 = 5300$ and standard

deviation
$\sigma \approx \sqrt{10000 \times 0.53 \times 0.47} \approx 50$.

(b) Since the center of the distribution is at
$Y = 5300$, the chances that we will lose
5300 times or more ($Y \geq 5300$) are
approximately 50%.

(c) The chances that we will lose
somewhere between 5150 and 5450
times (i.e., Y is within plus or minus 3
standard deviations from the center) are
99.7%.

(d) To break even or win we must have
$Y \leq 5000$ (i.e., Y must be more than 4
standard deviations to the left of the
center). The chances of this are
essentially 0.

81. (a) The standard deviation for the number
of votes for Mrs. Butterworth is
$\sqrt{800 \times 0.53 \times 0.47} \approx 14.12$. Thus, the
standard error is approximately
$14.12/800 = 0.0176$ or 1.76%.

(b) A 95% confidence interval is given by 2
standard errors above and below the
statistic obtained from the sample. In
this example, we have a 95%
confidence interval of 53% plus or
minus 3.52% which means that we can
say with 95% confidence that the actual
percentage of votes Mrs. Butterworth
will receive is between 49.48% and
56.52%.

(c) A 99.7% confidence interval is given by
taking 3 standard errors below and
above the sample statistic. In this
example, we can say with 99.7%
confidence that the actual percentage of
votes Mrs. Butterworth will receive is
between 47.72% and 58.28%.